Advance Praise for

Unleashing Suppressed Voices

on College Campuses

"This book is not only an excellent text to be used in higher education graduate classrooms across the country, but it offers exceptional case studies for new and seasoned administrators. It is clear that marginalized voices are still not being heard in the halls of our academy. This text provides an excellent vehicle to discuss the complex and layered issues of racism, prejudice, and discrimination that continue to be a part of what must be changed in today's colleges and universities."

Katherine Conway-Turner,
Provost and Vice President of Academic Affairs,
State University of New York at Geneseo

"This is a bold perspective on a topic that has been 'dammed up' far too long. The content and context of these writings provide an update on an agenda whose time has come. The case studies are a substantive aspect of this book that opens the world of diverse voices to even the least aware. *Unleashing Suppressed Voices on College Campuses* will strengthen the curriculum of schools of education and student affairs preparation programs.

Gregory Roberts,
Executive Director and Senior Operating Officer
ACPA–College Student Educators International

Unleashing Suppressed Voices

on College Campuses

Questions about the Purpose(s) of Colleges & Universities

Norm Denzin, Joe L. Kincheloe, Shirley R. Steinberg
General Editors

Vol. 19

PETER LANG
New York • Washington, D.C./Baltimore • Bern
Frankfurt am Main • Berlin • Brussels • Vienna • Oxford

Unleashing Suppressed Voices on College Campuses

Diversity Issues in Higher Education

EDITED BY O. Gilbert Brown, Kandace G. Hinton, Mary Howard-Hamilton

PETER LANG
New York • Washington, D.C./Baltimore • Bern
Frankfurt am Main • Berlin • Brussels • Vienna • Oxford

Library of Congress Cataloging-in-Publication Data

Unleashing suppressed voices on college campuses: diversity issues
in higher education / edited by O. Gilbert Brown,
Kandace G. Hinton, Mary Howard-Hamilton.
p. cm. — (Higher ed: questions about the purpose(s) of colleges
and universities; v. 19)
Includes bibliographical references and index.
1. College teaching—Social aspects—United States. 2. College teachers—
United States—Social conditions. 3. Universities and colleges—United
States—Administration. 4. Minorities—Education (Higher)—United States.
5. Education, Higher—United States. 6. Discrimination in higher
education—United States. I. Brown, O. Gilbert. II. Hinton, Kandace G.
III. Howard-Hamilton, Mary F. IV. Title. V. Series: Higher ed; v. 19.
LB2331.U79   378.1'9829—dc22   2006000641
ISBN 978-0-8204-8133-3
ISSN 1523-9551

Bibliographic information published by **Die Deutsche Bibliothek**.
Die Deutsche Bibliothek lists this publication in the "Deutsche
Nationalbibliografie"; detailed bibliographic data is available
on the Internet at http://dnb.ddb.de/.

Cover design by Sophie Boorsch Appel

The paper in this book meets the guidelines for permanence and durability
of the Committee on Production Guidelines for Book Longevity
of the Council of Library Resources.

© 2007 Peter Lang Publishing, Inc., New York
29 Broadway, 18th floor, New York, NY 10006
www.peterlang.com

Printed in the United States of America

Table of Contents

Part V Student Affairs and External Relations

Part 1   *Introduction and Analyzing Cases*

1. Unleashing Suppressed Voices at Colleges and Universities: The Role of Case Studies in Understanding Diversity in Higher Education

O. Gilbert Brown, Kandace Hinton
and Mary Howard-Hamilton

Since the founding of Harvard in 1636, the landscape of higher education in the United States has drastically changed. The system of higher education in this country has evolved into one that has become the model for nations to shape and reshape their own higher education organizational structure. The early colleges and universities were built for the purpose of educating and preparing young White men for the clergy and civic leadership.[1]

Women, African Americans, Native Americans, Latinos/as, Asian Americans, and other marginalized groups have varying levels of access because some policies have been created to include them. However, without the appropriate amount of assets (academic preparation, financial aid, social capital, mentoring, faculty of color) they continue to struggle in these often unwelcoming and indifferent environments.

With progress often come problems, issues, and concerns. The purpose of this book is to provide faculty, students, and staff with cases that address a variety of issues related to diversity in higher education. For the purpose of this book we describe diversity as the different sub-communities within college and university settings who are marginalized based upon factors like race, sexual orientation, and gender from the academic and social systems on campuses. With increased challenges of policies like affirmative action, Title IX, and other anti-discrimination laws, this book will offer the reality of diversity problems that occur on college campuses. *Unleashing Suppressed Voices . . .* will present cases that cover the landscape of higher education's diverse functional areas within student, academic, and business affairs as well as governance. White privilege, racism, and sexism are embedded in the very fabric of this country. The struggle to cure the "isms," in higher education began with small steps toward "unleashing the suppressed voices" silenced due to dejure and defacto policies and rules. There are constraints that have inhibited access and facilitators that have enhanced opportunities for marginalized groups to participate in higher education. This chapter will discuss several of those constraints and facilitators—White privilege, institutionalized racism, sexism, and heterosexism as well as policies that have maintained the status quo in higher education.

White Privilege

The concept of white privilege describes the reality that white Americans have implicit and embedded opportunities and power that have allowed them to maintain hegemony in different spheres of American life including higher education. White privilege, in conjunction with other environmental constraints, as well as national and international systemic hindrances has combined to shape the discourse on diversity over the past thirty years. Specifically, significant federal legislation has reversed educational opportunities for unrepresented groups and reduced the amount of aid to educational opportunity programs.

Constraints

Constraints are internal and external controls that impact and enable how institutions of higher education develop policies and make decisions. The following constraints have assumed a primary role in shaping the educational environment: (1) institutional beliefs, (2) state government, (3) federal government, (4) competing organizations, (5) university clients, (6) publics (alumni, parents, and social/political trends), (7) student clients, and (8) technology.[2] Four of the constraints have impacted how predominantly White institutions (PWIs) identify and address issues facing underrepresented students and they are: (1) federal government, (2) institutional ethos, (3) publics, and (4) student clients.

Public/Federal Constraints

Before 1968, most African American students seeking to earn their bachelor's degree matriculated and graduated from public or private historically Black colleges and universities (HBCUs) located in the southern and border states. In this chapter, we will use interchangeably the terms Black and

African Americans to describe Americans whose ancestors were kidnapped slaves from West Africa and the African Diaspora. The key public constraints were the Emancipation Proclamation, Morrill Acts I and II, the Civil Rights Movement, and Black student activism (1968–1974) at PWIs.[3] The key federal constraints were: (1)1954 Supreme Court case Brown vs. Topeka School Board, (2) the Civil Rights legislation including the 1964 Voting Rights Act, (3) Johnson's Great Society programs, (4) the 1965 Higher Education Act, and (5) the No Child Left Behind Act of 2001.[4] The combined public and federal constraints triggered the shift of college bound African American students attending primarily HBCUs to their attending predominantly White institutions.

In short, multiple constraints have combined to place racial diversity on the higher education agenda in the form of narrowing the racial gap in majority and underrepresented students' matriculation and graduation from traditional majority colleges and universities.

Racial and Ethnic Diversity

Constraints have had a major impact on observers' identification of subgroups to be defined as underrepresented. Originally, federal laws determined that underrepresented students were African American, Native Americans, and Latinos, especially Puerto Ricans and Mexican Americans. Underrepresentation is a term that was used to describe the disparity in the aggregate college matriculation and graduation patterns of traditional age (seventeen to twenty-four) Latinos (Puerto Ricans, Mexican Americans), Native Americans, and African Americans compared to White and Asian traditional age students. Consequently, the combination of different constraints influenced colleges and universities to begin attracting faculty and students from underrepresented populations.

Most research on underrepresented students and faculty focused on Latinos and African Americans. The research disparity is due to different factors including the unavailable data sets on Native Americans' high school graduation and college participation rates, small size of the Native American students who attend selective traditional white universities, absence of constraints (student and community demonstrations), small number of Native American Doctoral students, small pool of Native American faculty or other faculty who have research agendas on Native American issues.

Latinos and African Americans face similar and different problems regarding matriculation and persistence at predominantly White institutions. Moreover, Latinos relative to African Americans are a more diverse ethnic minority population because of the within group cultural differences, backgrounds, and circumstances. A rigorous study that included the Latino population would need to consider demographic and geographic distinctions.

There is considerable diversity among the different Latino subgroups as measured in matriculation and graduation data at four-year institutions. Aggregate matriculation data shows that Cuban American high school graduates compared to their Mexican American and Puerto Rican counterparts are highly represented in the undergraduate populations at selective colleges and universities. In addition, there is a considerable disparity in Latino subgroups' educational attainment of the four-year degree: Mexican origins, 6.9%; Puerto Rican origin 13%, Cuban origin, 23%; Central and South American origin, 10.6%.[5] Thus, in this chapter we defined underrepresented Latinos as Puerto Ricans and Mexican Americans.

Underrepresented populations' relative success in influencing predominantly White institutions to expand the presence of their subpopulations led to the institutions developing special student and faculty recruitment programs. In recent years, some Asian American student organizations and faculty sponsors recognized the relative benefits of the special student and faculty recruitment programs and they have sought to have different predominantly White institutions classify Asian Americans as underrepresented students.

Maintaining or Expanding the Definition of Underrepresented Groups

"People of color" is a term that describes racial ethnic minority populations. On a campus climate continuum, students of color share some similar and different perceptions of the environment for students who look like them at predominantly White institutions. We believe the underrepresentation includes the ethnic minority groups African American, Asian Pacific Americans, Native Americans, and Latinos. Unlike the case of Blacks and Latinos, the percentage of Asian Americans in selective colleges and universities is far higher than their percentage in the population at large.

Asian Americans have higher matriculation patterns than any other American ethnic group. The National Center for Education Statistics shows that the enrollment of nonwhites among U.S. college students increased from 16% in 1976 to 27% in 1996. Among African Americans aged 18–24, the percentage attending college went from 21% in 1972 to 30% in 2000, while the percentage of Latinos attending college increased from 17% to 22%. Statistics on Asians have only recently become available, but in 2000 they had the highest rate of college attendance of any ethnic group, with 55% of those aged 18–24 enrolled in school (compared to 36% for whites).[6]

During the late eighties and nineties different constraints including the rising Women's and gay, lesbian, bisexual movements influenced predominantly White institutions to begin shifting their focus from improving underrepresented and ethnic minority student and faculty presence on campus to focusing on the global definition and policy implications of diversity.

On the whole, racial and ethnic subgroups are not interested in becoming the underrepresented group just for the sake of having this unique status on college campuses. In fact, the subgroups are interested in maintaining their presences in the campuses student and faculty structural (numerical representation) diversity plans or achieving a presence in the campuses student and structural diversity plans.

Traditional Diversity Views

Gender

The diversity concept mirrors the movement at predominantly White institutions toward a wider conceptual and policy framework anchored on the marginalization of people from different race, sexual orientation, and gender backgrounds than from the majority heterosexual male population. Gender disparities between men and women have had a major impact on the power disparity within the majority and different ethnic minority populations. In general, white men compared to white women have more power and privileges in the higher education system. White women, compared to under underrepresented ethnic minority groups have more power and privileges at most predominantly white institutions. Thus, there are some similarities and differences regarding the status of white women and underrepresented ethnic groups.

The gender power vacuum exists within the underrepresented ethnic minority communities. Women from these populations face double and sometimes triple injustice in the form of racial and sexual discrimination.[7] Further, inside their racial and cultural groups women face gender secondary class status. The gender hierarchical structure in underrepresented groups is similar to and different from the gender hierarchical structure within the majority population.

Sexual Orientation

Regardless of ethnicity, gays, bisexual, lesbians, and transgender people have been the victims of harassment, physical abuse, and discrimination. The white gays and lesbians benefit from white privileges like their heterosexual counterparts through embedding themselves in the majority population without self-disclosing their sexual orientation. There is the luxury of an invisible status allowing one's sexual orientation to be minimized or ignored within the white community.[8]

Gays and lesbians from underrepresented/racial minority populations, like their white counterparts, have been and are victims of injustice in society. Gays and lesbians from underrepresented/racial minority populations face double (sexual orientation and racial/ethnic) or triple (gender, sexual orientation, racial/ethnic) jeopardy within society. Furthermore, they are attempting to integrate at least three social identities that have historically been stigmatized and oppressed: race, gender, and sexual orientation.

Race Still Matters

The authors agree with Cornell West's (1993) reconfirmation of W.E.B. Dubois's earlier view that race was the fundamental issue of American society in the twentieth century and race still matters in the twenty-first century American society.[9] Yet, race may be one layer of oppression to disguise inter-socioeconomic class differences between Blacks and Latinos versus Whites and Asians; race may be a layer in order to avoid intra-socioeconomic class differences among Blacks and the different Latino subgroups. Most of the cases in the book focus on different versions of the racial divide White/Black, Latino/White, Asian/Black impact on faculty, students, or professional staff and the many systemic layers that are part of the culture difference between and among ethnic groups.

Our case study book includes vignettes that allow writers concerned about suppressed populations to examine a range of diversity issues impacting these constituents in higher education. The organization of our book is as follows.

Part I Introduction and Analyzing Cases

Educators can make use of organizational, cultural, or student development theories as conceptual frameworks and maps to understand the complexity of human behavior. Mary Howard-Hamilton's chapter 2 "Applying Theory to Practice" discusses how educators can use different theories to enhance multicultural awareness, knowledge, and skills as well as assist in resolving difficult diversity issues that occur in higher education. Subsequently, institutions can make use of the knowledge to foster engagement with students, faculty, and staff in addition to increasing persistence and graduation from college. In chapter 3, "Using Cases for Teaching and Learning," Kandace Hinton discusses the multiple uses of case studies in a variety of institutional settings and examines the multiple uses of case studies in non-institutional settings.

Part II Institutional Mission, Leadership, and Racial Diversity

The eight cases in Part II address different aspects of the interaction between institutional mission, leadership, and racial diversity. An institution's mission delineates the purpose of its existence. The mission drives the academic programs, how faculty interacts in and out of the classroom, as well as the teaching, research, and service components. Understanding current campus initiatives is enriched when there is an understanding of the historical origins of the campus mission.

In the post-1968 context, some observers have suggested that HBCUs no longer play a significant role in the education of African Americans. Michelle McClure addresses the reexamination of HBCUs' role and relevance in "Can Historically Black Colleges and Universities Maintain their Mission, and Identity in the Midst of Desegregation?"

Artifacts, traditions, and symbols shape the campus climate throughout different historical periods.[10] Rachel Winkle-Wagner's case "Two Panels of Privilege: A Campus Mural Decision as White Privilege" addresses the placement of a controversial piece of art and how it impacts the campus climate for Latino and African American students at a large majority research institution located in the Midwest. Similarly, Susan Johnson's "In the Name of Honor: Impact of American Indian Mascot on Institutions of Higher Education" examines white privilege through the institution's use of an Indian mascot for their athletic teams. Some predominantly white institutions developed their athletic team mascots in an era when the dominant White held and widely disseminated caricature stereotypical views about Native Americans. The context-bound institutional mascots may impact the campus climate for Native American students and other progressively minded students.

Organizational Constraints

Institutional mission shapes the campus's approach to the adoption of organizational structures for academic and administrative divisions. Research universities are often made up of loosely coupled and fragmented academic and administrative centers and their core mission values are mirrored in the different autonomous academic schools.[11]

Student Affairs' general mission is to create learning environments outside the classroom that enhance student learning in the classroom. Student Affairs organizational structures and approaches can support, impede, or partially support students' perceiving satisfactory undergraduate experiences. Gilbert Brown's case "Organized Anarchy in Student Affairs: Organizational Structures Impacts Black Greek Letter Organizations' Experiences" highlights the disparities underrepresented organizations face when attempting to utilize campus venues for events. Patton's case, "Conflict in the Midst of Culture: The Transition from Cultural Center to Multicultural Center," raises the awareness of the impact of cultural centers on student persistence and the importance of providing counter spaces (see Chapter 2) for diverse student organizations.

The next three cases address the common theme of women administrators having uneven leadership experiences due to the embeddedness of sexism, racism, and heterosexism at different institutions. John Moore, in "Doing the Right Thing When Caught in the Crossfire," blends themes of organizational constraints, the veneer vs. substance of diversity, the governance process, and presidential leadership styles. Madhu Verma-Soin and Jerlando Jackson describe how women are often given position without voice or power in the case entitled, "Where do South Asian American Women Administrators Fit In?" Marie Miville and Madonna Constantine's "Negotiating Administrative Roles in Higher Education as a Woman of Color" examines the pioneering experience of a new academic dean who is pulled in different directions by internal and external stakeholders at the campus

Part III New Challenges Facing Faculty

Earning tenure and being promoted to full professorship are the major academic ranks and status available to faculty within an academic department, school, and the institution. The faculty core (teaching, research, and service) is a concept that describes faculty's general roles in an academic department at a college or university. The seven cases in Part III examine tenure track faculty perceptions of other constraints on their quest for tenure and later promotion. Eboni M. Zamani-Gallaher's case "Tick-Tock: The Convergence of the Biological and Tenure Clock in the Lives of Academic Women" examines three female faculty members' perceptions of demands and expectations of faculty that often impact the life and career choices that female faculty must make on the tenure and promotion track. Concomitantly, Benetta E. Fairley and Edward A. Delgado-Romero's case "Over-Commitment as a Way of Life for Faculty and Graduate Students" and Fabio Rojas in his case "Faculty Development Issues in a Department of Black Studies" both examine faculty members' perceptions of how they managed the different expectations that campus stakeholders (students, faculty, and staff) have of tenure track underrepresented faculty. The different expectations may contribute to junior faculty diverting mental and physical energy away from their research and scholarly production, thus derailing their tenure and promotion process.

Since 1968, many predominantly white institutions have devoted greater interests in attracting faculty from underrepresented backgrounds to their institution (Smith et al. 2004). The seven cases in Part III share a common theme of predominantly White institutions' efforts to attract underrepresented faculty to those campuses. Three cases address the thorny issues surrounding diversifying of ranks with persons from underrepresented backgrounds. Some observers believe that affirmative action principles explicitly or implicitly shape institutions' efforts to attract underrepresented faculty. Eckes and Smith 's case "Affirmative Action and Faculty Hiring" examines the impact of an affirmative action-related search, which sometimes has a negative impact on more qualified White candidates' job opportunities.

Some underrepresented faculty have reservations about the congruence between majority institutions formal commitment to hiring underrepresented faculty and the facts on the ground that they are still highly under represented in the faculty ranks. Three cases explore the theme of the congruence between institutional formal commitments and institutional action. Kimberly Lenease King-Jupiter and Devon Foster's case "Neo-Racism/NeoDiscrimination and Faculty Hiring," Robin Hughes and James Satterfield's case "Minorities are Encouraged to Apply . . . But We are Hiring the Most Qualified," and Edward Delgado-Romero's case "Perfecting the Status Quo" all address different aspects of the congruence between institutional statements and institutional action.

Underrepresented faculties, unlike their majority counterparts face multiple expectations from different internal and external stakeholders like: departments (internal stakeholders) expecting them to represent the "minority viewpoints" on committees, undergraduate/graduate underrepresented students often seeking out the faculty to serve as their mentors/advisors, or local (external stakeholder) racial/ethnic communities often expecting the faculty to serve as bridges/liaisons with the campus. Fairely and Delgado-Romero's case "Over-Commitment as a Way of Life for Faculty and Graduate Students of Color" and Fabio Rojas's case "Faculty Development Issues in a Department of Black Studies" both address the uneven impact of multiple stakeholders' expectations on professors' promotion and tenure.

Part IV Emerging Diversity Populations

Emerging stakeholder groups such as internal (disabled students) constraints and external (The 1990 Americans with Disabilities Act and the 1973 Vocational Rehabilitation Act) are shaping the context for institutions to expand the scope of their diversity issues beyond the so-called Big Three of race, gender, and sexual orientation. The cases in this section address students with disabilities and supplementary education curriculum as the many emerging areas of diversity at traditional majority campuses.

Disabled Students

Institutional responses to students with unique and special academic and social needs are the common theme of three cases in this subsection. Theresa Ochoa's case a "Special Case of Diversity: Students with Disabilities in Higher Education" allows different students to tell their own stories about how a campus responded to their different mental and physical challenges. Midge Madden's case "Speaking Out in the University" allows students and instructor in basic skills classes to share their similar and different views about being marginalized from the campus's academic and social communities. Adrienne Leslie-Toogood, Marilyn Kaff, and Teresa Miller in their case Student-Athlete or Athlete- Student dissect the challenges that a highly recruited student athlete (with special academic needs) faces trying to be successful in the classroom and in his sport.

Religious Constraints

Increasingly, Evangelical Christian organizations as external constraint are shaping the context of institutions' more accommodating responses to students' religious interests. Increasingly, institutions are paying greater attention to students' spirituality interests and needs. Ted Ingram's case "Faith in the Academy" examines students' spirituality interests in the context of the institution's responses to the student's development.

Marginalized Subpopulations

Asian Americans are absent from the institutional focus on underrepresented students and faculty at many majority campuses. Daisy Rodriquez's case "Asian Americans and Pacific Islanders a Displaced Minority" seeks to debunk the myth that Asian Americans are a monolithic group who fit the image as the perfect high achieving minority group. Some Asian American/Pacific Islanders groups are, indeed, underrepresented in high education and deserve consideration by merit based scholarship programs focused on underrepresented groups.

Lesbian, Gay, Bisexual, and Transgender Issues

The cases in this subsection address the fact that college bound LGBT students may face unique challenges with high school peers, teachers/school counselors, and parents both before and after college admission. They may have apprehensions about their sexual orientation and gender identity, about relationships with peers and faculty, and about finding a supportive infrastructure inside the university. Jeffery McKinney's case "Higher Education in Transition: Gender Identity on College Campuses" describes a transgender student's perceptions of marginalization by the Student Affairs Division, especially the LGBT Office, a research intensive university. Frank Ross and Julia Lash's case "Identity Development and Transition Issues in the First Year" describes the experiences of a young man from a small town and conserva-tive religious background as he enters a large university environment. Finally, Nancy Gimbel's case "LGBTQ" captures many of the conflicts and the perception of conflicts between Student Affairs administrators and students over an institution's unsatisfactory response to LGBTQ student concerns.

Part V Student Affairs and External Relations

The Student Affairs division portfolio often includes responsibilities for managing administrative units, overseeing first year experience programs (FYE), monitoring and enhancing the campus climate, managing the learning environment outside of the classroom that enriches the learning process inside the classroom between faculty and students. The seven cases in this section address a common theme of perceived uneven Student Affairs support of underrepresented and marginalized students at different predominantly White institutions.

Student and Alumni Organizations

Darnell Cole's case "Blue Diamond University" presents the scenario of numerous difficult interactions between a predominately white residential campus and historically black Greek lettered organizations. Brown and Riddick's case addresses African American Greek organizations' perceptions of unsatisfactory services, advising, and support from a Student Affairs Division at a major research university. Finally, Michele Scott-Taylor and Sara Dadlani's case "Student Governance and the Politics of Race" examines the inter-student organizational tension between student organizations that do not have access to institutional funds. For different reasons, majority white institutions are pondering over how to expand their underrepresented alumni's involvement in the alma maters. Angela Davis's case "Separate and Unequal" examines African American alumni efforts to establish an affiliate alumni organization in a mid-west majority institution.

Management

Transformational challenges facing senior and mid-level Student Affairs leaders who seek to improve the campus climate for all learners is the common theme of the next three cases. Michelle McQueen's case "Divine University" discusses senior Student Affairs Officer efforts to transform the campus climate for diversity. Joshua Power's case "Set Up for Failure" weaves threads of campus culture, gender, racism, and supervision/management in telling the story of the circumstances around the resignation of a mid-level African American Student Affairs/Service professional at a majority white institution located in the Deep South. Monica Galloway Burke's case "Implementing Diversity in a Challenging Organizational Climate" examines the reality that legal challenges to affirmative action has impacted a transformational oriented senior student affair leader implementation of a campus wide diversity plan.

Notes

1   Thelin, J. (2004). *A history of American higher education*. Baltimore, MD: Johns Hopkins University Press.

2   Weick, K. (2000). In M.C. Brown II (Ed), *Organization & Governance in Higher Education* (5th ed., pp. 36–49.). Boston, MA: Pearson Custom Publishing.

3   Brown, O.G. (1994). Debunking the Myths: Stories About African American College Students. Bloomington, Indiana: Phi Delta Kappa.

4   St. John, E., Paulsen, M., & Carter, D. (2005). Diversity, college costs, and postsecondary opportunity: An examination of the financial nexus between college choice and persistence for African Americans and Whites. *The Journal of Higher Education*, 76 (5), 545–569.

5   Gross, L. (2005). Creating meaning from intersections of career and cultural identity. In A. Ortiz (Ed.). *Addressing the unique needs of Latino students (New Directions for Student Services*, No. 105, 63–77). San Francisco, CA: Jossey Bass.

6   Massey, D., Charles, C., Lundy, G., & Fisher, M. (2003). The *source of the river: The social origins of freshmen at selective colleges and universities*. Princeton, New Jersey: Princeton University Press.

7   Robinson, T.L., & Howard-Hamilton, M.F. (2000). *The convergence of race, ethnicity, and gender: Multiple identities counseling*. Columbus, OH: Merrill/Prentice Hall.

8   West, C. (1993). *Race matters*. Boston: Beacon Press.

9   Hurtado, S., & Milem, J., & Pedersen, Clayton, A., & Allen, W. (1999). *Enacting diverse learning environments: Improving the climate for racial/ethnic diversity in higher education*. ASHE-ERIC Higher Education Report, 26 (8).

10   Birnbaum, R. (2000). The latent organizational functions of the academic senate. In M. C. Brown II (Ed), *Organization & Governance in Higher Education*, (5th ed., pp. 232–243.). Boston, MA: Pearson Custom Publishing.

11   Gollnick D., & Chinn, P. (2004). *Multicultural education in a pluralistic society*. Upper Saddle River, New Jersey: Pearson/Merrill Prentice Hall.

2. Applying Theory to Practice

MARY F. HOWARD-HAMILTON

The use of student development, social justice, and organizational theories should be the first step in assessing and identifying the issues that emerge when reading a case. Bell (1997) stated that "practice is always shaped by theory, whether formal or informal, tacit or expressed" (p. 4). Applying theory to practice allows the reader to detect what may be an underlying problem because a more global and empathetic perspective is taken. Theory allows readers to step outside of the frame of reference they operate from on a daily basis and allows them to view a situation from a broader world view. This allows the readers to approach the case from a higher level of cognitive complexity as well as creatively and sensitively provide suggestions for outcomes that could lead to an amicable conclusion to the dilemma.

It is imperative for professionals working in higher education to understand how the organization, environment, and behavior of the person all intersect to create a dynamic climate that can be compatible or clash with others in the institution. McEwen (2003, pp.154–155) noted that "it is our responsibility, both professionally and ethically, to know and understand the individuals, groups, and institutions with who we work. One important way to do this is through theory." Furthermore, Freire (1970) proffered that theory and practice intersect then become the interactive and historical process called praxis. It is the praxis that gives rise to sound case analysis outcomes and interventions.

Why Use Theory?

There are three reasons why administrators should integrate theory into their daily practices and decision-making processes according to McEwen (2003a, p. 154): 1) it provides a theoretical basis for knowledge, expertise, and practice serves as a foundation for a profession; 2) knowing and understanding theory provide a medium of communication and understanding among student affairs professionals; and 3) theory can serve as a common language within a community of scholars. Student development theory is a framework to inform thinking and understanding of the complexities of human development. Bell (1997) expounds upon the importance of theory stressing that it allows those reading the cases to clearly think about their intentions and how they manifest themselves in actions and outcomes. She also states that theory allows the reader to question old practices and create new techniques or paradigms. Last, theory forces people to learn from the past and stay conscious of how current situations can be viewed in a more imaginative and effective manner.

Clusters of Student Development Theories

There are several clusters of student development theories and they are psychosocial, cognitive structural, typology, and person environment (Evans, Forney, & Guido-DiBrito, 1998). Psychosocial development is concerned with the major challenges that impact an individual's personal and psychological oriented aspects of self and the relationships that exist between the self and society (Hamrick, Evans, & Schuh, 2002). According to Evans et al. (1998), "Psychosocial theorists examine the *content* of development, the important issues people face as their lives progress, such as how to define themselves, their relationships with others, and what to do with their lives" (p. 32). Primary theory in this cluster is the seven vectors of development (Chickering and Reisser, 1993) and they are: (1) developing competence; (2) managing emotions; (3) moving through autonomy toward interdependence; (4) developing mature interpersonal relationships; (5) establishing identity; (6) developing purpose; and (7) developing integrity.

Cognitive developmental theories attempt to understand the thought processes of individuals and how they construct or make meaning of the experiences in their lives (Evans et al. 1998). The major theoretical influence in this cluster is William Perry's forms of intellectual and ethical development. He determined that there were nine positions of intellectual development (1) basic duality; (2) multiplicity prelegitimate; (3) multiplicity legitimate but subordinate; (4a) multiplicity coordinate; (4b) relativism subordinate; (5) relativism; (6) commitment foreseen; (7–9) evolving commitments (Evans et al. 1998). Typology theory examines how individuals view and relate to their respective environment as well as to the persons within that sphere. The two theories in this cluster used by most higher education administrators are the Holland theory of vocational personalities and environments and the Myers Briggs Personality Inventory. Holland's six personality types are (1) realistic; (2) investigative; (3) artistic; (4) social; (5) enterprising; and (6) conventional.

Myers Briggs "suggests that there are eight preferences arranged along four bipolar dimensions: extraversion-introversion (EI), sensing-intuition (SN), thinking-feeling (TF), and judging-perception (JP)" (Evans et al., 1998, p. 246). The eight preferences can be grouped in a combination of sixteen different types (ISTJ, ENTJ etc).

Person environment theory examines the student and the environment as well as the interaction of the student with the environment. The formulae for this theory is bf = (p × e) and is often connected with the notion that challenge and support are important factors that should occur within an institutional environment to induce psychosocial and cognitive growth within the individual (Evans et al., 1998).

Cross' Psychological Nigrescence

While the vectors of development provide one perspective of the case, as reflective students, administrators, faculty in every discipline, as well as consultants the scope must be broadened within the realm of psychosocial understanding to include issues of race and identity development among college students. A widely used theory of identity development is William Cross Psychological Nigrescence. According to Cross (1991), nigrescence refers to the process of "turning Black". It defines the process of, "accepting and affirming a Black identity in an American context by moving from Black self-hatred to Black self-acceptance" (Vandiver, 2001, p. 166). Originally introduced in the 1970s during the latter portion of the Civil Rights Movement, this five-stage theory has stood the test of time and has since been reexamined and revised to four stages: 1) Pre-encounter is described as low race salience and there is very little connection to one's ethnicity and culture; 2) Encounter Blacks are faced with a racial crisis which causes considerable intellectual and personal disequilibrium, thus leaving them questioning their allegiance to the dominant culture; 3) Immersion-Emersion involves movement from a Eurocentric frame of reference to one that is African-centered. Within this movement, students deal with their racial discomfort and insecurities about the formation of a new identity, which may entail becoming Pro-black and/or anti-white. Pro-blackness may be seen by students immersing themselves in visible aspects of black culture such as the changing of hair, style of dress, and participation in all-Black events and organizations. Anti-white may be seen in students separating themselves from aspects of White culture; 4) Internalization finds Blacks becoming comfortable with their racial identity and culture. There is a commitment to changing the social order by investing time and energy in culturally relevant activities.

4) Internalization of the idea of creating a healthy black identity revolves around two major concepts, reference group identity and race salience. Reference group identity, the foundation of nigrescence, focuses on the complexity of social groups that individuals use to make sense of themselves as social beings (Vandiver, 2001). Race salience, "refers to the importance or significance of race in a person's approach to life and is captured across two dimensions: degree of importance and the direction of the valence" (Vandiver, 2001 p. 168). An individual can have, for example, "a high salience for race with a positive (pro-Black) valence or a high salience for race with a negative (anti-Black) valence" (Vandiver, 2001, p. 168).

Privilege, Multicultural Competence, and White Identity Development

McIntosh (1988) wrote a germinal article on privilege in which she defines it as the process of granting the dominant group opportunities that indiscriminately or blatantly acknowledge them systemically, politically, economically, and culturally. The unequal dissemination of these unearned privileges makes it difficult for marginalized or oppressed groups to gain any economic, personal, or cultural momentum in society (Hobgood, 2000; Howard-Hamilton & Frazier, 2005). Moreover, the effects of privilege "are so pervasive that they can be felt between people of color even when no white people are present, as well as between whites even when no people of color are present" (Hobgood, 2000. p. 36). Higher education administrators and faculty should examine their assumptions, biases, and privileges because who we are and what we believe may have a direct impact on how the cases in this text will be evaluated, deliberated, and reviewed. Moreover, when a recommendation is made regarding the outcome of how the individuals or organization in the case should be treated, the sanction could be too harsh or too lenient depending upon the personal world view of the reader. McEwen (2003a) insists that individual introspection and reflection is "important in relation to learning, critiquing, and using theories about student and human development (p. 174).

Student affairs professionals need to ask questions of themselves, such as Who am I, as an able-bodied, middle-class, educated White woman? or a second-generation bisexual Asian man? or an African American woman? or a person with any other combination of characteristics? Such self-reflection will help you discover and understand those frameworks you use in both the consideration and the application of theory. (p. 174)

Reading and memorizing theoretical stages and applying them randomly without personal reflection and purposeful planning could leave the administrator and student disappointed and bitter because a sensitive and thoughtful plan of action was not taken. Assumptions about a person's race, class, or gender is the mindset of a privileged individual. Multiculturally competent faculty, administrators, and staff would engage in personal reflection in addition to understanding and learning about other cultures, recognizing and deconstructing white culture, recognizing the legitimacy of other cultures and developing a multicultural outlook (Ortiz & Rhoads, 2000). Therefore, understanding and embracing the levels of white identity development become critical because they are foundation and framework for working with diverse groups. Furthermore, "identity development represents a qualitative enhancement of the self in terms of complexity and integration" (McEwen, 2003b, p. 205). The White Identity Development Model is a prime example of how one's identity becomes more complex when attempting to inculcate diversity issues with previous socialized perceptions of race.

The White Identity Development (WID) Model (Hardiman, 2001) was designed to explain "how Whites came to terms with their Whiteness with respect to racism and race privilege" (p. 111). The five stages of the WID are (1) No Social Consciousness of Race or Naiveté, (2) Acceptance, (3) Resistance, (4) Redefinition, and (5) Internalization.

The first stage is a naïve period in which whites have no understanding or recognition of other cultures and races. They are also unaware of how status and value is ascribed to one race over another. Acceptance, stage two, occurs when Whites recognize that "it is impossible in this society to escape racist socialization in some form because of its pervasive, systemic, and interlocking nature" (Hardiman, 2001, p. 111). Whites have an understanding that privilege exists and accept an understanding that they are perceived as superior to people of color. This is not a conscious choice by white people but oftentimes is an unconscious choice and a "by-product of living within and being impacted by the institutional and cultural racism which surrounds us" (Hardiman, 2001, p. 111).

The racist programming that has occurred unconsciously and consciously is questioned at the third stage called resistance. This is an action-oriented stage wherein Whites can become liberators for social justice and equal opportunity by fighting to ameliorate racism and other forms of oppression. This leads to a redefinition and clarification of why they are interested in working against racism, and they begins to embrace their whiteness rather than deny or denounce it. The new white identity is internalized in the fifth stage, thus raising their level of racial consciousness and integrating it into every aspect of their persona.

Social Justice Models

Social justice is a term used to describe a societal process in which there is a shared vision for the equitable distribution of resources and there is physical and psychological safety for all people (Bell, 1997). The individuals in a social justice system are self-determining and empowered. They "have a sense of their own agency as well as a sense of social responsibility toward and with others and the society as a whole" (Bell, 1997, p. 1).

Paulo Freire (1970) was the preeminent scholar who wrote about social justice issues in his germinal treatise "Pedagogy of the Oppressed". The book provided clear and direct goals to free the consciousness of oppressed people. Freire (Freire, 1970; Spring, 1999) argued that there were several significant steps that needed to take place in order for oppressed people to find their voices as they become critically conscious of how their lives are being determined by others rather than themselves. These steps are as follows:

1. *People are subjects of history*: All individuals make history and can change social, political, and economic conditions with a fully developed consciousness and understanding of their historical significance. "A subject of history is a conscious maker of history" (Spring, 1999, p. 148).

2. *Leadership and people work together to develop a Utopian vision*: Leaders work with all individuals to decide how the world should be transformed. There must be dialogue and conscious reflection on the ideas presented in order for problems to be solved.

3. *Dialogue*: The leaders may not understand the lives of the individuals who are oppressed. Therefore to heighten understanding, dialogue between leader and learner (or the oppressed) must take place. The dialogue helps to raise one's critical consciousness about social conditions, systemic oppression, and the way individuals perceive the world.

4. *Reflective—problematizing*: Reflection the oppressed allows them to expunge the oppressor from their consciousness. It also involves thinking about the consequences of one's actions and affects future choices and decisions. A transformation process occurs at this level and the oppressed become empowered. Concomitantly, the oppressor becomes more empathic.

5. *People who organize*: The oppressed and the oppressor become individuals who organize others so that social change may happen. There is a view that in order for the system to become transformed, groups of people must become empowered and conscious of what mechanisms can impact change. They have the ability to change the world.

6. *Revolution continuous*: When one problem is resolved there may be a tendency to become complacent rather than continuing to fight for more societal changes. There is an understanding that the dialogue is continuous and revolutions can transform the way people

behave, think, and act. Additionally, revolutions can help craft new policies for oppressed groups.

The importance of Freire's pedagogy is to stress the importance of action, reflection, and praxis. The list of goals clearly denote, how important it is to move into action and have a dialogue in order to resolve any conflict, dilemma, or stressful situation.

Critical Race Theory

Critical Race Theory is a theoretical framework generated by legal scholars of color who are concerned about racial oppression in society (Delgado & Stefancic, 2001; Smith, Altbach, & Lomotey, 2002; Solorzano, Ceja, & Yosso, 2000; Villalpando & Bernal, 2002). It explores how so-called race neutral laws and institutional policies perpetuate racial/ethnic subordination. This framework emphasizes the importance of viewing policies and policy making in the proper historical and cultural context to deconstruct their racialized content.

It challenges dominant liberal ideas such as color blindness and meritocracy and shows how these concepts disadvantage people of color and further advantage the whites. Critical Race Theory uses counter stories in the form of dialogue, chronicles, and personal testimonies because it acknowledges that some members of marginalized groups, by virtue of their marginal status, tell stories that are different from what white scholars usually hear. Counterstories are both a method to tell stories of often untold experiences and also a tool for analyzing and challenging the dominant discourse and the stories of those in power.

Critical Race Theory (1) recognizes that racism is endemic to American life; (2) expresses skepticism toward dominant claims of neutrality, objectivity, color blindness, and meritocracy; (3) challenges historicism and insists on a contextual/historical analysis of institutional policies; (4) insists on recognizing the experiential knowledge of people of color and our communities of origin in analyzing society; (5) is interdisciplinary and crosses epistemological and methodological boundaries; and (6) works toward the end of eliminating racial oppression as part of the broader goal of ending all forms of oppression.

Organizational Theory

Organizations perform smoothly or with tremendous problems because of the people who are responsible for the day-to-day functions within their systems. Organizational theory allows observers and those within the system an opportunity to view the behavior and create the culture within that unit.

There are four organizational models that "are useful for understanding the diversity of organizational approaches found in American colleges and universities" (Ambler, 2000, p. 122). These are the rational model, bureaucratic model, collegial model, and political model.

The rational model does not require a lot of structure and is based on academic values such as order, clear direction, logic, and rational as well as predictable behavior. The members within the organization are in synch with the mission of the institution and this model is found primarily in small, private, or religious-oriented colleges. The bureaucratic model emphasizes "hierarchical power, limits on authority, division of labor, specialization, technical competence, standard operating procedures, rules of work, and differential rewards" (Ambler, 2000, p. 123). The collegial process emphasizes a participatory process of decision making and openness to ideas. There is a reliance on professional autonomy and a normative compliance system, two enduring values of the academy. The political model focuses on "policy development as the means to resolve complex issues" (Ambler, 2000, p. 123). There is an emphasis on conflict resolution, authority, and power that is derived from the ability to control resources.

Conclusion

When analyzing the cases in this book, refer to the theories that will assist you in making a clearer and more critical analysis of what is occurring within the organizational structure. All cases should have a theoretical underpinning that will allow for an unbiased reaction and assessment by the reader.

References

Ambler, D.A. (2000). Organizational and administrative models. In M.J. Barr, M.K. Desler, & Associates (Eds.). *The handbook of student affairs administration*, (pp.121–133). San Francisco, CA: Jossey Bass.

Bell, L.A. (1997). Theoretical foundations for social justice education. In M. Adams, L.A. Bell, & P. Griffin (Eds.). *Teaching for diversity and social justice*, (pp.1–15). New York: Routledge.

Chickering, A.W., & Reisser, L. (1993). *Education and identity* (2nd ed.). San Francisco, CA: Jossey-Bass.

Cross, W.E. (1991). *Shades of black: Diversity in African American identity*. Philadelphia, PA: Temple University Press

Delgado, R., & Stefancic, J. (2001). *Critical race theory: An Introduction*. New York: New York University Press.

Evans, N.J., Forney, D.S., & Guido-Dibrito, F. (1998). *Student development in college: Theory, research and practice*. San Francisco, CA: Jossey-Bass.

Freire, P. (1970). *Pedagogy of the oppressed.* Continuum: New York.

Hamrick, F.A., Evans, N.J. & Schuh, J.H. (2002). *Foundations of student affairs practice: How philosophy, theory, and research strengthen educational outcomes.* San Francisco, CA: Jossey Bass.

Hardiman, R. (2001). Reflections on white identity development theory. In C.L. Wijeyesinghe & B.W. Jackson, III (Eds.). *New Perspective on racial identity development: A Theoretical and practical anthology,* (pp.108–128). New York: New York University Press.

Hobgood, M.E. (2000). *Dismantling privilege: An ethics of accountability.* Cleveland, OH: The Pilgrim Press.

Howard-Hamilton, M.F., & Frazier, K. (2005). Identity development and the convergence of race, ethnicity, and gender. In D. Comstock (Ed.). *Diversity and development: Critical contexts that shape our lives and relationships,* (pp.67–90). Belmont, CA: Thomson Brooks Cole.

McEwen, M.K. (2003a). New perspectives on identity development. In. S.R. Komives & D.B. Woodard, Jr. (Eds.), *Student services: A handbook for the profession* (4th ed., pp.203–233). San Francisco, CA: Jossey-Bass.

———— (2003b). The nature and uses of theory. In S.R. Komives & D.B. Woodard, Jr. (Eds.). *Student services: A handbook for the profession* (4th ed., pp.153–178). San Francisco, CA: Jossey-Bass.

McIntosh, P. (1988). *White privilege and male privilege: A personal account of coming to see correspondences through work in women's studies.* Working paper #189. Wellesley, MA: Wellesley College Center for Research on Women.

Ortiz, A.M., & Rhoads, R.A. (2000). Deconstructing whiteness as part of a multicultural educational framework: From theory to practice. *Journal of College Student Development,* 41(1), 81–93.

Perry, W.G. (1999). *Forms of intellectual and ethical development in the college years: A scheme.* New York: Holt, Rinehart & Winston.

Smith, W.A., Altbach, P.G., & Lomotey, K. (2002). *The racial crisis in American Higher Education: Continuing challenges for the twenty-first century.* New York: State University of New York Press.

Solorzano, D., Ceja, M., & Yosso, T. (2000). Critical race theory, racial microaggressions, and campus racial climate: The experiences of African American college students. *The Journal of Negro Education,* 69(1/2), 60–73.

Spring, J. (1999). *Wheels in the head: Educational philosophies of authority, freedom, and culture from Socrates to human rights* (2nd ed.). Boston, MA: McGraw Hill College.

Vandiver, B.J. (2001). Psychological nigrescence revisited: Introduction and overview. *Journal of Multicultural Counseling and Development,* 29 [3] 165–173.

Villalpando, O. & Bernal, D.D. (2002). A critical race theory analysis of barriers that impede the success of faculty of color. In W.A. Smith, P.G. Altbach, & K. Lomotey (Eds.). *The Racial Crisis in American Higher Education: Continuing Challenges for the Twenty-first Century,* (pp.243–270). Albany, NY: State University of New York Press.

3. *Using Cases for Teaching and Learning*

KANDACE HINTON

Unleashing suppressed voices often comes in the form of protest and public demonstration. This book is releasing suppressed voices out of a sense of protest for the lack of understanding of the changing demographics in the landscape of higher education through the use of case problems. This chapter specifically will discuss how to use and understand cases. First, an overview of the broad uses of cases will be discussed. Next, we will outline ways in which cases can be analyzed. Finally, an example of a case and analysis will conclude this chapter.

Cases have been used historically to teach lessons in a variety of disciplines. Law students learn from previous court cases; medical students often learn how to diagnose a patient's problem by examining the patient and comparing the symptoms to previous cases; business students find opportunities to learn lessons of accounting, management, marketing, and investment by studying real business problems presented as cases. The use of cases for teaching and learning within the field of education has always been a very practical approach to understanding students, systems or organizations, governance, and the general landscape of higher education. This section will focus on the importance of using cases as a pedagogical philosophy.

Historically, professors used the banking method for teaching and learning. Freire (1989) states that the banking method is when professors regard students as "receptacles to be filled by the teacher" (p. 58). In other words, as professors become more of the sage on the stage rather than the guide on the side (Barr & Tagg, 1995) "education becomes an act of depositing, in which students are the depositories and the teacher is the depositor" (p. 58). Freire further asserts that projecting or believing that students are ignorant and that they enter the classroom as blank slates, is "characteristic of the ideology of oppression" (p. 58) and opposes the viewpoint that education or the process of learning involves inquiry. This book and the cases therein provide tools for a more learning-centered approach to education.

Barr and Tagg (1995) suggest that there is a shift from an instruction paradigm to a learning paradigm. They parallel the banking or instruction paradigm to the learning paradigm asserting that the learning model should be the preferred pedagogical philosophy used for education. Some of the instruction model characteristics include: (1) the transfer of knowledge from faculty to students; (2) achievement of access for diverse students; (3) one teacher, one classroom model; (4) the idea that knowledge comes in chunks and bits and is delivered by instructors and gotten by students; (5) fitting into the storehouse of knowledge metaphor; (6) learning is teacher-centered and controlled; and (7) faculty are primarily lecturers. The instruction paradigm diminishes students' opportunity to "develop the critical consciousness which would result from their intervention in the world as transformers of that world" (Freire, 1989, p. 59).

The preferred learning paradigm is action-oriented and provides students and faculty experiences to heighten their sense of inquiry and transformation. Problem-posing learning is the approach embedded in the use of cases for teaching principles of the importance of diversity and hearing the voices of marginalized groups in our system of higher education. Freire (1989) states that the banking method "mythicizes reality, to conceal certain facts which explain the way [people] exist in the world," (p. 71) whereas the learning paradigm "demythocizes" and "unveils reality" (p. 71). He further asserts that the problem-posing approach encourages creativity and reflection, which stimulates action. The instruction approach often ignores the reality of student and faculty life experiences and history; the learning paradigm acknowledges, values, and invites the experiences of each participant to have a voice and importance. According to Barr and Tagg (1995), the learning paradigm

> 1) produces learning; 2) elicits students discovery and construction of knowledge; 3) creates powerful learning environments; 4) improves the quality of learning; 5) achieves success for diverse students; 6) quality of exiting students is the measure; 7) faculty are primarily designers of learning methods and environments; 8) learning environments and learning are cooperative, collaborative, & supportive; 9) knowledge exists in each person's mind and is shaped by individual experience; 10) knowledge is constructed, created; 11) learning is a nesting and interacting of frameworks; 12) fits learning how to ride a bicycle metaphor; 13) "active" learner required, but not "live" students required; 14) learning is student centered & controlled (p. 16–17)

Whatever learning experience works for students should be the ultimate goal of institutions of higher education.

We believe that the use of cases for learning purposes is a means by which students and faculty can explore possible solutions to problems situated in the context of broad and specific subject matter. Obviously, optimal theory-to-practice would involve working in real life situations. Because internships and cooperative learning experiences are not always available, course work can often involve simulated environments through collaborative, experimental, dialogue, and other active learning techniques. Furthermore, senior academic administrators, like deans and associate deans could find value in using case studies for training purposes for faculty and others involved in search committees and other recruitment and retention activities. Moreover, as student affairs leaders develop plans for retreats and extensive staff training, case problems within this text could be central to group discussion and program activities.

Cases can be used to build community within a traditional or virtual classroom. Students and faculty each have the opportunity to relate personal experiences of the problem being posed. For the purposes of this case book, academic programs are afforded the chance to "create [multi]culturally responsive learning environments" (Howard-Hamilton, 2000, p. 45). Howard-Hamilton affirms the learning paradigm, stating the importance of the use of cases for the inclusion of all voices. She states, "case study discussions in small groups can evoke moral dilemma decision-making and group consensus processes which lead to higher-level listening skills and multiple perspectives taking" (p. 51). As such the use of cases can be used to stimulate in-class and out-of- class time discussions, instigate action for relevant situations for students and faculty, and inspire inquiry.

Finally, we conclude this chapter with a sample case and a discussion on how to analyze subsequent cases. Stage and Dannells (2000) suggest eight questions to ask while considering a case problem. These questions are:

1. What are the decision issues presented in the case?
2. What facts are essential for understanding and dealing with the issues?
3. What additional information must be collected?
4. Who are the principal decision makers and what roles do they play?
5. Are there any theories that might be relevant to the decision issues?
6. What alternatives are available to the principal decision makers?
7. What are the advantages and disadvantages associated with each alternative?
8. What course of action (long-term and short-term) will be taken (p. 42)?

In addition to asking these eight questions, each contributor in this book has added a set of discussion questions to consider when analyzing cases in order to offer thoughts or remedies to each situation. Cases often reflect personal experiences. Students and faculty have vast experiences within the context of formal education. One of the most significant uses of case studies is to author your own cases to serve as reflection, catharticism, and learning.

The Gateway Center: Institutional Response to a Community Need

Kandace G. Hinton

Institutional Setting

The University of Southtown Indiana (USI) is a medium size public regional comprehensive institution. Previously, it was primarily a commuter campus with student apartments located in close proximity to campus; however, recently, the university has erected at least one on campus residence hall. The University of Southtown Indiana was founded in 1965 as a branch campus of State University and gained its independence in the mid-80s. Since its founding the campus has grown to nearly 10,000 students. There are approximately 3.3% African Americans, .26% American Indians, .73% Asian Americans, .68% Latinos, .61% international, and 94.35% European Americans.

Description of Surrounding Community

The institution, in southern Indiana, is located in the outlying county area nearly eight miles from the central city of Whiteville with a population of approximately 150,000 residents. Whiteville is nestled on the banks of the Ohio River. The city is rather segregated in that a majority of the African American community resides in the central city area. There is a considerable amount of industry in the area including a major pharmaceutical plant, appliance manufacturer, an automobile manufacturer, and power plants. There are approximately 13,000 African Americans residing in the city of Whiteville.

Key Characters

Dr. Korn—president of the university
Dr. Jonesey—associate vice president of Academic Affairs and Extended Services
Mr. Baldi—community activist
Ms. Fly—director of the Gateway Center
Shirley Herdman—Director of University Division

Information Germane to the Case

Historically, residents in the central city of Whiteville (which is predominantly African American) had not participated in postsecondary education. Because the university was established as a regional comprehensive institution to serve the needs of the immediate population, Mr. Baldi approached the president about establishing outreach program efforts to encourage higher educational attainment within the African American and low socioeconomic community. After months of discussion, the president presented the idea of establishing an adult access center in the community.

Dr. Jonesey's task was to research the need for such a center, seek external funding, and form a search committee for a director. His office subsequently surveyed parents of Headstart children (approximately 200) asking whether or not they would participate or enroll in college courses if there was a center located in close proximity to their homes. The survey was favorable toward establishing an access center—the Gateway Center.

The Case

The establishment of the Gateway Center was to serve a two-fold purpose, one to extend the university into a community that had not overwhelmingly participated in postsecondary education, and the other, to increase African American enrollment at the USI. To this end the search committee hired Ms. Fly, as the center's director. Ms. Fly had grown up in the community, earned a bachelor's degree from an HBCU, and worked on the main campus of USI as an admissions counselor for two years. The Gateway Center's initial budget was approximately $70,000 (in cash and in kind), which was to cover the director's salary, a secretary's salary, a part-time academic advisor's salary, a janitor's wages, facility leasing, and other operating costs, including purchasing instructional software.

The director of Gateway was charged to establish a curriculum so that students enrolled at the center could get nearly two years of transferable general education courses, recruit students and faculty, provide financial aid counseling, schedule courses, assist with academic advising, budgeting, and overall marketing of the program to the community and the university.

The center opened mid-semester with 30 students enrolled. The university established a numeric goal of 100 students per semester (because of the previous survey of Head start parents). Most of the students were African American women and women who were being forced off public assistance because of welfare reform policies. Each semester the enrollment increased to reach its pinnacle of 80 students and finally leveling to an average of 50 per semester. Initially, university officials were ecstatic because of the significant overall increase in "minority" enrollment.

The Gateway Center offered certificates to students completing 28–30 credit hours of courses. Some of the courses were remedial but many of them were indeed college level and could be transferred to the main campus, the state community colleges, and the local private four-year liberal arts institution. Cumulatively the center enrolled nearly 300 students over a five-year period with about a third completing the certificate program. Furthermore, many of the students who completed the program continued their studies at the main campus or transferred to the community college and completed associate and bachelor degrees in nursing, business, and other academic and vocational areas. Also, some student who did not complete the certificate program became employed due to their enrolling and completing general math, communication, and writing courses at the center.

Early on, Ms. Fly established an advisory board comprised of Mr. Baldi, community pastors, directors of other service-based not-for-profit organizations, university faculty, community college administrators, and students, to assist with the planning, assessment, marketing, and development of the center.

In the fourth year of the center's existence Dr. Jonesey requested the director of the University Division and an academic advisor and faculty member from that department to conduct an audit and assessment of the program. One year later, their findings were presented stating that the center consistently had low enrollment numbers and was not cost effective for the university to continue its support. Dr. Jonesey reestablished the advisory board with only two community representatives and several university faculty and administrators. He informed the new advisory board and Ms. Fly in March that the center would close at the end of the academic year. Ms. Fly was given the option of continuing with the university in janitorial services or as an admissions counselor, the part-time advisor had already moved on to a position outside of academe, the secretary and janitor were not going to be provided for. Subsequently, Ms. Fly negotiated positions for her staff (the janitor and secretary) on the main campus.

Dr. Jonsey informed the advisory group that the funding previously used for the Gateway Center would be directed toward the newly established multicultural office which would begin service the next academic year and that the university would offer a program similar to the Gateway Center on the main campus.

Dr. Jonesey had only visited the site twice in the five years of the program's history. He was initially supposed to be Ms. Fly's immediate supervisor, and met with her annually to "see how things were going." The second year of the program, Dr. Jonesey asked Shirley Herdman, the director of the University Division to serve as Ms. Fly's supervisor and to provide assistance and direction to the program as needed.

Discussion Questions

1. What are the issues or problems presented in this case?
2. How does the institution demonstrate commitment to multicultural issues?
3. How does the institution demonstrate commitment to serving the minority and low SES communities?
4. What tools (knowledge and skills) were necessary for the Gateway Center to continue serving the center city of Whiteville?
5. What are some alternatives to the Gateway Center's demise?
6. How would you evaluate the institution and the key persons/decision makers in this case as being multiculturally competent or incompetent?

Research Activities for Further Exploration

1. What is the history of the institution you are attending (or one that is close to your hometown) as it relates to community service in low income and minority communities?
2. How many extended service projects or programs does the institution have in place outside of the university community and what are those programs designed to accomplish?

What is the community's perception of college or university established programs and how effective have these programs been in improving community quality of life?

References

Barr, R.B. & Tagg, J. (1995). From teaching to learning: A new paradigm for undergraduate education. *Change, 27* (6) (November/December), 13–25.

Freire, P. (1989). *Pedagogy of the oppressed.* New York: Continuum Publishing.

Howard-Hamilton, M.F. (2000). Creating a culturally responsive learning environment for African American students. In M.B. Baxter Magolda (Ed.). *Teaching to promote intellectual and personal maturity: Incorporating students' worldviews and identities into the learning process,* (pp. 45–53). San Francisco, CA: Jossey-Bass.

Stage, F.K. & Dannells, M. (Eds.). (2000). *Linking theory to practice: Case studies for working with college students,* (2nd ed.). Philadelphia, PA: Accelerated Development.

Part II Institutional Mission, Leadership, and Racial Diversity

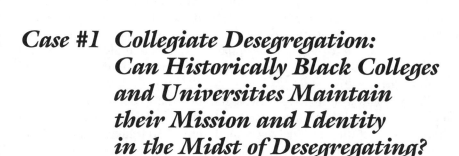

Case #1 Collegiate Desegregation: Can Historically Black Colleges and Universities Maintain their Mission and Identity in the Midst of Desegregating?

Michelle L. McClure

The United States prides itself on its diversity of higher education, which not only creates greater access for its citizens, but for those who choose to come to America to study from abroad. One unique aspect of U.S. higher education, which speaks to the ideals of diversity and creating greater access are America's minority serving institutions, in particular historically black colleges and universities (HBCUs). HBCUs have made a significant contribution in educating a group of people that were historically discriminated and marginalized. Furthermore, black colleges and universities have produced graduates who not only made a significant difference within the black community, but have impacted society as a whole. Yet, despite the contributions to providing education to black people and producing leaders, scholars, and agents of social change, these institutions' missions, legitimacy, and existence have been questioned and challenged, which has always posed a threat to their survival. However, today, these institutions are faced with their greatest challenge; the policy of collegiate desegregation, which heightens the threat to their existence and function as black institutions.

Historical Background Information Regarding Collegiate Desegregation Policies

Desegregation is not a new policy issue that both predominantly white institutions (PWIs) and HBCUs have had to address (Brown & Hendrickson, 1997; Haynes, 1978; St. John, 1997). Desegregation laws and policies have forced PWIs to make a concerted effort to diversify their student bodies in order to maintain their federal funding (Skyes, 1995). Likewise, HBCUs have had to abide by diversity initiatives since 1970; however, these initiatives have not posed a problem until recently. *United States V. Fordice* (1992), also known as the *Ayers* case, serves as the judicial guidepost for desegregation in states that operated racially segregated, dual systems of higher education. Collegiate desegregation, as a result of the *Ayer* case, mandates the "adoption of collegiate desegregation compliance policies that aid in remedying the continuing vestiges of *de jure* (by law) segregation in higher education" (Brown, 2001, p. 50).

The problem with the *Ayers* case is that the final settlement that sets the precedent for black institutions located in the South does not reflect the original intent of the case Jake Ayers filed in the 1970s. Jake Ayers sued the state of Mississippi because of the inequalities that existed between the state's PWIs and HBCUs, for fear that his children would receive an inferior education if they decided to attend one of the HBCUs. Over the course of twenty years, the case has evolved from establishing equality and equity between PWIs and HBCUs to desegregating HBCUs. As mandated by the courts, HBCUs represent ideas of separation and segregation, therefore, in an effort to provide a remedy HBCUs must increase their white student population to 10% in order to receive funds allocated by the state.

Black institutions find themselves struggling to abide by mandates that are not clear and concise. In the midst of uncertainty, HBCU administrators question if they are designing proper desegregation plans that will be approved by state judges (Hollis & Wright, 1997). Without the approval of these initiatives to diversify their institutions, public HBCUs are denied funding, which triggers a debilitating reaction. This situation perpetuates a cycle, which further cripples these institutions (Brown & Hendrickson, 1997). Without adequate funding, these institutions are not able to meet the needs of their African American students as well as attract white students. Without the ability to attract white students they are unable to receive their funding by the state—a Catch-22 situation.

The Setting

Mid-Southern State University (MSSU) is a historically black university founded in the mid-1880s. Designated by the Commission of Higher Education as the urban institution of the state, this research-intensive university "functions as a community of learners in which teaching, research, and service are central to its total environment" (Charge to the Mid-Southern State University Community, 2001). Moreover, it maintains a commitment to serving diverse students from various academic, ethnic, social, and geographic backgrounds to create leaders who are capable of addressing and meeting the needs of a global community (Charge to the Mid-Southern State University Community, 2001).

Mid-Southern State University is the only four-year public institution located in the mid-southern part of the state and is the second largest institution of higher learning in the state. With its new mission as an urban institution, the Commission on Higher Education has granted Mid-Southern State University permission to offer new programs, thus expanding its academic offerings. Mid-Southern State University offers bachelors through doctoral degrees in allied health, business, education, engineering, liberal arts, science and technology, and social work. Mid-Southern State University is ranked nationally among all institutions of higher learning as a top producer of baccalaureate degrees to African Americans. In addition, it is ranked in the top 10 category in the nation and the top 10 among HBCUs as a top producer of African American PhDs.

Mid-Southern State administrators view the new charge and new degree programs as a "welcomed" opportunity. However, this new opportunity comes with some costs and expectations. The new charge and new degree programs were granted to this institution with the expectation that they would use these new changes as an opportunity to attract a more diverse student body. According to *Ayers* legislation, black colleges and universities located in the state must increase their white student population to 10 percent in order to receive their state allocations, as well as monies set aside by the *Ayers* case to help black colleges achieve a "level playing field" with their white counterparts.

The Characters

Dr. Belinda Turner: the Associated Vice Chancellor of Academic Affairs at MSSU has been at MSSU for over twenty-five years. As an alumna of MSSU she takes pride in witnessing how much her institution has grown since she first set foot on MSSU as a first-year student. For educated black people of her generation, MSSU and other HBCUs were the only form of access to higher education available. Dr. Turner is a strong advocate and supporter of MSSU. The university gave her the confidence, support, and academic preparation to pursue graduate school. After completing her doctoral degree, Dr. Turner returned to her alma mater so that she could touch and mold young minds and give them what MSSU gave to her, which is pride, confidence, and ability to achieve anything that they set their minds to accomplish.

As Associated Vice Chancellor of Academic Affairs, Dr. Turner's major responsibilities include implementing the new degree programs designed by the state and monitoring students' academic status. This year, Dr. Turner is faced with new challenges and duties because of new policies created from the *Ayer* case. Her new responsibilities include ensuring that the new policies of the *Ayers* case are fully implemented by the institution so that they are in compliance to receive the funds allocated to them. Dr. Turner has had to create many new diversity initiatives to attract and recruit white students to MSSU. Some of her new diversity initiatives are the creation of white scholarships and the Summer Academy, which is a summer bridge program that admits students who do not fully meet the new admissions policies after completion of the nine-week program. The Summer Academy only allows for thirty perspective students to participate. With MSSU's mandate to attract white students, most of the slots have been set aside for white students with learning challenges and disabilities, thus displacing many qualified black students who would benefit from the program.

The new diversity initiatives have caused Dr. Turner to feel in conflict as an alumnus and administrator. Often times, she finds herself asking, "How can I stay true to the mission of my institution, while trying to attract white students? Do I not take the money as a result of *Ayers* litigation and watch the doors of my institution close? Or, do I take the money and see the doors of MSSU remain open?"

Dr. Keith Beckley: a white faculty member who serves as the chair of the engineering department has been at MSSU for over fifteen years. He is not fully aware of the *Ayers* case. He does know, however, that the *Ayers* case is helping to diversify the study body, which he believes is great for the university. Furthermore, he knows that the *Ayers* case has brought new monies and new programs to the institution, which in his opinion is a "welcomed opportunity." According to Dr. Beckley, he has witnessed MSSU operate with inadequate funding for academic programs for some time. Dr. Beckley states, "The state has allowed for MSSU to create new programs, yet did not provide the funding necessary to house the programs. For instance, the state allowed for us to create an engineering program. However, the program had to sit dormant until we raised the funds necessary to offer such a program. And, in my opinion that is not how you run a program."

Dr. Dwayne Smith: the Associate Vice President for Community Relations. His primary responsibilities include maintaining positive relations between the university and the community. In addition, he serves as senior spokesman for the university. As the *Ayers* litigation settled, his duties were expanded to include informing supporters and alumni of the impact the new policies would have on MSSU.

Dr. Smith believes that the *Ayers* case will bring welcomed change in how the university is perceived by the community. For many years, MSSU has had a negative image with the white community. Much of this negativity stemmed from the history of racism that has not only plagued this community, but the nation as well. Dr. Smith has spent a great deal of work trying to decipher how the university can improve its reputation with the state's white residents. He hopes that the new degree offerings and the possibilities of expanding the campus to other sections of the city will make MSSU more accessible and appealing to whites who, perhaps, would consider MSSU as an option for higher education.

Some of the alumni have voiced their concerns with Dr. Smith. Many of them have shared that they do not want MSSU to become a predominantly white institution, which is what has happened to some other HBCUs. Some alumni have accused Dr. Smith of "selling out the university" and have told him that his actions are reflections of "Uncle Tomism!" Dr. Smith believes that their accusations are far from the truth. He states, "MSSU is a black college, it was founded as a black college, and it will remain a black college." He believes he is doing his job; to move the university into the twenty-first century.

Mr. Khalid Thomas: a junior who serves as president of the student government. He is a highly intelligent young man who keeps the students very informed of the actions of administration and the board of directors. Some of his actions may be viewed as those of an instigator or rebel rouser. He has been informing the student body about the new *Ayers* policies. Furthermore, he has been passing out flyers to organize the student body to protect the mission and identity of the institution because he believes that the administration is trying to make MSSU a predominantly white institution through its diversity initiatives such as the creation of white scholarships. Most of his activities have led to racial tension between black and white students on campus. Many of the white students do not feel that they are welcomed to participate in many of the activities sponsored by the student government or student organizations. Therefore, most of the white students remain commuter students and just come to campus to attend classes.

The Problem

You are the new Vice Chancellor of Student Affairs and Enrollment Management for Mid-Southern State University. As the new enrollment manager you are charged with the duty of developing a recruitment plan to help diversify MSSU to achieve 10 percent white student enrollment. In addition to attracting white students, you are still held accountable to attracting, recruiting, and retaining traditional students that the university has historically served. Furthermore, you are responsible for the following functional units: student union, student activities and organizations, orientation, and the summer academy. Serving as the Vice Chancellor of Student Affairs, your responsibilities extend to collaborating with academic affairs so that the mission and identity you are trying to create for your functional units are aligned with the mission and identity of the university.

Discussion Questions

1. How do you accomplish your duties when you have a student body and broad alumni base who are fearful that the new legislation will change the historical mission of the university, thus making MSSU a predominately white institution?
2. How will your recruitment initiatives achieve the goal of recruiting both black and white students, while maintaining the mission and identity of the university?
3. How do you accomplish collaboration between student affairs and academic affairs so that faculty can have more ownership in the programs and activities that you have charge over in an effort to get more students involved?
4. It is apparent from your investigation, that the mission and identity of the university are not quite clear among faculty or students. Furthermore, there are racial tensions brewing between black and white students. How do you get both black and white students, and other students of color, engaged with the university so that no student or ethnic groups are marginalized?
5. Can a black university maintain its historical identity and mission, while attracting diverse students? Or must a black university let go of its historical past, in order to have a future?
6. What are the policy implications that *Ayers* legislation has on your responsibilities?
7. What steps can you take as the Vice Chancellor of Students Affairs and Enrollment Management to get your key players aligned with your vision for your department, which also supports the identity and mission of the university?

References

Brown, M.C. (2001). Collegiate Desegregation and the public black College: A new policy mandate. *The Journal of Higher Education, 72* (1), 46–62.

Brown, M.C. & Hendrickson, R. (1997, January). Public historically black colleges at the crossroads. *Journal for a Just and Caring Education, 3* (1), 95–113.

Charge to the Mid-Southern State University community one (2001). [online]. Available: *http://mssu.edu/Mission-statement%5B1%5D.htm.* [December 4, 2001].

Haynes, L. (Ed.). (1978). A *critical examination of the Adams case: A source book.* Washington, D.C: Institute for Services to Education.

Hollis, M. & Wright, S. (21 April, 1997). Quirky desegregation court orders caps Alabama colleges' enrollment. *Community College Week*, 9 (19), 10.

Sykes, M. (1995, August). The origins of affirmative action. [online]. Available: *www.now.org//nnt/08-95/affirmhs.html*. [December 6, 2000].

St. John, E. (1997). Desegregation at a crosswinds. *Journal for a Just and Caring Education*, 3 (1), 127–134.

United States v. Fordice, 112 S. Ct. 2727 (1992).

Recommended Readings

Adams v. Richardson, 356 F. Supp. 92 (D.D.C.1973).

Allen, W. & Jewell, J.O. (2002). A backward glance forward: Past, present, and future perspectives on historically Black colleges and universities. *The Review of Higher Education*, 25, (3) 241–261.

Anderson, J. (1988). *The education of blacks in the south, 1860–1935*. Chapel Hill: The University of North Carolina Press.

Ayers v. Fordice, U.S. District Court for Northern Mississippi (1994).

Ayers v. Musgrove, U.S. District Court for Northern Mississipi (2001).

Brown, M.C. (2001). Collegiate desegregation and the public black College: A new policy mandate. *The Journal of Higher Education*, 72 (1), 46–62.

——— (1999). *The quest to define collegiate desegregation: Black colleges, title VI compliance, and post-Adams litigation*. Westport: Bergin & Garvey.

Brown, M.C. & Hendrickson, R. (1997, January). Public historically black colleges at the crossroads. *Journal for a Just and Caring Education*, 3 (1), 95–113.

Darden, J.T., Bagaka, J.G., & Kamel, S.M. (1996). Historically black institutions and desegregation: The dilemma revisited. *Equity & Excellence in Education*, 29 (2), 56–68.

Fleming, J. (1984). *Blacks in college*. San Francisco, CA: Jossey-Bass.

Hossler, D. (1997). Historically black public colleges and universities; Scholarly inquiry and persona reflections. *Journal For a Just and Caring Education*, 3 (1), 114–127.

Lum, L. (2001, March 29). Will historic inequalities ever be remedied? *Black Issues in Higher Education*, 18 (3), 32–39.

Merisotis, J.P. & O' Brien, C.T. (Eds.). (1998, Summer). *Minority Serving Institutions: Distinct Purposes, Common Goals*. San Francisco, CA: Jossey-Bass.

McDonough, P.M., Antonio, A.L. (1997, January). Black students, black colleges: An African American college choice model. *Journal for a Just and Caring Education*, 3 (1), 9–36.

Preer, J.L. (1982). *Lawyers v. educators: Black colleges and desegregation in public higher education*. Westport, CT: Greenwood Press.

Redd, K.E. (1998, Summer). Historically black colleges and universities: Making a comeback. *Minority-serving institutions: distinct purposes, common goals*, 26 (2), 17–32.

St. John, E. (1997). Desegregation at a crosswinds. *Journal for a Just and Caring Education*, 3 (1), 127–134.

St. John, E. & Musoba, G. (2001, October). Academic access and equal opportunity: Rethinking the foundations for policy on diversity. Policy Research Report #01–06. Bloomington, IN: Indiana University.

Stefkovich, J. & Leas, T. (1994). A legal history of desegregation in higher education. *Journal of Negro Education*, 63 (3), 406–420.

Taylor, E. & Olswang, S. (1999). Peril or promise: The effect of desegregation litigation on historically black colleges. *The Western Journal of Black Studies*, 23 (2), 73—81.

United States v. Fordice, 112 S. Ct. 2727 (1992).

Williams, J.B. (1997). System-wide desegregation of public higher education: A research agenda. *Journal for a Just & Caring Education*, 3 (1), 63–76.

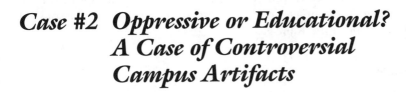

Case #2 Oppressive or Educational?
A Case of Controversial
Campus Artifacts

RACHELLE WINKLE WAGNER

Campus artifacts, such as murals, art, and buildings are a representation of the campus ethos and mission. This case, at a large public predominantly white institution, provides an example of how keeping a racially volatile classroom mural, was viewed as educational for some and as oppressive for others.

Introduction

This case will examine the decision-making process regarding a controversial classroom mural. Some students, staff, and faculty of the institution felt that the final decision to keep the mural intact in the classroom represented academic freedom, free speech, and the need to educate about the state's volatile history of race, ethnicity, and culture. On the contrary, others felt that the decision was oppressive or even an example of white privilege.

Institutional Setting and Background

Middleton University (MU) is a large, research extensive university, with over 38,000 undergraduate and graduate students in a mid-south state. Middleton University is a predominantly white institution in the charming college town of Burnsville with a population of approximately 70,000 people. Burnsville is a predominantly white community where over 85% of the community is white.

In the 1920s, a prominent artist, Randall Frist, painted a mural depicting the history of the state in a public theater in Coolidge Hall, which later became a large lecture classroom on the MU campus. The 250 foot long mural, "Education, the Klan, and the Press," included a central image of the Ku Klux Klan beside a flaming cross. At the time, the depiction of the Ku Klux Klan was considered progressive by many because of its honest portrayal of an ugly period of the state's history. During the 1920s, the state was a Ku Klux Klan stronghold. The surrounding area of Burnsville continued to be at the center of Klan activity from the post-Civil War period through the Civil Rights Movement of the 1960s. The painting of the Ku Klux Klan also includes images of journalists, who eventually broke some of the political power of the Klan.

Key Characters

Talia James: an African American senior sociology major, originally from Florida, is the president of the Black Student Union (BSU). Since her first year in college, the BSU has discussed the Frist Mural. As part of her platform upon becoming president of the BSU, James decided to lead a movement against the continued display of the mural. Since becoming president of the BSU, she has attempted to build unity among the masses of black students on campus. She also has collaborated with other organizations to build a multi-racial anti-mural front among student organizations on campus. Talia's first class at MU was held in the classroom with the Frist mural. It made her very uncomfortable to look up and see Ku Klux Klan depictions while she was trying to learn about sociology.

Dr. Cynthia Felder: a white woman, has been the Chancellor of MU for three years. Felder has been particularly interested in trying to diversify the images on campus through artwork and the recruitment of students and faculty. She is committed to diversity on campus and has been instrumental in recruitment policies to help diversify the faculty, administration, and student populations.

Dr. Gonzalez: a Latino professor of journalism, is the current president of the Faculty Senate. His research interests include academic freedom and first amendment rights as they are portrayed in the media. He sees his role as the faculty senate president as trying to ensure that these rights are maintained within MU.

Dr. Frank Malone: an African American man, is a professor in criminal justice and chair of the Racial Incidents Team. His research interests include racial policies and legislation and the imprisonment of African American males. He is committed to making the campus a more safe and welcoming place.

Timothy Saunders: a white undergraduate man from Ohio, is a junior telemarketing major. He is a member of the track team and does not understand the racial division within his team. He feels that the debate over this mural will only work to further divide students along racial lines on campus.

Kara Edwards: an African American sophomore communication studies major from North Carolina feels that the mural should continue to be displayed. She believes that African American students should face their history in the United States and move beyond it. Her opinion is that covering the mural would only work to keep students from understanding the reality of historical racism in the state and in the country.

Jonathan Cooper: an African American man, is a junior music major. He is a member of the Black Student Union and supports the covering or removal of the mural. Cooper, originally from New York, does not feel comfortable in Burnsville. He constantly feels like he is being watched and has heard stories about overt racism in the surrounding towns.

Michelle Johnson: a white female senior Spanish major opposes the display of the mural. Johnson grew up in Kansas and has traveled extensively internationally. She believes that the mural portrays domination and oppression and students should have the right to choose if they want to view it.

Case

Almost seventy years after the mural had been painted, in March 2002, students on the MU campus, led by the Black Student Union, argued that the mural should be removed or covered because it brought pain to many of the students who saw it. The Black Student Union president, Talia James, asserted "Students understand that art is controversial . . . But in a classroom where I'm trying to learn about sociology, I don't need to be confronted with images of the Ku Klux Klan to be enlightened."

There were thirty-five complaints to the Middleton University Racial Incidents Team regarding the mural. Dr. Frank Malone, chair of the University Racial Incidents team reported that the vast majority of the reports favored covering the mural during classes, or removing it for display in a museum or elsewhere. For example, Malone explained, one African American student reported feeling as if she was in danger of violence when she saw the mural in the classroom. Another African American student reported to the Racial Incidents Team that when he sat in the classroom, he did not feel that it was safe to speak his mind because of the mural. Malone explained that white students also complained to the Racial Incidents Team. One student explained that she felt continuing to display the mural kept her from moving past the racism of her family members who lived in the state during the time that the mural was painted. Malone reported that the Racial Incidents Team held the position that the mural should not continue to be displayed in a prominent classroom where students did not have a choice of whether or not they saw it. Dr. Malone advocated for the covering of the mural.

Some proponents of the mural, like junior telemarketing major, Timothy Saunders, contended that to remove it would represent an act of censorship. Saunders claimed that the removal, or covering, of the mural would deny first amendment rights on campus. Dr. Fredrico Gonzalez, president of the faculty senate concurred with this viewpoint asserting that the denial of free speech on campus could jeopardize academic freedom.

The Decision on the Mural

On March 25, 2002 the MU Chancellor, Cynthia Felder, announced that the mural would remain in the classroom and that removing it would hide the shameful aspects of the state's past history. Some students, like Timothy Saunders and Kara Edwards, praised Felder's decision. Both Saunders and Edwards strongly felt that the mural could be used as an educational tool for all students, regardless of ethnic background. Saunders argued that if the mural were removed, it would negatively impact the educational experiences, especially of white students, to fail to understand the shameful history of racism. Edwards argued that African American students needed to face the painful past in order to move on from it.

In an attempt to appease the upset students, a small sign was placed near the mural explaining that it was not intended to glorify the Klan. Professors teaching in the classroom were mandated to show students a video explaining the work at the beginning of each semester. Dr. Fredrico Gonzalez, the Faculty Senate President considers this mandate to be a violation of academic freedom in the classroom. Gonzalez maintained that forcing all faculty to show a particular video encroaches on the choices of faculty to choose the content of their courses.

Following the decision for the mural to remain, Felder further emphasized the importance of diversity on the Burnsville campus saying that now MU should be compelled to act on its commitment to diversity. She further outlined a three-part diversity plan to include an education program, the establishment of a fund to raise private support for more diverse campus art, and the inclusion of a diversity section in the new student orientation sessions.

The Frist Mural as Educational or Oppressive?

The mural decision split the students, staff, and faculty into two camps which were both racially diverse: those who considered the decision to be in the interest of education, academic freedom, and free speech; and those who considered the decision to be an example of white privilege and oppression of minority students. To date, there is little reconciliation on campus between these two predominant views regarding the Frist Mural decision.

Michelle Johnson, an opponent of the mural was concerned that the mural may hinder learning in the classroom. She maintained that while she did not want to run from the history depicted by the mural, artwork that makes some students uncomfortable and/or unable to learn does not belong in the classroom. Further, Johnson considered the remaining mural to be an example of white privilege: the privilege of whites to decide what is oppressive or educational on campus. Jonathan Cooper, a junior music major described his feelings upon seeing the mural in his entry-level psychology class. Cooper explained that the mural made him feel like he stood out or that he didn't belong in his predominantly white lecture classes.

During the controversy surrounding the mural, Chancellor Felder, a white woman, noted that if students do not have the context with which to interpret the mural and do not have a choice of whether or not they can view it, it is likely going to cause discomfort for some students. She continued that it could be particularly uncomfortable for African American students who comprise only 3% of the campus population. However, Felder maintained that in the interest of free speech, academic freedom, and educating students about history, even painful history, the mural would remain.

Was this an example of white privilege? Privilege consists of the ability to define social norms. Relying on this privilege allows the avoidance and objection to oppression, and the blinding of rarely seeing the self as privileged (Wildman and Davis, 1997, p. 316). White privilege is defined as an invisible package of unearned assets, often unseen by those who are privileged, or the invisible standard by which everything is measured (Delgado & Stefanic, 1997; Frankenburg, 1993; Giroux, 1997; Keating, 1995; Mahoney, 1997; McIntosh, 1992).

Talia James, President of the BSU argued that the audience for this mural was arguably a white audience as the depictions seem to be educating those who did not know about, or those who desired to ignore, the Klan's history in the state. She asserted that as an African American student, this assumption about educating white students left her out, almost assuming that she would not be present in the classroom. Dr. Malone, concerned about all of the reports about the mural that had been turned into the Racial Incidents Team concurred that this assumption could work to privilege white students on campus.

On the contrary, some considered the mural to be necessary to maintain education, academic freedom, and free speech on campus. For example, academic freedom can be defined as, "the freedom of the individual scholar in his-her teaching and research to pursue truth, wherever it seems to lead, without fear of punishment or termination of employment for having offended some political, religious, or social orthodoxy" (Berdahl, 1990/1997, p. 470). Dr. Gonzalez, as President of the faculty senate, argued that the removal of the mural would lead to a "slippery slope" where professors would eventually be told what they could teach, say, or research. Further, Gonzalez maintained that it was the responsibility of educational institutions to confront sometimes harsh realities of past history, even though some history is painful.

Timothy Saunders, as a white student on campus, explained that he did not understand why it was a problem to display the mural. He asserted that it is part of history, and white people historically did have power over other groups, so this reality should be displayed. Another student, Kara Edwards, questioned why the African American students would want to make a big deal about the mural. She claimed that the uproar about the mural would only work to separate the student body along racial lines.

Summary

The Frist Mural provides an example of ways in which campus artifacts can spur discussions about race, oppression, white privilege, academic freedom, free speech, and education. In this case, the decision-making process was seen as an example of white privilege and discrimination by some; and as an example of a necessary educational tool representing academic freedom and free speech by others. The final decision was to allow the mural to remain. This case provides an example of the complexity of decisions regarding campus artifacts and ethos.

So, was the decision-making process and remaining mural an artifact of Middleton University's commitment to education, even in the face of painful history and controversy? Is it an illustration of a commitment to academic freedom and free speech within a public institution? Or, was the remaining mural and decisions made regarding it a symbol of oppression and white privilege?

Discussion Questions

1. The following are example decision options concerning the mural in the classroom: cover the mural, destroy the mural, allow the mural to remain, or stop using the lecture hall. Of these options, or others you develop, which option would you choose as a student affairs administrator? Who does the option represent or fail to represent?

2. The mural decision is asserted as representing two opposing viewpoints: education, academic freedom, and free speech versus white

privilege and oppression. In what ways can student affairs practitioners make themselves aware of these issues? Can these opposing viewpoints be reconciled?

3. List some solutions to this controversy and the action steps necessary to make them happen.

4. After a campus controversy like the one mentioned in this case study, there is a need for healing on campus. What are some strategies that could be used to help the students, staff, and faculty heal from this controversy?

5. One of the solutions listed by Chancellor Felder was to restate the campus commitment to diversity. What are some ways that a campus can display a commitment to diversity in light of this decision?

6. What is the role of student affairs practitioners in diversity initiatives?

7. Discuss other examples of white privilege that may exist at predominantly white institutions of higher education. Do some of these examples come into conflict regarding academic freedom and/or free speech?

References

Berdahl, R. (1990/1997). Public universities and state governments: Is the tension benign? In L.F. Goodchild, C.D. Lovell, E.R Hines, & J.I. Gill (Eds.). *Public policy and higher education: ASHE reader series*, (pp. 470–475). Boston, MA: Pearson Custom Publishing.

Delgado, R. & Stefanic, J. (1997). *Critical White studies: Looking behind the mirror.* Philadelphia, PA: Temple University Press.

Frankenburg, R. (1993). *White women, race matters: The social construction of whiteness.* Minneapolis: University of Minnesota Press.

Giroux, Henry. (1997). Rewriting the discourse of racial identity: Towards a pedagogy and politics of whiteness. *Harvard Educational Review*, 67 (2), 285–320.

Keating, A. (1995, December). Interrogating "whiteness," deconstructing "race." *College English*, 57 (8), 901–918.

Mahoney, M.R. (1997). Racial construction and women as differentiated actors. In Richard Delgado & Jean Stefanic (Eds.). *Critical white studies: Looking behind the mirror*, (pp. 305–309). Philadelphia, PA: Temple University Press.

McIntosh, P. (1992). White privilege and male privilege: A personal account of coming to see correspondence through work in Women's Studies. In M. Anderson & P.H Collins (Eds.). *Race, Class, Gender*, (pp. 291–299). Belmont, CA: Wadsworth Publishers.

Wildman, S.M. & Davis, Adrienne, D. (1997). Making systems of privilege visible. In Richard Delgado & Jean Stefanic (Eds.). *Critical white studies: Looking behind the mirror*, (314–319). Philadelphia, PA: Temple University Press.

Recommended Readings on White Privilege and Academic Freedom

Altbach, P.G., Berdahl, R.O. & Gumport, P.J. *American higher education in the twenty-first century: Social, political, and economic changes.* Baltimore, MD: The Johns Hopkins University Press.

O'Neil, R.M. (1999). Academic freedom: Past, present, and future. In P.G. Altbach, R.O. Berdahl, & P.J. Gumport (Eds.). *American higher education in the twenty-first century: Social, political, and economic changes,* (pp. 89–108). Baltimore, MD: The Johns Hopkins University Press.

Delgado, R. & Stefanic, J. (2001). *Critical race theory: An introduction.* New York: New York University Press.

Hill, M. (Ed.) *Whiteness: A critical reader.* New York: New York University Press.

Giroux, Henry. (1997). Rewriting the discourse of racial identity: Towards a pedagogy and politics of whiteness. *Harvard Educational Review,* 67 (2), 285–320.

Maher, F.A. & Tetreault, M.K. Thompson. (1997). Learning in the dark: How assumptions of Whiteness shape classroom knowledge. *Harvard Educational Review,* 67 (2) (summer), 321–349.

Case #3　In the Name of Honor: Impact of American Indian Mascots at Institutions of Higher Education

SUSAN D. JOHNSON

Mascots have long been a source of pride for institutions of higher education. Yet, certain mascots, particularly those using American Indian imagery, can be a concurrent source of both pride and anger for students at institutions of higher education. Such is the case with the Golden University campus. The campus has utilized an Indian head logo for the last fifty years of its existence. The initial mascot was changed per the request of the athletic department to portray a more menacing image to opposing teams. Over the years, the number of American Indian students on the campus has increased and with that, so has greater opposition to an American Indian mascot. The controversial issue has come to the forefront again with a recent proposal to finance an American Indian Cultural Center with a special fund-raising campaign through the alumni association. Students, faculty, and staff opposed to the American Indian mascot have organized a protest calling for the retirement of the mascot concurrently with the construction of the proposed American Indian Cultural Center.

Institutional Setting

Golden University is a doctoral research-intensive university located in the southwest. Founded in the late 1800s, the student population has grown to approximately 20,000. Known for its athletic tradition, Golden University is a top-ranked school in football and basketball—winning division and/or national titles for the last fifteen years. Over the last decade, the enrollment management division has made strides in the recruitment of students of color to the University, which has been a priority of President Aims and the university's strategic long-range plan. Located near several American Indian reservations (including Navajo, Pueblo, and Zuni tribes), Golden University's minority student population currently makes up 10% of the total student population (American Indian, African American, Latino, and Asian students make up 5%, 2%, 2%, and 1% respectively). With the increased number of students of color has come greater opposition to the university's use of an American Indian mascot: controversial depictions of American Indians against opposing team mascots on T-shirts; a "tomahawk" chop and chant at athletic events; and a student portraying "Chief Golden" at various school athletic events.

Recently, several student and faculty organizations, including the American Indian Student Association (AISA), the Black Student Union (BSU), and the Multicultural Faculty Association (MFA), have proposed a special campaign to fund the building of an American Indian Cultural Center. Despite the fact that American Indian students comprise most of the minority student population, no cultural center is currently dedicated to programs and practices to service the needs of American Indian students at Golden University. Separate cultural centers currently exist, however, for African American, Latino, and international students.

One section of the proposal calls for the removal of the institution's American Indian mascot out of respect for the American Indian culture. To further their cause, organizers have invited the president of the Movement for American Indian Rights to campus for a lecture. Following the speech, organizers staged a protest the next day in front of the administration building. Several student participants were detained by the Department of University Police. Andrea Collins, the Dean of Students and Multicultural Affairs, has asked President Aims repeatedly to address this by holding public forums to discuss the mascot issue, yet has been repeatedly rebuffed by him and other administrators.

Key Characters

Sherman Sage: President of the American Indian Student Association (AISA) and one of the students detained by the Department of University Police during the protest.

Brendon Aims: is in his tenth year as President of Golden University. During his tenure, Golden University has experienced increased student enrollments, record-setting private donations from alumni, and a more diverse faculty, staff, and student population. He considers the mascot issue to be very divisive. Although he addressed the possibility of retiring the mascot with the Board of Trustees when he first arrived, he has not raised the issue since with the Board or any other constituents.

Andrea Collins: Dean of Students and Multicultural Affairs, is an African American alumnus of Golden University. Prior to becoming a dean, she advised both the American Indian Student Association and Black Student Union in her former position as director of Student Activities. She has often expressed her dislike of the use of an American Indian mascot.

Lexi Monroe: President of the Black Student Union was also detained by the University Police following the protest. She has been instrumental in rallying African American students to support the removal of an American Indian mascot and to build an American Indian Cultural Center.

Peter Franklin: Vice President of Student Affairs, is a trusted advisor to President Aims and has been with the university for the past twenty-five years.

Owen Yates: Director of the Alumni Association is opposed to starting a fund-raising campaign for an American Indian Cultural Center and feels alumni money should instead go toward building a new seating addition to the football stadium.

Karen Givens: Vice President of Enrollment Management, is the only female senior administrator at Golden University. Karen and her department have exceeded the president's goal to increase the ratio of students of color at Golden University. She has also worked diligently to mentor Andrea whenever possible and to prepare her as a senior administrator.

The Problem

You are Peter Franklin, Vice President of Student Affairs, and the direct supervisor of Andrea Collins. You are in the process of preparing for an accreditation site visit from the Department of Education's Civil Rights Office (CRO). The site visit was instigated by repeated comments and complaints from students, faculty, and staff about how the use of an American Indian mascot promoted a racially hostile environment at Golden University—a direct violation of the Title VI federal guideline.

Key Facts

Monday. You have a meeting with Andrea Collins, dean of Students and Multicultural Affairs, and two student leaders, Sherman Sage, president of the American Indian Student Association, and Lexi Monroe, president of the Black Student Union, to discuss a proposal for an American Indian Cultural Center. Andrea and several faculty members have worked closely with the students to prepare the proposal. One concern you raise is the request for the university to cease the use of an American Indian mascot prior to building a cultural center for American Indian students. The students argue that an American Indian Cultural Center would have little to no value or meaning if an Indian mascot continued to exist on the campus. They site instances of harassment, lewd comments and gestures, and the overall insult of a white student dressed as "Chief Golden." You state that the center would be a definite asset to the campus and that you can appreciate their argument against the mascot. You further state that this is not a decision you can make alone. Since the proposal calls for the use of alumni funds to build the cultural center and the president sets the priority for usage of alumni funds, you state that you will discuss the proposal at the next cabinet meeting with the president and other senior administrators on Wednesday. Sherman and Lexi note that they are willing to take action to keep this topic in the forefront and not rest until the mascot is retired.

Wednesday. The cabinet gathers for its weekly meeting. In attendance are you, President Aims, Vice President Givens, and Alumni Association Director, Owen Yates. At the top of the agenda is the upcoming site visit from CRO on Friday. The cabinet reviews the various reports on students of color from enrollment management and the institutional research office. Vice President Givens mentions that the CRO has arranged to interview several American Indian student leaders while at Golden University. You mention your earlier meeting with Sherman Sage and Lexi Monroe about the proposed American Indian Cultural Center. Owen Yates immediately expresses his opposition to the use of alumni funds for yet another cultural center. He reminds the cabinet that the next presidential priority for alumni funds is the addition of a new seating section for the football stadium. The president interrupts and stresses to the cabinet that the CRO is a more immediate concern and should be the primary focus for now.

Thursday. The President of the Movement for American Indian Rights speaks in the university auditorium. He recounts the efforts of people across the country attempting to retire American Indian mascots at institutions of higher education. Several white students gather outside the auditorium with signs saying "Go back to the reservation if you don't like it here!" before the lecture.

Friday. You are in a site visit meeting in the administration building with members of the CRO when you hear a disturbance outside. Hundreds of students, faculty, and staff have gathered outside the building chanting "Hey, hey, ho, ho, the Indian mascot has to go!" The protest occurs during a prime class period and draws the attention of many teachers and students in the surrounding academic buildings. Because of the noise level, the Department of University Police arrives to disperse the crowd. Still chanting loudly, several people, including Sherman and Lexi, refuse to leave. After several hours, the students are detained by the University Police for failure to comply with an officer.

Following weeks. The protest has received local and national attention, including write-ups in national higher education magazines and newspapers. The Civil Rights Office delivers a negative report to Golden University with several guidelines—one of which is the retirement of the mascot. Failure to address the guidelines by the end of the following year could result in a loss of the federal funding amount currently available to Golden University.

Lexi and Sherman are said to have violated the Code of Student Conduct. Because of her ties to the students, Andrea has removed herself from hearing their cases. Consequently, you must hear the cases in her place.

Multiple Perspectives

Alumni. Even though the institution did not always have an American Indian mascot, the current mascot has become an inherent part of the traditions at Golden University. Alumni are strongly opposed to the idea of being known as something other than the "Golden Warriors" and many have written to the Alumni Association to indicate their withdrawal of financial support should the mascot be retired.

American Indian students. While many American Indian students want the mascot retired, not all American Indian students are opposed to the use of the mascot. Some argue that it is honorable to use the image of a warrior as the university's mascot. This has created some division amongst the American Indian students on the campus. Some administrators, particularly Owen Yates, use this division to support keeping the mascot. Sherman is doing what he can to present a united front from the American Indian Student Association. However, he will graduate in six months and is concerned about others stepping up to continue the cause.

Other students of color. The BSU has been the most avid supporter among other students of color in the retirement of an American Indian mascot. Other student organizations have not been as vocal. The BSU has done joint programming with the American Indian Student Association to further educate the campus about the racist connotation of an American Indian mascot and will continue to support the AISA in any way they can.

White students. Most white students wish the problem would simply go away. They do not see the problem with being "Golden Warriors." They claim to use the mascot in a respectful manner and argue that they cannot help what opposing teams do at athletic events. In the past, white Greek organizations have placed teepees in their front lawn and held cowboy and Indian parties during homecoming. While this has not happened for a number of years, it is still a point of contention between white and American Indian students on the campus.

Faculty. The Multicultural Faculty Association has organized rallies in conjunction with the student groups. Other faculty support has been one rise. Just recently, the faculty senate approved a resolution in opposition to the use of an American Indian mascot.

Administration. President Aims has not addressed the mascot issue since he first arrived. The previous university president made some sweeping changes in regard to the mascot without consulting the Board of Trustees and President Aims is well aware of the potential consequences of defying the Board of Trustees. Vice President Givens has tried to support Andrea as a mentor, but cautions her about knowing which battles to fight—especially as a female administrator.

Discussion questions

Campus Climate

1. What are the campus climate issues in this case? How should the administration address these issues in the present and in the future?
2. How should the administration work with various university constituents (i.e., alumni, students, faculty) to address these issues?

Student Development

1. What student development theories are most pertinent to the issues in this case?
2. What sanctions, if any, should the students involved in the protest receive?
3. Consider the impact of an American Indian mascot on the ethnic/racial identity development of American Indian students. Will an American Indian Cultural Center sufficiently address the cultural needs of students on a campus with an American Indian mascot? If not, what other alternatives should the campus consider?

Organizational Theory

1. How is the use of an Indian mascot congruent or incongruent with CRO and other accreditation standards?
2. What are some group dynamic issues among the senior administration?

Resource

Rosenstein, J. (Writer/producer). (1996). *In whose honor?* [videorecording]. Ho-ho-kus, NJ: New Day Films.

Recommended Readings

Baca, L.R. (2004). Native images in schools and the racially hostile environment. *Journal of Sport and Social Issues*, 28, (1) 71–78.

Brooks, J.F. (2002). *Confounding the color line: the Indian-Black experience in North America.* Lincoln: University of Nebraska Press.

King, C.R., & Springwood, C.F. (2001). *Team spirits: the Native American mascots controversy.* Lincoln: University of Nebraska Press.

Pewewardy, C. (1993). The tomahawk chop: The continuous struggle of unlearning "Indian" stereotypes. *Multicultural Education*, 1 (2), 14–15.

Spindel, C. (2000). *Dancing at halftime: Sports and the controversy over American Indian mascots.* New York: New York University Press.

Springwood, C.F. (2004). I'm Indian too!: Claiming Native American identity, crafting authority in mascot debates. *Journal of Sport and Social Issues*, 28 (1) 56–70.

Case #4 Organized Anarchy in Student Affairs: Organizational Structures Impact Black Greek Letter Organizations' Campus Experiences

O. GILBERT BROWN

Organized anarchy is a sense making theory that seeks to explain the paradox (centralization and decentralization) of colleges and universities academic and administrative organizational systems. Organized anarchy's distinctive features are: ambiguous goals, unclear technologies, loose coupling, fluid participation, highly educated professional work force, and clients who participate in institutional governance Baldridge et al., 1977; Birnbaum, 1988; Cohen and March, 1974; Weick, 1976, 1979 (as cited in Kuh, 2003).

Traditionally white Greek letter organizations (TWGLO) host many social events in fraternity or sorority houses located on or adjacent to the campus. Since historically black Greek letter organizations (HBGLO) do not have fraternity and sorority houses, they must host their social events in different university facilities. The university's approach to HBGLO' facilities challenges is complicated by three different administrative divisions' control of facilities that have been used or could be used for the organizations' weekend parties. The purpose of this case is to describe Mid-Western University's triad Student Affairs model's impact on historically HBGLO having unsatisfactory experiences creating and delivering academic support programs and social programming for the entire campus, especially undergraduate African Americans.

Many large institutions have adopted centralized, not decentralized, Student Affairs models to put into operation Student Affairs major functions (See Appendix A). Presently, Mid-West's triad Student Affairs model is composed of Student Development, Upward Mobility for All, and Auxiliary and Administrative Services divisions (See Appendix B). Mid-West's decentralized model varies from how many large institutions have organized their Student Affairs Division. Each autonomous division is lead by a Vice Chancellor, Vice Chancellor/Associate Vice President, or Associate Vice Chancellor administrative officer. In the last thirty years, Midwest' triad model is the fourth Student Affairs/Services model that the campus has implemented in an effort to provide Student Affairs functions to undergraduates. Previous organizational models were: (1) traditional centralized Student Affairs/Services model, (2) decentralized organizational model, (3) centralized Student Affairs model, (3) triad Student Affairs model, and (4) centralized Student Affairs model.

Mid-west's central administration and board of trustees have offered different reorganization rationales (benchmarking the best business practices to higher education, re-allocating funds from non-degree units to degree granting units, leveraging the campus resources to serve new sub-cohorts among undergraduates) to different internal and external stakeholders. Mid-West's re-organization pattern has created a leadership vacuum that has unintentionally contributed to HBGLO receiving unsatisfactory leadership/advising, logistics/facilities support, and regular resources from the campus.

Institutional Setting

Mid-Western University is a doctoral-intensive university with over 38,000 undergraduate and graduate students. U.S. News and World Report regularly highlight the South Hoisington campus as a premier research institution that offers excellent undergraduate education as well as an array of outstanding graduate programs. The campus is located in the picturesque college town of South Hoisington. South Hoisington is a predominately white community of 60,000 people, excluding the students. Respectively, Whites, Asians, Latinos, African Americans, and others make up 85%, 2%, 3%, 6%, and 4% of the South Hoisington population. In this case, we use the terms African American and black interchangeably. During the 40s and 50s, President Lucas Williams provided the watershed leadership that helped Mid-Western evolve from a regional university into an international university.

In addition, President Lucas played an exemplary role in creating a campus that welcomed all students regardless of race, sexual orientation, and gender. Emeritus and senior black faculty fondly recall President Lucas's role in establishing the black faculty presence on campus. In particular, President Lucas supported the founding of a watershed historically black Greek letter fraternity at Mid-Western. The founding of the fraternity contributed to the development of a climate that eventually welcomed the other eight historically black Greek-letter organizations called the Divine Nine.

The Divine Nine

The Divine Nine is an umbrella term that describes the nine HBGLO that are present on traditionally white institutions (TWIs) and historically black colleges and universities (HBCUs). TWGLO' charters prohibited Jewish, Blacks, and other underrepresented racial minorities' students from seeking membership in their organizations. The Divine Nine were shaped in the era of dejure (law) racial segregation around the country. Three of the organizations were established by students attending TWIs. At majority campuses, students sought to developed fraternities and sororities to meet students' multiple (support, group affiliation, or shared cultural interests) needs in these often hostile and chilly campus environments. At HBCUs, Six/Nine were developed by black students to provide undergraduates more affiliation and involvement options outside the classroom at warm and welcoming campus environments (Kimbrough, 2003; Ross, 2000).

Currently, Mid-West has eight/nine of the organizations who have active chapters who are making a difference inside and outside the campus community in the following areas. In the post Civil Rights era, the Divine Nine through their programs for affiliated and nonaffiliated students continue to facilitate diverse (low SES/majority black high schools, middle/SES students from racially mixed high schools, and upper SES who attend majority white public and private high schools) African American students having satisfactory transitional experiences going from high school to college. Then too, the Divine Nine at most campuses are responsible for organizing most of the social events for African American students and other students who enjoy the black cultural traditions.

Moreover, the Divine Nine through their service programming help narrow the town and gown divide between the campus and the larger Mid-West community. Also, the organizations create a welcoming environment that encourages African American, Asian, Latino, and White students' opportunities to develop common ground through their inclusive programs and activities. Next, alumni members of the organizations and the campus contribute to the strategic goal of African Americans using BA/BS attainment as an initial social escalator to foster their upward mobility in society. Thus, alumni members contribute to narrowing the well documented SES divide between the white majority and the black minority. Finally, senior institutional leaders appreciate the active organizations contributions to the campus' historic diversity and multicultural mosaic and traditions. HBGLO's continuous presence shows the organization's creativity in building sisterhood or brotherhood without the presence of an enduring physical structure. The reality is that HBGLO and the campus cannot seem to move forward in finding a way to ensure their regular access to campus facilities.

Many or Few Facilities: For Whom and For What

The mid-level Student Development administrators' recent facility survey agrees with HBGLO's informal assessment that Mid-Western has a range of academic and administrative facilities that could be made available to historical HBGLOs for their weekend social events. For example, the Eatman Student Recreation Center and the Volleyball Gym are facilities managed by the Wellbeing and Instruction Physical and Recreation Department and the Athletic Department. The academic department's vast spaces serve as teaching facilities for the different degree programs between 8:00 AM–4:00 PM throughout the regular academic week. The Student Recreational arm of the division offers informal and formal recreational opportunities for students between 4:00 and 11:00 PM throughout the week and between 8:00 AM and 12:00 PM on the weekend.

The quagmire in the campus has a range of facilities that HBGLO could potentially use for weekend parties, yet, the organizations cannot get regular access to the facilities for weekend parties. HBGLO's unsatisfactory experiences do not fit with the institution's analysis of its historical place in creating equity for all at Mid-Western.

"Talking the talk" or "walking the walk"

Historically, Mid-Western has not been shy in promoting a reputation of being in the vanguard regarding removing barriers that have impeded African Americans' attainment of satisfactory academic and social experiences on campus. However, Mid-Western's current policies toward HBGLO could be viewed by many as talking the talk, but not walking the walk. On the one hand, the campus's commitment to diversity and educational benefits for all students is publicly expressed in the Board of Trustee's publications, administrative units' web pages, and school catalogs. On the other hand, Mid-Western appears to support a de facto restrictive policy that places a significant burden on HBGLO.

Mid-Western's de facto policy is mirrored in these indicators: (a) support of a security policy that places a heavier financial burden on HBGLO than on TWGLO; (b) acquiescence to different units which place unfair financial burdens on HBGLO as a condition for the student groups' usage;

(c) establishment of in-effect consensus that HBGLO will be steered away from hosting weekend parties in the Descendants of West Africa Cultural Center and other select units; and (d) the disparity in resources (advising, logistical, and financial) allocated to TWGLO and HBGLO.

The university's approach to HBGLO's facilities use is challenged and complicated by three different administrative divisions' control of facilities that have been provided or could be assigned for the organization's weekend parties.

Administrative Structure

Five years ago, Mid-Western senior level administrators, with the approval of the Board of Trustees, reorganized non-instructional revenue and non-revenue-generating units that provide student services. The divisions are: Student Development, Upward Mobility for All, and Auxiliary and Administrative Services (See Appendix B). Administrative responsibility for the facilities rests with three different Vice Chancellors. Student Development was one of the largest non-degree-granting units on campus from the mid-80s to the late 90s. The Chancellor and his senior cabinet, with the support of the Board of Trustees, created Upward Mobility for All and Auxiliary and Administrative Services essentially by removing revenue-generating and high-visibility units from the traditional Student Development Division.

The Division of Student Development

In the last twenty-five years, the campus has developed four different configurations for the Student Development Division and Vice Chancellor Winfred has served the campus throughout the four configurations. Winfred earned his three degrees from Mid-Western Hills. Vice Chancellor Winfred is "the alumni's alumnus who has served as Vice Chancellor for ten years." Winfred is well respected by diverse students for his willingness to attend all student organizational events.

During his tenure, Winfred has been close to the vest in developing new programs, services, or implementing different administrative practices. Presently, Student Development's portfolio includes units like Disability Services, Judicial Affairs, Counseling Psychology Services, Student Legal Services, and the Student Activities/Greek Affairs Office (Appendix C). The Assistant Dean for Greek Affairs has not been shy in saying to colleagues that Dr. Armstrong, the Upward Mobility Vice Chancellor, could 'wave his magic wand' to solve the access problem by giving HBGLO regular access to the Adams/Moore Center Multi-purpose Room." Thus, Vice Chancellor Winfred can play an important role in developing short-and long-term solutions to the long-standing issues involving HBGLO' access to campus facilities.

Upwardly Mobility for All Division

Six years ago, the campus lured back Dean Armstrong as a "favorite son" black alumnus to serve as Vice Chancellor for Upward Mobility Services and Vice President for Excellence and Equity (Appendix D). Mid-Western really needed an administrator like Armstrong, following several negative newspaper articles about the low graduation rates of underrepresented students, especially black students; public wrangling between black faculty, students, and administrators regarding the Dean of the Afro-American Affairs Department's alleged ineffectiveness; several fights among black athletes and HBGLO members; and organizational fragmentation between units serving underrepresented students.

    Dr. Armstrong's dual rank reflects his leadership roles at the flagstaff South Hoisington campus as well as the five campus Mid-Western system. Armstrong is an important campus leader due in part to his previous tenure as Chancellor of two regional campuses in different states. Armstrong also has deep informal and formal connections to the Board of Trustees. His long administrative experience and political acumen have helped him to navigate the expectations and tensions associated with being a high-ranking black who had a foot in the "Big House" (main administrative building) and a strong presence on the "Yard" (undergraduate environment) with the rank and file brothers and sisters.

    Several years ago, the campus built a large Adams and Moore Academic and Support Center, which combined a new Descendants of West Africa Cultural Center and a new home for the Theater and Arts Department. Adams and Moore Center's multipurpose room is large enough to host HBGLO' weekend parties. HBGLO have asked the Upward Mobility Division for permission to have weekend dances in the multipurpose room. Entry level staff often gave HBGLOs vague reasons to justify turning down their requests to rent the facility for the weekend. Front line staff developed different diversions from keeping HBGLO leaders from appealing their negative decisions to Vice President Armstrong. Black student leaders have asked "How can Upward Mobility believe that the rest of the campus will let us use facilities, when our groups cannot use the Descendants of West Africa Cultural Center facilities?"

Division of Auxiliary and Administrative Services

Seven years ago, the campus consolidated all revenue-generating student services units, including the Union, Residence Halls, and the Auditorium, under new Associate Vice Chancellor Potter. For unknown reasons, central administration assigned the newly consolidated residence (management and student life) hall system to be part of the new Division of Administrative Services (See Appendix E). The new Associate Vice Chancellor served as an Associate Dean of Students under the current Vice Chancellor for Student Development. Potter served the campus in numerous capacities before assuming his current position. By Mid-Western standards, having served ten years, he is still "new" to the campus.

Most of the venues suitable for weekend dances belong to Potter's division. Vice Chancellor Potter's meteoric rise to senior leadership makes him a key player in the campus' crafting of short-and long-term approaches to the facilities issue.

Action

Recently, the descendants of West Africa Cultural Center held a leadership retreat for incoming black student leaders. Student leaders' simmering frustrations about Greek organizations access to campus facilities for weekend parties disrupted the question-and-answer session which followed the keynote speech. Students sought the keynote speaker's advice on how to address the continuing problems over facilities access.

Discussion Questions

Following are some key questions that should be considered regarding the case:

1. Organized anarchy's characteristics are ambiguous goals, unclear technologies, loose coupling, fluid participation, highly educated professional work force, and clients who participate in institutional governance. What are the indicators of organized anarchy in the Mid-Western University's triad Student Affairs organizational structure? What role do the campus's traditions and culture play in central administration and the board of trustees' tendency to frequently re-organize the Student Affairs functions? How does the triad Student Affairs model impact the white and black racial divide that exists above and below the surface at the campus?

2. What are the indicators that the triad Student Affairs model has impacted HBGLO and its supporters' perceptions and feelings about the campus?

3. Senior-level and mid-level professionals in two of the three divisions appear to have different collaboration approaches with each other regarding HBGLO's usage of campus facilities. What leadership

and organizational theories would you draw upon to help mid-level professionals maximize their cooperation in this organized anarchy environment?

4. How are the three Student Service-related divisions' practices toward TWGLO and HBGLO congruent or incongruent with the Council for Advancement of Standards in Higher Education (CASE)? What are opportunities and challenges of benchmarking Mid-Western's triad Student Affairs model with their peer institutions' organizational models for Student Affairs?

Outside Consultant

You are an outside consultant for Mid-Western University.

1. Who are the decision makers(s) in the case?
2. What are the constraints (political, economic, and undergraduate demographic composition,) impacting stakeholders' decisions?
3. What options (helping HBGLO to gain more resources, establishing a campus-wide commission, or developing a centralized campus-wide facility resource center) are more desirable than others?
4. Provide five recommendations that will move the campus toward developing a Student Affairs organizational model that fosters undergraduates having more satisfactory social experiences that contribute to their graduation.

Appendix A

Mid-Western University
Student Affairs Organizational Benchmarking Study

Introduction

On many campuses institutional leaders (Boards of Trustees and President/Chancellor) established Student Affairs as a free standing centralized division reporting to the president or chancellor. Briefly, Student Affairs major functions are: Academic advising, Admissions, Assessment/Research/ Program Development, Athletics, Campus Safety, Career Development, College Unions, Service Learning Programs, Commuter Services/Off Campus housing, Student Legal Services, Counseling/Psychological Services, Dean of Students Office, Dining and Food service, Disability Support Services, Enrollment Management, Financial Aid, Fundraising and Fund

Development, Greek Affairs, Health Services, International Student Services, Judicial Affairs, Leadership Programs, Lesbian, Gay Bisexual and Transgender (LGBT) Student Services, Multi Cultural Services, First Year Experience Programs, Recreation and Fitness Programs, Religious Programs and Services, Registration Services, Residence Life/Housing, Student Activities, and Women's Center (Dungy Jordan, 2003). For different reasons, IHEs especially in large campuses began downsizing their Student Affairs functions from a centralized into several different organizational structures like Housing/Residence Life, Support Services Programs for Underrepresented Students, Enrollment Management, and Student Affairs Divisions.

Mid-Western is a long time member of comprehensive athletic conference composed of 11 major research universities. The aim of the benchmarking study is to compare and contrast Mid-West distribution of Student Affairs functions against its peer institutions in the conference. False institutional names are listed in order to preserve the confidential nature of aspects of the study. The frequency of X in the table's categories illustrates the degree of centralization or decentralization of an institution's Student Affairs functions: (1) 1X Highly Centralized (0), (2) 2X Centralized 5(f), (3) 3X Decentralized (3f), and (4) 4X Highly Decentralized 3(f). The table shows that conference is roughly evenly split between centralization (5/11) and decentralization (6/11) in the organization of their Student Affairs functions:

Peer Institutions	Traditional Student Affairs Organization	Housing/Residence Life Department either free standing division or linked to another not Student Affairs division	Underrepresented Students division either free standing division or affiliated with Provost	Enrollment Management Division either free standing division, linked to another division, or affiliated with Provost
Pearson University	X		X	X
Blue Chip University	X	X		
Mid-Western University	X	X	X	X
Fab Four University	X		X	
Magic University	X	X		X
McHale University	X	X		
Heal University	X			X
Raiders University	X		X	X
Larned University	X	X		
Holmstrom University	X	X	X	X
Harris University	X	X	X	X

Appendix B

Campus Organizational Chart

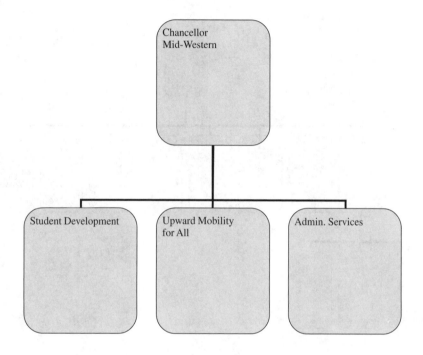

Appendix C

Student Development Organizational Chart

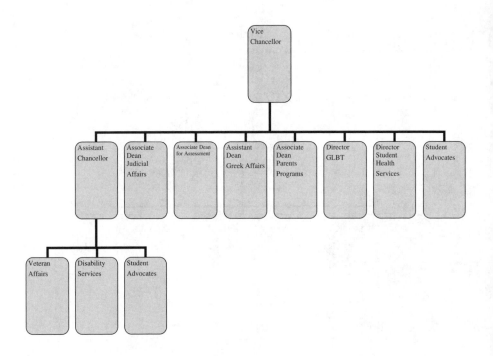

Appendix D

Upward Mobility for All Organizational Chart

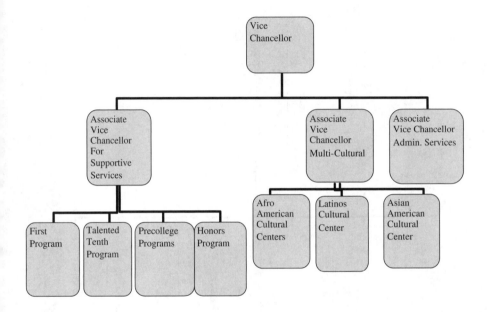

Appendix E

Admin. Services

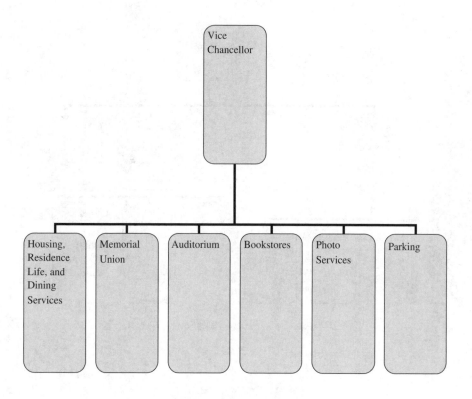

References

Dungy Jordan, G. (2003). Organization and functions in student affairs. In S. Komives, D. Woodward, Jr., and Associates, (Ed.), Student Services: a handbook for the profession, (4th ed.pgs 339–357). San Francisco: Jossey Bass Publishers.

Kimbrough, W. (2003). *Black greek 101: The culture, customs, and challenges of black fraternities and sororities.* Danvers, Mass.: Rosemont Publishing & Printing Corp.

Kuh, G. (2003). Organizational theory. In S. Komives, D. Woodward, Jr., and Associates, (Ed.), Student Services: a handbook for the profession, (4th ed.pgs 269–296). San Francisco: Jossey Bass Publishers.

Ross, L. (2000). *The Divine nine: The history of African American fraternities and sororities.* New York NY, Kensington Publishing Corp.

Recommended Background Reading

Astin, A.W. & Helen S.A. (2000). Leadership reconsidered: Engaging higher education in social change. Battle Creek: W.K. Kellogg Foundation.

Eckel, P., Green, M., & Hill, B. (2001). On change V: Riding the waves of change: Insights from transforming institutions. Washington, D.C.: American Council on Education.

Hurtado, S., Milem, J., Pedersen-Clayton, A., & Allen, W. (1996). Enhancing campus climates for racial/ethnic diversity: Educational policy and practice. In C. Turner, A. Lising Antonio, & M. Garcia (Ed.), Racial and ethnic diversity in higher education, (pp. 671–685). Boston, MA: Pearson Custom Publishing.

Kuh, G. & Whitt, E. (1988). The invisible tapestry: Culture in American colleges and universities. Washington, D.C.: ERIC Clearing on Higher Education.

Miller, T. (2003). CAS: The book of professional standards for higher education. Washington, DC: Council for the Advancement of Standards in Higher Education.

Peterson, M. W., Dill, D.D., Mets, L.A. & Associates. (1997). Planning and management for a changing environment. San Francisco, CA: Jossey Bass.

Tinto, V. (1993). Leaving college: Rethinking the causes of student and cures of student attrition. Chicago and London: The University of Chicago Press.

West. C. (1993). Race matters. Boston, MA: Boston Press.

Case #5 Conflict in the Midst of Culture: The Transition From Cultural Center to Multicultural Center

Lori D. Patton

Introduction

Black culture centers have been present on college campuses since the late 1960s. Resulting from the Black Student Movement (BSM), these facilities have long been revered as "a home away from home" for some black students, particularly at predominantly white institutions (PWIs). Black culture centers were a portion of the larger list of demands that black students urged university administrators to meet. The desire to have black studies in the curriculum, a greater black faculty presence and revised admissions policies were also critical in demands by black students. Following a host of legislative changes, such as the Civil Rights Act and the Higher Education Act, PWIs saw a huge influx of black students. However, these same institutions were severely under-prepared to deal with the challenges and needs of this incoming population. As a result of the isolation and invisibility that black students felt in the environment at PWIs, they organized to take matters into their own hands to make these institutions more relevant for their collegiate experiences.

One demand that African American students made, that black culture centers be established on white campuses, made a significant impact on other underrepresented groups at PWIs. Subsequently, Latino, Asian and Native American culture centers were established. While each of these centers is designed to meet the needs of specific populations, they also serve a greater role in sharing the culture, traditions, and values of these populations with the larger campus community.

In the following case, it becomes evident that tighter budgets and the push toward a campus multicultural center will have a major impact on current students and alumni of this university. A lack of understanding of historical roots and different cultures, coupled with protest and resentment, led to a heated conflict in the midst of culture.

Institutional Setting

Phillips University (PU) is a large, public institution located in the Midwest. Founded in 1865, Phillips boasts a number of nationally ranked academic programs within the disciplines of business, agriculture, and music. The university serves approximately 42,000 students, representing all fifty states and many other countries. There are approximately 35,000 undergraduate and 7000 graduate students. About 70% of Phillips students are white. The remaining breakdown includes 10% African American, 7% Latino/Hispanic, 8% Asian American, and 2% Native American. International students represent 3% of the student population.

Phillips University has a strong reputation of being a diverse university. It has three ethnic culture centers (black, Hispanic and Asian), an office of Native American Affairs and a center for international students. Several of its academic programs and student support services were featured in a 2002 edition of *Time* magazine's fifty Best Colleges for Students.

Historical Context

Phillips University was the fifth in the nation to establish a black culture center. The Dewitt Black Culture Center (BCC) was named in honor of the first black student to enroll and successfully graduate from PU. The center was established in 1969 and has existed since then. It is a hub of African American student activity. The Dewitt BCC was founded following a massive African American student protest. The students demanded that the administration create the center to support African American students. When this demand along with several others was refused, the African American students under the leadership of the Black Student Union (BSU) President, Joe Witherspoon, staged a major sit-in at the administration building. Following the three-day sit-in, massive news coverage, and at the urging of some supportive white faculty and staff members, PU agreed to establish the center in a residential property owned by the university once the students agreed to play an active role in its establishment. This resulted in extensive fund-raising activities and solicitation of donations for items and resources that would be housed at the center. The students worked diligently to build ties within the growing black community located near the university. Through creative means, they secured posters, decorations, music recordings, a typewriter, and a host of other resources. Moreover, through their dedication and diligence in contributing to the foundation of the Dewitt Black Culture Center, they had created strong ties with the local black community. Over the next fifteen years, the Hispanic and Asian culture centers were established. By 2000, the Office of Native American Affairs was created.

While PU receives accolades for the creation of the centers, below the surface there are several issues. The Dewitt Black Culture Center is in terrible physical condition. Several students use the center and participate in its programming, but have complained for years about its poor condition and location. The university has not been supportive of renovating the center and insists that it will cost too much money. The other centers on campus are also located in small homes on the periphery of campus and are in poor physical condition.

Each of the center directors has managed to keep his or her respective centers afloat and maintain student involvement despite the poor conditions. However, the students have on numerous occasions made it clear that they want more space, resources, and a location that is more centrally located on campus.

The Issue

Phillips University receives a huge amount of support from alumni. One of the largest alumni support groups is the Black Alumni Alliance (BAA). The BAA has established scholarships and produced major funding to assist PU in its recruitment and retention of African American students. The BAA has also been instrumental in donating money to the Dewitt BCC to assist with its services and programs. The president of the BAA is none other than Joe Witherspoon, the greatest track runner in PU's history. Witherspoon is an avid supporter of PU and was an instrumental member of the BSU in the late 1960s. Witherspoon is also a close friend and colleague of Matthew Lawrence, a PU alumnus and the Vice President of Student Affairs at PU.

Lawrence has recently been informed that over the next eight years, his budget will be incrementally reduced. Moreover, after a lengthy meeting with PU's president, it was highly recommended that the campus culture centers be combined into one unit and established as a multicultural center. Such a move would allow Lawrence to shift monies in the budget toward other programs and offices within Student Affairs. When Lawrence explained that there would be an outcry if the university created a multicultural center, the president clearly states, "I know it will be difficult at first. Students don't like change, but they will get over it. Lawrence, you have good rapport with the campus community. I am entrusting you to make this happen."

Breaking the Bad News

After serious contemplation, Lawrence schedules a meeting with the directors of the culture centers and the Native American affairs office on September 9. In the meeting, he explains the current budget crisis facing Student Affairs and shares his plan of merging the centers into a multicultural center. The directors share their disagreement with the proposal, explaining that although the centers are for use by any campus member, at their core, they serve the needs of specific student populations. The directors are clear in their argument that it would be a huge mistake to merge the centers into one. Dr. Janice Baptiste, the Director of the Dewitt BCC, firmly explained the immense struggle and sacrifice that went into establishing the center. She commented that merging the culture centers would weaken the strong identities that each center currently has and the special relationships that the directors have formed with the students. Her arguments for the continuance of the Dewitt Center as a free-standing facility hinged upon its historical significance to current students and alumni, the consistent feedback she received from students about the positive impact of the programming and services, the relationships that had been established between the center and blacks in the surrounding community, and the significant role that the center played in the university's recruitment efforts of black students and the establishment of other culture centers on campus.

Andrew Sanchez, Director of the Latino Culture Center and Michelle Rodriguez, Director of the Asian Culture Center expressed similar reasons for maintaining the individual identities of the centers. Both had recently established programs, which focused on helping international students from Latin and Asian countries deal with English language barriers. Sanchez began to explain the many ethnicities that existed among Latino students and the need to have a space that focused on creating a stronger sense of community among this population. He talked about the high traffic of the center and the students' commitment and involvement with the center's programming. Rodriguez shared that the Asian culture center had done a significant amount of programming and had made an impact on the campus-wide understanding of Asian cultures.

Angela Rogers, coordinator of Native American student services, was extremely disappointed with the news. This office had only been established for two years. In that time, she had reached out to several students who identified with Native American culture. She had major concerns about the resources she had been given to develop the office and agreed with the culture center directors in maintaining their current status. She summarized much of what had been stated in the conversation and asked Lawrence about alternatives beyond establishing a multicultural center.

Lawrence noted each of their concerns. However, he explained that there was no reason why all of the great things that each shared about the centers could not take place in a multicultural facility. Their explanations, in his opinion, were more compelling in favor of the multicultural center. He told the directors that merging the centers was not up for debate; it was inevitable. He asked them to work on a strategy to create a center that could meet multiple and individual needs and assured them that their voices would not go unheard.

The directors, unhappy with Lawrence's decision, suggested that he hold an open forum to share the university's plans with the students. One week later, on September 16, the Vice President for Student Affairs, VPSA, held the open forum. Despite his efforts to maintain a peaceful forum, the students began to chant their disagreement with the plan for a multicultural center. The VPSA insisted to the crowd that the establishment of the multicultural center committee would include student, staff, and faculty voices in order to create a space for everyone.

Word Gets Out

Later that evening, the BSU President, Miles Shaw facilitated a meeting. The major topic of concern was the new multicultural center. The students discussed a strategy for maintaining the BCC. Amidst the audience, Kim Owens says, "It's really not a bad idea. Hear me out! I know that some of you use the Dewitt culture center. I've even been over there a time or two, but the reality is that we don't even use that building. When we want to have parties, we use the union. When we want to study, we go to the library. I love Dr. Baptiste and I know she doesn't want the center to go, but think about it . . . They are promising us a state of the art building with more resources, things we haven't and won't get at the Dewitt Center. I think we should support this." While some agreed with Kim's point, it was not enough to quell the students' decision to plan a campus protest. Overwhelmingly, the students wanted to keep the Dewitt BCC because of its historical significance to PU and to African Americans at the institution. They felt that collapsing the centers into one would erase the struggle that had characterized the creation of the Dewitt BCC. They also discussed the lack of personal space they would have in a multicultural center and commented that everybody would want to use the space, making it an impersonal environment. Adrian Witherspoon also spoke up about the importance of the center to his father (Joe) and all the black alumni of PU.

Prior to the close of the meeting, the BSU had come up with what they termed the, "Old' School Protest Plan":

- Miles Shaw would meet with the presidents of the Latino and Asian student associations to get them on board with the protest.
- Arrange a meeting with the President and the VPSA to discuss keeping the center.
- Contact the Black Alumni Alliance for support and to inform them of what was going on.
- Contact the local black churches and black business owners for their support.
- Contact the media to get a story in the paper and to have them present at the upcoming march and sit-in.
- Conduct a march in October and a sit-in in November.

When Dr. Baptiste heard the plan, she agreed to support the students and explained that a plan like that would only work if everyone was on board. She shared that it would take organization and communication. She also warned the students that there was no guarantee that the plan would be successful because the VPSA had made up his mind, but that it was worth a try.

Within two weeks of announcing the plans for a multicultural center, the PU campus was in an uproar. It was front-page news in the student newspaper and had also reached local newspapers.

Adrian Witherspoon had contacted his father, Joe to share the news. As expected, Joe was highly upset and placed a call to Vice President Lawrence. Inspite of several attempts, Witherspoon's calls went unanswered. Witherspoon immediately, shared the announcement with those on the BAA list serve and called an emergency meeting of the BAA executive council.

When the BAA convened, they invited Dr. Baptiste and the BSU President. The group decided to write a letter to the president of PU. Later that evening Witherspoon received a call from Vice President Lawrence. After a brief exchange of niceties, Witherspoon asked him what was going on and why PU was trying to get rid of the Dewitt BCC. Lawrence explained, "We are not trying to get rid of it. We will be merging the centers together to create a multicultural center with resources and facilities for all of our minority students". Witherspoon blatantly disagreed with the decision. He said, "Matthew, you were with us in 1969. You saw all that we sacrificed and went through to get the BCC established. You knew what it meant then and you know what it represents now. PU has gained recognition for having three culture centers and a Native American office. It's gained recognition through the work of the staff, students and more specifically, the alumni. It has been years since the university has supported the center with real financial dollars. Now, you want to just do away with it? We will not just stand by and watch it happen. I suggest you go back to the President and rethink this whole thing!"

Getting Others On Board

Following the BSU meeting, Miles Shaw, BSU President, met with the leaders of the other ethnic student associations. In the meeting, Shaw stresses that they have to stick together and that saving the culture centers has to be a top priority for all groups involved. The Latino Student Association President, Joseph Perez and the Asian Student Union President, Paul Young, say that they have each met with the directors of their centers and have already decided that the multicultural center is a good idea. They commented that most of the attention and support usually goes to the Dewitt Black culture center anyway. So, the multicultural center would allow more opportunities and benefits for all students, not just the black students. Shaw was surprised at their response, but tried to encourage them to help out with the protest. He said that this would be a team effort that would benefit African American, Latino, Asian, and Native American students. Through this protest, all voices would be heard. Shaw was convinced that this was a chance for students to really make a difference in a university decision that would affect them. Shaw gave his word that despite the end result, they would work together as student leaders to ensure equitable distribution of resources. Joseph and Paul maintain their stance, but agreed to allow Miles to discuss the issue with the general body of their respective organizations.

Discussion Questions

There are some key issues that must be addressed when examining this case:

1. Should the culture centers be merged into one multicultural center?
    a. What are the ramifications for such a shift?
    b. Can the things that are accomplished within the individual centers be accomplished within a multicultural center?
    c. Who is ultimately affected if the shift takes place?
    d. Can a multicultural center effectively serve all racial populations?
    e. If the center is implemented, does the definition of multicultural change to include GLBT communities, women, international students, and other populations?
    f. What type of structure would need to be in place for a multicultural center to be successful in transition from individual centers?
    g. What roles do university constituents (alumni, people in the local community, parents) play in decision making?

2. How will Miles Shaw get the other ethnic student organizations on board?

   a. Is the plan outlined by the Black Student Alliance relevant on today's college campus?

   b. How does this case represent solidarity among students of differing ethnic backgrounds on today's college campus?

   c. If the students were to work together as a team, would their voices be loud enough to save the culture centers?

   d. Are the facilities worth saving if the students do not use them and they remain in poor condition?

   e. What role can the center directors play in salvaging the centers and student relations on campus?

   f. Are the justifications that the directors give relevant enough to maintain individual centers?

   g. What factors may have lead to VPSA Lawrence perceiving the justifications as further evidence of creating a multicultural center?

   h. What are some of the perceptions of individual culture centers relative to promoting campus separatism and multiculturalism?

3. Will the Black Alumni Association and community allies step up?

   a. How much power and influence do these entities have?

   b. Will PU suffer the loss of their support as a result of the merger?

   c. Are there other subgroups of the Alumni Association that can get involved in this discussion?

4. What will it take for VPSA Lawrence and the President to change their minds?

   a. What are the essential factors that are driving the creation of a multicultural center?

   b. How can a decision such as this lead to the marginalization and suppression of certain voices on campus?

   c. Given the pending financial constraints, what alternatives exist besides creating the multicultural center?

   d. What larger issues might be considered a greater priority than the culture centers within the student affairs division? Within the university?

   e. Can the money that would be used for the merger, be used for each individual center?

   f. What else can the VPSA do to salvage the division budget?

    g. If the merger is an inevitable reality, what do the President and VPSA have to do to foster a consensus on campus about the change? Who needs to be involved with building the consensus?

    h. How will PU's image among racial/ethnic populations be affected as a result of the merger?

    i. How will student experiences be affected by the merger?

    j. What are the ramifications of this merger for an institution that has a positive rapport with communities of color?

Recommended Readings

Black Culture Centers and Student Experiences

Ancis, J.R., Sedlacek, W.E., & Mohr, J.J. (2000). Student perceptions of campus cultural climate by race. *Journal of Counseling and Development*, 78 (2), 180–185.

Anthony, E. (1971). *The time of the furnaces: A case study of Black student revolt*. New York: Dial Press.

Benet, J. (1971). Introduction. In D. Karagueuzian (Ed.). *Blow it up!: The Black student revolt at San Francisco State College and the emergence of Dr. Hayakawa*, Boston, MA: Gambit, Inc.

Bennett, W. (1971). The Afro-American cultural center. *Harvard Journal of Afro-American Affairs*, 2 (2), 18–29.

Exum, W.H. (1985). *Paradoxes of Protest: Black student activism in a white university*. Philadelphia, PA: Temple University Press.

Hefner, D. (February 14, 2002). Black cultural centers: Standing on shaky ground? *Black Issues in Higher Education*, 18 (26), 22–29.

Lewis, A.E., Chesler, M., & Forman, T.A. (2001). The impact of "colorblind" ideologies on students of color: Intergroup relations at a predominantly white university. *Journal of Negro Education*, 69 (1/2), 74–91.

Miller, K.K. (2001). Negroes no more: The emergence of black student activism. In A. Bloom (Ed.). *Long time gone: Sixties America then and now*, (pp.123–143). New York: Oxford University Press.

Morgan, G.D. & Preston, I. (1990). *The edge of campus: A journal of the black experience at the University of Arkansas*. Fayetteville: University of Arkansas Press.

Princes, C.D.W. (1994). *The precarious question of black cultural centers versus multicultural centers* (Report No. HE 028386). Harrisburg, PA: Annual Conference of the Pennsylvania Black Conference on Higher Education. (ERIC Document Reproduction Service No. ED383273).

Smith, R., Axen, R. & Pentony, D. (1970). *By any means necessary: The revolutionary struggle at San Francisco State*. San Francisco, CA: Jossey-Bass.

Young, L.W. (1986). The role minority student centers play on predominantly white campuses. In C.A. Taylor (Ed.). *Handbook of Minority Student Services*, (pp.14–22). Madison, WI: NMCC, Inc. Publications.

Young, L.W. & Hannon, M.D. (February 14, 2002). The staying power of black cultural centers. *Black Issues in Higher Education 18*, Last word.

Theoretical Perspectives

Bergerson, A.A. (2003). Critical race theory and white racism: Is there room for white scholars in fighting racism in education? *International Journal of Qualitative Studies*, 16 (1), 51–63.

Crenshaw, K.W., Gotanda, N., Peller, G., & Thomas, K. (1995). *Critical race theory: The key writings that formed the movement*. New York: New York Press.

Cross, W.E. (1991). *Shades of black: Diversity in African American identity*. Philadelphia, PA: Temple University Press.

Delgado, R. (1995). *Critical race theory: The cutting edge*. Philadelphia, PA: Temple University Press.

Solorzano, D.G. (1998). Critical race theory, race and gender microaggressions, and the experience of Chicana and Chicano studies. *International Journal of Qualitative Studies in Education*, 11 (1), 121–136.

Solorzano, D., Ceja, M., & Yosso, T. (2000). Critical race theory, racial microaggressions, and campus racial climate: The experiences of African American college students. *Journal of Negro Education*, 69 (1–2), 60–73.

Leadership

Wolf-Wendel, L.E., Twombly, S.B., Tuttle, K.N., Ward, K., & Gaston-Gayles, J.L. (2004). *Reflecting back, looking forward: Civil rights and student affairs*. Washington DC: National Association of Student Personnel Administrators.

Kezar, A. (2000). Pluralistic leadership: Bringing diverse voices to the table. *About Campus*, 5 (3), 6–11.

Scott, R.A. & Bischoff, P.M. (2000). Preserving student affairs in times of fiscal constraint: A case history. *NASPA Journal*, 38 (1), 122–133.

Case #6 Doing the Right Thing When Caught in the Cross Fire

JOHN W. MOORE

Dr. Jack Morris was in the middle of his seventh year of a very successful presidency of Midwestern State University (MSU) when he found himself in a cross fire of controversy regarding the appointment of an Athletics Director. The controversy involved the Board of Trustees, the Athletics Director Search and Screening Committee, the Athletics Department, athletics boosters, alumni, and community members, among others. At the core of the controversy were the equitable consideration of a highly qualified female candidate for the position and the ability of the president to make personnel appointments within the purview of his delegated authority.

Institutional Setting

Midwestern State University is a comprehensive doctoral public university with an enrollment of approximately 13,000 students. The institution was founded shortly after the Civil War as a normal school responsible for the education and training of public school educators. As has been typical of such institutions MSU evolved during the twentieth century from a single purpose teachers college into a comprehensive state university offering instruction in a variety of academic disciplines and fields of study. The instruction of undergraduate students has been understood to be the primary mission of the university since its inception. With the expansion of MSU's mission and scope over the years increasing priority has been placed on graduate education, scholarship, and service to the State and beyond.

The University has often been referred to as the State's "Opportunity University." The University's admission policies have encouraged students of diverse academic, socioeconomic, racial, and ethnic backgrounds to enroll. Many students are the first in their families to attend college and come to MSU from large urban industrial centers of the state and also from small and modest-sized rural agriculturally-based communities. Over the years the University has been thought to be the most racially and ethnically diverse institution in the State's public system of higher education. The University's faculty and staff have taken great pride in the emphasis it has placed on "adding value" to the lives of Midwestern's student body. It has not been uncommon to hear faculty define the University's purpose as that of "transforming the lives of students."

The diversity reflected in MSU's student body has not, however, been reflected in the University's faculty and professional staff which is essentially white. The institution's policies convey a commitment to equal opportunity and affirmative action, but any assertive or special efforts by the administration to recruit people of color to the faculty have been resisted. Despite its lack of diversity, the faculty genuinely has been dedicated to serving and supporting the institution's diverse student body. The achievements of students of color have been a source of pride over the years.

Midwestern State University is located in Centerville, a blue-collar town of about 70,000 people. Centerville is a Democratic stronghold in the middle of a state that is considered to be very conservative socially and politically. Centerville residents who traditionally vote for the Democratic Party, however, are thought to be quite conservative socially. African Americans make up a very small percentage of the Centerville's population. In Centerville, race relations are not considered to be particularly progressive, and from time to time incidents with racial overtones have occurred in town and on the campus.

MSU Administration and Board of Trustees

The Board of Trustees at MSU consists of nine trustees appointed by the Governor for four-year terms. The board is required by law to have at least one female trustee. Currently there are two white women and two African American men on the board. Judge John Stevenson serves as chair of the board. Stevenson has been a staunch supporter of President Morris and is well connected politically in the community. Three of the nine trustees, including Stevenson, are from Centerville and are very attuned to and sensitive about the town's perceptions of what is going on at MSU.

The board's responsibilities and authority are typical of public university governing boards. The board employs the president, establishes policy, and oversees the educational program, personnel, and financial resources of the institution. The board enjoys a reputation for supporting the administration, delegating appropriately, and only occasionally micro-managing. President Morris has worked hard to build supportive relationships with all board members and is thought of highly by the board.

The University level administration consists of four vice presidents, an attorney, an Affirmative Action/EEO officer, and an executive assistant to the president. When President Morris arrived all of these positions were filled by White males with the exception of the AA/EEO officer who was a White female. President Morris made significant changes at this level early in his tenure by appointing the first woman vice president at the University. Morris also hired a woman to fill the attorney's position and hired an African American woman to serve as the new Special Assistant to the president for Ethnic Diversity. Appointments at the dean and director levels followed a similar pattern as women and people of color were hired and promoted in increasing numbers over time.

President Morris had come to MSU from a successful presidency on the west coast where among other things he had a reputation for being very committed to "diversity issues." The MSU Board recruited Morris aggressively and found his experience and academic profile very compatible with MSU's needs and culture. Morris' strong commitment to equal opportunity and affirmative action were well known to the MSU Board at the time of his appointment. If this was a concern of Board members when he was appointed it was not a subject of discussion with Dr. Morris.

Relationships between President Morris and the board could not have been better during his presidency. The board, community, and campus were pleased and impressed with Morris' open and consultative style of administration, his energy and imagination, and his commitment to helping MSU be the best it could be. The University's strategic plan was developed in an inclusive way, and the plan included a commitment to ethnic and international perspectives initiatives. Progress was made on many important strategic goals and Dr. Morris continued to enjoy the full support of the Board and other key constituencies. At the conclusion of the president's third year a comprehensive review of Morris' performance resulted in very positive conclusions and the Board extended his contract for another three years.

Given the very favorable performance review President Morris found it curious that the only cautionary feedback that he received from the leadership of the Board was advice that "he might want to slow down a bit with his emphasis on diversity." Morris heard Board members counsel that "change comes slowly around here." A year later, Morris heard more direct comments from the Board and people in the community when he appointed the first African American athletics coach in the history of the institution. To the amazement of many, including African American students and alumni, MSU had a black basketball coach. President Morris again was reminded to slow down on the "diversity agenda" while the Board continued to praise his overall leadership of the University.

Athletics

Inter-collegiate athletics is a high priority for the Board, the alumni, and the community. Of particular priority is the men's basketball program which had been faltering badly for over a decade. Morris was determined to accomplish two goals in athletics namely, bring men's basketball back to winning ways, and increase opportunities for women student-athletes. In the case of men's basketball his first move was the appointment of Sam Johnson as Men's Basketball Coach. Sam was selected from a national search and was considered one of the bright and promising African American coaches in the country. Bringing Sam Johnson to MSU was considered to be a real achievement and it signaled that MSU was serious again about its basketball program. People in the community were less enthusiastic about the Johnson appointment than people on campus but had to admit that Johnson's credentials were impressive. The all white coaching staff was surprised by Johnson's appointment but generally welcomed Sam to the department. After an NCAA compliance review and a similar Title IX review by the U.S. Office of Civil Rights, the University took deliberate steps to increase athletics opportunities for women. President Morris skillfully used the leverage provided by these external reviews to push changes that in his judgment were long overdue.

President Morris' Dilemma

A year after the appointment of coach Johnson, the current Athletics Director announced his plans to leave MSU. President Morris established an appropriate search and selection committee, consisting of a cross-section of individuals from the campus and external community, to conduct a national search. Among the members of the committee was Sally Slaughter, the Associate Athletics Director (AD). The search proceeded on schedule, candidates were interviewed, but in the end none of the current candidates was deemed suitable. During the process the committee found itself comparing the candidates with Sally Slaughter. Committee members were quoted as saying "why are we doing this search when we have a terrific person right here, Sally." After accepting the fact that the search had failed President Morris extended the search process and the committee began its work again. Sally Slaughter, however, resigned from the committee and announced her candidacy. The second search produced two excellent candidates, a White male Associate AD from a sister institution and Sally Slaughter. The search and screening committee submitted both names to President Morris with a strong recommendation that he appoint Sally

Slaughter. The committee's recommendation was inadvertently leaked to the local newspaper and quickly became a hot topic in the community, among athletics boosters, and of course, the Board of Trustees. Controversy erupted immediately as some boosters expressed strong feelings in favor of the other candidate. Sally Slaughter was well liked and respected; she had played, coached, and served as Associate AD at MSU over many years. But a number of key boosters, and as it turned out trustees didn't like the idea that Slaughter would be the new AD. The word was out that the President was about to make another of his "affirmative action appointments."

President Morris had been impressed with Sally Slaughter from the time he arrived at MSU. In the absence of the AD she had served superbly as the interim AD. She had held high offices within the NCAA and was especially well respected within MSU's athletics conference and throughout the nation. Morris thought she had the "whole package."

Following the newspaper article identifying the two finalists for the position Dr. Morris's phone began ringing off the metaphorical hook. Alumni, boosters, community leaders, and respected faculty called to give their conflicting opinions and advice to the president. Finally, a call came from one of the local trustees who requested a meeting with Dr. Morris. When the trustee arrived he immediately reported to the president that he and other board members would be very upset if the president appointed Sally Slaughter. He went on to say that "their position had nothing to do with Slaughter's gender or reported unconventional lifestyle," implying that she was a lesbian. Their opposition was simply about her qualifications. The trustee indicated that he felt so strongly about the issue that he had lobbied other members of the Board who were equally opposed to Slaughter and that they intended to have their way on this issue. He told the President not to create division within the Board by bringing Slaughter's name forward. President Morris was quick to point out Slaughter's impressive credentials, that the search and screening committee had recommended her unanimously, and that her record of service to MSU athletics was outstanding. "On what grounds could the Board object to her appointment?" he asked. Morris further stated that "the Board had delegated to him the authority to appoint administrative personnel and that the Board had no basis for reversing that policy." The conversation concluded abruptly as the trustee again indicated his intention to oppose the president on Slaughter's appointment and to rally the full Board against the president. Later that day President Morris received numerous calls from people on both sides of this emerging issue. Two trustees called to express concerns that the president might proceed with his desire to appoint Slaughter; none called to support her possible appointment.

President Morris' Reflections

That evening President Morris sat in his study thinking about the dilemma in front of him. He had worked hard to build an effective Board of Trustees and to establish a mutually respectful and supportive relationship with the Board. He was well aware that legally the Board was "the boss" and that his success and survival depended on the continuing support of the Board. The issue of the AD appointment risked putting that important relationship in jeopardy. It had been Morris' practice to never bring issues or recommendations to the Board that would create fractures among the Board or between the Board and the administration. He had always been successful in finding the common ground on tough issues and as a result the Board had never failed to support his recommendations. The president understood that it might not be possible to find common ground on the AD issue. He was worried.

President Morris was familiar with the research and writings of Robert Birnbaum (1988) presented in *How Academic Leadership Works*. Birnbaum reported that effective presidents enjoy and require the support of not only the governing board, but the administrative group and the faculty as well. He knew that his credibility with these important constituencies depended on how he handled this personnel decision. The president knew that they expected him to honor the results of the search process, to act in accord with the University's equal employment and affirmative action policy, and to insist on his right to make this appointment without inappropriate interference from the board. President Morris also knew that other external constituencies had a stake in this issue. The boosters wanted the best AD available. The alumni would be interested but would reflect conflicting opinions. In the community and on campus there were groups concerned about the advancement of qualified women and would see this issue as a real test of the president's commitment and resolve on the institution's diversity agenda.

The president searched his mind for solutions. He asked himself how he could resolve the matter without seriously dividing the board, the campus, and the community. On what basis should he decide what to do? What values were at stake? What was the right thing to do?

Possible Resolutions

The next morning President Morris jotted down the options he saw before him. He could:

- Recommend the alternate candidate to the Board for appointment with the hope of avoiding a fight with the Board. He realized though that the two female board members might decide to make things difficult;

- Ask Slaughter to withdraw her candidacy, thus leaving the president with only one viable candidate to recommend to the Board;
- Reopen the search and ask Slaughter not to apply for the position so as to avoid a recurrence of the problem at hand;
- Recommend Slaughter to the Board and let them resolve the matter one way or the other;
- Lobby the board members individually in search of support for Slaughter, and after doing so allow the Board to make its determination; or
- In addition to lobbying board members, ask members of the campus and larger community to lobby the Board (something he had never done previously) on behalf of Slaughter, and then have the Board act on his recommendation in support of Slaughter.

Discussion Questions

1. Looking first at this case from a governance perspective:

   - What should be the appropriate roles and purviews of authority of the governing board, the president, and others in the selection and appointment of senior administrative officers, such as the Athletics Director?
   - What criteria or principles should be used to prescribe the appropriate roles, responsibilities, and purviews of authority in personnel matters?

2. Accepting the importance of the relationship between a president and the governing board:

   - What principles should guide administrators in facilitating both the governing board and the administration to fulfilling their mutual accountabilities?
   - What principles should guide both parties when attempting to resolve contentious issues?

3. Playing the role of advisor to President Morris, how would you advise the president with regard to these questions:

   - What values and principles should inform his actions and his ultimate decision?
   - With regard to the alternatives President Morris is considering, what are the implications of each alternative (i.e., advantages, disadvantages, and consequences)?

- Which alternative would you recommend that he pursue and why?
- How would you define what would be a constructive resolution (i.e., success)?
- What are tactics to be the employed in order to achieve a constructive resolution of the matter?

Recommended Readings

Birnbaum, R. (1992). *How academic leadership works: Understanding success and failure in the college presidency.* San Francisco, CA: Jossey-Bass.

Chait, Richard, Holland, Thomas, and Taylor, Barbara. (1993). *The effective board of trustees.* Phoenix: Oryx Press.

Fisher, James. (1991). *The board and the president.* New York: The American Council on Education and the Macmillan Publishing Company.

Heifetx, R. (1994). *Leadership without easy answers.* Boston, MA: The Harvard University Press.

Case #7 Where do South Asian American Women Administrators Fit in? The Case of Jasmine Kaur at Mega University

Madhu Verma Soin and Jerlando F.L. Jackson

Institutional Setting

Mega University is a Predominantly White Institution (PWI) located in the state capital of a rural Midwestern state in America. Bandar (population of 350,000), the city in which Mega University is located, lacks ethnic and cultural diversity with 90% of the population being white and 10% being people of color. Mega University attracts approximately 40,000 students internationally and across the United States, while a large nucleus of students are in-state residents. As a land grant, research-extensive institution, Mega University takes pride in its world-class research, teaching, and public service/outreach.

A closer examination of the student population demographics shows that 10% are students of color, 10% international students, 52% female students, 3% LGBT students, and 2% are classified as physically or mentally disabled. As it relates to the university workforce, approximately 10% of the administrators are people of color. Of the 2000 faculty employed at Mega University, only 6% are people of color. When taking gender into consideration, there is a 70/30 (men to women) gender-gap across the university workforce.

In acknowledging its long-standing problem with racism on campus—attracting and retaining students, staff, and faculty of color—the Mega University administration developed a university-wide diversity program: Diversity for the Future (DFTF) which focuses on improving the social climate and presence of students, staff, and faculty of members of four targeted ethnic groups—American Indian, African American, Latina/o, and Southeast Asian American.[1] In addition, the goal of the program is to increase awareness of the broader university community toward understanding the targeted groups' values, customs, and experiences.

The history and intention behind the DFTF program are important in making sense of the campus politics and culture. During the 1980s there were a series of overt racist acts against students of color; from 1985–1987 alone there were 200 racist acts, some of which received media attention. Students of color activists began demanding that the university take action and be responsive to the student needs. It was not until 1990 that the university officials created the DFTF program, which was more of a reaction to subdue students of color activists. While there have been well-intentioned administrators involved, there has been a lack of concrete improvements in the campus climate and accountability to the program's goals.

Key Characters

Jasmine Kaur: the assistant director for the Biology[2] and Molecular Biology undergraduate programs has been at Mega University ten years. She has a bachelors degree in biochemistry and masters degree in Sociology from Mega University. She is a second-generation Indian Sikh[3] immigrant and her father is a professor in Mathematics at Mega University. Consequently, she knows the campus system well and is highly regarded in the community by students, staff, and faculty. During her time at Mega University, she has become known for her social justice activism and compassion for students.

Jasmine is one of three South Asian[4] Americans in administrative non-faculty positions at Mega University. She does not fit into any neat categories; she is a U.S. citizen, born and raised in the United States, considered an American "minority," yet not defined as part of the "targeted minority" groups outlined in the DFTF plan and other diversity/affirmative action efforts at Mega University. This creates a unique dilemma for her when she sees that Asian American undergraduates, including Indians, are one of the fastest growing ethnic groups on college campuses yet they are seriously underrepresented in positions of administrative leadership.[5] In fact, national statistics indicate that Asian Americans hold the least number of postsecondary education administrative positions as compared to African Americans, Chicanos/Latinos, and Whites (U.S. Department of Education, NCES, 1999). Consequently, as a South Asian American woman, she does not get much support on campus and remains invisible in many ways.[6]

Todd Schwartz: a plant pathology professor in the College of Life Sciences, co-director for the Biology Major, Director for the Biotechnology Center, and the main force behind creating the Biology Major, an intercollege major, on campus. He is the primary supervisor for Jasmine's position.

He is a world-renowned researcher, but has struggled with the supervision and management aspects of the center. Nonetheless, Dr. Schwartz has dedicated a large amount of his personal and professional time to create the new Biology Major.

Stephen Olson is a professor in Dairy Science in the College of Agriculture, chair for the committee for diversity in the College of Agriculture, and the co-director for the Biology Major. He is new to his role as co-director of the major and supervisor for Jasmine. He is eager to get on board and help out however he can to dispel the negative myths about the Biology Major in his college.

Katie Johnson is Jasmine's student assistant. She is from a small town in the Midwest, a pre-medicine junior at Mega University, and has been working with the Biology Major since its inception. She works hard, is reliable, and loves her job. This is the first time she is working so closely with a person of color.

The Case

January, 2001

Jasmine was thrilled about assuming her first position after completing her masters degree. She had a long history with the university, particularly when it came to social justice issues on campus. Since she struggled with feeling marginalized as a woman of color[7] at Mega University during her undergraduate and graduate school experience, she wanted to minimize similar experiences for other students. Subsequently, she was committed to ensure that all students felt welcomed and empowered to grow personally and professionally. Therefore, her present position seemed perfect to serve as a student advocate.

Jasmine and Katie shared an office; they were solely responsible for managing the Biology and Molecular Biology programs. Katie was particularly helpful in this process since she was a Biology Major student. Katie enjoyed working in the program, even though it was a new and strange experience working for an individual with a different ethnic and racial background from herself.

For the first time, Jasmine felt like a professional and a member of the university community. Dr. Schwartz and Jasmine met weekly to review the programs' progress. At that point in time, there were approximately 300 declared Biology majors and Dr. Schwartz projected that the program would grow to accommodate a maximum of 500 students. Although everything seemed new and there was not much on-the-job-training, Jasmine was excited about the work of the program. She was responsible for all the administrative work (e.g., student advising, budget management, website development, program planning, publications updates, and obtaining grades). Jasmine made every effort to ensure that her office was inclusive and welcoming, including putting out resources for students of color and other disadvantaged groups. Dr. Schwartz was thrilled to find an ideal candidate in Jasmine for this position; she was competent and possessed the perfect background in the biological sciences. The Biology Major was his passion and she was just as excited and committed. He was confident that she would be fine working autonomously.

June 2001

Something did not feel right to Jasmine. She was happy to be a real "professional" and enjoyed her job, yet she was becoming aware of the resistance to the Biology Major from the College of Agriculture. A few administrators (who are all white and male) were spreading the word that the major was "bad," giving incorrect advice to students, and discouraging them from majoring in Biology. Furthermore, some students were even being treated disrespectfully. For example, an assistant dean scolded a student who was not sure what he wanted to do for a career and told him that he was wasting his life away and would get nowhere in life with a Biology Major. Another administrator hassled a pre-medical Latina student about switching out of Genetics into Biology and then grilled her on her credentials for even attending Mega University. Dr. Schwartz was aware of this and was quite disheartened. He decided to keep fighting for the major and with Jasmine's help he felt that they would be successful.

It was Jasmine's sixth month in her position and the work pace was quite hectic since the Biology Major had grown to 500 students (and Molecular Biology had a steady 125). She was expecting some feedback and possibly job performance evaluation, but did not receive any formal assessment. This seemed to be a part of departmental culture since she received so little supervision for all the work she had been doing. Because she felt so isolated, Jasmine had begun to create her own professional support network of colleagues on campus. This was easy for her to do, since she knew so many people and had been around for quite some time.

Jasmine also participated in an activist group that was raising awareness about racism and hate crimes on campus. Race issues were ever-present in her mind. When she went to meetings with other science advisors or other campus meetings, she was the only person of color. No one ever talked about diversity, multiculturalism, students of color, first-generation students, or any other marginalized groups. In the building that she worked in, she was one of two people of color. At least some of her students were from diverse backgrounds;

otherwise, it was a sea of white. She tried to discuss how she felt oppressed on campus with Dr. Schwartz and he did acknowledge that Bandar was a racist place. At that point, Jasmine felt her boss was supportive. Dr. Schwartz felt that he was a very open-minded non-racist person since he had adopted a Chinese child and had many Asians working in his laboratory.

September 11, 2001

September 11, 2001 was a tragic day for Jasmine. As she was listening to the radio getting ready for work, she heard about the airplanes that crashed into the Twin Towers of the World Trade Center in New York City. On hearing this tragic ordeal, she did not anticipate how it would change her life. While at work she became aware of the dismal state of affairs; therefore, she talked with her students who came into her office seeking council. Jasmine asked how they were doing and could tell that each student was both sad and afraid. Nonetheless, she wanted to be there to support them.

Post-September 11, 2001

Over the next few days, Jasmine too, became afraid. She feared for her father, her brother and other family and friends who looked like her. She was especially scared for those family members and friends with beards and turbaned Sikhs, since they could be mistaken for being Arab, Muslim, or Middle Eastern.[8] Then, on September 15, she read in the local newspaper that Balbir Singh Sodhi, a Sikh gas station owner, an American citizen, was shot dead in Arizona while planting flowers in front of his shop. Following the Sikh tradition, he wore a turban and a beard. He was killed merely because of the way he looked and it was reported to be a "hate crime" fueled by prejudice after 9-11.

Jasmine felt the pain and fear in the pit of her stomach and cried; these were her people. Who would be next . . . her brother? Herself? Jasmine now feared for her own safety. She was not safe in the United States or on campus. The face of racism had just shifted. Earlier, Indians[9] were an invisible ethnic/racial group and now her people were targeted because of the way they looked. In addition, mosques[10] and gurudwaras[11] were being vandalized across the country. She felt uncomfortable walking on campus and felt people's stares filled with hatred. Jasmine decided not to walk home alone at night and to stay home as much as possible. Unfortunately, that was not enough to keep her from being targeted. On her way home on September 16th she was leaving her office at 5:30 pm and walking toward the ramp where her car was parked. Jasmine was watching people carefully and was hyper vigilant of her surroundings. Then, half a block ahead she spotted three white male students intensely glaring at her. She became more nervous and tried to not look at them. As she passed by all three gave her the middle finger and one man hissed at her calling her a terrorist and another screamed "Go back to your country!" Jasmine felt fear pulse through her and she bolted to her car. She escaped to her car, but what happened kept replaying in her head. Terror enveloped her and she did not know where to turn.

A few days after her traumatic experience and the shooting of Balbir Singh Sodhi, the University Health Services held a brown bag session to discuss how advisors could be supportive to their students. Jasmine went to connect with others and poured out her heart about her own fears for her safety. She held back her tears as she spoke about the pain of discrimination and hate crimes, even those occurring in Bandar. The director for International Affairs retorted, "This cannot be true, we have not heard about this happening. No students have informed us about anything on our own campus." Other advisors were upset that Jasmine dared speak up and were in denial, "I did not hear about any murder and you have to understand that people are upset." They did not want to believe that this could happen in America, but more specifically in Bandar. They did not want to believe Jasmine's stories, her comments were dismissed and she was treated with suspicion. Jasmine expected at least some of her colleagues to understand and care; she was disappointed and deeply hurt. Only one woman, the director of the student union, came up to her afterwards and hugged her and said: "Sorry to hear that you have to go through this." The session facilitator felt compassion for Jasmine and hoped that people would have been more validating to her.

Jasmine went back to her office, shaken, and depressed. Over the course of the next few months after the attacks, people from Arab, Muslim, Sikh, Middle Eastern, and South Asian American groups (and those who appeared Middle Eastern) were targeted for harassment, threats, and assaults, including attempted murders, murders, property damage, and arson.[12]

Jasmine heard disturbing stories from her students who fit the picture of looking "like the enemy." They also did not report what happened to them and asked Jasmine to keep it confidential. Overall, other students, faculty, and staff were not supportive of these students' experiences and actually created a hostile environment for them, affecting their schoolwork and safety. Two stories in particular stand out for her. Farah, a Persian American who wears a headscarf, was with three other Muslim women at the Islamic center on campus when they were verbally harassed and their veils were pulled off. She explained to Jasmine how she did not feel comfortable being on campus or in Bandar and wished to go back home to her family. The other student, Manpreet, a second-generation Sikh American with long hair pulled back in a bun, told Jasmine:

I stayed home for two weeks after 9–11. I was so scared! I received two death threats and I knew I would be targeted by the way I look, especially with my beard. The first time it was by a bunch of White guys in a truck yelling out racial slurs and threats and the second time I was walking down campus and again a group of White men who were behind me said: "We're going to walk behind you until you are dead." The same week my older brother who wears a turban, was driving in Chicago when a Black man all of sudden blocked his car and said "Lower your eyes. Lower your eyes. Lower your eyes. I am an American" and then pointed a gun to my brother's face. So, it's been really bad. I try to be safe and only go places with my posse of other people of color, but we have to go in small groups because otherwise people will think we are celebrating. I feel that I can't tell anyone. None of my teachers understand.

Jasmine was saddened to hear about the students' experiences and let them know that she was there to support them. She could be there for her students, but whom could she turn to? Jasmine's needs were not being met, yet she was working hard to meet the needs of her students.

Things were hard enough before 9-11. Her efforts to improve the major were met with resistance and the oppression added to the marginalization that she already felt as a woman of color, especially as a South Asian American woman. She had to deal with being ignored in meetings, not receiving credit for things she said or did, and being treated as inferior. The worst aspect was the feeling of being invisible and not being asked about how she was doing, especially by Katie, Dr. Schwartz, and others she worked with on a daily basis. It was frustrating and a difficult position to be in because she was so committed to "saving the major" and she was also expected to be the voice of diversity, especially for students of color.

Jasmine even went to all three of the Mega University President's Listening Sessions, where the president was requesting feedback from the campus community about the university's response to September 11 and the related hostilities toward Muslims and other minorities. She spoke up about the harassment she faced and how she was treated at the staff meeting. Other students, faculty, and staff of color talked about receiving death threats, being called names, staying home from work and class, and being physically accosted. A Muslim American student with parents from Iran described how his professor and other students called him out in front of the entire class, asked him if he was Muslim, and demanded that he explain why his people wished to kill Americans. "I don't feel safe going to class or being with my classmates. I feel that they are judging me and that I have no rights. I am paying to be here at school and I deserve to feel safe and not be harassed and blamed." President O'Reilly was touched by Jasmine's story and all the other stories, and he seemed concerned about campus climate, but not enough to facilitate a change.

June 2002

Work became more difficult[13] as her responsibilities enlarged; she needed help in carrying out the additional duties. One person was no longer enough to do all the work. Also, since the College of Agriculture was derailing intended Biology majors at the freshmen and transfer orientation, she decided to attend the orientations herself and advise those students. She started Peer Advising Workshops to streamline advising during registration time. At this point, the Biology program had grown to a total of 900 students, so the sheer numbers were overwhelming. The students liked Jasmine and came to see her regularly, plus the word was out on campus that she was very helpful. Additionally, Dr. Schwartz recognized Jasmine's commitment and nominated her for an advising award, which she did not receive, but she was thrilled nonetheless. She was however, presented with a TRIO mentor award from a first-generation Hmong college student.

Jasmine was struggling to gain support from the faculty and administrators in her program. She sent Drs. Schwartz and Olson an article on the supervision of women of color staff on campus and asked if they could set a meeting to discuss it. The article expressed how important it is to retain women of color and that they should be supported, especially since most are required to perform additional non-formal duties associated with people of color on campus. After sending them the article twice, Drs. Schwartz and Olson still did not address these issues with Jasmine and ignored her request for a meeting. They understood that Jasmine was working hard, but they were extremely busy themselves. Dr. Schwartz just needed to make sure that the Biology Major was appropriately administered. He was concerned that it had grown so large and that more space, resources, and staff were needed to maintain the major. Plus, he himself was in crisis trying to manage his research and teaching load. Although at times he was concerned about Jasmine, he really did not make the time to help her.

Jasmine was depressed and even started applying for other jobs. San Francisco sounded nice; it was more diverse and much warmer. She was so overwhelmed with her job responsibilities and had no support that she went home crying many times. When she told Dr. Schwartz he really did not know what to do. In addition to the stress at work, Jasmine was becoming very concerned about her brother who was receiving threats at his workplace and called names such as "sandnigger" and "Osama."

Jasmine decided to stick with her job and thought that Dr. Schwartz would be there to support her and hopefully give her a raise or some other promotion soon. Then, one day at a Biology Major Executive Committee Meeting, the members were nominating faculty for the next term. Jasmine noticed that it was all white men and said "It would be a good idea to have some diversity on our committee. We should name some women and people of color." Drs. Schwartz and Olson looked at her, ignored her comment and moved on listing off white men. After that day, she did not feel the same way about Dr. Schwartz; it was clear that he did not get it.

Then, the last straw was a few months later when Jasmine hired a white woman as her assistant who had a problem being supervised by a woman of color. She intimidated, lied, and disrespected Jasmine and it came as a shock to her when Dr. Schwartz took the assistant's side. She felt crushed and became severely depressed. She had been there two years and this woman was here for only two months and Dr. Schwartz basically stabbed Jasmine in the back. Jasmine wanted to leave her job. She felt burnt out, isolated, disrespected, invisible as if she had no feelings. She did not feel like a whole person anymore; therefore, she submitted her letter of resignation.

Discussion Questions

1. What are some of the unique issues that Jasmine faced as a South Asian American woman employed at Mega University?
2. What happened at the post 9-11 staff meeting? How could staff have shown support to Jasmine's expressed experiences?
3. What institutional dynamics fostered and allowed the post-9-11 racism at Mega University?
4. How would you describe the collective campus culture? In addition, please describe staff and student level culture?
5. How much of the resistance that Jasmine experienced in her job can be attributed to her being a second-generation immigrant and how much do you think was associated with her status as non-faculty at Mega University?
6. If you were Dr. Schwartz, how would you have handled this matter differently?
7. What are some retention strategies that might have helped Jasmine stay at her job? What strategies might have helped to develop Jasmine's leadership skills and advancement in the university?
8. How can Mega University change the DFTF to be inclusive of non-targeted minority groups?

Other Resources

80–20 Initiative (2004). *Glass ceiling evidence.* Retrieved September 9, 2004, from http://www.80-20initiative.net/glassc.html

Catalyst (2003). *Advancing Asian women in the workplace: What managers need to know.* New York, NY. Retrieved April 3, 2005, fromhttp://www.catalystwomen.org/knowledge/titles/files/fact/WOCAsiaFactsheet%20Final.pdf

Hune, S. & Chan, K. (1997). *Minorities in education special focus: Asian Pacific American demographics and education trends. Annual Status Report*, No. 15, Washington DC: American Council on Education.

Department of Justice's Federal Bureau of Investigation (2002, February 13). *FBI Press Release*. Retrieved March 13, 2004, from http://www.fbi.gov/pressrel/pressrel02/director021302.htm

NCES (Fall, 1999). *Table 224. Employees in degree-granting institutions, by race/ethnicity, primary occupation, and employment status, sex, and type and control of institution*. Retrieved March 13, 2005, from http://nces.ed.gov/programs/digest/d02/tables/XLS/Tab224.xls

SAALT, South Asian American Leaders of Tomorrow (2001). *American backlash: Terrorists bring war home*. Washington, D.C. Retrieved March 13, 2004, from http://www.saalt.org/abr.htm

Sikhnet (2004). *Introduction to Sikhism*. Retrieved March 13, 2004, from http://www.sikhnet.com/s/SikhIntro

US Department of Education, National Center for Education Statistics (1999). *Integrated Postsecondary Education Data System (IPEDS)*. "Fall Staff 1999" survey. Retrieved March 12, 2004 from http://nces.ed.gov/programs/digest/d02/tables/XLS/Tab224.xls

United States Census Bureau (2002). *The Asian Population: 2000*. Retrieved March 13, 2004, from http://www.census.gov/prod/2002pubs/c2kbr01-16.pdf

United States Equal Employment Opportunity Commission (2001, December 12). *EEOC confers with minority groups on combating September 11, backlash discrimination*. Retrieved March 13, 2004, from http://www.eeoc.gov/press/12-12-01.html

Wong, J.M. (2002). Asian American leaders in higher education: Career aspirations in student affairs, DAI-A 63/12, ProQuest *Digital Dissertations* (Pub No. AAT3073864).

Notes

1   These are the racial categorizations as outlined by the DFTF.

2   The Biology major was initiated in July 2000 and Jasmine began six months later in January 2001.

3   Sikhs follow Sikhism, which is a distinct world religion that was founded by Guru Nanak Dev (1469–1539) over 500 years ago. The five important articles of their faith are the : (1) *kesh* (uncut hair) which is covered with a turban; (2) *kirpan* eremonial sword) (3) *kangha* (a wooden comb for the hair); (4) *kara* (steel bracelet); (5) *kachh* (undershots). Sikh communities throughout the world still maintain these symbols (Sikhner, 2004)

4   South Asians include people from India, Pakistan, Maldives, Bhutan, Nepal, Sri Lanka, and Bangladesh.

5   Asian Indian students are not underrepresented in higher education. When we break it down by sectors of the university they are overrepresented in certain fields (like medicine and engineering), but underrepresented in other fields (like education and English). This numerical representation is largely unrelated to experiences of discrimination and racism and unrelated to white privilege. There are many examples of affluence and prosperity within the Asian American population, but in many ways they still face the same types of racism, social inequality, and institutional discrimination that other groups of color face. For Indian Americans, there is an added challenge of a lack of political power and an absence of a national civil rights safety net. Therefore, the image

that the entire Asian American community is the "model minority" is a myth. "The model minority myth of success has effectively deracialized Asian Americans as a group and created a dynamic where they have become visible on campusyet marginalized in positions of power" (Wong, 2002, p.ix).

6. A report by Catalyst (2003) shows evidence that Asian and Asian American women feel overlooked by their workplace's diversity programs and policies, most likely due to the perception that Asians and Asian Americans do not require specific diversity efforts. Also, Asian American women, compared to other women of color, are more likely to have a graduate education and be in entry levels in leadership (NCES, 1999; 80-20 Initiative, 2004). A lack of mentors, a positive relationship with their manager, cultural differences, and inadequate informal networks are some of the barriers that have prevented advancement in their jobs and careers. Wong (2002) also found that Asian American women experienced a glass ceiling and subtle racism in academia.

7. Woman of color remains a widely accepted term for women who are non-White and non-European.

8. "For Americans of South Asian or middle Eastern descent . . . their fear was compounded by the possibility that they would be unjustly held responsible for the vile acts of terrorists for no reason other than the spelling of their name, the color of their skin, the clothes that they wore, the religion they practiced or the accent which they spoke English" (SAALT, 2000, p. 3).

9. Asian Indian immigrants did not come to the United States in sizeable numbers until the 1965 Immigration and Nationality (or Hart-Cellar) Act which ended discriminatory immigration policies that purposely limited the number of immigrants from Asia and instead established a system based on preference categories which favored professionals and highly educated professionals. The Indian American population stands at 1,678,765 as of the 2000 U.S. Census. The majority are U.S. citizens and most live in New York and California. The overall growth rate for Indian Americans from 1990-2000 was 106 percent, the largest growth in the Asian American community (United States Census Bureau, 2002).

10. Mosque is the place of worship and religious activities for muslims who follow the religion of Islam.

11. Gurdwara is the name given to the temple where Sikhs worship and hold community fgatherings. It means ëGateway to the Guruí or house of God. There are over 300 gurdwaras in the United States.

12. From September 11, 2001 to February 14, 2002 the FBI began investigating 414 hate crimes towards Arab, Muslim, Sikh, Middle Eastern, and South Asian groups (Department of Justiceís Federal Bureau of Investigation, 2002). Also, as of December 6, 2001 the EDOC had received 166 formal complaints of workplace discrimination specifically related to the September 11 attacks (United States Equal Employment Opportunity Commission, 2001). In the first week alone, from September 12 to September 17, there were at least 645 reported bias incidents directed at people who appeared to be from the Middle East (SAALT, 2001). The incidents include those that were reported by media organizations and do not include the experiences of Jasmine and numerous others who were suffering in silence.

13. Authors would like to note that it is unclear how much of the difficulty encountered by Jasmine was related to her non-faculty status or her race/ethnicity.

Case #8 Sin Fronteras: Negotiating Administrative Roles in Higher Education as a Woman of Color

MARIE L. MIVILLE AND MADONNA G. CONSTANTINE

Dr. Mariana Lucha is the Dean of the College of Arts and Sciences in a large, four-year university in the Southeast region of the United States. Dean Lucha, an Afro-Latina, is the first woman and person of color to serve in a deanship at Southeastern State University (SSU). During her first semester, Dean Lucha, along with other Deans, was asked by the University president to play a highly visible role in the university's capital campaign, which was set to kick off in late September. This role entails seeking out known and new donors and alumni to set up scholarships, endowed chairs, and the like. At the same time, several local private advocacy groups have been calling attention to the low admission, retention, and graduation rates of students of color at SSU. These rates are particularly low in comparison to the population ratios of the state. Similarly, public attention had been drawn in national publications to the low rates of faculty of color that are hired and subsequently tenured at SSU, particularly in comparison to their white colleagues.

Institutional Setting

Southeastern State University is a large public university which was chartered in the mid-1800s as part of a federal land grant initiative. From the beginning, SSU was viewed as the state's flagship university, hiring faculty and admitting students who could maintain the university's tradition of "scholarly excellence." The university has long been regarded as a premier research institution, not just within the state, but also in the Southeast. One of the goals of the current capital campaign is to broaden the scholarly reputation of SSU beyond the region. Thus, a major emphasis of the capital campaign is to bring in funds that will help recruit top faculty who are able to establish highly productive research programs that are well-positioned to earn top grant funding. A related goal is to recruit top students who will facilitate the establishment of research programs, and who will themselves go on to similarly successful careers in academia.

Although SSU originally admitted only male students, beginning in the 1950s, after bowing to legal pressure, the university began to admit female students. Current enrollment remains split at 55% male and 45% female. With respect to students of color, although individual students of color (generally African Americans) had been admitted in very small numbers in the early part of the twentieth century (the first Ph.D. was granted in 1948 to an African American), it was only in the 1970s with affirmative action policies in place that SSU began to admit students of color in larger, more representative numbers. Latino/a students recently have begun to be admitted to SSU in higher numbers due to the demographic changes in the state, with Latinos/as being the fastest growing racial/ethnic group.

Southeastern State University's Administration/Board of Trustees

The University is led by the president, the provost, and several vice presidents (e.g., Research, Finance, and Student Affairs). For the most part, these top administrators have been male and white, except for those administrators representing diversity-related topics (vice president of Multicultural Affairs/Director of Affirmative Action). Its administrators meet regularly and work to promote the continuing scholarly reputation of the university. As well, the University president often lobbies the state legislature and governor for more funds. Lately, these political entities have grown increasingly conservative and less interested in promoting affirmative action at SSU. The administration also has close ties with the University's Board of Trustees, which is comprised primarily of lay people, many of whom are wealthy and powerful alumni of SSU. By far, the board is overwhelmingly white and male, although there are generally one or two people of color who, by virtue of their solitary status, generally are rendered invisible in the decision-making process.

Dean Lucha

Dean Lucha was born and raised in San Juan, Puerto Rico. When she was ten, her parents moved their family to the Bronx, New York City to live with her uncle and aunt. Dean Lucha left behind her grandparents, aunts, uncles, and several cousins with whom she was very close. Upon arriving in New York, Dean Lucha attended public schools, developing friendships that were racially mixed, including African American, Latino/a, and Asian peers. Although she mostly spoke English at school and with friends, Dean Lucha spoke primarily Spanish at home with her parents. Dean Lucha later attended the Community College of New York and won a prestigious fellowship to study sociology at Ivy League University A, where she earned her M.A. and Ph.D. degrees. She subsequently took a faculty position at Ivy League University B, and was eventually promoted, tenured, and selected as department chair. Dean Lucha has authored over fifty refereed articles and two books, and her areas of study include African and Latino/a studies, immigration, and poverty. Dean Lucha is married to Dr. Marcus Reed, an African American man from the Southeast, who is a full professor at a small liberal arts college. They have two children.

Dr. Lucha's hiring as dean at SSU was not without controversy. Her application for the position was clearly the strongest of the pool, as seen by her stellar scholarly output, national service as a top officer in her professional organizations, and solid administrative experiences in a highly regarded department and university. However, some SSU faculty members in the College openly vocalized their concern about Dean Lucha's ability to maintain the university's and college's "academic excellence." These faculty members called into question the true nature of the scholarship in Dean Lucha's areas of study, stating that they wanted someone with clearer credentials that were closer to the mission of the college. As well, some trustees quietly expressed reservations about Dean Lucha's ability to network with SSU alumni and long-time donors. Student of color organizations and local citizen groups mounted a public campaign to hire Dean Lucha, believing her to be someone who could "make a difference at SSU." Moreover, the president felt strongly about the need to hire a "highly qualified" woman or person of color in a top administrative position; Dean Lucha, in his estimation, more than fit the bill.

The College of Arts and Sciences

The College of Arts and Sciences is a primary college of the university, providing essential coursework for all SSU students in their first two years. The College was a founding unit of SSU and has many diverse programs for both graduate and undergraduate students, ranging from the arts (e.g., English) and social sciences (e.g., psychology, sociology), to the so-called "hard" sciences (e.g., biology, chemistry). Departments range in number of faculty, students, and available scholarship monies. However, most departments emphasize scholarship at all levels. The faculty in the College is predominantly white (about 80%), with most faculty of color being located in the Ethnic Studies and Foreign Languages programs. Women make up

30% of the college faculty and are located primarily in the Arts and Social Sciences Departments, as well as the nascent Women's Studies program. The majority of tenured faculty are white (90%) and male (80%).

Students of Color at Southeastern State University

Most students of color in the state typically attend community colleges or regional universities, due to both financial and family concerns. However, given the growing national prominence of SSU (which also has a top-ranked football team), many students, including students of color, have become more strongly interested in attending SSU. In addition, school boards and parents have begun a campaign to see their children attend the top-notch university in their state. However, many students of color, as well as their parents, privately acknowledge some concerns about the support and visibility of people of color at SSU. These concerns were most recently fueled the previous year by a series of cartoons published in the SSU student newspaper, *The Knight Rider*, lampooning the academic abilities of "students of color" at SSU. Administrators at SSU responded somewhat slowly, though ultimately in favor of students of color. The administrators, stating their hands were tied legally, were unable to forbid any such future cartoons from being published, but required the newspaper staff to attend diversity training workshops.

Black/African American students. By far, African American students are students of color with the longest association with SSU. African American students were among the earliest graduates of SSU, and they developed numerous student organizations over the years based on political activism, profession/major, and socializing (e.g., black fraternities/sororities organize the annual Step Show in February). The major student group, Afro America!, began with the Civil Rights Movement of the 1960s, becoming a primary force leading to further desegregation of SSU via more open admission policies. Many of the original officers and members of Afro America! have gone on to lead successful professional careers and public lives, with the current mayor of the state's largest city having served as the first treasurer of the student group. The alumni wing of Afro America! also has become a consistent financial contributor to SSU, setting up a number of scholarships, as well as an endowed chair for the African American studies program (an interdisciplinary program in Dean Lucha's College). The student group and alumni wing of AfroAmerica! were primary vocal supporters of Dean Lucha's hiring.

Latino/a students. Because of the state's location in proximity to several Latin American countries, along with recent national trade agreements, SSU has experienced a major increase in the number of enrolled Latino/a students within the last decade. Initially, the increase was seen in small migrant groups who came and settled to work in the rural areas. However, in the last ten years, the number of Latinos/as seeking employment and permanently settling in urban and suburban areas first doubled, then tripled, and now represents 20% of the state's population. For many Latinos/as, education is viewed as the door to the "American dream." Although many Latino/a parents fear losing their children via physical distance and loss of language and cultural values, they generally encourage their children to continue on to college. To be sure, some Latinos/as prefer their children to remain close to home, even as they pursue higher education. However, a number of Latinos/as are pushing for increased enrollment of Latinos/as in the state universities, including SSU. At SSU, Latino/a students have recently organized to develop student groups similar to those of African Americans based on political activism, profession/ major, and social support (last year, the first Latino fraternity was officially chartered). As well, a student services unit was created at SSU three years ago devoted especially to the needs of Latino/a students.

Asian and Pacific American students. As with Latinos/as, Asian and Pacific Americans represent a fast growing segment of SSU's population. Due to the location of the state, however, the rise in population growth is much slower than in other parts of the United States. Nevertheless, many Asian and Pacific American parents are committed to sending their children to top universities in the state and country. Many of SSU's residents view Asian and Pacific Americans in terms of the "model minority" myth (i.e., quiet, unassuming, and hardworking). At SSU, this perception is evident in the lack of specific services for Asian and Pacific American students, unlike those that exist for African American and Latino/a students. At SSU, Asian and Pacific American students generally organize via their ethnic identity (e.g., Chinese, Japanese, or Vietnamese), although an Asian American student group with more activist goals recently has been formed.

American Indian students. Although small in number at SSU (less than 1% of the student body and two tenure-track faculty), American Indian people have lived in the SSU region for centuries. One of the largest tribes in the country has national headquarters in the state, and a tribal college exists about forty miles from SSU (many transfer from this college to attend SSU upon receiving their Associate's degree or to pursue a graduate degree). Tribal scholarships are a significant source of funds for many American Indian students at SSU. There is a single student group organization at SSU for American Indian students. Over the years, American Indian and African American student groups developed a strong working relationship in calling for needed changes for people of color at SSU.

White Students at Southeastern State University

White students have comprised the bulk of SSU's student body for most of its existence. There is a strong fraternity tradition at SSU for white male students, and many SSU students strive to belong to these organizations, often seeing them as a stepping stone to meeting professionals in the field and becoming involved in the power elite of the state. The school mascot, the Knight, is viewed by some as representing the historical significance of whites in the state, and a number of school songs are geared to present the Knight in an all positive light. Without a doubt, white students at SSU are among the top students academically in the state. Many of them selected SSU based on reputation, scholarship funds, and loyalty to the state (e.g., history and values). As well, a large proportion of white students come from families who can count several generations as SSU alumni. The large majority of white students (as with students of color) come from top percentages of their high schools, having maintained near 4.0 GPA's, and with standardized admission test scores in top percentile ranks. Within the past twenty years, and especially within the past five years, a number of white students have voiced strong concern about the "loss of academic excellence" at SSU. They point to "quotas" that apparently exist for students of color (vehemently denied by the administration) that provide separate admissions standards. Some also have proposed the need for "White History Month" in response to various racial/ethnic celebrations sponsored by SSU in the past decade. Relatedly, alumni groups consisting mostly of whites were among the strongest opponents of the hiring of Dean Lucha, agreeing with some white faculty members about concerns related to the potential loss of academic excellence of the University and detracting from the overall mission of SSU. At the same time, many white alumni have been very generous with SSU, providing millions of dollars of extra funding for scholarships, faculty and administrative positions, and student athletics. The SSU administration has strong close ties with a number of wealthy families who are both SSU alumni and generous contributors.

The Administrative Dilemmas

At the first Dean's Council meeting of the Fall semester, SSU's President, Dr. John Smith, proudly introduces two new deans: Dean Lucha and Dean Robert Stern of the College of Veterinary Medicine. He welcomes both to the Council, and notes that many great things are expected at SSU that year. He pointedly looks at Dean Lucha in remarking how he hopes the perceptions of SSU continue in a positive scholarly light, being capable of leading an increasingly diverse student body into the next generation of the state's leaders and scholars. This positive perception, President Smith continues, will be critical to mounting a successful capital campaign at SSU over the next five years. Dean Stern quickly jumps into the dialogue, adding that he believes his college already has taken the lead in these efforts, having recently set up a $5 million fund from alumni members for scholarships and laboratory funds. Athletic Director Jim Baker immediately adds that his department clearly is the leader at SSU in recruiting diverse students via needed scholarships, and these students reportedly go on to lead highly successful careers. Dean Lucha is initially surprised by the quickness and vehemence of these statements, but then adds herself that the College of Arts and Sciences is about to kick off an "Academic Excellence Through Diversity" campaign, aimed at both alumni and potential new donors, in support of the upcoming SSU capital campaign. Her remarks are greeted with silence from other Council members, which is then broken by President Smith coughing, adding that he is looking forward to a productive year at SSU.

That same week, Dean Lucha presides at the College's first faculty meeting. Among the agenda items are the capital campaign, new faculty hires, and the existing admission policies of the College. Dean Lucha welcomes the faculty, expressing her excitement about the new goals of SSU and College. She presents her "Academic Excellence Through Diversity" program for the College (no surprise to the faculty because this was a central part of her application materials), which emphasizes targeting the many groups and programs currently supporting the College. "No donor shall be left out of the campaign!" is Dean Lucha's rallying cry. She is met at first with silence from the mostly white male faculty, after which Dr. Carl Fromm, professor of sociology, speaks up, stating that although he is supportive of the new campaign, he does not want to see the standards of the College for either hiring or admissions "continue to slide by the wayside." Dr. Javier Gomez, Director of Latin American Studies, quickly counters with a comment regarding recent faculty hires as not reflecting the "pool of qualified applicants" and applauding Dean Lucha for her "beginning" efforts. Dean Lucha intervenes, stating that she will empanel a Task Force consisting of faculty, staff, and students to examine these issues, and then adjourns the meeting. Still later that week, Dean Lucha meets with the officers of several student groups of color who call upon her to help make "needed changes" at SSU.

Possible Resolutions

Dean Lucha was hired in part as a response to the increasing diversity of the state's population and the student body at SSU. Furthermore, she brings a great deal of scholarly and administrative experience to her position. Dean Lucha has begun to establish ties with a number of SSU alumni and members of the Board of Trustees across a variety of racial/ethnic lines. Her initial tasks as dean of one of the largest colleges at SSU are complex and many. Like any dean, a primary task is:

Establishing power, influence, and organization in the role of Dean of College of Arts and Sciences. Taking an organizational/systems approach, Dean Lucha imagines she can successfully achieve this task by doing the following:

a. Networking with administrators within the College (e.g., department chairs, directors of admission, directors of Ethnic Minority Recruiting Programs, etc.);

b. Networking with faculty (identify concerns, problems, begin to confront hiring and retention inequities)

c. Networking with students (identify concerns, problems, confront admissions inequities);

d. Networking with administrators within SSU (e.g., president, provost, other vice president, deans, etc.);

e. Networking with constituent groups (alumni, Board of Trustees/ trustees, local and state politicians, relevant state agencies and boards, private advocacy groups);

f. Developing a support base at SSU for various initiatives; and

g. Gaining a thorough knowledge of the budget and external resources.

Some of her duties also clearly relate to the two initial issues that may eventually characterize her leadership at SSU and which may or may not conflict with each other:

1. Meaningfully contributing to the SSU Capital Campaign—
   • Utilizing above networking efforts
   • Identifying programs/means of gathering funds

2. Rectifying admissions, retention, and graduation rates of students of color—Establishing perception and/or reality of the situation:
   • Review current admissions procedures
   • Review current support services/retention programs for students
   • Identify successful graduates of color from the College
   • Institute new programs/structures that effectively review and promote admissions, retention, and graduation rates of all students
   • Review hiring and tenure policies in the College
   • Place supportive people of initiatives in important places, such as program directors and department chairs

One approach Dean Lucha might take is to combine the two initiatives by incorporating her central theme, "Academic Excellence Through Diversity:"

- Encourage scholarship funds and endowed chairs on a whole range of topics
- Establishing groups across existing racial/ethnic ties groups for various purposes (social, academic)

Discussion Questions

1. Common barriers to success for women of color in administrative roles have been identified by a number of scholars. These include:

   - Lack of support network/chilly climate
   - Marginalization
   - Tokenism
   - Stereotypes/biases about women of color, including the Double Bind of race/gender
   - Clash of cultural values (cultural background/values vs. institutional setting/values)
   - Differing communication or working styles (e.g., collaborative vs. independent)
   - Feeling squeezed or pulled among different constituencies

Describe how each of these barriers already exist to Dean Lucha's ultimate success in achieving both goals at SSU (raising funds, rectifying long-standing inequities)?

2. What suggestions would you offer Dean Lucha to overcome these barriers?
3. What conflicts might you expect among the various constituencies described in the chapter?
4. Who might be important allies for Dean Lucha to establish? Why?
5. How can Dean Lucha make a positive difference at SSU, both in helping to raise needed funds and in confronting long-established inequities in the system?
6. The title of the chapter is based on a recommendation by Gloria Anzaldua, a Chicana scholar and poet, who states, "To survive the borderlands you must live *sin fronteras* (without borders), be a crossroads" (Anzaldua, 1987, as cited in Delgado-Romero, Flores, Gloria, Arredondo, & Castellanos, 2003, p. 280). How might Dean Lucha be a crossroads for the initiatives and challenges she faces at SSU? What are potential costs and benefits of this approach for Dean Lucha both personally and professionally?

Recommended Background Readings

Racial/Ethnic Issues in Higher Education

Davis, J.D. (Ed.). (1994). *Coloring the halls of ivy: Leadership and diversity in the academy.* Boston, MA: Anker.

Turner, C.S.V., Garcia, M., Nora, A., & Rendon, L. I. (Eds.). (1996). *Racial & ethnic diversity in higher education.* Boston, MA: Pearson.

People/Women of Color as Faculty and Administrators in Higher Education

Arredondo, P. (2002). Mujeres latinas—santasy marquesas. *Cultural Diversity and Ethnic Minority Psychology*, 8 (4), 308–319.

Benjamin, L. (Ed.). (1997). *Black women in the academy: Promises and perils.* Gainesville, FL: University of Florida.

Bowen, R.C. & Muller, G.H. (Summer 1996). *New Directions for Community Colleges: Achieving Administrative Diversity, No. 94.* San Francisco, CA: Jossey-Bass.

Castellanos, J. & Jones, L. (2003). *The majority in the minority: Expanding the representation of Latina/o faculty, administrators, and students in higher education.* Sterling, VA: Stylus.

Padilla, R.V. & Chavez, R.C. (Eds). (1995). *The leaning ivory tower: Latino professors in American universities.* Albany, NY: SUNY Press.

Turner, C.S.V., & Myers, S.L. (2000). *Faculty of color in academe: Bittersweet success.* Boston, MA: Allyn & Bacon.

Part III New Challenges Facing Faculty

Case #9 Affirmative Action and Faculty Hiring

Suzanne E. Eckes and Christi M. Smith

Most educational systems seek to support a diverse student body and to provide an educational setting that encourages diversity. In order to achieve diversity, oftentimes universities adopt affirmative action programs. Affirmative action has been used in faculty hiring to remedy past discrimination and to employ a more diverse faculty. Once such programs are established, the question in moving beyond the initial steps of embracing affirmative action becomes how to create a system which addresses race, class, and gender in tandem. For example, when considering faculty hiring, how should universities prioritize amongst a variety of diversities? Can and should a hierarchy of valued characteristics be created to enhance student interaction in an increasingly pluralistic society? To what extent should race, class, and gender be considered in hiring to increase diversity and to rectify past injustices?

This case explores whether race and gender should be considered in hiring university faculty. Specifically, a fictitious public university seeks increased faculty diversity in all of its academic departments. The rationale provided by the university is two fold. The administration feels that it is vital to take steps toward remedying the effects of past discrimination in academic departments and believes that there are great benefits in maintaining a racially diverse faculty. As such, Green Acres University has decided to consider race as one of many factors in faculty hiring. The case specifically challenges university administrators to consider how to implement affirmative action policies when there are two or more applicants from groups which are historically marginalized.

When reading this case, take on the role of the program chair, department chair or dean. Consider how you would address these issues in faculty hiring. In this role, be sure to answer whether race and gender should be a factor in hiring faculty and how each criterion should be weighted.

Institutional Setting and Faculty Background

Green Acres University is situated in the Southwest region of the United States and enrolls 25,000 undergraduate and graduate students. The student body is 48% Latino, 32% white, 15% African American, and 5% other. Green Acres is a research-extensive university. The numbers of students of color and women have risen each year for the past five years.

Between 1998 and 2003, only 1% of the University's full-time faculty was Latino, and 94% of the full-time faculty was white. Five percent of the full-time faculty was Native American, African American or Asian American. Nineteen percent of the full-time faculty was women.

The Physics Department, the focus of this case, had no people of color employed as full-time faculty members. Twenty percent of the full-time faculty was female; however, none of the female faculty members were tenured.

The University Policy

The University was concerned about the high number of Latino/ students enrolled and the low number of Latino/a faculty members employed. In order to rectify the racial imbalance of Latino/a faculty members, the University instituted the "minority bonus program," an unwritten amendment to its affirmative action policy which allowed a department to hire an additional faculty member following the initial hiring of a Latino/a candidate. This program was used as an incentive for the University departments to hire more Latino/a candidates.

The Issue

The University published an announcement regarding an impending faculty vacancy in the Physics Department. The announcement for the faculty position emphasized a need for a doctorate degree in Physics, a number of quality publications and at least two years of teaching experience. Teaching experience through a post-doctoral program or working as a teaching assistant during graduate school counted toward the two-year requirement. The announcement indicated that applicants with external grant money would be looked upon favorably. There was a stipulated salary range between $52,000 and $59,000, dependent upon experience and qualifications. Although both publications and teaching experience are considered during hiring, research is most scrutinized during tenure and promotion.

The University's hiring guidelines required each department to conduct more than one interview. The University interviewed Mary Scott, a thirty-three-year-old white woman from Minnesota and Ruben Ortiz, a twenty-nine-year-old Latino immigrant from Mexico. Mary earned her Ph.D. from a prestigious research-extensive East coast university. At the time of the interview she was participating in a post-doc program at a research-extensive university in the mid-South. At the mid-South university, Mary spent twenty hours per week on her research and the other twenty hours on teaching undergraduate courses at Charles Hamilton Houston, a historically black college located in a neighboring town. During her time in the post-doc, Mary had two articles accepted for publication in reputable research journals. These publications are considered impressive but they were not in the field's top journals. Even though these publications were not in the top journals, Mary is still considered above-average based upon her years of experience.

Ruben was a doctoral candidate at a research-extensive university on the West coast where he was scheduled to defend his dissertation one month after his interview at Green Acres University. While at the university, Ruben had been a teaching assistant for three years. Ruben had won the Trustee's Excellence in Teaching Award all three years and his advisor believed that Ruben had a great chance of winning the prestigious dissertation of the year award. Ruben was a co-author of one article that was published in a top-tier journal. Ruben is also considered an above-average candidate based upon his years of experience. Neither candidate had any external grant money.

Due to the perceived shortage of Latino Ph.D. candidates, coupled with Ruben's strong academic and teaching achievements, the search committee sought approval to initially offer Ruben $60,000, with an increase to $65,000 upon completion of his Ph.D. This initial offer exceeded the advertised salary range. Even though Ruben had not accepted any competing offers, the University justified its premium offer as a method of preventing a bidding war between two prestigious universities slated to interview Ruben. This strategy, according to the University, was designed to preempt other institutions from hiring Ruben. Ruben accepted the offer and was hired as a new assistant professor.

Ruben and Mary were more qualified for the position compared to the department's other recent hires. The curriculum vitae for both candidates revealed comparable strengths with respect to their educational backgrounds, publishing, areas of specialization, and teaching experience. The university concluded that despite some inequalities, their strengths and weaknesses complemented each other; hence, as a result of the additional position created by the minority bonus policy, the department hired Mary one year later. Mary was offered $59,000, which, according to the dean, was slightly above the mean for new hires in physics.

Mary's Argument

Mary claims that she was more qualified for the position initially offered to Ruben because she had already earned her Ph.D. and had published more articles. She found the disparity in pay discriminatory when she was offered the position one year later. Mary filed a compliant against the University alleging gender and race violations under Title VII of the Civil Rights Act as amended in 1991.

Mary argued that the university relied too heavily upon race and pointed out that gender was of equal importance when seeking to remedy past injustices and in promoting an inclusive atmosphere on campus. Mary cited a study by the American Institute of Physics, which states that only 3% of full-ranking physics professors were women between 1994 and 1998. She stated that due to long-standing gender discrimination in the physical sciences, female undergraduates needed more role models.

During Mary's doctoral work at the mid-South university, a study was conducted at that institution which profoundly shaped some of her concerns regarding gender discrimination in the academy in general and in the arena of science in particular. In 1999, the university undertook "A Study on the Status of Women Faculty in Science at Mid-South University" to examine disparities in the academic careers of women faculty. The study concluded that "the percentage of women faculty in the School of Science (8%) had not changed significantly for at least ten and probably twenty years." The study noted that "Even if we continue to hire women at the current increased rate in Science, it will be 40 years before 40% of the faculty in the School of Science could be women." Mary argued that the situation at Green Acres University was not dramatically different from Mid-South University.

The University's Argument

The University argued that the implementation of a race-conscious affirmative action policy was designed to remedy the effects of past discrimination against a traditionally disadvantaged group, namely Latinos. In particular, the university also sought to remedy a manifest imbalance in a traditionally segregated job category. In making this argument, the University pointed out that only 1% of the faculty was Latino/a. The University also articulated the benefits of maintaining a diverse faculty. Within the diversity argument, the University cited research and Supreme Court precedent to demonstrate that the "minority bonus program" was both necessary and legal. The university contended that a failure to attract Latino/a faculty perpetuates the university's white enclave and further limits student exposure to a multicultural environment. Although the university conceded that women were underrepresented in the physics department, it argued that the lack of people of color was even more dramatic.

The University also noted that both candidates were equal in most respects and given the aspect of subjectivity involved in choosing between the candidates, the University should be given the latitude to make its own employment decisions provided they are not discriminatory. This recognized deference arguably relates to the academic freedoms afforded under the First Amendment, including who may teach and what may be taught. Accordingly, in this case, the university had good reason to consider race as a factor in faculty hiring. Mary argued that the situation at Green Acres University was not dramatically different from Mid-South University.

The Research

One of the most recent studies on diversity, conducted by Patricia Gurin (2003), professor of psychology, identified the value of classroom diversity in higher education. Gurin's analyses demonstrated a pattern of consistent, positive relationships between student learning in higher education and both classroom diversity and informal interactional diversity. The Gurin study also revealed that the scores of white students increased on the measures of complex thinking and social thinking when they interacted with students of other races. Gurin relied on data from approximately 200 colleges and universities for the purpose of this study. Green Acres relied on the Gurin study and argued that the same findings could be applied to a diverse faculty. Mary, on the other hand, contends that this research only pertains to student body diversity and should not be extended to faculty hiring.

The Law

The permissible contours for affirmative action plans are blurred. Although Title VII of the Civil Rights Act of 1964 presents an obstacle in this scenario, the issue of diversity as a compelling state interest in recent case law is worthy of discussion. The University of California v. Bakke decision permitted the consideration of race as one of many factors for student admissions in higher education. The University of Michigan affirmative action cases, Grutter v. Bollinger and Gratz v. Bollinger, also permitted this type of affirmative action for higher education admissions. Although Bakke, Grutter and Gratz focused on student admissions, several scholars contend that the spirit of these decisions should also apply to faculty hiring. In other words, if the Court found student body diversity to be a compelling state interest, it should also find faculty diversity equally valuable.

Supreme Court decisions regarding the remedying of past discrimination are also unclear. Although the Supreme Court noted the importance of eliminating patterns of racial segregation in occupations that have been traditionally closed to minorities, this rationale has been questioned in several employment court cases.

The Affirmative Action Debate

Concerns about diversity in higher education are not to be limited to the student body. As with student body diversity, a well-documented case can be made for hiring a diverse faculty. Alger (1999) and Ryan (2003) argue that a diverse faculty would play a pivotal role in breaking down stereotypes and improving race relations at the university. Faculty members break down these stereotypes as they influence through their teaching, research, and service activities. Through these activities, a diverse faculty could arguably improve race relations on campus.

Likewise, Eckes (2005) contends that employing a diverse faculty could lead to a more robust exchange of ideas during faculty-to-student exchanges and faculty-to-faculty exchanges. In other words, there are certain benefits to the student body that could not be provided by a nearly all-white faculty. Indeed, universities are premised upon the creation of a holistic learning environment as part of the institution's educational mission, promoting a sense of community among faculty and students. Such a sense of community would be more difficult if a university lacked diversity.

Conversely, one could argue that such plans operate against whites and unfairly favor certain minorities, creating reverse discrimination. The concern in this case is not only over whether affirmative action is inherently a worthwhile venture, but the complications which arise in its implementation. The question of how much weight should be given to race as opposed to gender is also pertinent to this discussion. Given these difficult questions, discuss the following issues as they relate to this case.

Discussion Questions

1. What lessons can we draw from recent court decisions regarding the ways in which affirmative action affects faculty hiring at public colleges and universities?
2. Do the arguments which support affirmative action in selecting a student body have equal merit when applied to faculty hiring?

3. How can the consideration in faculty hiring be implemented in a fair and unbiased manner?
4. How do we determine whether race or gender needs further representation due to changing demographics over time?
5. How do we make such hiring practices "uncontroversial?" Specifically, under such a policy, is it possible to avoid a hostile work environment for minorities and women?
6. Can a fair tool for evaluating faculty applicants be developed? How do we create a tool which is both dynamic enough to adapt to change and sufficiently binding to provide unbiased guidance to Promotion and Tenure Committees?
7. As dean/department chair, what leadership model should be applied when making this hiring decision?
8. How do these policies impact the governance of colleges and universities?

Gender

Committee on Women Faculty, 1999. A Study on the Status of Women in Science at MIT. Retrieved March 1, 2004, from the MIT Web site: http://web.mit.edu/fnl/women/women.html#The%20Study

Legal

Gratz v. Bollinger, 123 S.Ct. 2411 (2003) (focused on diversity).
Grutter v. Bollinger, 123 S.Ct. 2325 (2003) (focused on diversity).
Johnson v. Transportation Agency, 480 U.S. 616 (1987) (focused on remedial interest).
Regents of University of California v. Bakke, 438 U.S. 265 (1978) (focused on diversity).
United Steelworkers of America v. Weber, 443 U.S. 193 (1979) (focused on remedial interest).

Affirmative Action Research

Alger, J. (1999). When color-blind is color-bland: Ensuring faculty diversity in higher education. *Stanford Law and Policy Review*, 10 (2), 191–199.
Eckes, S. (2005). Diversity in higher education: The consideration of race in hiring university faculty, *Education and Law Journal*, 2005(1), 1–21.
Gurin, P. (2003). The Compelling Need for Diversity in Higher Education. Expert Report for University of Michigan Pending Lawsuit Gratz & Hamacher v. Bollinger. Retrieved July 10, 2003, from the University of Michigan Web site: http://www.umich.edu/~urel/admissions/legal/expert/gurintoc.html.

Recommended Background Reading

Race

Ancheta, A. (2003). *Revisiting Bakke and diversity-based admissions: Constitutional law, social science research, and the University of Michigan affirmative action cases.* Cambridge, MA: The Civil Rights Project at Harvard University.

Ryan, J. (2003). What role should courts play in influencing educational policy? The limited influence of social science evidence in modern desegregation cases. *North Carolina Law Review,* 81 (2), 1659.

West, C. (1993). *Race matters.* Boston, MA: Boston Press.

Case #10 Neo-Racism/Neo-Discrimination and Faculty Hiring: Chronicling the Perpetuation of Racial Privilege

KIMBERLY LENEASE KING-JUPITER AND DEVONA L. FOSTER

Much attention has been paid to the lack of representation of African Americans among the faculty ranks at predominantly white institutions (PWI) across the country. While the institutions cite the lack of African Americans in the pipeline, another cause is the ways in which search committees are constructed and the un-stated criteria that the European American faculty uses to make these decisions.

Institutional Setting

Southern University has been classified as a doctoral/research-extensive university. It is a land grant institution with over 33,000 undergraduates and graduate students. Southern University offers an array of undergraduate and graduate programs from its twelve degree-granting schools. The campus is located in Buffington Hills which is a mid-size deep southern city still haunted by the shadow of defacto racial segregation in housing and education.

While the U.S. News and World Report have consistently ranked Southern University in the top 100, turmoil among the administration led to a two-year probation by the Regional Accrediting Board. This turmoil was most apparent in the number of senior administrative positions filled by interim candidates and unwillingness on the part of the Board of Trustees to launch search committees to permanently fill a number of positions. Interim deans headed six of the twelve colleges; the president and provost were interim as were a number of other positions. Many campus leaders contend that the positions have been filled by interims in order to allow the 'good ole boy' network to prevail. More specifically, by not launching national searches, the board and other well-placed European American men in the administration could promote members of their clique. Not surprisingly, that clique predominantly consists of European American men with some women.

Much of this turmoil emerged when President Johnson resigned in 1995. Instead of launching a national presidential search, the Board of Trustees preemptively fired President Johnson and installed the provost as interim President—John Ballard. President Ballard's promotion led to the elevation of a number of European American males to positions on an interim basis. Those positions have not been filled permanently. Similar attempts are made among faculty ranks inevitably resulting in an overwhelmingly European American faculty.

Relative to the deans' searches, various constituent groups believe that the chairs of search committees have been constructed to select the interim deans on a permanent basis. After all, they have all applied for the positions. This became an issue when one of the interim deans launched a campaign to remove the only African American selected to chair one of the dean's search committees. In a letter written to Interim President Ballard, Interim Dean Barbara Ann Chambley wrote, "I believe that the search for the Dean's position in the College of Liberal Arts has been structured to prevent the hiring of anyone white. By selecting an African American to chair the search committee, it is unlikely that my candidacy will be given a fair and impartial evaluation." Meanwhile, the best friend of the interim Dean in the College of Sciences—Candra Brands, chaired the dean's search committee in the College of Sciences. Those opposed to Brands' candidacy complained that this unfairly privileged her in the selection process.

Question Set #1:

(a) What do you think Interim President Ballard did in response to the letter? What would you have done in response to this letter?
(b) What does the comment say about the role of race in the selection process?
(c) Do you think the relationship between the chair of the College of Science search committee and the interim Dean influenced the selection process?
(d) Should close relationships between chairs of search committees and candidates mean that the chair should remove him or herself from the committee?

Stalemate in the Foundations Department

As is typical of most predominantly white universities, Southern University contends that the lack of racial diversity among faculty and the senior administrative ranks exists because they cannot attract 'qualified' candidates of color. Employing approximately 1200 faculty, fewer than 50 are of African American descent. Of those fifty faculty, fewer than five are full professors with the majority occupying the rank of assistant professor. Southern University's formal and informal recruitment processes hinder the recruitment of racially diverse applicant pools. National searches are formally launched and job announcements are published in nationally circulated publications like the *Chronicle of Higher Education*. On the other hand, Southern University's faculties use their social networks to encourage their colleagues, their colleagues' students, or their protégés from other institutions to apply for current or anticipated openings. Consequently, in the formal search committee proceedings, faculty members rely on unpublished criteria when determining what candidates to invite for interviews or to determine what candidates to eliminate from the competition.

Within the College of Education, Dean Jasper has been adamant about the need to develop a faculty that is racially diverse. At the College of Education faculty meeting in 1996, he said, "thirty percent of the population of the state are African American and the fastest growing population in the state is of Hispanic descent. This is a state institution. That means that we have to respond to the circumstances within the state. Of the 7 departments in the college, only 2 departments can boast of racial diversity among their members. This is problematic because we know that a diverse faculty is better equipped to prepare educators to cope with diversity in the classroom. We must do better and I am inclined to ensure that we will do better".

After the meeting, Dean Jasper said to Charlotte Taffy (one of only two African Americans tenured in the College, current president of the Southern University Black Staff and Faculty Association (SUBSF) and the College's Director of Human Resources, "the departments have proven resistant to hiring someone who is not European American, so we have made very little progress. However, with the number of positions we are hiring for this year, the faculty could look very different next year. I want you to review and sign off on all faculty searches before any offers are made. I'll send out letters notifying the department heads." "How aggressive would you like me to be?" asked Charlotte. Dean Jasper responded, "Searches that don't have any racial diversity will not go forward unless the chairs of those committees can explain why."

The Role of Search Committees in Promoting Diversity among Faculty Ranks

Out of seven faculty departments, four of them have searches underway. In the Foundations Department alone there are three searches underway. The only other African American tenured in the College besides Charlotte Taffy chairs one of the searches; Kiya Dale chairs that search and they are looking for someone to teach history of education. There is also a search in that department for someone who can teach educational psychology. Dick Talbort chairs that search. The department is also looking for someone who can teach in the area of technology. Janet Childs chairs that search committee. In a meeting between Bennett King (the Foundations department head), Kiya Dale, Dick Talbort and Janet Childs, Bennett said "It appears the Dean means what he said. We have been told that if the candidate pools are not diverse, we will not be able to move on the searches. To avoid any problems, we should conduct the searches so that we attract some level of racial diversity." Dick Talbort responded, "I'm more concerned about finding a qualified candidate. That usually means that the best candidate will be white. This is just another effort to control what we do." Kiya Dale said, "Are you suggesting that you would never be able to find qualified candidates who are black, Hispanic or Asian?" Dick frowned, turned red and retorted, "that isn't what I said". "But is that what you meant?" replied Kiya Dale. In an effort to diffuse the discussion between Kiya and Dick, Bennet asked Janet about the status of her search. After all, her search had been underway for the last three years. Two offers had been made and declined. Janet said, "I just hope this is the last year for this search!"

In order to recruit a large and racially diverse candidate pool, the announcements for all three positions were submitted to the *Chronicle of Higher Education*, Black Issues in Higher Education, and to a number of professional electronic list servers. The deadline for applications was March 1st. Kiya and Janet contacted potential candidates whom they had met at national conferences to further encourage them to apply and contacted department chairs at universities around the country with programs commensurate with the program for which they were hiring. Their efforts resulted in a pool of sixty and fifteen candidates, respectively. {The pool for the history of education search included eight African American and two Hispanic candidates. For the technology position, there were two African Americans. The search for the educational psychology position netted only four candidates. Two of those candidates did not complete their applications by the March 1st deadline leaving one European American male and one Asian American male in the pool.} Since Kiya Dale's experiences as chair of the history of education search committee clearly exhibits the myriad of ways that faculty work to prevent the development of racially diverse faculties, that search will be highlighted in the remainder of the case study.

The Real Criteria

Included in the history of education candidate pool was someone who completed a fellowship in the department several years prior to the search—Jordan Eagle. After the fellowship, Jordan maintained relationships with prominent people both within the Foundations Department and in the College of Education. Although Kiya was not a faculty member in the department when Jordan was at Southern on fellowship, they were acquainted through the American Comparative Studies Association (ACSA). At the annual meeting in November, Jordan mentioned to Kiya that he would be applying for the position. He submitted his application early and then visited the campus to spend time with his friends in January—almost two months before the application deadline. During his visit, he individually met with every faculty member in the Foundations Department with the exception of Dr. Bennet; he was out of town. When Jordan requested a meeting with Kiya, she inquired as to the nature of the meeting, after all, they had a discussion about the position at the ACSA national conference in November. Jordan said he was interested in discussing the position. Kiya was suspicious. She had said what she had to say about the position when they saw each other in November and Jordan hadn't mentioned his visit to campus. She also didn't know that he had a fellowship at Southern University before her arrival. Bennett King informed her of Jordan's fellowship.

In addition to the meetings with faculty, Associate Dean Jeffries arranged for Daphne Elders, a tenured member of the Foundations Department and, incidentally a member of the history of education search committee, to organize a brown bag luncheon wherein Jordan Eagle would discuss his research. Kiya declined going to the brown bag because Jordan's activities during the visit sounded suspiciously like a campus interview for the position even though the application deadline had not passed and the search committee had yet to convene.

Jordan's meeting with Kiya took place immediately following the brown bag luncheon. In the meeting, Kiya thought Jordan was very aggressive. Jordan asked about the qualifications for the position. Kiya responded by giving him a copy of the position announcement and discussing the teaching expectations for the new position. Jordan kept telling Kiya that he was really interested in the position and wanted to know his chances. She explained to him several times that the application deadline had not passed, no one had reviewed the application pool in its entirety, and even if they had, it would be inappropriate to answer such a question. Jordan asked again what she thought about his chances. Frustrated, Kiya repeated her response and ended the meeting. She was already late for another meeting in the dean's office with Charlotte Taffy. Charlotte wanted an update on the history of education search. As Kiya walked down the hallway towards the dean's office, she saw Jordan in the hallway whispering to the Associate Dean Jeffries and Daphne Elders. Kiya acknowledged the threesome as she entered the Dean's office and wondered if this signaled problems to come.

Meanwhile, Bennett King met with Dick Talbort about the educational psychology search. Bennett was inclined to double the recruitment efforts or halt the search until the following year. Dick said, "Bennett we've got a viable candidate who really wants to come here. If you are just trying to satisfy the dean, we also have diversity. What's the problem?" Bennett expressed concern about the paucity of candidates but wrote a letter to Charlotte regarding the status of each search committee.

Question Set #2:

    (a) What do you think Bennett King said in his letter to Charlotte?
    (b) How many applications constitute a "viable" pool of candidates?
    (c) In the meeting with Charlotte, should Kiya inform her about the activities surrounding Jordan Eagle's candidacy?

Reviewing the Applications Begins

The committee members for each search were instructed to review the applications in their respective pools and vote for the top candidates. Given the size of the history of education candidate pool, Kiya told the committee that the candidates receiving at least three votes (votes from half the committee) would remain in the competition for the second round of reviews. Committee members were given an evaluation sheet listing the criteria appearing in the job announcement. They were instructed to rate each candidate on a scale from one to five. The criteria included the following: 1) completed terminal degree; 2) whether or not the terminal degree was in the appropriate field; 3) experience in teaching/experience in teaching courses expected for this position; 4) strength of recommendations; and, 5) potential or demonstrated ability to conduct research. The evaluation forms also left room for the committee members to comment on each candidate. See the following table for a summary of committee members' comments on selected candidates from each the history of education search.

Search Committee Evaluations: History of Education

Compilation of Committee Evaluations for Selected Candidates

Candidate	Terminal Degree	Teaching Exp	Strength of Recom	Research Potential	Comments	Avg. Score
Terry Askew	yes/yes	yes/yes	strong	yes	Teaches history of educ and has 3 articles	4.5
Faber Cabinet	no/yes	yes/no	average	yes	ABD; exp teaching in different subject area; presented at 2 national conferences	4
Nagina Cabour	no/no	no/no	poor	no		0
Jordan Eagle	yes/no	yes/no	poor	no	Degree in Comp and no work in history; no exp teaching in U.S. context or under-grads; no recs from colleagues just from Southern; Ph.D. for 4 years and no publications	4

Candidate	Terminal Degree	Teaching Exp	Strength of Recom	Research Potential	Comments	Avg. Score
Dabney George	yes/yes	yes/yes	excellent	yes	Ph.D. recently but has 3 pubs; has taught history of educ for undergrads & grads	5
Nadine Hamilton	yes/yes	yes/yes	excellent	yes	New Ph.D.; no pubs but lots of conference presentations; taught with undergrads & grads	4.5
Gene Hawkins	yes/yes	yes/yes	excellent	yes	New Ph.D.; 2 journal and book	5
Vincent Iwards	yes/yes	yes/no	good	yes	Recs don't really stand out	4.5
Sasha Jackson	no/yes	no/no	excellent	yes	ABD; no teaching experience; glowing recs; 2 pubs and lots of conf presentations.	4

Name						
Bailey Jefferies	no/yes	yes/no	good	no	ABD; no pubs or conf presentations	3
Adrian King	no/yes	yes/no	good	yes	ABD; no teaching in area but lots of teaching exp; no pubs or conf presentations	3.5
Alexandria Lennox	yes/yes	yes/no	good	yes	Taught K-12 and undergrad courses but none in history; only 2 conf presentations	1.5
Cheryl Osborne	yes/no	no/no	poor	no	Degree in Sociology; no teaching exp.; advisor says not disciplined; no pubs or conf presentations No teaching	2
Taylor Smith	yes/yes	no/no	good	no	exp.; generic recs; no pubs or conf presentations.	
Dabney Stunt	yes/no	no/no	poor	no	no pubs or conf presentations.	1
Deborah Williams	yes/yes	yes/yes	excellent	yes		5

Question Set #3:

(a) Which candidates do you think received at least three votes?
(b) If you were to conduct a phone interview with five candidates, whom would you select?
(c) Did/should prior relationships influence the search process?
(d) Who do you think the committee recommended for hire?

When the search committee convened, fifteen candidates received a minimum of three votes. In addition, Nandi Sally (a tenured faculty member in the department) felt that she needed more information on a potential candidate—Faber Cabinet. The candidate was ranked highly by most committee members, but his advisor didn't provide an anticipated completion date for the Ph.D. Since that was the primary concern, Nandi agreed to contact the candidate's advisor to get additional information before the committee completely excluded the candidate from the process. At the end of the first round, Jordan Eagle was excluded from the competition. He received his terminal degree from a university in the United States but had never taught a course on the American education system nor had he been involved in the preparation of pre-service teachers. Additionally, although receiving his Ph.D. three years prior to this search process, Jordan Eagle only had two publications. Also, he submitted two more recommendations than the job announcement requested, yet, none of the recommenders were his colleagues or administrators at the university with which he had been previously or currently employed. All of the recommenders were from Southern University faculty and administrators. Concerns were expressed regarding his ability to meet the tenure and teaching expectations of the position. Although Jordan held his terminal degree longer than anyone else in the candidate pool, comparatively speaking he had fewer publications. Several of the candidates that had recently completed their degrees had more publications and/or conference presentations than Jordan. Sasha Johnson hadn't completed her Ph.D. yet but had two publications in very prestigious refereed journals. Gene Hawkins received his Ph.D. during the fall preceding the search process, yet he had already published a book and had two journal articles. Dabney George and Terry Askew both completed their degrees a year ago yet they had more publications than Jordan. The committee agreed that the pool was very qualified. There was, however, some discrepancy about who the leading candidate was.

News of Jordan's exclusion from the second round of considerations spread quickly through the department. When Daphne Elders returned from the committee meeting, waiting for her was an email message from Associate Dean Jeffries. Instead of returning his email, she went down to the dean's office to speak with him directly. As soon as she walked into his office, he said, "How did Jordan do?" "He has been eliminated from further consideration." said Daphne Elders. Stunned Jeffries asked, "What criteria were used to exclude him from the competition?" Daphne delineated the concerns regarding the paucity of Jordan's publications; his lack of teaching experience with undergraduates; and, the fact that none of his recommenders had ever really worked with him. Jeffries thanked Daphne for the information, expressed his dissatisfaction and excused himself from the impromptu meeting. As Daphne exited his office, Jeffries said, "Jordan is a good friend of mine and several of the full professors in the department. He really wants to be here and whatever his shortcomings, he would do better here than anyone else. That is all that should matter, after all, I wrote him the strongest recommendation I've ever written for anyone." Daphne left the dean's office committed to bringing the issue up again when the committee met the following week.

Kiya Dale called the next selection committee for the history of education position to order. Before they could address issues pending from the previous meeting, Daphne said, "I think we unfairly eliminated Jordan Eagle from the selection pool. I don't think he was given adequate consideration." Kiya Dale responded, "If you can get two other members of the committee to agree with your assessment, he can remain in the pool. Every candidate remaining in the pool has to have support from at least half of this committee. Does anyone else agree with Daphne's position?"

Question Set #4:

(a) Do you think Jordan Eagle was retained in the competition after the first round?
(b) Do you think the associate dean or other senior members of the department contacted other members of the selection committee?
(c) Should Jordan be excluded from the search because of his behavior while on campus?
(d) Why or why not?

Other Search Committees in the College

During the March departmental faculty meeting, the chairs of the search committees were asked to make a short report. Kiya Dale reported the following:

> We had a total of sixty applicants. After two rounds of elimination, we have five candidates that will be contacted for phone interviews. The goal is to identify the top two candidates to invite for a campus interview.

Dick Talbort said, "I'm assuming that Jordan Eagle is in that group". Kiya Dale looked directly at Dick Talbort and retorted, "What would make you think that? Have you seen the applicant pool?" Around the room you could hear people mutter "But we like Jordan and he really wants to be here!" Looking at Bennett King, Kiya said, "Would you like me to review the criteria used in the selection process and discuss how Jordan compares relative to those criteria?" "That won't be necessary", said Bennett. Anxious to move the meeting along, Bennett asked Janet Childs to report. Disappointed, Janet reported that their top three candidates called to remove themselves from the competition. They already had job offers. Satisfied that there might still be viable candidates in the pool, Janet recommended that the process proceed. Faculty members expressed their appreciation for Janet's efforts—"We know how long and arduous the task of chairing this committee has been for you", someone said. When it was Dick Talbort's turn to report, he reported the following:

> As you know we had four candidates. The committee met and conducted phone interviews with two of the candidates. We have decided to bring one of the candidates to campus for an interview.

Nobody had any comments in response to Dick Talbort's report. Kiya Dale, concerned about the small applicant pool asked, "Did the committee consider contacting the chairs of departments around the country to increase the candidate pool"? Dick replied, "We advertised and that is the extent of my responsibility as chair of the committee. The fact that the position is at Southern University should be enough." "So you are going to hire from a pool of four candidates?" said Kiya Dale. Almost too soft to hear, Bennett King said, "Actually there are only two candidates in the pool."

One of the candidates met Kiya Dale at the national meeting of the American Educational Research Association (AERA) and was an African American male—Texas Crenshaw. Texas Crenshaw's mother was ill making a job at Southern University his highest priority. After all, his mother lived thirty miles from Southern University. Texas had just received his degree from an Ivy League institution and already had four publications in the best journals in the field. Kiya suggested that he contact Dick Talbort to ask further questions about the status of the search. Unfortunately, in Texas' conversation with Dick Talbort, he was discouraged from applying. Dick told him that there was no way Southern University could offer him a salary commensurate with his record. Texas immediately contacted Kiya to inform her of the information he received from Dick Talbort. In their conversation Texas said, "Why apply to Southern when it is clear they don't want me?" Kiya responded by contacting Bennett King and encouraging him to contact Texas regarding his candidacy. Bennett was unsuccessful. The other candidate was a Latina—Guadalupe Vazquez. She was a Holmes Scholar and was recruited to the pool by Charlotte Taffy. Several of her family members were avid Southern University football fans and were enamored with the idea that their daughter might one day teach at the flagship university in their very own state. However, like Texas, Guadalupe was advised to contact Dick Talbort. Kiya knew of Guadalupe's interests from conversations with Charlotte Taffy. After learning that she did not complete the application, Kiya wondered what Dick might have said to her on the phone. Concerned about hiring from a pool with only two candidates and influenced by Kiya's persistence the department agreed to review the candidates' applications. Kiya was scheduled to have lunch with Charlotte Taffy the following day and resolved to discuss the matter with her.

Application

Thomas Wang

425 Cheersville Road
Bloomington, Indiana

Education: Ph.D. in educational psychology conferred in January, 1997 from Indiana University-Bloomington. Research interests: racial identity development formation and role of statistics in the perpetuation of privilege.

M.S. in Measurement conferred in May, 1990 from Harvard University.

Professional Instructor, Indiana University from August, 1993 to present. Teaching courses in
  Experience educational psychology to pre-service teachers.
Instructor, Indiana University from August, 1996 to December, 1996. Co-taught graduate statistics course.
Visiting Assistant Professor, Indiana State University, from August, 1996 to present. Taught courses in educational psychology for pre-service teachers.
Research Assistant, Educational Testing Services, May, 1990 to July, 1993. Coordinated efforts to revise the SAT so that it was less culturally biased. Piloted the revised SAT.

Publications:
Taylor, B. and Wang, T. 1995. Race and the SAT: Can we develop an unbiased standardized test? *American Educational Research Journal*, pp. 30–52.
Taylor, B. Wang, T., Simons, K. and Bridges, A. 1996. Is the SAT really revised?: An examination of students' performances on the revised SAT. *Harvard Education Review*, pp. 170–195.

Taylor, B., Wang, T. and Bridges, A. 1996. Alternative ways to determine college admissions. *NASPA Journal*, pp. 10–21.

Conference:
    Seven presentations at the national conference of the American Educational

Presentations:
Research Association
Three presentations at the national conference of the Association for the Study of Higher Education.
One presentation at the National Association of College Admissions Counselors.

Application

Marcus Shepard

Education: Ed.D. in educational psychology, Southern University, May, 1995. Research interests are structural equation modeling.

Professional: Assistant Professor, Sage Regional College, January, 1996 to present. Teach

Experiences: Statistics for a professional certification program.

Research Assistant, Southern University, August, 1993 to May, 1995. Conducted research with Dick Talbort and Ty Jeffries

Publications:
Jeffries, T., Talbort, D., Fringe, S., Wilson, D., and Shepard, M. 1995. Treating critical brain injuries: Does the treatment make a difference? *Journal of Social Psychology*, pp. 10–12.
Talbort, D., Wilson, D., Resin, B., Wilson, Q. and Shepard, M. 1996. The self esteem issues of non-traditional students enrolled in a traditional education program. *Journal of the Aging*, pp. 100–115.
Taylor, A., Vixen, J., Alexanders, B., Shepard, M. 1997. Self-efficacy of teachers: Does collaborative teacher training make a long-term difference? *International Journal of Teaching*, pp. 200–225.

After reviewing the applications, the department was asked to vote on one of three possible actions: (1) accept the advice of the committee and bring Marcus Shepard to campus; (2) bring both candidates to campus; or, (3) close the search and start the process again next year.

Question Set #5:

(a) Do you think the department would have decided to review the work of the committee without Kiya Dale's insistence? Why or why not?

(b) Was it ethical for Dick Talbort to retain his position as chair of the selection committee given his relationship with one of the candidates?

(c) How would you explain the paucity of candidates in the educational psychology pool?

(d) If you were the department head, would you have taken actions to curtail Dick Talbort's behavior?

Charlotte Taffy pressured the department to bring both candidates in for a campus interview or try again next year. Bennett King met with Dick Talbort to update him on the status of the search committee he chaired. Even though Kiya's office was six doors down from Bennett King's office and her door was shut, she could hear Dick Talbort's response clearly: "They can't tell us what to do. The entire committee decided that Marcus was the best candidate. That other guy can barely speak English. This is bullshit". Inside the office, Bennett tried to calm Dick down, after all he was responsible for contacting the candidates to arrange their campus visits. Bennett said, "Do you want me to contact the candidates or do you feel up to doing it"? Muttering under his breath, Dick walked out of Bennett's office slamming the door.

The campus visit for Marcus Shepard departed from protocol. Instead of the typical itinerary—meetings with all faculty members in the department, the dean and the provost, and a research presentation—the candidate offered to conduct a guest lecture for a graduate course during his visit. Several members of the search committee attended the class. In conversations with members of the department, Dick was asked why he hadn't scheduled a similar activity for Thomas Wang. Dick Talbort assured everyone that he "extended the same opportunity to both candidates but Wang declined".

Question Set #6:

(a) Was the interview process fair to both candidates?

(b) Do you think Talbort extended the same opportunity to both candidates?

(c) The Full Faculty Makes a Decision

The search committee reports were delivered in the April department meeting. The chairs of the search committees again presented the committee's recommendation. Janet Childs declared her search a failed one and suggested that they try again the following year. Kiya Dale discussed the status of her search. The committee interviewed five candidates by phone, three were invited for campus visits: Nadine Hamilton, Terry Askew and Gene Hawkins. Kiya said, "After much discussion we agreed to offer the position to Gene Hawkins. However, the day the committee made its decision, Dr. Hawkins called to tell me that he accepted a position at Teachers College. I called an emergency meeting of the committee the following day and the committee unanimously decided to offer the position to Nadine Hamilton". Although Kiya fully expected someone to raise issues regarding the candidacy of Jordan Eagle, no one did. Finally, Dick Talbort described the activities of his search committee. Dick said that the committee unanimously recommended Marcus Shepard. Surprised, the faculty began discussing the recommendation. The department was split regarding the recommendation. Several members supported the candidacy of Thomas Wang on the basis of the superiority of his research agenda and teaching experience. As the conversation went back and forth, several members complemented Marcus Shepard on his teaching based on the classroom observation. Janet Childs said, "Why didn't Wang guest lecture?" Dr. White said he declined the offer to do so. Kiya Dale asked whether or not the committee established teaching a course as a standard interview criterion. Dick Talbort said "Marcus Shepard offered. I called Thomas Wang and gave him the same opportunity. He decided not to do so". Kiya Dale said, "I have two issues. First, as an African American teaching at this institution and knowing the response of many of our students towards faculty who aren't white, I think that was a wise decision. Our students have difficulty receiving black, Hispanic and Asian faculty in the same way they do white faculty. If you recall student complaints about Maya Gupta, students complained that she couldn't speak English clearly. The funny thing was that English was her only language. Second, is it fair to use classroom teaching as an interview criteria?" Kiya was concerned that the criteria had not been established by the committee or agreed upon by the department prior to the process and that it might unfairly disadvantage certain candidates. However, the news that Thomas Wang declined the offer to teach a course was damaging to his candidacy. Anxious to divert the discussion away from this issue, Kiya said, "If you look at their research records, only Wang's record suggest that he actually has a research agenda. Shepard simply does research with whomever needs him to run statistics. Furthermore, he doesn't have any publications on which he is first author".

Question Set #7:

(a) Who do you think was selected for the position in Educational Psychology?

Hidden Racism and the Ways of Faculty Hiring

The reality of American society is that most European Americans are isolated from members of other racial groups. While they grow up exposed to racist and discriminatory messages, the notion of political correctness has made it unpopular to overtly express racial preferences. The result is that European Americans have had to learn the language of equality while developing covert racist and discriminatory practices. Evidence of this is seen during the hiring, tenure, and promotion processes.

In this particular case study, faculty attempted to manipulate the selection process. They used prior relationships to determine who would be the 'best fit' or 'most qualified' addition to the department. Thus, Dick Talbort, in his position as chair of the search committee, worked to exclude competitors who might interfere with the hiring of Marcus Shepard. The candidate whom he couldn't exclude he discredited by adopting a selection criteria that had the potential to disadvantage candidates of color. Secondly, in the case of Jordan Eagle, the associate dean and a host of others attempted to maneuver to hire Jordan even though he wasn't the 'most qualified' candidate in the pool. Instead of determining these things based on the stated criteria like demonstrated or potential to conduct research or teaching experience commensurate with the targeted position, faculty worked to maintain their comfort level within the department by hiring people whom they could envision as 'one of us'. If faculty reside in racially or class homogenous environments, they are likely to establish professional relationships consistent with this existence. That means that when they are asked to invite someone new into the department, faculty will have difficulty seeing someone perceived as 'one of them' as a desirable colleague. However, instead of admitting their biases, they find alternative ways to eliminate people who might make them uncomfortable. Thus, the most 'qualified' and best suited candidate for the department is oftentimes a candidate that resembles the majority of those residing in the department. This represents neo-racism and neo-discrimination—the new forms of racism and discrimination in this era of political correctness and discrimination lawsuits. More specifically, instead of overt articulations regarding the inferiority of those who are not of European American descent, faculty find other, not necessarily ethical, ways to reproduce racially homogenous environments. Ironically, even those European Americans who adopt an anti-racist posture are less aware of neo-racist and neo-discriminatory practices. In effect, even faculty opposed to racism and discrimination will fall prey to excluding African, Hispanic and Asian Americans on grounds that they would not be successful here or they would detract from the departmental climate. The responsibility for protecting the ethics of the hiring process falls to faculty aware of the many forms that racist and discriminatory discussions take and who have the willingness to champion ethical procedures. In this case study, Kiya Dale plays that role. However, what is the toll that occupying such a role takes on 'the champion'? The 'good ole boys' network requires us to substitute the stated criteria and evoke less formal criteria designed to reproduce and protect the status quo. This is accomplished by adopting practices that privilege members of the status quo, shaping position announcements that privilege candidates that we already have in mind, or senior faculty using their power to coerce junior faculty to take the unethical road for fear of reprisals during the promotion and tenure process. Dismantling the 'good ole boy' network requires the work of 'champions' committed to equity

Action

Statewide litigation charging the higher education system with institutionalized discrimination resulted in a strategic plan designed to remove vestiges of racial discrimination. To this end, the District Court Judge required all higher education institutions in the state to report their status relative to diversity. In response, the Provost's Office required each college and department to submit a strategic plan for diversity. Included in the plan was a discussion of each department's status relative to diversity—numbers of African and Hispanic American students and faculty, a description of efforts to increase these groups representation on campus, and plans to improve the likelihood that members of these groups would be successful in their careers at Southern University. The real challenge has been how to encourage departments and colleges to implement the plans in good faith.

Discussion Questions

1. What are the environmental issues germane to this case?
2. What leadership and organizational theories would you draw upon to help guide practice decisions you would make if you were the provost? The dean? A department chair?
3. Do popular leadership and organizational theories adequately address the nature and nuances of racism and discrimination?
4. Can a strategic plan address the issues raised by this case? Explain your response.
5. If you were an outside consultant, what five suggestions/recommendations would you make to help redress the issues raised in this case?
6. Who should be involved in the design of the strategic plans at each level—the department, the college, or the university?

7. Does one's status in respect to the promotion and tenure process influence the ability to act as "the champion?"
8. If you decide to champion equity in your department and you do not have tenure, what steps can you take to mitigate challenges to your success?
9. What are the similarities and differences between Southern formal and informal faculty hiring processes with their faculty colleagues at peer institutions?

Recommended Readings

Bonilla-Silva, Eduardo. (2003). *Racism without racists: Color-blind racism and the persistence of racial inequality in the United States.* Lanham: Rowman & Littlefield Publishers, Inc.

Cleveland, D. (Ed.). (2004). *A long way to go: Conversations about African American faculty and graduate students.* New York: Peter Lang Publishing, Incorporated.

Davis, Wanda, M. (1998). Toward civility: Assessment as a means toward improving campus climate. *College Student Affairs Journal, 18* (1), 72–83.

Green, A.L. & Scott, L.V. (Eds.). (2003). *Journey to the Ph.D.: How to navigate the process as African American.* Sterling: Stylus Publishing.

Gudeman, Roxane Harvey. (2001). Faculty experience with diversity: A case study of Macalester College. In G. Orfield (Ed.). *Diversity challenged: Evidence on the impact of affirmative action,* (pp.251–276). Cambridge: Harvard Education Publishing Group.

Hurtado, S., Milem, J., Clayton-Pedersen, A., Allen, W. (1999) Enacting diverse learning environments: Improving the climate for racial/ethnic diversity in higher education. ASHE-ERIC Higher Education Report, 26 (8), 140.

Mabokela R.O., & Green, A.L. (Ed.). (2001). *Sisters of the academy: Emergent black women scholars in higher education.* Sterling: Stylus Publishing.

Milem, Jeffrey, E. (2003). The educational benefits of diversity: Evidence from multiple sectors. In M.J. Chang, D. Witt, J. Jones, & K. Hakuta (Eds.). *Compelling interest: Examining the Evidence on Racial Dynamics in Colleges and Universities.* Stanford, CA: Stanford University Press.

Orfield, G. & Kurlaender, M. (Eds.). (2001). *Diversity challenged: Evidence on the impact of affirmative action.* Cambridge: Harvard Education Publishing Group.

Orfield, G. & Miller, E. (Eds.). (1999). *Chilling admissions: The affirmative action crisis and the search for alternatives.* Cambridge: Harvard Education Publication Group.

Case #11 "Tick-tock": The Convergence of the Biological and Tenure Clock in the Lives of Academic Women

Eboni M. Zamani-Gallaher

For academicians, preparing for promotion and tenure review is the most daunting tasks facing nearly all faculty members in their careers. While more women and people of color enter academic careers, institutions of higher learning remain "ivory towers" tailored toward the upward mobility of white men as the representation of women and minorities among the faculty ranks is stratified and subsequently unbalanced. According to a CNN report, women make up 58% of the nation's thirteen million college undergraduates and outnumbered men in 2002 for doctorates earned (CNN, 2004). However, only 10% of tenured faculty are women with a miniscule amount accounting for women of color; case in point, the University of Michigan (n.d.) reports that women hold one-third of assistant and associate professorships combined and one-sixth of full professorships while women of color hold 6% of all tenure and tenure track positions. Although more women are earning Ph.Ds, there still remains a highly disproportionate number of women entering academia in tenure-track positions (Trower as cited in HGSE News, April 12, 2004).

Teng (2003) reported that fewer women professors who have children earlier in their careers obtain tenure than their male counterparts do (i.e., nationally 77% of male professors who have children earlier in their careers obtain tenure compared to only 56% of female professors). Unfortunately being married and having children has been associated with reducing the likelihood of achieving tenure for female faculty members (Lee, 2004). Far fewer women, particularly at research universities, become tenured and/or obtain full professorships.

Many female faculty members express mixed feelings regarding policies that affect their decisions about whether and when to have children in lieu of tenure (Armenti, 2004); for instance, several institutions of higher learning have installed practices that allow expectant women to petition for an additional year on their tenure clock (i.e., the average five to six-year probationary period granted to Assistant Professors in tenure-track positions before undergoing review for promotion and tenure). Nonetheless, it can sometimes be a damned if you do, damned if you don't situation for junior faculty who are completely honest regarding their plans to conceive whereby colleagues may judge their choice to start a family negatively, even questioning their career commitment. Thus, a good number of women exercise the added year option with great trepidation; as often, the expectation is that with the additional time the female faculty member should have produced more scholarly works as opposed to time needed for childbearing and childrearing responsibilities (Ward & Wolf-Wendel, 2004).

Organizational Setting

The context of this case takes place at the annual meeting for the National Society of Social and Educational Inquiry (NSSEI). This is an organization that boasts a large membership of social science researchers, educational leaders, and policy analysts. Every year a wide cross-section of professionals from various colleges and universities, governmental agencies, and policy think tanks convenes to participate in sessions presenting cutting-edge research and commentaries on current educational dilemmas.

NSSEI has a variety of divisions targeted to particular segments of their membership, such as the Division of Women and Equity in Education (WEE). This year as a part of the pre-conference workshops, the WEE Division has decided to sponsor a half-day session on women and tenure. The focus of the workshop is to discuss the ability of women faculty to obtain tenure and provide participants with a forum in favor of actualizing the full inclusion of women at all levels within higher learning institutions. Furthermore, the primary aim of the workshop is to not only give voice to participant concerns regarding gender equity in the academy but to encourage those attending to return to their respective campuses and form a taskforce on women and tenure.

The WEE-sponsored workshop has drawn a diverse group of female academicians. Individuals attending are primarily junior faculty seeking promotion to the Associate level, though quite a few Associate Professors are in attendance to share lessons learned, frustrations associated with tenure and post-tenure. The faculty members attending this workshop represent a variety of institutional types; they also differ in terms of age, years in academia, marital status, and motherhood.

The Characters

Bethany Thompson: A forty-six year-old white Associate Professor of five years in the Department of Educational Psychology at a research university in the South. Bethany is also a divorced mother of two young children ages 4 and 1 that desires an appointment to full professorship and wishes to become Dean of a School of Education in the near future.

Jessica Hernandez: A thirty-five 35 year-old Latina junior faculty member in Mathematics Education completing her second year at a comprehensive, doctoral granting institution in the Midwest. She is a newly wed woman with hopes of starting a family soon.

Sojourner Paxton: A forty-four year-old African American newly minted Associate Professor of Sociology at an elite Liberal Arts institution in the Northeast. Sojourner has never married and has no children.

The Predicament

Sharing Stories: Three WEE Workshop Participants Speak

Bethany registered for the WEE sponsored pre-conference workshop in order to network with other women who have aspirations to receive full professorship and move on to positions of academic leadership. Bethany began her academic career at the age of thirty-five. Previously she had been a school counselor for little over five years when she decided to pursue a doctorate in Educational Psychology. During her fourth and final year of graduate study, she met and married Tory who had a budding career in Advertising.

While searching for academic positions, it was clear to her that she would have to relocate to find gainful employment. Tory agreed to move though the transition was not a smooth one. The new market proved to be less profitable for Tory and provided few professional development opportunities in advertising given the smaller college town venue. Tory's discomfort with their locale placed a strain on their relationship. Additionally, Tory was ready to start a family though Bethany had been advised by her faculty mentor to wait until after tenure. Nonetheless, Bethany gave birth to their first child the summer before her fourth year as an Assistant Professor. She had been highly productive prior to this point, therefore, when she applied for tenure during year five it was granted. Given that she had planned for a May baby, she did not miss much time away from her academic responsibilities though it was very taxing on her mentally and physically to adjust to motherhood while still preparing manuscripts for publication and preparing for fall courses.

Bethany became pregnant again shortly after being granted tenure and was scheduled to deliver her second child mid-January of the spring term. Much to her surprise, some of her colleagues appeared annoyed with the fact that she was expecting and made judgments regarding her commitment to academia and what they perceived to be a decline in her productivity. One year after their youngest child was born Tory announced that he wanted to separate. He admitted that he considered her a workaholic that lacked the ability to balance work and family given her post at a research-extensive university. He also contended that in her quest to obtain tenure and become widely known in her field, their relationship suffered and they grew apart. Tory thought he sacrificed his own career ambitions given the limited opportunities that existed in their small college town.

Bethany and Tory later divorced. Now that she is the primary custodian of their children she really feels more than ever as a single parent that she performs hidden work (i.e., working 1st, 2nd, and 3rd shift without acknowledgment). Bethany shares her concern of whether or not she will get full professorship as she still produces but recognizes that she submits far fewer manuscripts these days. Bethany told others attending the workshop that she has attempted to step up her service and strengthen her teaching but finds that the time required to do everything well eludes her. She states, "I attempt to be community involved and of service much of the time, while being a teacher/scholar full-time, when my reality is that I am Mom all the time". A major concern of Bethany is that the glass ceiling and good ole' boys' network continues to persist. The vast majority of campus administrators and the bulk of tenured professors on her campus are white males. Although this is the case across many institutions of higher learning, it seems even more pronounced to the New York native that presently works at a research university in the deep South. To what extent is leadership gendered and why is Bethany finding that unlike her male counterparts aspiring administrative posts, striking the balance between paid work and family work appears to be a non-issue?

Jessica came to the WEE workshop hoping to find a sounding board and suggestions for two major concerns. First, are her anxieties surrounding third-year review; she is currently at a unionized Midwest comprehensive doctoral granting university that has fewer than ten doctoral programs. While doctoral study in her area of specialization is not available, she and a few other faculty members have been arduously working on a proposal to offer a Ph.D. in Mathematics Education. A product of Ivy League institutions, all of Jessica's postsecondary training was at highly selective, elite institutions. At present she is satisfied with the departmental culture and overall campus climate. However, she does lament that she really would like the opportunity to work with doctoral students and direct student research beyond the master's level.

Jessica has been highly productive and has published several articles, monographs, and book chapters. In fact, she recently secured a contract to author a textbook. Though at her current institution, she attempts to go above and beyond the norm in order to have greater mobility should a position at a research institution strike her interest. Despite how well regarded Jessica is, she continues to worry about her upcoming review. Her colleagues have suggested that she should have a very favorable third-year review given her high teaching evaluations from peers, students, and the department chair in addition to recent awards for her service as well as leadership on local and national committees/organizations.

The other issue of primary concern Jessica shares with WEE participants is the lack of what she considers "family-friendly" policies at her home institution. Her husband, an attorney serving as university counsel at a neighboring research university, is anxious to start a family. Whereas many women must return to work a short six weeks after delivery, Jessica would not have the luxury of the standard six-week maternity leave should she become pregnant. One of the reasons she thought her institution would be ideal for juggling career and family was because though research is required and publications are encouraged, it is not a "publish or perish" environment. However, she was troubled to find that despite having what has been considered a strong bargaining unit and faculty contract, there is jury duty leave, military leave, political leave, and various other forms of faculty leave but no maternity leave.

Faculty negotiations have begun as the current contract expires in five months. At a recent campus AAUP information meeting, Jessica expressed her concerns regarding faculty leave policies and was encouraged to join and chair the Leaves Committee. She is hesitant to chair the committee since she is an untenured junior faculty member. However, she did agree to attend the first meeting of the Leaves Committee. There were seven faculty (including her) that were in attendance. She quickly noticed that she was one of only two female faculty members present, the only person of color, less than forty-five years old or untenured.

During the meeting most members were concerned about time limits for professor exchange and sabbatical leaves. When asked what concerns she would like the committee to address, she brought up the challenges and considerations for childbirth and childrearing. She explained that there should be more options for employees to take advantage of and new alternatives for faculty such as maternity leave and short-term disability that would benefit all faculty as well as women that may experience difficulties during their pregnancies. She encouraged the others to consider that "family-friendly" policies and practices could stimulate greater interest in potential male and female faculty applicants. She noted that many Baby Boomers will be retiring in the near future and most faculty today begin their professional lives in their late-twenties to mid-thirties. Her contention was that many prospective faculty may not want to put their personal lives of starting a family on hold. Hence, the need to have maternity leave addressed in the new contract.

After having addressed the committee, one of the male full professors commented "While that is fine and dandy, we are on an 8-month contract and we have gotten along without this for years just as other area institutions. The need is more perceived than real because you gals need to plan your babies for the summer". Needless to say, Jessica was livid but without recourse to fully challenge her senior colleague. Furthermore, she looked for support from the only other female faculty in the room (an Associate Professor in the College of Technology) and was further dismayed to hear, "Why I assumed that maternity leave was standard but its neither here nor there to me since I never opted to have children in lieu of my professional goals". How can Jessica be on the mommy-track while being on the tenure-track without bumping her head on the glass ceiling?

Sojourner shared that she fully understands the implications of delaying promotion and tenure review and subsequently struggled with deciding which clock should chime louder (i.e., tenure clock or the biological clock) very early on in her academic career. While her family is very proud of her professional accomplishments, at forty-four years of age she continually feels pressure from her parents to become a wife and mother. As the only child of her parents, they have eagerly wanted grandchildren and don't understand her seemingly casual attitude about marriage and parenthood. She contends that if someone were to post a sign that expressed her parents' thoughts it would read, "Grandbabies wanted"!

Sojourner had also longed for the right man to come along. However, there are not many African American single men in the small, rural community where her institution is located. As such, she has made peace with her decision to move full speed ahead with her career advancement in lieu of a committed relationship and/or embarking on motherhood. In a recent conversation with her parents, they expressed their disappointment that she has never married and did not have any children. She told them that they have grandkids, stating one's name is "Tenure" and the other will be "Promotion".

After sharing the aforementioned with the WEE participants (many of which could relate to her tussle with personal and professional choices), she expressed two central concerns that brought her to the meeting. One was the concern regarding what she feels is double jeopardy: the intersection of gender and race in the over-extending of faculty of color. The other matter dealt with the gender gap in faculty salaries. Recently, Sojourner found that overall the women in her department had lower salaries than their male counterparts of the same rank with similar educational and professional backgrounds. She wanted to ascertain exactly how sex/gender gets figured into a paycheck and to what extent should faculty of color expect acknowledgment let alone compensation for the "invisible work" she is called to do on committees, with students and in the community that their white male colleagues are not expected or sought out to perform.

Discussion Questions

1. How would you respond to each faculty members' situation?
2. What is the best solution for each faculty member and how different would your approach be in ensuring that new policies and practices are formed?
3. What are the ethical ramifications and legal issues surrounding this case?
4. How should new faculty assess the culture of a prospective college/university employer in terms of person-institution fit and whether an institution is a family-friendly employer?
5. With regard to juggling work and family, what are the personal duties/rights of academic women?
6. How different are the career advancement concerns of female academicians in contrast to their male counterparts?
7. Why should the academic community be concerned about the increasing trend of women stratified along tenure lines?
8. To what extent does faculty rank mitigate the effects of work–family balance?
9. Converse about the nexus between race/ethnicity with gender as well as the possible impact of each on faculty promotion and tenure; next, consider and discuss how race and the variation of cultural backgrounds shift the challenges, expectations and demands facing those in pursuit of tenure?
10. What can institutions do to rectify the disproportionate number of women (particularly women of color) that are awarded tenure and promote upward mobility?
11. While many view the promotion and tenure review process as subjective and ambiguous, talk about the perceived and real differences across institutional types (e.g., Carnegie Classification: two-year vs. four-year, public vs. private, research institution vs. teaching institution, unionized vs. no faculty bargaining unit).
12. How can the overall institutional environment and campus climate improve or exacerbate the glass ceiling regarding women's promotion and tenure?

13. Which conceptual frameworks (e.g., social mobility theory, human capital theory, etc.) and/or student affairs theories might provide a useful lens in impacting institutional policies, revising current practices, and aiding administrative decision making?

14. To what extent are departmental sex compositions "equitable"? To what extent are women and men in similar positions?

15. To what extent are women and men in gender equitable departments and positions?

16. As a social system, how have universities (particularly research institutions) perpetuated gender inequities as it relates to a woman's ability to achieve tenure in concert with motherhood?

Theory-to-Practice Activity

Investigate common tenure practices, at your institution and elsewhere; additionally, speak to junior and senior women faculty regarding their concerns and experiences with the tenure process. Finally, evaluate the implications of these practices for women faculty. Upon gathering your findings, consider what theoretical frameworks may have utility in dealing with the issue of gender inequity among faculty. Afterwards, give consideration to relevant conceptual underpinnings of the problem, share the facts with your academic community and propose policy and practice reforms where needed.

References

Armenti, C. (2004). May babies and post-tenure babies: Maternal decisions of women professors. *The Review of Higher Education*, 27 (2) 211–231.

CNN (February 17, 2004). *Women a minority of tenured faculty and administrators*. Retrieved January 25, 2005 from www.cnn.com/2004/EDUCATION/02/17/women. on.campus.ap/

HGSE (Harvard Graduate School of Education) *News* (2004, April). Major Universities Discourage Women Seeking Tenure: New Harvard Study Finds Universities Need Instruction on Making Workplace Equitable. Retrieved June 24, 2004 from, http://www.gse.harvard.edu/news/features/trower04122004.html

Lee, J.T. (2004, July). Tenure route longer for women in science. *The Boston Globe*. Retrieved August 2, 2004 from, http://www.boston.com/news/education/higher/articles/2004/07/06/tenure_route_longer_for_women_in_science/

Teng, S. (2003, December). Fewer women than men with kids get tenure. *Yale Daily News*. Retrieved April 4, 2004 from, http://www.yaledailynews.com/article.asp?AID=24421

University of Michigan (n.d.). [Women *at the University of Michigan: A statistical report on the status of women students, faculty and staff on the Ann Arbor campus*. Retrieved August 19, 2004 from, http://www.umich.edu/~hraa/womenatum/execsum.html

Ward, K. & Wolf-Wendel, L. (2004). Academic motherhood: Managing complex roles in research universities. *The Review of Higher Education*, 27 (2) 233–257.

Recommended Background Reading

Aguirre, A. Jr. (2000). *Women and minority faculty in the academic workplace: recruitment, retention, and academic culture. ERIC digest.* Washington, DC: George Washington University Press.

Corcoran, M. & Clark, S.M. (1986). Perspectives on the professional socialization of women faculty: A case of accumulative disadvantage? *Journal of Higher Education,* 57 (1), 20–43.

Crosby, F.J. & VanDeVeer, C. (2000). *Sex, race, and merit: Debating affirmative action in education and employment.* Ann Arbor, MI: University of Michigan Press.

Ely, R.J., Scully, M., & Foldy, E.G. (2003). *Reader in gender, Work and organization. center for gender in organizations.* Simmo Ent.

Friedman, S.D. & Greenhaus, J.H. (2000). *Work and family—allies or enemies?* New York: Oxford University Press.

Gilmartin, S.K., Korn, W.S., Astin, A.W., & Sax, L.J. (1999). *The American College Teacher: National Norms for the 1998–99 HERI Faculty Survey.* ERIC Documents Reproduction No. 435272

Harvard Business Review on Work and Life Balance (2000). Boston, MA: Harvard Business School Press.

Parasuraman, S. & Greenhaus, J.H. (1999). *Integrating work and family: Challenges and choices for a changing world.* Westport, CT: Greenwood Publishing Group.

Patitu, Carol, L. & Tack, Martha, W. (1992). *Faculty job satisfaction: Women and minorities in peril. ERIC digest.* Washington, DC: George Washington University.

Rapoport, R., Bailyn, L., Fletcher, J.K., & Pruitt, B.H. (2001). *Beyond work-family balance: Advancing gender equity and workplace performance.* San Francisco, CA: Jossey-Bass.

Rieke, R.D. (1982). Women faculty members in a world of male administrators. *Association for Communication Administration Bulletin,* 41, 64–68.

Smith, N.D. & Tamer, M. (March/April 1999). Women and Tenure at the Institute. *MIT Magazine of Innovation.* Retrieved August 19, 2004 from, http://web.mit.edu/newsoffice/nr/1999/trwomen.html

Stafford, F.P. & Johnson, G.E. (1974). The earnings and promotion of women faculty. *American Economic Review,* 64 (6), 888–903.

Stevens, D.D. & Cooper, J.E. (2002). *Tenure in the sacred grove: Issues and strategies for women and minority faculty: SUNY series in women in education.* Albany, New York: SUNY Press.

Tidball, E.M. (1976). Of men and research: The dominant themes in American higher education include neither teaching nor women. *Journal of Higher Education,* 47 (4), 373–389.

Varner, A. & Drago, R. (2002). *The Mapping Project: Preliminary Results from the National Survey of Faculty.* ERIC Document Reproduction No. ED468783.

Wilson, R. (November 9, 2001a). For women with tenure and families, moving up the ranks is challenging: Many say they lack the time to finish that next book or secure that key grant. *The Chronicle of Higher Education.* Retrieved April 4, 2004 from, http://chronicle.com/free/v48/i11/11a01101.htm

Wilson, R. (November 9, 2001b). A Push to Help New Parents Prepare for Tenure Reviews. AAUP wants colleges to grant them extra time—even if they don't take leaves. *The Chronicle of Higher Education.* Retrieved April 4, 2004 from, http://chronicle.com/free/v48/i11/11a01001.htm

Zemsky, R. (2001). Gender Intelligence. *Policy Perspectives,* 10 (2).

Related Web-based Resources

AACU Diversity Web
    http://www.diversityweb.org/
Advancing Women in Leadership Journal
    www.advancingwomen.com
American Council on Education (ACE)
    www.acenet.edu
Association of University Professors (AAUP)
    www.aaup.org
The Feminist Majority Foundation
    www.feminist.org
Institute for Women's Leadership
    www.womensleadership.com
National Association for Equal Opportunity in Higher Education (NAFEO)
    www.nafeo.org
National Association for Women in Education (NAWE)
    www.nawe.org
Race, Gender, and Affirmative Action
    http://www-personal.umich.edu/~eandersn/biblio.htm
Sex Roles: A Journal of Research
    http://www.kluweronline.com/issn/0360–0025/
U.S. Census Bureau
    http://www.census.gov/
Women's Studies Database: Bibliography
    http://www.inform.umd.edu/EdRes/Topic/WomensStudies/
    Bibliographies/

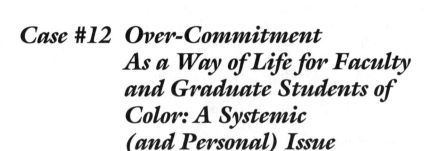

Case #12 Over-Commitment As a Way of Life for Faculty and Graduate Students of Color: A Systemic (and Personal) Issue

BENETTA E. FAIRLEY AND EDWARD A. DELGADO-ROMERO

"Human Progress never rolls in on wheels of inevitability; it comes through the tireless efforts of men". Dr. Martin Luther King, Jr. (1962)

Institutional Setting

The setting is the School of Education (SOE) at a large, comprehensive university in the Midwestern United States. The SOE has adopted the goal of diversity as one of the five strategic goals of its mission statement. The SOE is led by a Latino Dean, an African American female associate dean for the graduate school, and a white male executive assistant dean. The University recently hired an African American President, a first for the university.

The University is located in a mid-size town of 69,291 people, and is located fifty miles from a major urban city. The SOE for the academic year had 1192 graduate students with 65% female and 35% males. This pool consisted of 792 white American, 246 International (mostly from Korea, Taiwan, Japan and India), 69 African American, 36 Latino/a, 30 Asian American, and 4 Native American students. There are 95 faculty in the SOE, 44% female and 56% male, eighty of whom are white, nine African American, five Latino/a, and one Asian American.

Key Characters

Sherilyn: a twenty-six-year-old African American graduate student in her second year in the counseling psychology Ph.D. program. As a full-time second year doctoral student, Sherilyn is taking courses, completing twelve hours of practicum work each week, assisting with several research projects, facilitating two support groups, and developing her dissertation proposal. In addition to her academic duties, Sherilyn has a twenty hour a week assistantship working with a student support services program. Within this role she teaches a course for freshman education majors, coordinates a bi-annual newsletter, programs events, maintains a scholarship database, and assists students with academic and personal concerns. Sherilyn has also decided to become involved in a number of extra-curricular activities involving community support and student involvement. Within this past year she has been active with the Faculty and Staff Enrichment (FASE) Mentoring Program, Minority Education Student Association (MESA), Association of Multicultural Concerns Division (AMCD) part of the American Counseling Association, as well as various cultural activities on campus and community activism.

Sherilyn has chosen to take on these roles because she feels like it is her responsibility to become active in the enrichment and development of the community around her. Nevertheless, there have been situations where Sherilyn has taken on roles that were not initially her choice of involvement. Just before the start of the fall semester, Sherilyn was given the title of president of MESA. This title was given to Sherilyn not through personal choice, or a student body vote, but through a declaration of the title by a faculty advisor. It was not surprising that this title was given to Sherilyn considering that she was the only active member of the organization who took an interest to ensure its existence. Initially Sherilyn wanted to take on a lesser leadership role because she had never taken on such a position, but because she was the only individual who expressed an interest in the organization, taking on the role of president became her only option in attempting to maintain the organization's survival.

Carlos: a thirty-seven-year-old Latino assistant professor in the department of Counseling and Educational Psychology, has spent five years in the counseling center at another university before deciding to concentrate on teaching and research. Carlos is in his second year in the tenure-track position. He is Sherilyn's advisor, in addition to advising ten other doctoral and masters students, serving on seven dissertation committees, holds several ethnic minority related professional leadership positions both nationally and locally, serves on the SOE diversity committee and is on the advisory board of the Latino/a cultural center.

Over-commitment

The problem of over-commitment became apparent when after having unsuccessfully tried for two weeks to schedule a research meeting, Sherilyn and Carlos were only able to see each other at several ethnic and racial minority related service/volunteer events. Successfully completing research is the key for Sherilyn to get her Ph.D. and for Carlos to achieve tenure, yet consistently research was relegated to secondary importance to service activities. Several colleagues offered advice: "say no", "don't do service", "it's up to you to protect your schedule, you have to put research first".

Thus they were both feeling unhappy, overcommitted, and blamed for their inability to set personal and professional boundaries that would help them succeed. When Sherilyn and Carlos projected these trends over several years they could imagine not meeting their goals, feeling burned out or perhaps even leaving academia. And yet both Sherilyn and Carlos were disciplined people who had achieved many things, were well-respected, sought after, and constantly asked to serve on committees or take on leadership roles.

They decided to take some time out and examine this issue. The first thing they noticed was that many of their peers colleagues of color felt the same way, while at the same time their white colleagues would often be the ones to offer the advice to "just say no". What was going on?

Background

As aspiring academicians of color at a Predominately White Institution (PWI), the knowledge of the sacrifice and heroic efforts of their forefathers and foremothers in breaking down racial barriers is a strong motivating factor for ethnic minorities work. For many people of color it is this recognition that sends them into the arms of community and campus involvement geared toward the uplifting and encouragement of other persons of color within their respective institutions. This recognition of past struggle, wanting to continue the tradition of social change, while maintaining a strong involvement in both campus and community organizations alongside advancing within an academic career often creates a paradox that may lead to over-commitment.

In his letter written from the Birmingham jail to several Alabama clergymen, Martin Luther King, Jr. addresses the point that progress is not something that comes without will, it occurs because individuals place effort into making it happen. Beyond the previous statement and the echoes from family and community regarding the need for strong involvement in the development of people of color, there are several other key perspectives that have an influence in the increased level of involvement that occurs with a number of people of color.

An informal survey was completed with graduate students in the SOE in order to asses the level of over-commitment and feelings of being overwhelmed. During this self-report, informal survey researchers asked students several questions regarding accomplishing tasks, being able to say "no", their level of involvement in campus and community organizations, as well as their rating of feelings of being overwhelmed because of being unable to meet desired daily goals and feeling pulled in too many directions.

Feelings of being overwhelmed are not a novelty to any graduate program across the country. From the information provided by the students, the average ranking of feelings of being overwhelmed was at 6.2 (moderately overwhelmed) ranging from 2.5 (score listed between being moderately overwhelmed and not overwhelmed) and 10 (being extremely overwhelmed). If students in general are reporting fairly high levels of being overwhelmed, taking into account how factors such as low-representation and high need for students of color in programming endeavors and diversity/multicultural initiatives may escalate their feelings of being overwhelmed needs to be addressed.

In addition to the opportunities being provided, there is also the personal want for camaraderie and collectivism.

> there is no need for repayment, only the grasping of opportunity to aid someone else, just as I have aided you,

The above quote is not the sole reason as to why people bind themselves to involvement. There is the desire to be in an atmosphere where there are people who look alike, talk alike, think, dress, behave, and have histories that are similar. Because of this desire it is not unlikely that persons of color will become involved in activities that are geared toward persons of color because of a need to be in the company of persons who have characteristics similar to their own.

Decision Options

There are several decision options that may be useful in working with persons of color who are encountering this circumstance.

Before addressing issues of over-commitment, over-involvement, or burn out it may be helpful to understand why individuals need to become involved. An important question to consider is, "What is occurring with this individual where involvement is necessary for him or her?" Processing the value of involvement for this individual will help in understanding the perspective of the person you are attempting to assist.

After this understanding has been obtained, possibly addressing the individuals on how over-involvement may serve as a detriment to their goals of assisting because of their increased chances of burn out may be beneficial.

Discussion Questions

1. Can this issue be addressed without placing blame on the individuals (i.e., stating that it is due to their lack of will power and poor boundaries that results in their current circumstance)?
2. How does the quote mentioned above relate to this issue of over-involvement?
3. Are developments in multicultural concerns the responsibility of persons of color?
4. What are the systematic issues that are encompassed within the two hypotheses proposed by the authors, high demand, low supply, and overuse of resources? For example, do recruitment, retention, and affirmative action policies relate to this issue?
5. Why don't they "Just Say No"?
6. How do you see various developmental and other theoretical frameworks fitting with this phenomenon of over-commitment with persons of color within academia? What aspects of the model fit with this issue? Do you think there is a model that better addresses this subject?

Recommended Readings

Smith-Maddox, R. & Solorzano, D.G. (2002). Using critical race theory, Paulo Freire's problem-posing methods, and case study research to confront race and racism in education. *Qualitative Inquiry,* 8(1) 66–84.

Lynn, M. & Adams, M. (2002). Introductory overview to the special issue critical race theory and education: Recent developments in the field. *Equity & Excellence,* 35(2) 87–92.

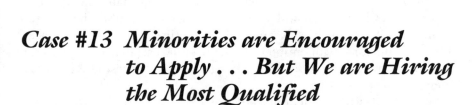

Case #13   Minorities are Encouraged
to Apply . . . But We are Hiring
the Most Qualified

ROBIN L. HUGHES AND JAMES SATTERFIELD

Key Characters

William Georgia: President Georgia is on his second presidency. His first was
at a large private institution in the northeast where he was credited with
increasing research funding and minority faculty recruitment by 30%. He
has been the president of Midwestern State for less than a year. His academic training is in chemical engineering.

Robert Flowers: internationally known scholar, works in the area of student
retention. Resigned a position from a prominent institution because of the
elimination of affirmative action programs on campus. An anonymous donor
and philanthropist donated $70 million to support his efforts to retain students.
He is also the department chair and a full professor.

Letty Shoemaker: associate professor. Married to Robert Flowers. Moved
to the university with Robert. Letty's research interest is also in the area of
student retention. She has worked in the field with Robert for more than
twenty years.

Arnold Redlette: associate professor. Research methodologist. A long time
friend of Robert's, he was hired when Robert left the university.

Judith Lange: a third-year assistant professor and is the only African
American on the search committee. She has the benefit of not having any
previous personal knowledge of the candidates.

The Candidates

Marvin Pickette—white male doctoral student, completing dissertation with
an internationally known scholar in the field. Marvin is from Dakota. He

knows the chair of the search committee, Robert Flowers. Marvin will defend his dissertation in a couple of months (March 22). He has one publication in a journal edited by his mentor, and no national presentations. He has taught one graduate course.

Cynthia Baldwin—African American female candidate and doctoral student from Chicago. She will defend her dissertation within the next few months (April 12). She has presented at several (five) national conferences. She currently works with an internationally known scholar in higher education. Cynthia teaches courses in college student success at a research-extensive University.

Max Sliver—white male applicant from Michigan. He is currently the assistant director of a student retention program. He is also the editor of one book. He has presented at three local conferences.

Laura Rodriguez—Latina applicant from Dallas successfully defended her dissertation and currently teaches at a historically Black university. She was recruited by Letty at a national conference. She has several publications in four refereed journals. The journals traditionally publish articles that focus on issues of race. She has presented at several national conferences.

Institutional Setting

The city of Melville is small college town located in the northern most portion of a Midwestern State. The university marketing material boasts a student population of 25,000, a nationally ranked school of education, and a diverse student population (from thirty states and nineteen foreign countries). The Melville campus, one of the flagship institutions and a main campus in system comprised of eight colleges, offers 120 majors and a diverse student population from all over the state, country, and world.

The state, too, recognizes a level of diversity not experienced in other states. The population is 18% African American, 50% White, 30% Mexican American and 2% other. Paradoxically, the university does not share the same diverse demographics. For example, according to the Office of Institutional Studies and Planning, there were 15 Executive Administrative positions filled by Blacks or 4.82% of the total 311 potential positions. On the other hand, service and maintenance positions filled by Blacks accounted for over 40% of the population and those filled by Hispanic accounted for 31%—while only 27% of those service maintenance positions were filled with Whites. Interestingly enough, the demographic composition of Melville, suggests that Blacks are disproportionately employed in non-professional positions by the University. According to the Census Bureau figures for 1999, blacks and Hispanics comprise a large proportion of the residents of the city, 30% of the total 134,213 population. Black citizens constitute 16,418 of the population and Hispanics 23,840. These figures become more interesting in light of the fact that the total number of white staff employees far exceeds that of either blacks or Hispanics. Whites comprise 90% of the total administrative and professional staff employed by the university, and 97% of the faculty. In addition, out of a total of 782 blacks employed at the Melville campus, 65% are relegated to service and maintenance positions, yet account for only 1.91% of the executive administrative staff. In contrast, of 3,409 whites employed in non-faculty positions, only 8.8% are employed as service maintenance staff.

The university's student population does not reflect the ethnic or racial diversity of the city or state. Although the brochure boasts a high level of diversity for the state, one quickly finds out that diverse students population refers to the city or state from which the student matriculated In fact, in terms of racial diversity, the institution is quite homogeneous. The current student population consists of approximately 89% white students, 3% African American, 3% Mexican American and 5% other and international.

Last month, the Chronicle of higher education noted that although the Melville campus was one of the largest in the county, it was also one of the most homogeneous, and most likely to report incidents of racial intolerance. According to faculty and administration, since the recent attacks on affirmative action, the university has been unable to attract many students or professors of color to the university.

The Case

William Georgia, the new president of the university, has made increasing institutional diversity a priority for the institution's strategic plans. He has called for faculty and administrators to make efforts to increase the enrollment of students of color. He has also initiated and called for departments to begin to make better efforts for recruiting, attracting, and retaining students and faculty of color. According to President Georgia, during the fall convocation address, "A diversity strategic plan is an institutional priority, without which, the institution will be left behind as a well intentioned footnote and afterthought in the cultural and organizational history, sad monuments to a forgotten orthodoxy" (Lincoln, 1999, p. 21). The final words from the president's convocational address noted that funds would be earmarked to promote the diversity campaign.

Faculty and staff, however, are divided on the formation of such a plan. According to one large faction, faculty hiring in the name of diversity and students recruited and admitted for reasons of diversity is illegal. This group of faculty and staff center their arguments on the fact that law prohibits discrimination on the basis of race, color, and national origin in any program or activity receiving federal financial assistance. According to some faculty and staff members, this plan has utterances of reverse discrimination.

Faculty who support the president's strategic plan for diversity and are proponents of hiring a diverse staff, cite the equal protection clause of the constitution's fourteenth amendment to strengthen their position. During a recent faculty senate hearing, one member reminded the participants that the ruling in the Bakke case stated unequivocally that, "Racial discrimination is constitutional, if it is narrowly tailored to a compelling government interest." And, that the interest here is diversity—compelling! These discussions among faculty and administrators have caused serious tension. Administrative and faculty members are threatening some form of protest.

Meanwhile, the president of the university is supporting a faculty senate initiative that calls for a university-wide charge to hire diverse faculty. He says effectively that by the year 2010, "we should increase our faculty of color such that it reflects the student population, and we should increase the population of students of color such that they reflect those of the state." He has asked that faculty make it a priority to hire faculty of color this year.

The following scene takes place in the College of Education at Big State University in Melville. The College of Education is seeking an assistant professor, tenure-track to teach, conduct research, and serve in the higher educational administration student affairs program. The search committee has narrowed the search to four candidates—Laura, Cynthia, Max and Marvin. And of course, minorities are encouraged to apply.

The Scene

The reviews of the final candidates are somewhat mixed. The faculty are divided on several issues. The most controversial issue, according to the faculty, is that of hiring people of color—just because they are people of color. Some faculty members believe the president is forcing them to hire faculty of color, when in fact, they should always hire "the most qualified". Nevertheless, the faculty search committee in the College of Education have narrowed the search to four candidates—two candidates of color, and two candidates who are white and male.

> **Judith:** I really like Laura!
> **Arnold:** She hailed from an HBCU, you know what that means?
> **Judith:** No, I don't. What does it mean?

Some of the faculty argued that since the applicant's doctoral degree was from an HBCU, their views, research and pedagogical style may be "different" from that of the other faulty. Still, other faculty members commented on where the applicants chose to publish.

Arnold: Well, for starters, take a look at her publications. Do you notice anything?

Judith Lange: Yes, she has several publications in prestigious journals; what is your point?

Arnold: Well, the journals are not mainstream journals. Are any of those journals on the tier-one list for our department?

Robert: Well, I can say that at least she does have more teaching experience, but Martin clearly has some very nice publications in more prestigious journals, you know, tier-one journals—besides, I know his advisor personally. He is on one of my editorial boards.

Judith: (sarcastically) hmmmm. Let's see . . . wonder why he would have more publications in those "tier-one journals"? Who says those journals are tier-one anyway? Robert, please! By the way, he has one publication, since we are [emphasis added] counting.

Robert: (genuinely puzzled) What are you saying?

Judith: I believe you know. Them that have, get . . . It's not what you know, but who you know. Need I be any clearer? Privilege is such a wonderful thing . . . for some.

Letty: Well Judith, Robert, Arnold and I just noted in an instant that we somehow felt more comfortable with the candidate from Michigan and Dakota, than we did with the either of the candidates from Dallas or from Chicago. They just seemed like a better fit. (Uncomfortable laughter from Letty) Perhaps we just like cold weather . . . ha ha ha (uncomfortable laughter around the table).

Judith: It is easy to feel comfortable with someone that has similar backgrounds and interests as you. You just mentioned that Marvin's mom is one of your oldest friends. You are the candidates Godfather? So in essence, he is a part of that network that we all shun. Robert, you know the one that you ran away from—the good ol' boys network. Now you are a leader of the same gang (Judith looks disgusted—Robert seems puzzled). You even casually stated that he publishes in the same journals as well—the ones that you are the editor or are on the editorial board. Now talk to me again about why do you think that you feel more comfortable?

Arnold: Well, Judith, both Cynthia and Laura teach diversity courses. You know, here we go again. I do not think that we need another critical theorist or multicultural person here. Don't you teach those classes? Do we really need another one? I mean both the applicant from Chicago and Dallas can teach multicultural courses.

Judith: Actually no, considering the demographics of this campus, and the demographics of this region, I would say no. Apparently, we do not offer enough courses that explore different perspectives. Also, I would hope that we are all incorporating diverse perspectives throughout all of our curriculums. For instance, how do you teach law, leadership theory, developmental theory or organizational theory without talking about race, class, gender, sexual orientation? My class titled diversity in higher education is not the only class where I incorporate diverse perspectives, theories, and philosophies. I just assumed that you all did too. If not, it is not my job to teach everyone about all of the diversity in one class—during one semester. Not fair, too stressful for me, and just not smart as a department or university.

Robert: (somewhat nervously) Remember, Arnold, what old Georgie, the president, said last week, we are beginning to sound like footnotes and an afterthought.

Arnold: Well, their research agendas certainly do not fit within the charge of the university. Laura is singing to the choir by publishing in those journals—critical race theory or whatever they call it.

Judith: What!? So the university is determining what we research now. Oh no, I am outta' of this business if that ever comes to fruition.

Arnold: I just mean, do we really need another critical researcher? I guess that's what they call that line of research . . . ha ha. What is that they do anyway? They never seem to fix the problems. They just cite the problems.

Judith: Oh no Arnold, not this argument. The same could be said of most research—in any discipline. That is why the boys in Washington want to get rid of all of us. You are just providing them with more ignorant and uninformed ammunition. Listen to what you are saying, and better yet why you are saying it. Citing the problems, isn't that what we all do—theorize? How many of us are in the field fixing the problems? When did you last take your cause to the streets? Remember that person at the open forum meeting last week who questioned Dr. Lampard in Educational Leadership? He said, "You have written a plethora of books about the principalship, but when were you a principal?" He went on to question his ability to conduct research in an area where he claimed Lampard had no 'practical experience'. I despise that ignorant argument, but you are doing the same thing. When we start battling with our own about how we research we enter some very sacred grounds called academic freedom. I would like to believe that it is more reality than myth.

Letty: Thank you Judith, but can we get back to the issue at hand.

Judith: This is the issue at hand. What do you mean? Better yet, where have you been during the past few minutes of this conversation?

Letty: I have been right here. I want to get back to this notion of pre-ferential hires.

Judith: Oh my father. I am either in the wrong field, the wrong campus or in a time warp. Who is talking about preferential hires? And who is being hired preferentially—this time?

Letty: I just take issue with these preferential hires; we should be able to hire the most qualified!

Judith: Letty, what do you think has occurred in higher education over the past couple of hundred years? Our campus looks the way it does because of preferential hires—preferential recruitment. Call it good old boys network, spousal hires, or hiring a friend. It is all preferential hiring. 'Minorities are encouraged to apply' is a sad sound bite. Please tell me that you must know that you are a preferential hire? You are qualified, but you were hired when your husband was hired. And also explain what you mean by most qualified.

Letty: (exasperated and somewhat unnerved). Exactly that, the most qualified. And I would like to believe that I was hired because of my qualifications—not my husband's qualifications (Letty looks dazed).

Judith: I am certain that you were, but most spouses negotiate spousal hires . . . right? Did you not Robert, or did the university recruit Letty?

Arnold: (under his breath) Exactly. The most qualified—no matter what color or gender. Let's get back to that.

Judith: And sexual orientation . . . and how do you go about deciding who is the most qualified? Don't get me wrong; I do agree to some extent. The most qualified should be hired.

However, most of the time, it seems like the white candidates are the most qualified—according to our campus, and most campuses throughout the United States. Take a look at the faces on this campus, and most others, most of the professors, administrators, and students are white. Go to any college of education website . . . who do you see?

Letty: Perhaps they were the most qualified at the time? Perhaps there were not many people of color in the pool.

Robert: Yes, the number of applicants in the pool is very important.

Arnold: The number and the quality of the pool too. Don't forget that!

Judith: It must be nice to be that naïve about racial preference and privilege. Not the pool myth.

Letty: Naïve? We are just color blind!

Judith: No, you are just privileged, and you are calling it color blind. You do not have to think about how your race affords you some privilege, so you call it being color blind. And by the way, you are not color blind. We would not be having this conversation about who is qualified, and where the candidates publish, and where they attended school if you were. So let's just be honest here. We are really talking about privileging one candidate over another because of our, your, racial preferences.

Letty: Oh wait just a minute! I really resent being called racist!

Judith: You should resent benefiting from racism.

Letty: How do I benefit from racism?

Robert and Arnold:
(looking somewhat astonished) Yeah, wait a minute. You are calling us all racists.

Judith: No I am not. I am saying that you benefit from a racist system. Take a look around this table, the conversation that we are having about the candidates of color. Then take a look at the student demographics, the professors of color on this campus—all twelve of us. Look at most institutions of higher education, administrators, faculty; do you actually believe that all of these people were the brightest and the best? Certainly not. So all of the folks of color were just not as qualified? Take a look at hiring trends in general, at housing patterns, who purchases what house in what neighborhood and who cannot—Ever heard of red-lining? The bottom line is that, people tend to hire people who look, and act, exactly like themselves. By the way, that is what the "mainstream" [sarcastically] literature says. I can give you the references. The publication appears in a mainstream journal.

Letty: I am really getting uncomfortable with this conversation. Let's just stick with the facts. Let's take another look at the CV's.

Robert: Me too, can we move on please. Get me those CV's.

Judith: I hope we can move on, but I do not know how we can make a decision with a hiring committee such as it exists now. Perhaps we need to speak to the dean or EEO about reconfiguring this team. It is simply unfair to the candidates of color. Yes, let's get those CV's.

Discussion Questions

1. Discuss the president's agenda to hire a diversity faculty. Effectively he asks the entire university faculty to make significant efforts to move toward a more diverse campus. Some faculty are remiss, noting that the undertone appears to be reversely discriminatory. Discuss what the faculty mean by reverse discrimination and the phrase minorities are encouraged to apply. Some faculty members claim that the phrase, minorities are encouraged to apply is misleading and discriminatory. Discuss (see Clegg, 2002; Guinier, 2001 and Milem, 1999).

2. Why should the university hire a diverse faculty? Or should they, companies, institutions, hire based on merit and the most qualified? Using literature and other resources, divide into two groups. Prepare a well-argued case that outlines why it would or would not be important to hire a diverse faculty (see Guinier, 2001 and Milem, 1999). In addition, read the Clegg article. Also see Grutter v. Bollinger case.

3. How do search committees, we as institutional faculty and administrators determine who is the most qualified? Develop a rubric that would help determine who is the most qualified. Outline some potential parameters that may constitute why one candidate may be more qualified versus someone who may be less qualified. For instance, a propensity to get along may be considered a criterion. However, how do you determine from an interview, who gets along well with others? You may even incorporate a new guideline for determining what constitutes a tier-one journal.

4. Arnold notes that one of the candidates does not publish in mainstream journals. Robert chimes in by adding that Martin clearly has publications in more prominent journal—besides I know his advisor personally. He is on one of my editorial boards. Discuss Judith's

response—"Privilege is such a wonderful thing." How do faculty on your campus or department go about deciding what publications are considered to be tier-one or mainstream? Talk about some institutionalized assumptions that individual departments would have to make when selecting where one is to publish. Alternative exercise—request a copy of the promotion and tenure document from your college. Invite promotion and tenure committee members in to discuss how and why they have decided why particular journals are considered to be tier-one.

5. Examine the statement from the Bakke ruling, can we successfully translate the government ruling to institutions of higher education? How? In other words, how does governmental compelling interest necessarily reflect institutional interest? Or does it and should it? (see Bakke case, Clegg, 2002 and Milem, 1999).

6. Judith refers to whites as having a psychological footing in terms of being hired. Effectively, people who look alike or are of the same phenotype tend to hire each other. Discuss this notion. (Read Mcintosh and Jensen's article. Also read Hughes chapter). If this is true, then how do you determine the most qualified despite the desire to hire someone who looks and acts like the employer? Discuss how race might privilege one candidate over another (see Hughes, 2004 and Staple, 1995. In addition, see Madsen and Mabokela, 2000).

7. What does Judith mean when she states that teaching the diversity course is too stressful and not fair? (See William Smith's Chapter).

8. Aside from fiscal support for minority faculty hiring, what are some ways in which the institution can increase its outreach efforts?

9. What are some ways in which the president's budgetary process can promote the hiring of minority faculty?

10. As funding for higher education across the country decreases and the ability to earmark funds for specific outreach dissipates, what are some ways this president can build sustainability for hiring new minority faculty?

References

Clegg, R. (2002). When faculty hiring is blatantly illegal. *Chronicle of Higher Education*, 49 (2), 20.

Grutter v. Bollinger, et al. United States Court of Appeals for the Sixth Circuit. Nos. 01–1447/1516. 2002 [http//www.umich.edu/urel/admissions/legal/grutter/gru-ap-op.html]

Guinier, L. (2001). Colleges should take "confirmative action" in admissions. *Chronicle of Higher Education*. B10–12.

Regents of the University of California v. Bakke, 438 U.S. 265; 98 S. Ct. 2733; 1978 U.S. Lexis 5; 57 L.Ed. 2d 750; 17 Fair Empl. Prac. Cas. (BNA) 1000; 17 Empl. Prac. Dec. (CCH) P8402 (1978),

Barbara Grutter, Petitioner v. Lee Bollinger, et al. 539 U.S. 306; 123 S.Ct. 2325, 156 L.Ed.2d 304, 71 USLW 4498, 91 Fair Empl. Prac. Cas. (BNA) 1761, 84 Empl. Prac. Dec. P 41, 415, 177 Ed. Law Rep. 801, 03 Cal. Daily Op. Serv. 5378, 2003 Daily Journal D.A.R. 6800, 16 Fla.L. Weekly Fed. S 367

Hughes, R.L. (2004). The dwindling pool of qualified professors of color: Suburban legends. In D. Cleveland, (Ed.). *A long way to go: Conversations about race*, 81–93. New York: Peter Lang.

Madsen, J. & Mabokela, R. (2000). Organizational culture and its impact on African American Teachers. *American Educational Journal* 37 (4), 849–876.

Milem, J. (1999). The educational benefits of diversity: Evidence from multiple sectors. In M. Chang, D. Witt, J. Jones, & K. Hajuta (Eds.). *Compelling interest: Examining the evidence on racial dynamics in higher education*, (pp.1–41). Stanford, CA: American Educational Research Association and the Stanford University Center for Comparative Studies in Race and Ethnicity.

Smith, W. (2004). Black faculty coping with racial battle fatigue: The campus racial climate in a post-civil-Rights era. In D. Cleveland, (Ed.). *A long way to go: Conversations about race*. New York: Peter Lang.

Staples, R. (1995). Black deprivation-white privilege: The assault on affirmative action. *The Black Scholar*, 25 (3), 2–6.

U.S. Supreme Court University of California Regents v. Bakke, 438 U.S. U.S. 265 (1978)

Recommended Readings

Altbach, P.G., Gumport, P.G., & Johnston, D.B. (Eds.). (2002) *In defense of American higher education*. Baltimore, MD: The John Hopkins University Press.

Altbach, P.G., Berdahl, R.O., & Gumport, P.G. (Eds.). (1999). *American higher education in the twenty-first century: Social, political, and economic challenges*. Baltimore, MD: The John Hopkins University Press.

Chemers, M.M. & Murphey, S.E. (1995). Leadership and diversity in groups and organizations. In M.M. Chemers, S. Oskamp, & M.A. Costanzo (Eds.). *Diversity in organizations: new perspectives for a changing workplace*, (pp.157–190). Thousand Oakes, CA: Sage Publications.

Cose, E. (1993). *The rage of a privileged class*. New York: Harper Collins.

Hackman, J.D. (1985). Power and centrality in the allocation of resources in colleges and universities. *Administrative Science Quarterly*, 30 (March), 61–77 Cornell University.

Jensen, R. (1998). White people need to acknowledge benefits of unearned privilege. *Baltimore Sun Times*. Dawn/LAT-WP News Service (c) Baltimore Sun.

Layzell, D.T. & Lyddon, J.W. (1990). Budgeting for higher education at the state level. *ASHE-ERIC Higher Education Report*, Number 4, The George Washington University School of Education and Human Development.

Mcintosh, P. (1988). *White privilege: Unpacking the invisible knapsack*. Working paper 189.

Olivas, M. Olivas, Michael A. (1996). The decision is flatly, unequivocally wrong. *The Chronicle of Higher Education*. p. B3.

Tatum, B. D. (2003). *Why are all the black kids sitting together in the cafeteria? and other conversations about race: A psychologist explains the development of racial identity.* New York: Basic Books.

Trow, M. (1994). Comparative reflections on leadership in higher education. In P.G. Altbach, R.O. Berdahl, & P.J. Gumport (Eds.). *Higher education in American society* (3rd ed., pp. 269–288) Amherst, NY: Prentice-Hall.

U.S. Supreme Court University of California Regents v. Bakke, 438 U.S. U.S. 265 (1978).

Case #14 Perfecting the Status Quo

Edward Delgado-Romero

Case Overview

This case examines the involvement of a student affairs staff member of color in an academic search committee targeting diversity. Furthermore, it examines the politics, institutional racism, and inequitable outcomes in the process. This is the story of how a search for a faculty person of color ends in the hiring of a white man.

Key Characters

Luis: a Latino student affairs staff member with an academic background in the academic discipline.

John: a white full professor, head of the search committee.

Ben: a white full professor, a member of the search committee, long-time rival of John.

Reed: a white untenured assistant professor, a member of the search committee.

Institutional Setting

State University—A large, public, research-extensive university in one of the most demographically diverse states in the country.

The Case

The academic department consisted of twenty-four faculty members, twenty of who were men and twenty-two of whom were white. The department had a history of trouble in retaining, recruiting graduate students and faculty of color. Consequently, when a position became open in the department, the department chair (a white male) insisted that diversity should be a criterion in the hiring. Therefore, he recruited Luis, a Latino who had a doctoral degree in the same discipline as the department, to serve on the search committee. Luis, who worked in student affairs, was an affiliated faculty member of the department and sometimes taught courses. He was also a locally and nationally known leader in the area of multiculturalism.

The department chair explained that the motivation for hiring a faculty person of color was there: the population of the state and to a lesser extent, the student body, was rapidly diversifying; the current faculty was almost exclusively white men; and recent success in recruiting racial and ethnic minority graduate students raised the question about the need for mentors and role models of color given that the two faculty of color were inundated with requests for personal and professional guidance. In addition the larger profession was espousing the need for diversity, inclusion, and multicultural competence among faculty, students, and administrators.

Luis felt somewhat uneasy when the composition of the search committee was announced. There were two white male full professors (John and Ben), one untenured white male professor (Reed) and Luis, an adjunct faculty of color from Student Affairs. Luis was concerned because he heard about the rigidly hierarchical power structure of faculty life in this department. Tenure marked a line between those who were "insiders" in the department (associate and full professors) and those who were not (assistant professors—who were in a probationary period, and adjunct faculty—who would never be a permanent part of the department). And of the insiders the full professors wielded all the power in the department.

Luis was concerned that John would try to control the process and outcome of the search, despite appearances of collaboration. John had a single-minded devotion to getting his way, this single-mindedness had served him well in the research world. In particular he enjoyed besting Ben, who was a long-time rival.

The charge to the search committee was to identify and recruit one, and possibly two senior multicultural scholars, preferably people of color. Luis was relieved at first that his opinion was sought out and that his connections to multicultural scholars was utilized. Luis was able to use his contacts to convince some prominent, exceptionally well-qualified and established faculty members to apply for the position.

Once the application deadline passed, the search committee met to review folders. The job ad had been clearly written to emphasize the need for expertise in multicultural research and the resulting pool had a bimodal distribution: multicultural scholars of all races and white male faculty who had applied regardless of the focus of the search. Luis was relieved when the committee agreed to create a short list of two tenured multicultural scholars of color and two promising graduate students, one a person of color and the other with a diverse ethnic background. However, he was concerned that there was also a white male included in the short list, and his work was not in multicultural area. Luis recommended that he should be cut from the list. John eloquently defended keeping the person on the list as a backup, because he was "too good to pass up". Given the strength and match of the other candidates, Luis dropped the matter. He was to learn later that this white male candidate was a former mentee and personal friend of the search chair, a fact that was not discussed in the meeting.

Luis found the interview process disturbing especially given the way that racism was perpetuated under the guise of intellectual rigor and supposed scientific detachment. The established candidates of color were brought to campus and subjected to a hostile reception. For example one candidate was asked if he was "really" a minority, because he "looked White". During the job talks, the white male faculty came in late, carried on side conversations, and addressed the candidates by their first names. This type of reception made it difficult for the job candidates to perform well.

In the search committee meeting after the presentations the search chair criticized the job talks and presented negative feedback from the general faculty. John even went as far as to imply that the candidates may not have done their own work, and that other (white) people had actually done the sophisticated statistical analyses. Luis strongly challenged this notion, but once the accusation was out there, like a foul odor, it was hard to cover up. John and Ben insisted that these candidates, despite being tenured at comparable institutions, were not "going to work out". Both Reed and Luis felt that they could convince them otherwise. Had this been a democratic process, then the vote would have been tied, however, the reality was that John and Ben held all of the power.

John and Ben decided that the committee would move on and interview the two graduate students. John stated that he had talked to one of the candidates and that this candidate had accepted another position and was "off the market". The remaining candidate was invited. This candidate was young and straight out of graduate school, but seemed to have a genuine interest in multicultural research. This candidate was not a person of color, but was considered ethnically diverse.

The one reservation about this candidate was that an initial motivation had been to bring in a more senior person who could be a mentor and contribute to the program immediately. Using this reasoning John invited the white male professor who had been included in the interview pool. Luis became irate, but was assured that this was just a precautionary move and that the search was still focused on diversity. Luis began to get a realistic sense of the limited power he had in this process and was considering resigning from the search committee in protest.

The white male candidate was invited to campus. In person his demeanor was that of someone who felt he already had the job, his arrogance and overconfidence culminated in a job talk that was an unqualified disaster. Certainly not something that one would expect from a seasoned scholar. Yet, rather than intellectually dissect him like had been done with the previous candidates, the white male faculty helped, encouraged, and supported this faculty member during the presentation. They went out of their way to save the presentation. And they addressed him as "Doctor".

At the next search committee meeting John and Ben nearly came to blows. On the surface the disagreement was about the search, but beneath the surface it was about egos and imposing one's will. Accusations of manipulating the search process were made, and both full professors began a battle for dominance that quickly was made very public (through email) in the department. The most noticeable aspect of the fight was that neither John nor Ben seemed to care about the precarious situation that the untenured faculty and the adjunct faculty were in, and the potential damage that could be done to their long-term future with the department. Luis received phone calls from both John and Ben late at night and was repeatedly asked to take sides. Luis had his integrity publicly questioned many times, most memorably in an email from Ben accusing him of being a coward.

There were different prices to pay for what happened. Luis chose to distance himself from the department, thus cutting off chances to teach or work with graduate students. Reed was not so lucky. Despite a strong record of publications, after the search he was (informally) led to believe that he was not going to get tenure and he opted to leave for a comparable university that welcomed him with open arms and tenure. Reeds leaving turned out to be a significant event as subsequent events showed.

The economic situation for the state was dire, and a hiring freeze went into effect after the new faculty person was hired. Reed resigned his position to go elsewhere, which resulted in a vacancy in the department. Incredibly John convinced the dean of the college that since the white male had already interviewed, that he was not subject to the hiring freeze. In addition, the white male candidate was hired (again during a hiring freeze) and granted tenure (the first time a faculty member has not had to wait a probationary period). Without a doubt the candidate had the qualifications to be tenured, this was not in doubt. However, every rule in the book had been rewritten so this candidate could be hired and handsomely rewarded. Luis wondered if John could be so Machiavellian as to manipulate the entire process just to get what he wanted? Luis came to the conclusion that he was. For his part John felt he did nothing wrong, and in fact he stated that he should have been congratulated for his resourcefulness.

Therefore, the search committee that had once held the promise of diversifying the department had a made a small but significant step in hiring a ethnically diverse, multiculturally focused junior faculty. However, they also took a giant step backwards by subverting every safeguard in place by hiring a white male faculty with personal connections and no professional interests in diversity. Small but significant progress with regards to diversity would immediately be offset by a major reinforcement of the status quo. This tenured faculty member was granted immediate insider status, with the promise of lifetime employment and would be one of the people to vote on the future of the department (which included subsequent tenure decisions and new hires).

Summary

As Luis reflected on the events of the search, he had two distinct reactions, one logical and one very personal. In terms of a critical analysis, Luis learned a great deal about institutional racism. The same criteria that were used to eviscerate the candidates of color were bent to benefit the white candidate. The perception of a bad job talk was an obstacle for the candidates of color, but chalked up to a "bad day" for the white candidate. Insinuations were made that the candidates of color were second-rate scholars who might have had white peers and students do their work for them. However, the white candidates' qualifications or personal connections were never questioned, their qualifications were beyond reproach. Finally the candidates of color were publicly humiliated and dropped from consideration with their credibility impugned. The white candidate seemed immune from criticism and received the benefit of a welcoming and supportive faculty, in essence he was treated as an "insider" from the beginning. It seemed that the criterion of what constituted an acceptable candidate literally shifted from candidate to candidate, but always in favor of the white candidate.

Despite the initial intention of diversifying the faculty, the outcome led to another white male joining the powerful elite in the department. Was this the original intent of the department or search chair? Did they "mean" for this to happen? Luis came to believe that this interaction was an example of aversive racism. Aversive racism happens when white people have the best of intentions but perpetuate racism through a mental filter that keeps racist outcomes out of conscious thought. The person, who espouses egalitarian beliefs, fails to see how objective criterion is shifted to produce an outcome that is unfair and biased. In this example it would be the way that performance criterion was consistently shifted (e.g., the value of the job talk) to benefit the white candidate. The most insidious aspect of aversive racism is that, in the end, the aversive racist believes that he or she acted fairly and without bias.

In terms of a personal reaction, Luis felt that he had been used in the process as a token person of color. He felt responsible for helping to humiliate the scholars of color who were personal friends of his. He felt that his status as a person of color was used to legitimize the search and the outcomes, and that he had very little power and everything to lose in the process (as adjunct faculty his promotion depended on the vote of the faculty). Luis was also frustrated for having wasted precious time and energy that could have been used in Student Affairs where there was a genuine commitment to multiculturalism. Initially he had been flattered to have his academic department, which occupied a higher status in the hierarchy of the university, turn to him for help in implementing diversity and instead he had helped perfect the status quo.

Decision Options

Were there things that Luis could have done differently? Where there decisions that Luis could have made to change the outcome? He had most seriously considered resigning from the committee and perhaps this would have been the best option. However, as a token, Luis was unclear of his power to affect the process in any way. Perhaps in retrospect, he should have asked about the composition of the search committee and insisted that he had a trusted ally on the committee to attenuate the power imbalances. And perhaps he should have suggested that they find a (tenured) faculty of color to serve on the committee.

It seems that one of the critical decisions is how involved the Student Affairs practitioner should be with academic departments given the real power differences between faculty and staff. It seems to be in the nature of Student Affairs to be more receptive to diversity issues and far more inclusive in hiring, retention, and promotion. Perhaps Luis had assumed that his experience with Student Affairs (he had been hired in search directly targeting diversity) would translate into academic life. So the real decision seems to be how much one tries to change a system that one is not fully part of and that is a perplexing question.

Discussion Questions

1. What are some ways to negotiate the inherent power and status differences between Student Affairs and academic departments?

2. People of color are often asked to take on roles across the university related to diversity interests. What is the best way to address this systemic issue and involve white staff and faculty in diversity initiatives?

3. How does one confront aversive or unintentional racism? This is particularly challenging for people of color whose concerns are often dismissed as personal or political.

4. How does one promote a social justice agenda within a hierarchical power system such as Student Affairs or Academia?

5. Job searches are often contentious because of the advantages that insider candidates have in the process. Is this contentiousness unavoidable, even in the search for faculty of color? That is, can any search be truly fair?

Recommended Readings

Dovidio, J.F. & Gaertner, S.L. (2000). Aversive racism and selection decisions: 1989 and 1999. *Psychological Science*, 11(4), 315–319.

Lynn, M. & Adams, M. (2002). Introductory overview to the special issue critical race theory and education: Recent developments in the Field. *Equity & Excellence*, 35(2), 87–92.

Niemann, Y.F. (1999). The making of a token: A case study of stereotype threat, stigma, racism, and tokenism in academe. *Frontiers: A Journal of Women Studies*, 20 (1),11–34.

Niemann, Y.F. & Dovidio, J.F. (1999). *Tenure, race/ethnicity and attitudes toward affirmative action: A matter of self-interest?* Sociological Perspectives, 41(4) 783–796.

Reyes, M.D. & Halcón, J.J. (1996). Racism in academia: The old wolf revisited. In C. S. V. Turner, M., Garcia, A., Nora & L.I. Rendón (Eds.). (1996). *Racial and Ethnic Diversity in Higher Education*, (pp. 337–348) Needham Heights, MA: Simon & Schuster.

Ridley, C.R. (1996). *Overcoming unintentional racism in counseling and psychotherapy: A practitioners guide to intentional intervention.* Thousand Oaks, CA: Sage.

Smith-Maddox, R. & Solorzano, D.G. (2002). Using critical race theory, Paulo Freire's problem-posing methods, and case study research to confront race and racism in education. *Qualitative Inquiry*, 8(1), 66–84.

Case #15 Faculty Development Issues in a Department of Black Studies

FABIO ROJAS

Black Studies programs are torn between the demands of the academy and student needs. Scholars hired to teach and manage Black Studies units are expected to pursue research agendas, and faculty members who fail to demonstrate research success are not promoted. However, Black Studies faculty members often feel that they have a special obligation to support African American students, which can detract from the successful completion of their research. The Department of Black Studies at Midwest Research University (MRU) suffered from this tension. Attention given to students detracted from the department's ability to retain and promote faculty. This case study describes the history of the MRU's Department of Black Studies and problems recruiting and promoting faculty. The case study discusses efforts of Dr. Glee to develop the department and its faculty as well as the problems some scholars had in getting promoted with tenure.

Historical Background

African American intellectuals had been proposing something like "Black Studies" for decades (Carr, 1998; Rojas, 2002). Early proposals for something resembling Black Studies include W. E. B. DuBois' research center at Atlanta University (1910), the Association for Negro History founded by Carter Woodson (1927), the emergence of "Nile Valley" scholarship with Chiekh Anta Diop (1950s), Afro-history at Lane College proposed by Bobby Seale and the Soul Brothers Association (predecessor organization of the Black Panthers; 1966), and various demands for the inclusion of "Black topics" in the college curriculum (mid-to late 1960s).

The first fully formed Department of Black Studies was created in Fall 1969 after San Francisco State College students organized a strike for a Department of Black Studies during the 1968–1969 academic year. The strike at San Francisco State was successful because students had already created a functioning Black Studies curriculum as part of an experimental college. Student strikers were also successful because two years of conflict between the College's Board of Trustees, Governor Ronald Reagan and legislative leader Jesse Unruh weakened the administration. Black Studies' success at San Francisco State College motivated students across the country. Students soon mobilized to demand the establishment of Black Studies as an academic department at hundreds of campuses. Students offered the following justifications for Black Studies: (1) the existing college curriculum excluded Black students, (2) Black Studies should be a resource for all students, (3) Black Studies should help students in their transition from high school to college, (4) Black Studies should have an academic and social component and (5) Black Studies would emphasize the value of Black Culture.

There is much evidence that Black Studies has found a place in American higher education. Although very few universities adopted the most radical demands for all-black colleges inside existing predominantly white colleges, many started to offer Black Studies courses and about 150 created degree-granting programs now exist. Research shows that 48% of research universities have degree-granting Black Studies programs although they comprise only 10% of all institutions of higher education (Rojas, 2004). Research universities are four times as likely to have a Black Studies degree program as a liberal arts college, of which 12% have a Black Studies degree program. Institutions classified as "doctoral universities" or "masters college" in the Carnegie classification of institutions of higher education have very few Black Studies programs. A few universities offered master's degrees and five universities offer doctoral degrees (Temple University, University of California, Berkeley, Harvard University, University of Massachusetts, Amherst, Michigan State University). Some reports even suggest that the field has gained legitimacy because administrators see it as a tool for attracting Black students and managing racial tensions on campus (Hine, 1990).

Institutional Setting

The Midwest Research University is a public university located in a large urban area and was created in the mid 1960s as a branch campus of the larger flagship campus, which is located in a "downstate" rural area. The University was originally housed in an industrial facility in 1963 and moved to its current location in the late 1960s. Its administration recruits students from the immediate metropolitan area and offers a wide range of academic and professional degrees. The university is located near major transportation routes and it is walking distance from downtown, allowing it to retain its urban character. Known originally as a regional university, the administration has recently tried to bolster the institution's research reputation by hiring an internationally known scholar to be the Dean of the College of Arts and Sciences, who has shown some success in attracting academic luminaries to the campus.

The University is organized much like others. The University's College of Arts and Sciences contains the Humanities, Social Science, and Physical Science Departments. Durring the 1960s and early 1970s, the College of Letters and Science experienced a quick expansion adding new academic programs and faculty. Like most other universities, the expansion was halted because of the financial crisis of the 1970s, and many departments had difficulties paying for new faculty positions and support staff. The situation stabilized somewhat in the 1980s.

The university has shown a willingness to attract and educate African Americans, Latinos, Asians and Native Americans. The university has made efforts to attract ethnic minorities as students and faculty. For example, students and faculty supported the establishment of a Black Studies Department and the Educational Opportunity Program. African American enrollments were initially low. An internal report from 1970 suggests that only about 200 students out of approximately 6000 were African American. This number peaked in the 1978 when approximately 3200 African Americans enrolled at the University. Since then, the African American student population has numbered approximately 2000 per year. By the 1990s, the student population included a wide range of ethnic minorities and immigrants from Eastern Europe, who were settling in the city where MRU is located.

The Creation of the Department of Black Studies

The Department of Black Studies was approved in the 1969–1970 academic year by the State Board of Higher Education. At the time, there were at least two proposals for Ethnic Studies at MRU. One proposal was developed by faculty members in the Education College. The proposal described a teacher education program aimed at developing urban education and community development experts. Students were to combine ethnic studies courses with an internship in a school or community organization. The proposal encountered strong opposition because of personal conflicts between the Education College dean and faculty members who sponsored the proposal. Another reason was the strong language of the proposal, which was viewed as extreme, and the demand that the Ethnic Studies program have a governing board consisting of "community" members from outside the university. Unsurprisingly, the proposal never moved past the ad hoc committee and the bitter dispute surrounding the proposal resulted in resignations by some of the involved parties.

The successful proposal was drafted by students in consultation with faculty members and administrators. The proposed Department of Black Studies was closely modeled on existing departments. The proposed academic unit offered an undergraduate degree and had a series of courses, including an introductory course, electives and a senior seminar. Most importantly, the proposal emphasized that Black Studies must develop intellectually and move beyond its roots in protest. The Department of Black Studies was to be indistinguishable from other departments in its teaching, research, service, and internal organization. The proposal was approved by the faculty Senate and then the State Board without fanfare in the spring of 1970. The meetings of the faculty Senate indicate that the Black Studies was approved because it was seen as a modest expansion of the university's existing degree offerings.

Evolution of the Department and Faculty Development

The Department started offering courses during the academic year 1970–1971 and awarded its first bachelor's degrees in 1973. The Chair, Dr. Glee, an African American social scientist with a Ph.D. and an established scholarly reputation was already tenured in another department. Until her death in the 1990s, she held a joint appointment in Black Studies and Speech. Like most Black Studies advocates, she was acutely aware of the need to move away from student activism and develop academic legitimacy. She cultivated the Department's status by hiring a well known poet who could teach literature and junior faculty who were earning Ph.D.'s in the humanities and social sciences.

Dr. Glee tried to articulate guiding principles for the department. She started by gathering data on department activities to help her understand what the department was doing. Dr. Glee surveyed undergraduate students to find out what attracted students to the department's classes. She surveyed faculty members about the books they assigned in class to inventory what was taught in the various courses. Her findings noted that there was little thematic consistency in the department course offerings. Attempting to remedy the situation, Dr. Glee, like many other Black Studies scholars, formulated an intellectual framework for Black Studies, where courses would be organized around topics (e.g., the Civil Rights Movement or the Harlem renaissance) and intellectual rigor (e.g., introductory courses versus senior seminars).

Further attempts to develop Black Studies were stymied by financial and bureaucratic difficulties in the late 1970s and 1980s. Although Dr. Glee and later chairs such as Dr. Kufu, an African historian, were successful in recruiting some permanent lecturers and two senior faculty members with joint appointments in other departments, bureaucratic delays prevented the recruitment of junior and senior scholars. Although the Dean of Arts and Science approved these faculty searches, the approval often came in the late winter or summer. The department did not have the opportunity to recruit from deepest pool of candidates. An internal evaluation of the program criticized the administration's poor recruitment efforts. In one instance, these delays discouraged a nationally recognized literary critic from considering taking an appointment at MRU.

Disorganized recruitment was not the department's only problem. The few tenure-track faculty members in the department found promotion to be elusive. For example, Ms. Treadwell, a humanities scholar, arrived at the department in the late 1970s without completing her doctoral dissertation. When Dr. Glee abruptly resigned her position as department chair for reasons not made clear at the time, none of the tenured faculty members associated with the department assumed the position as department leader. Ms. Treadwell reluctantly became the department's acting director during her second and third years at MRU. Administrative duties prevented Ms. Treadwell from completing her doctoral degree in a timely fashion, which in turn prevented her from developing a research portfolio meriting a promotion with tenure. Faculty meeting records indicate that the Department's steering committee, composed of tenured faculty in Black Studies and other Departments, were fully cognizant of the problem but did little to address the issue other than recommend to the College of Arts and Sciences that Ms. Treadwell's tenure schedule be extended. Archival records do not indicate if this request was approved but Ms. Treadwell left MRU for another university after finishing her time as acting director and completing her dissertation.

Attention given to students slowed the development of a core Black Studies faculty. Faculty members in the department reported that they felt a special obligation to help black students. For example, faculty members sponsored cultural events such as gospel and jazz concerts along with different plays and various symposia. The assistance given to black students often consumed a great deal of time for junior faculty. An external committee report in the early 1980s lauded the faculty's desire to help students, but also noted that excessive time dedicated to students detracted from the department's ability to promote junior faculty members. Junior faculty members simply didn't have the time to develop the required publication record. Although MRU is a research university and the university's academic handbook from the 1970s clearly states that research is an important promotion criteria, the department never developed norms that would help its junior faculty allocate time for research. Staffing problems such as Dr. Glee's abrupt retirement from the chair position routinely trumped junior faculty research needs, such as Ms. Treadwell's need to have light teaching and administrative duties.

After Dr. Glee's retirement and death in the early 1990s, her successors sensed change in the department's atmosphere. The emphasis on student support has declined and new faculty cohorts are, in their words, "more professionalized." More recent recruits come from strong Ph.D. programs or have already earned tenure elsewhere, giving them the experience needed to succeed in the research university environment. Recent junior faculty hires have more clearly understood that success at MRU depends on scholarly output, as well as quality teaching. The curriculum has changed with its new faculty, resembling more closely a focused interdisciplinary program, rather than a survey of the Black experience organized around topics such as the Civil Rights movement.

Since the 1970s, students have changed demographically, socially, cognitively, and psychologically. Also, faculty members believe that black students are now less radical, less challenging in the classroom, and they make fewer demands of the department. Older faculty members can remember class sessions when students would openly challenge their authority in classroom and assert their political opinion. One faculty member reported to me that black Muslims enjoyed his class because he was comfortable with their confrontational styles. This sort of radicalism is now less frequent. There are now fewer demands on the department for Black student support, although many still feel the department should play a vital role in advising black students. Student demography has changed as well. Significant numbers of non-black students now take courses in the department and students are more willing to declare Black Studies as a double major. Both changes lessen the department's obligation to closely mentor undergraduate students. Overall, this had a predictable effect: junior faculty had more time for research.

Although the department is now better prepared to mentor its faculty through the tenure process and students are less demanding, the department has still found it difficult to expand its program. Early in its history, some administrators proposed merging Black Studies with related programs such as urban studies or to assign some of its core courses to other academic units. Later attempts to establish a master's program and a joint Ph.D.

with Speech and Drama never came to fruition because the department's faculty members were mostly lecturers and assistant professors. In comparison with other programs, the department has not developed beyond its initial role as an undergraduate program. In 2004, there is still no master's degree program or significant links to any of the university's doctoral programs.

Discussion

Dr. Glee successfully cultivated the department's standing by hiring qualified scholars. However, MRU's department didn't develop its potential as a center for scholarship because the department failed to assign its administrative tasks in ways that would allow junior faculty members to establish themselves as researchers. The weak faculty presence meant that the department never developed a reputation within the university that would allow it to develop a graduate program. In later years, the changing student population lessened the mentoring load within the department, which allowed some junior scholars to earn tenure. The appointment of more senior scholars also helped lessen the administrative load placed on junior faculty.

Discussion Questions

1. MRU's Black Studies Department experienced problems recruiting and promoting junior faculty members. What theories of faculty recruitment and promotion would you draw upon to guide the decisions you might make? What factors facilitate the School, Department, and the campus to have tenuring expectations different from other departments?
2. An important theme in the case study is the Department's efforts to establish an identity distinct from the "activist" identity associated with the protests that brought Black Studies to the university. How would you advise the department chair with respect to this issue?
3. What theories of student support would you draw upon to design student support services that would relieve the Department of Black Studies from a perceived obligation to help minority students? How did the school and Black Studies department socialize and mentor junior faculty about the tenuring requirements?
4. How would you advise individual faculty members in their attempt to serve students while successfully building a case for tenure?
5. How would you advise black students who want to use the resources provided by the Department of Black Studies?

References

History of Black Studies

Carr, Greg Kimathi. (1998). *African philosophy of history in the contemporary era: Its antecedents and methodological implications for the African contribution to world history.* Doctoral dissertation. Department of Afro-American Studies, Temple University. Chapter 8 is a history of the idea of Black Studies.

The Academic Organization of Black studies

Hine, Darlene Clark (1990). Black studies: An overview. In *Three Essays—Black Studies in the United States*, New York: The Ford Foundation.
Rojas, Fabio. (2004). Social Movement, "Organizations and the Diffusion of African-American Studies". Manuscript. Department of Sociology. Indiana University, Bloomington.

Studies of Department Stability

Rojas, Fabio. (2004). "Embedding Durable Movement Outcomes in Organizations— The life and death of black studies in two American universities". Manuscript. Department of Sociology. Indiana University, Bloomington.

Recommended Readings

History of Black Studies

Alkalimat, Abdul. (1984). *Introduction to African-American: A people's college primer.* Chicago: *Twenty-first Century Books and Publications.* (Chapter 1, Pages 1–30).
Asante, Molefe and Ama Mazama. (2005). *Encyclopedia of black studies.* Philadelphia, PA: Temple University Press.
Crouchett, Earl. (1971). Early Black Studies Movements. *The Journal of Black Studies*, 2 (2): 189–199.
Orrick, William H. (1970). *College in crisis, A Report to the National Commission on the causes and prevention of violence.* London: Aurora Publishers. (Most thorough account that exists of the San Francisco State College Strike for Black Studies.)
Van Deburg, William. (1992). *New day in Babylon: The black power movement and American culture, 1965–1975.* Chicago: University of Chicago Press. (Chapter 3 is about the Black Student movement.)

The Academic Organization of Black studies

Conyers, James. (1994). *The evolution of African-American studies.* Lanham, Maryland: The University Press of America.
Ford, Nicholas Aaron. (1973). *Black studies: Threat or challenge.* Port Washington, NY: Kennikat Press.

Frye, Charles A. (1976). *The impact of Black studies on the curricula of three universities.* Washington, D.C.: University Press of America.

Huggins, Nathan Irving. (1985). *Afro-American studies: A report to the Ford foundation.* New York: The Ford Foundation.

Studies of Department Stability

Benjamin, Richard M. (1995). The revival of African-American studies at Harvard. *The Journal of Blacks in Higher Education,* 9: 60–67.

Cunningham, Jo Ann. (1991). Black studies programs: Reasons for their success and non-success from inception to the present. *National Journal of Sociology,* 5 (1)]: 19–41.

Small, Mario J. (1999). Departmental conditions and the emergence of new disciplines: Two cases in the legitimation of African-American studies. *Theory and Society,* 28 (5): 710.

Faculty Development

Goldsmith, John A., John Kolmos & Penny Schine Gold. (2001). *The Chicago guide to your academic career: A portable mentor for scholars from graduate school through tenure.* Chicago: The University of Chicago Press.

Jarvis, Donald K. (1991). *The faculty development handbook.* Modern Language Association of America.

Part IV Emerging Diversity Populations

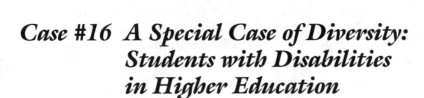

Case #16 A Special Case of Diversity: Students with Disabilities in Higher Education

Theresa A. Ochoa

Federal special education policy (e.g., IDEA and ADA) assures students with disabilities access to a free and appropriate public education and protection against discrimination. But while the doors to public education have been thrown open more than thirty years ago for students with disabilities at the elementary and secondary level, access to postsecondary education has come more slowly and at lower rates. What are the experiences of students with disabilities in higher education? How can institutions of higher education improve the experiences of students with disabilities in higher education? The author provides a brief description of the special education laws in higher education and their provisions in higher education; describes the services available in one institution; and highlights the dilemmas of teaching students with disabilities in higher education through cases.

A Special Case of Diversity: Students with Disabilities in Higher Education

Differences related to ethnicity, religion, and socioeconomics can, and often do, result in cruelty towards others, according to Hallahan and Kauffman (2003). But differences can also be an opportunity to enrich our interaction with others. Since 1973, the United States has instituted special education policy (i.e., Section 504 of the Rehabilitation Act, the Individuals with Disabilities Education Act, and the Americans with Disabilities Act) to minimize mistreatment of individuals with disabilities in public and private institutions. Despite more than thirty years of special education mandates that prohibit discrimination, students with disabilities continue to face obstacles that limit their participation in higher education. What experiences and challenges do students with disabilities face in higher education? More importantly, what can institutions of higher education do to minimize discrimination against students with disabilities?

The intent of this chapter is to provide a brief description of the special education laws in higher education and their provisions in higher education; to describe the services available in one institution; and highlight the dilemmas of teaching students with disabilities in higher education through cases. The chapter begins with a discussion on the number of students with disabilities in higher education.

Number of Students with Disabilities in Higher Education

If entrance to college is viewed as an indicator of success, then the IDEA, the most comprehensive federal special education policy that provides educational safeguards for students with disabilities in elementary and secondary schools, is in fact achieving its goal of making education accessible to individuals with disabilities. Because of IDEA, students with disabilities mainstreamed into public schooling since 1975 are now, albeit gradually, entering higher education (Otis-Wilborn, Cates, Proctor, & Kinnison, 1991). National figures provided by Thomas (2000) of first-year college students who indicated having disabilities in 1996 reached an all time high of 9% (a total of 140,142 students with disabilities) of the freshmen student body population, a rise from 2.6% in 1978. However, the 2001 College Freshmen with Disabilities report from the HEATH Resource Center, the same report used by Thomas (2000), indicates a drop in enrollment, showing that only about 6% of first-time freshmen attending college in the year 2000 reported having a disability. The 3% drop from 1996 to 2000 is disconcerting: What accounts for the drop in enrollment? Are those students attending two-year colleges, as suggested by the HEATH Resource Report? Despite fluctuation in the number of students with disabilities in higher education in any given year, one thing is certain, they are present in postsecondary education and there are laws that guarantee access to higher education.

Special Education Policy in Higher Education

Magdalene was diagnosed with ADHD and a severe reading disability in the third grade. She has highly supportive and involved parents, strong self-advocacy skills, and a clear understanding of her learning strengths and limitations. Her mother helped her with difficult reading assignments. In high school she received individualized math tutoring from her teacher, and she took advantage of academic resources provided by her school. She was admitted to a number of high-ranking public universities but opted to attend Cornfield University based on her understanding of the services available for students with disabilities.

Process Questions

- What are Magdalene's rights under Section 504 and ADA?
- If she is accustomed to IDEA's provisions, what is likely to be problematic for her at the university level regarding the accommodations she is likely to expect under IDEA that are no longer applicable at the University level?

Section 504 of the Rehabilitation Act of 1973 (Section 504) and the Americans with Disabilities Act (ADA) of 1990 are the two pieces of legislation that provide access to higher education and special education services to students with disabilities. Both Section 504 and ADA are basic civil rights provisions similar in language to Title VI, prohibiting racial discrimination (Scott, 2001). Under Section 504, a person with a disability is anyone who has a physical or mental impairment that substantially limits one or more major life activities, has a record of such impairment or is regarded as having such impairment. According to Thomas (2000), "with respect to higher education, a qualified student with a disability is one who is able to meet a program's admission, academic, and technical standards (i.e., all essential non-academic admission criteria) either with or without accommodations" (p. 250).

According to Scott (2001), non-discrimination against individuals with disabilities in higher education is not about 'disregarding' the disability or treating students as though they were like their counterparts without disabilities. Instead, Section 504 is about awareness of the wide range of individual abilities and handicapping conditions manifested in varying degrees and severity" (p. 399).

Differences between IDEA, Section 504, and ADA

It is important to understand the differences between IDEA, the primary federal education policy pertinent at the elementary and secondary levels, and Section 504 and ADA, as they relate to the educational provisions and requirements. Students who enter college with a special education diagnosis were served by IDEA through secondary school and they need to understand that their services and accommodations fall under Section 504 and ADA, not IDEA, in college. Compared to IDEA, ADA restricts services to 13 categories of exceptionality, Section 504 and ADA have a broader definition of a person with a disability. While Section 504 and ADA are broader and more inclusive, these laws protect students from discrimination but are more limited in their educational provisions. In other words, Section 504 and ADA provide less, not more, in terms of educational services. In contrast to IDEA's requirement that special educational services ensure a meaningful benefit from education, Section 504 and the ADA are not designed to provide individualized instruction. IDEA requires schools to provide supplemental aids and services without charge, including diagnostic testing and evaluation, specialized tutoring, books on tape, counseling, and note taking and testing accommodations. In comparison, postsecondary students, served under Section 504 and ADA are not entitled to specialized tutoring or counseling. Furthermore, the cost of the evaluation is the responsibility of the student. According to Simon (2001) students with disabilities at the postsecondary level are entitled only to reasonable accommodations in the form of academic adjustments, or auxiliary aids and services (e.g., readers, interpreters, real-time captioning, note takers, testing modifications, alternate text, priority registration, and audio taping of lectures).

Additionally, while the IDEA requires schools to identify students with disabilities and service them according to their individual needs, Section 504 and ADA place the responsibility of identification on the students. By law, then, professors and instructors are under no obligation to make modifications in their teaching until students identify themselves and indicate the types of services they need. Put differently, in colleges, students must self-identify, after they gain admission, in order to receive any services or accommodations from the university.

Special Education Services at Cornfield University

Rosa Isela is in your class. For the past three years, she has had difficulties in courses that require heavy reading. Biology and geography have been particularly challenging for her. When she takes a test, she finds that the questions on exams are tricky. When she reads, she has trouble understanding concepts, remembering information she knows she has read, and explaining herself to others verbally. Her writing skills are weak. She is frustrated in class because despite spending considerable amount of time studying for tests and writing assignments, she is still receiving low grades. As her instructor, you suspect she may have a learning disability and decide to approach her.

Process Questions

- What university services are available to her?
- What office can you refer her to for assistance?

- How might you approach her to inquire if she has an evaluation for special education or needs to seek one from the office of services for disabilities?
- What might you tell her are the benefits of having an evaluation to determine special education eligibility?
- How many students with disabilities are in your class?

Cornfield University provides a variety of services for students with disabilities. The starting place for services is the Office of Disability Services for Students (DSS) where students can obtain verification to show their instructors when and if instructional accommodations are required, arrange to have a note-taker, or are provided documentation of their disability that allows them access to assistive technology services. While the exact name for this office varies according to university, all universities have it and it is this office that provides information or services for students who need an initial educational evaluation to determine the existence of a disability.

The Adaptive Technology Center (ATC) at Cornfield University operates within the school library and offers students with disabilities services ranging from reading software programs like the *Kurzweil 3000* that transforms written text into speech for students with visual impairments or decoding difficulties and *Dragon Naturally Speaking*, a voice recognition program that allows students with visual physical impairments, capabilities to dictate verbal commands that are transformed into text. These software programs are installed on students' personal computers under a user license purchased by the university. Additionally, the ATC has a lending system whereby students without financial resources have access through a lending service to the software programs and a laptop. Other services include signing services for students with hearing impairments, and walking guides for students with visual impairments.

Among the most important services a university can provide to students with disabilities is an increase of awareness among university personnel about students with disabilities' learning characteristics and needs. According to Thomas (2000) professors, administrators, and staff will need awareness and skills training as they encounter students with disabilities. Professors will need to understand the characteristics of students with disabilities in their courses, the policies of their university regarding students with disabilities, as well as the accommodations the law requires them to make for students with disabilities.

If the intent in not merely to meet the letter of the law but its spirit, then professors who know that many students with disabilities find it difficult to disclose that they need accommodations, can facilitate the process through a combination of statements included in the syllabus about disabilities and his or her approach to making modifications. Additionally, the syllabus may contain the phone number for the center for students with disabilities in their university.

Considerations about Special Education Accommodations

Carrie, an education major has significant challenges in her teaching field experience. She was unable to read out loud from a fifth grade reading level book when her supervising teachers handed a book over to her; she had difficulty explaining directions and answering student questions about the directions for the math problems she had developed, and made computational mistakes when correcting her students' work. Despite hard work on her part she is not passing. The supervising faculty member and teacher are in a dilemma considering her rights as an individual with disabilities and their responsibility for the students she will teach.

Process Questions

- What accommodations should be made for pre-service professionals with disabilities (like Carrie) who are unable to meet the essential requirements of their program of study?
- At what point is the accommodation made for pre-service teachers with disabilities (like Carrie) diminishing their ability to meet the challenges of their profession?
- As a professional educator, what are your responsibilities to the students Carrie (or teachers like her) will teach?

As noted by Gilbert (1998), one of the hallmarks of learning disabilities is difficulties in academic skills and performance. All occupations have requirements and essential components and most individuals, either before or after they enter an occupation consider what is required of them to succeed. A significant number of students with disabilities consider careers in education. Gilbert (1998) reported that in 1996, 9.2% of secondary students with disabilities had aspirations of becoming teachers.

Certainly, there are benefits to having diversity in the teaching force (McGee & Kauffman, 1989), and as Otis-Wilborn et al. (1991) have pointed out, the benefits parallel those of having teachers from minority cultural backgrounds by serving as role models for their students to follow. Additionally, they may have a greater understanding of the challenges their students face and can provide academic and emotional support because they can identify with the students on a more personal level. Nonetheless, there are also potential concerns in having students with disabilities as educators.

In conclusion, by law, universities have the responsibility to assist students with disabilities to pursue any educational career they are qualified to enter. Students with disabilities will be better served if their instructors at the university level understand the legal requirements of special education law, the services available for students with disabilities in their institution, and possess an understanding of the characteristics of the students they teach and the skills and inclination to make modifications without compromising the preparation of students with disabilities for their future occupation. Consider the last question of the chapter: What is the likelihood that you would be accused of discrimination against a student with a disability?

References

Americans with Disabilities Act of 1990, 42, USC 12102.

Gilbert, S.L. (1998). Another type of diversity: A student teacher with a learning disability. *Qualitative Studies in Education*, 11 (2), 323–340.

Hallahan, D.P. & Kauffman, J.M. (2003). *Exceptional learners: Introduction to special education* (9th ed.). Boston, MD: Allyn and Bacon, Chapters 3 & 13.

HEATH Resource Center. (2001). College freshmen with disabilities: A biennial statistical profile. Washington, DC: American Council on Education.

IDEA Amendments of 1997, Pub. L. No. 105–17, 111 Stat. 37.

McGee, K.A. & Kauffman, J.M. (1989). Educating teachers with emotional disabilities: A balance of private and public interests. *Teacher Education and Special Education*, 12 (3), 110–116.

Otis-Wilborn, A.K., Cates, D., Proctor, T., & Kinnison, L. (1991). Preparing students with disabilities as special educators. *Teaching Education*, 4 (1), 89–101.

Rehabilitation Act of 1973, Section 504, PL 93–112.

Scott, S.S. (2001). Coming to terms with the "otherwise qualified" student with a learning disability. *Journal of Learning Disabilities*, 23 (7), 398–405.

Simon, J.A. (2001). Legal issues in serving postsecondary students with disabilities. *Topics in Language Disorders*, 21 (2), 1–16.

Thomas, S.B. (2000). College students and disability law. *The Journal of Special Education*, 33 (4), 248–257.

Case #17 "Speaking Out" in the University: A Case Study of Basic Skills Students and Their Teacher Enacting a Critical Literacy

MIDGE MADDEN

Class ends but three students stay. Tamica bangs her fist on the desk. "We need to change things, Dr. M. These basic skills courses just don't work! They don't *speak* to us. They don't give a chance to really get into our learning. We need to think more about what is happening in our world . . . we want to talk about prejudice, racism, and why we are always discriminated against if we're black or Puerto Rican. I think it's only if we talk about these things that we can work together to solve them. We must . . ."

Nicole angrily interrupted, "I hate talking about discrimination and racism. It seems that anymore that's all we hear. I'm sick of being blamed for everything—I'm not racist."

Katina burst out, "Well, you're not the one being looked at suspiciously at stores in the malls. You can go anywhere and not fear being discriminated against because you're white!"

Nicole muttered, "Oh, forget it. I'm not going to listen to this," and left.

Tamica shrugged. "Come on, Katina, let's go." Her parting words were, "How we going to get anywhere if no one wants to face facts? Being in college is really no different. And in a way it's worse. We're thought of as less not only because we're black or Puerto Rican, but because we have to take basic skills courses—courses that shout out *You're dumb*! All we want to do is succeed!"

~~~

This is a case study of my classroom and my evolving understanding of what it means to teach literacy critically. In this study, I narrate my attempt to create a democratic classroom with college basic readers and writers. I sought to create a space wherein I, as well as my students, could freely come to voice and examine ways in which we perceived ourselves as empowered or powerless to control events in our lives. I envisioned a classroom where issues hitherto unspoken, such as race and inequity, or more specific to all my students and to my concerns, positions of marginality created by basic skills programs, could be safely explored. Freire's (1988) critical pedagogy intrigued me for it described a practice in which excluded and often silenced groups could challenge dominant approaches to learning.

Furthermore, I had a goal of "constructively disrupting the culture of the university" (Lytle and Cochran-Smith, 1995) by trying to change the university's stance towards basic skills programs and the students placed within them. Listening to the expressions of marginality voiced by many of my minority students, I knew that there must be a better way to teach reading and writing to these students. Cognizant that students in my courses—often their first college classroom experience—came to class with questions, fears, and illusions about gender, race, and inequities, I wanted a classroom that would privilege insider knowledge and become a place of contact between the text/ interpretive world and the worlds beyond the classroom, a classroom that put basic skills and issues of marginality and other at the center.

The Research Setting

During the course of the study, I listened to the institution—the official voice of Bracey—and to the academic departments responsible for writing basic skills curricula. I heard as well the stories of Special Support staff and faculty. And I listened to my students.

The Institution

In 1996 Bracey College was at a crossroads in its history. Begun in 1890 as a "normal school" for the training of teachers, Bracey was formerly known for many years as Godwin State College. In the 1980s through a challenge grant, GSC began to broaden its vision towards becoming a regional university. Then, in the 1990s, benefactors Lawrence and Wilma Bracey's generous gift to advance the development of the college further widened its horizons. Not only did the name change to Bracey College, but now an Engineering School could be established, the communications programs could be developed into a School of Communications, and the goal of reaching university status came within reach.

When I and others in the college community read *Beyond 2000: The Bracey Vision*, many of us in the college community agreed that Bracey's vision statement named admirable and ambitious dreams; but we wondered how and if these dreams might translate into reality. Against this backdrop of future visions, fellow colleagues and I observed that real change in the Bracey community moved slowly. The Bracey College of 1994 and 1995 wherein I conducted my study contrasted in many ways with its newly voiced vision; moreover, this very dissonance between the dream [of learning communities, critical thinkers and co-constructed curriculums] and the reality created important tensions that effected and impacted my study.

Reading and Communication Departments

Concerning basic skills courses, both the reading and communications departments made it clear that their primary interest revolved around high numbers of passing students. Acceptable test scores and grammatically finished essays indicated good teaching and successful learning in the Bracey basic skills program. Basic skills instructors were generally left to their own pedagogical interpretations of what might best help struggling college readers and writers. New and different pedagogies were not encouraged, but neither were they discouraged as long as they "worked" and students passed the courses.

The Office of Testing and Basic Skills

As the basic skills reading coordinator, I served as the liaison between the reading department that designed the syllabi for basic reading courses and hired basic skills faculty and the Office of Testing/Basic Skills whose responsibility was to test and place freshmen students in basic skills courses. Although I shared the common goal of helping these students achieve academic success in college, there existed some important differences in my beliefs about students and literacy learning from those of the Office of Testing and Basic Skills.

Testing and Basic Skills

The Testing and Basic Skills office labeled the basic skills student as somehow deficient, requiring remedial assistance. This view of students was supported by Bracey College's definition of basic skills that read in part:

> . . . *Students with measurable deficiencies are required to complete successfully special basic skills courses to remediate those deficiencies.*

I had long questioned this model of the deficient learner in need of remediation. Having worked with struggling readers and writers for fifteen years, I wondered why they must first experience a sense of failure and asked if this failure was prerequisite to eventual success. And, if so, at what price? Did we allow these students into college and then fail to allow them full participation (Rose, 1985)? At Bracey, students enrolled in basic reading and writing courses were first admitted to the college; then, they were informed that they would be required to take the NJCBSPT to place out of (or into) basic skills courses. Further, the Office of Testing and Basic Skills accepted a single test score on the New Jersey College Basic Skills Placement Test as a valid indicator of reading competency. Students who scored below the predetermined cutoff score were placed in non-credit basic skills courses which did not count toward the minimum number of semester hours needed to complete the student's major and/or degree, but required regular tuition. This practice elicited feelings of marginalization and frustration for many entering freshmen. As one student remarked, "It's like being tracked all over again, only this time we have to use our college loans and pay to be called "basic skills". It doesn't seem right to me."

I argued that the college needed other ways of determining reading and writing proficiencies beyond a single test score. And, although other basic reading and writing teachers agreed with me, we were part time and overpowered. State and college policy mandated that the New Jersey College Basic Skills Placement Test (NJCBSPT) score determine proficiency in reading.

Students

In considering the breakdown of students enrolled in basic skills courses, we see that this group of students enrolled in Level A reading [only Level A students were involved in my study] was comprised entirely of EOF/MAP students, special admits, and English as Second Language (ESL) foreign students. These students historically had lower GPA's and SAT scores than the traditional students; additionally, they comprised the largest student group requiring basic skills courses. Ninety-seven percent (152 out of 156) failed to achieve a passing score on the NJCBSPT and were placed in at least one basic skills course, but usually these students needed to take two or more remedial courses. Thus, these students were those who, although admitted, were most certain to be denied full acceptance at the university.

Such was the context in which I conducted my study: an institution in transition, reading and communication departments who, for the most part, conceived of teaching literacy as learning skills and strategies, and a diverse [and divided] student population. Working with marginalized students while the college pursued more elite academic status and facing my own vision—one of academic success for *all* students—I began to understand the difficulties ahead in trying to achieve this goal.

The Curriculum

In the course content, I eschewed traditional "how to improve reading and writing" texts and we examined oppression across race and gender. Together students and I selected texts that included news articles, poems, short essays and stories, and a memoir. As we read, wrote, and talked, black and white issues surfaced, but sexual abuse and women's powerlessness dominated much class time as well. We also entered into a semester-long study of the basic skills program at Bracey, its assumptions about learning, and its implications for those classified as basic skills.

Secondly, out-of-class meetings became an important component of the course, numbering fourteen [12 involved the focus group]. The table [found in the appendix] provides lists of the texts read in each class, examples of written responses and descriptions of out-of-class meetings in the course.

Research Processes

I began collecting data by listening more closely to faculty and administration. I collected college brochures and documents that would provide me with deeper insights into the workings of the college. Statements of the college vision, memorandums, and reports of committee findings all deepened my understanding of the context. I also talked closely with EOF counselors, other reading and writing faculty, and basic skills staff. I questioned students about basic skills courses, both those enrolled in my classes and former students.

As reading basic skills coordinator, I also had access to unpublished reports on racial and ethnic distributions of basic skills populations at Bracey, attendance, test and academic transcripts, reading departmental meeting minutes, and Basic Skills staff meetings and faculty decisions. All of this served to support or contrast the descriptive data that I collected within the classroom context.

A critical piece of data became my reflective journal that I began in 1994 and continue, now, in 2004. Other artifacts included audiotapes [class talk, student conferences, and focus group sessions] and student writing [response journals, drafts, and final portfolios].

The analysis of data for this study occurred in three phases: ongoing analysis from 1994–1996, topical, thematic sorting from 1996–1998, and portraiture analysis and writing from 1998–2000.

During Phase I, I used a topical, thematic sorting, searching for key ideas and emergent themes around which I wrote my first drafts. During the second phase of analysis, I conducted a topical, cross-cut analysis. Finally, during the third phase, I changed the organization of the study from topical to chronological. And I used the methodology of portraiture (Lawrence-Lightfoot, 1997) to write the story of my classroom.

The Story

> *Acting as if our classroom were a safe space in which democratic dialogue was possible and happening did not make it so . . . . We needed classroom practices that confronted the power dynamics inside and outside of our classroom that made democratic dialogue impossible.*

(Ellsworth, 1989, p.313)

Teaching to transgress. Making connections. Voicing conflicts. Students as teachers. Teacher as learner. Impassioned outbursts and quiet reflections. The power of literacy.

This narrative chronicles how fifteen students and I negotiated a course, striving to reach a practice, such as described above. A co-constructed curriculum, shared authority, connecting with students in new ways, teaching for change. I believed strongly in all of these abstractions. And I also understood the challenge.

"O Yes": March 8, 1996

March 8, 1996 had been quite a day! A moment in the spotlight for four focus group members. *Their* opportunity to be heard. The University of Pennsylvania Ethnography Forum.

We glanced at one another as we faced an audience of fifteen teachers. Positioning ourselves in a semi-circle at the front of the room, we were ready to go. "We're here, today, to tell you about our experiences as researchers. This past fall we constructed and critiqued our basic reading and writing course . . ." Shi-Kia confidently began, and I breathed a sigh of relief. I watched the audience as Monique, Minerva, and Brenda performed dramatic readings and talked about what they had learned. And I thought back over these past few months . . . *We had compiled students' surveys, searched for important findings, and planned the presentation. We had written a script. We had practiced again and again, working on proper articulation and expression of our parts. . . .* Shi-Kia's resonant voice reciting her poem brought me abruptly back to the present:

Pain

First image, bright, smart, successful, making it
As you succeed, problems: special, under prepared,
Retard, incapable . . . WHAT? Unable . . .
Mind confused over a test
But under circumstances didn't do your best.
Anger, upset, maybe a little depressed.

Can't understand why you failed a test.
Words linger around the bias request.
The curve of the bell . . . OOPS!
I mean the bell curve might explain the rest—
A label stamped on you.
Making you feel a little blue because you
want an education to compete too.
What can I do to change the fall?
Speaking to you, may help too,
But deep down inside I cry to you.

The audience clapped and I beamed with pride for my students. The questions began. Monique and Shi-Kia took over. "What are your next steps?" asked an older black woman from the back. "Are you going to try to make some changes at your school?" Monique answered with a list of ideas that we had talked about as possibilities. She stood poised and in control. She had committed these ideas to memory and she spoke them with conviction.

A young white man, peering intently through wire-rimmed frames, nodded repeatedly. He looked at Shi-Kia. "Can you talk some more about your feelings as a basic skills student?" Shi-Kia leaned comfortably against the blackboard, arms crossed, and eager to speak. Beaming in her bright red sweater, her vibrant personality shone through as she spoke passionately of her feelings of being an outsider at Bracey. As the session wound to a close, a basic skills teacher at a Philadelphia high school connected with Monique, eager to have the focus group visit her school and share their stories with high school students.

The audience clapped again. It was over. And Brenda, Shi-Kia, Monique and Minerva exited, heads held high.

An Afterward

Monique, Dave and I sat around a small table. Wearing earphones and wired with small microphones, we smiled nervously at one another. Denis Mercier, the radio producer, mouthed "Ready?" His technician whispered, "Testing, one, two, three . . . you're on!" "Welcome to Community Voices," began Denis. "Today's guests will talk about students here at the college, basic skills students whose voices until now have remained unheard. Briefly, let me introduce our guests: Dave Townsend, a writing instructor, Midge Madden, the reading basic skills coordinator, and Monique Horn, a basic skills student. Monique, why don't you tell us about your research this semester?" As Monique outlined the role of the focus group and its findings, I wondered who was listening to this broadcast. *Would we reach the right people? Would our appeal to other faculty to help us make basic skills courses count towards graduation be heard? We had found a public forum at the college, but would anything come of our "going public"?*

The Ethnography Forum, the "Community Voices" broadcast, and the Bracey Spring Research Seminar represented three different forums that we had used to make our concerns public in the months following the reading/writing course. The focus group presentation had been a success: intrinsically for me, filled with pride for my students, and extrinsically for my students, basking in the approval of an interested audience. But feedback from the radio broadcast had never been received, and no faculty had come forward to work with us. And in the Research Seminar, faculty had listened politely but had argued that their courses "really couldn't link with basic readers and writers." Despite a combined student-teacher effort, little tangible change had resulted.

That April, a month after the radio show, Monique abruptly left school and moved to Virginia. The following fall Brenda did not return to Bracey, electing to study at a nearby community college. And Ryan and Shi-Kia failed basic writing. [Ryan would eventually be dismissed from college two years later because he had not passed basic writing.] I returned to teach at Bracey for another year, but spent little time there. I resigned as basic skills coordinator in June 1997. Shi-Kia, Minerva and Brian still remain at Rowan in 1999.

Conclusions of the Study

Two major themes emerged as findings of this study: 1) sharing power or negotiating curriculum and 2) exploring the relationship between teaching critically and literacy.

Sharing Power: Evolving Understandings of Critical Teaching

In this basic skills reading and writing course, I had articulated two goals: achieving democratic dialogue in the classroom and negotiating the course with my students. I had learned that the teacher's moves were critical and that I would have to understand the power dynamics inside and outside of the classroom to make open talk possible. Assuming control of much of the class discussions, all of the reading assignments, and all of the requirements for the course at the beginning, I had not begun on the right foot. But I backtracked as the course continued, slowly sharing control with the Focus Group and encouraging all students to voice ideas and opinions.

The creation of a Focus Group (FG) distinguishes this course as quite different from other basic skills courses that I had taught. At its inception,

I had no idea where the notion of a small outside group of student-researchers had come from. But I knew that my students and I would need outside opportunities to form closer relationships if a sharing of power could honestly take place. Once the FG began, the dynamics of the course radically shifted. And power sharing was born—a "homemade, hands-on invention" (Shor, 1996, p.123). Seven students and I met every other week for one to two hours. We chose topics of discussion, made reading selections for the class, interviewed basic skills students and tabulated results, and collaboratively wrote a presentation for the Ethnography Forum at the University of Pennsylvania [although only four students actually attended]. It became imperative to insure that the Focus Group would see themselves as legitimate—as co-researchers, working with me to plan and critique meaningful class practices. By the end of the course, I wrote, "The FG has tasted power and I'm hard put to gain it back!" Although half of the class had joined the FG, rather than allow the remaining students to feel like outsiders, the FG drew their classmates into heated discussions about racist and sexist practices and freely shared ideas spawned in FG meetings.

A sharing of power happened in this course; students began speaking heatedly about unfairness, making connections of racial and class subordination with basic skills identity. The FG pushed us to unpack the assumptions behind Bracey's basic skills program and they pushed for some sort of a critical agenda to change the system of placement and assessment. In the end, despite a conference presentation, appearances on the college radio station, and a call to other faculty to link a credited course with ours, nothing changed. But, perhaps change was not the point. My students and I had learned together, side by side, to speak across differences and to believe in the power of ourselves.

Critical Teaching and Literacy

A second theme that emerged during my study became the relationship between teaching critically and literacy. As a basic reading and writing teacher, improving the understanding of literacy must, by the very nature of the subject, be of primary importance. Thus, I first held consistent notions about a critical literacy: A critical literacy is about teaching in the contact zone, making the classroom a place where "cultures meet, clash, and grapple with each other, often in contexts of highly asymmetrical relations of power" (Pratt, 1991, p.38). It is about seeing literacy as political, having an advocacy role, and connecting in multiple ways with racism and sexism and it is characterized by provocative, potentially inflammatory texts that demand serious wrestling with in order to fully understand. Texts rich in content that challenge the reader and provoke the writer to hard, painful

thought. My students experienced all of these things . . . *and* they all passed
the basic skills reading proficiency exam.

Power and Voice: Implications of Teaching Critically in a Basic Skills Classroom

Ira Shor (1996) speaks often of his classes as Siberia, alluding to what he
calls the students' instinctive reaction to crowd themselves into distant corner seats. He interprets this behavior as a socially constructed response to
unequal power and institutional authority. Like Shor's classes, my own basic
skills students often headed for the corner and back seats in the room.
They grudgingly had moved desks into a haphazard circle when asked, but
some invariably sought to remain outside—in the corner. Shor wonders if
he can change his windowless Siberia to a "constitutional convention"
where he and his students will share authority and power. I, too, had looked
around my basement classroom and asked my students, "What do you want
to get out of this course?"

I evoke the notion of classroom as Siberia to underscore the deeply
entrenched ideas of school and authority that my critical pedagogy pushed
against in my basic skills classroom. Not only was I faced with enacting an
untried, different pedagogy, but I had to "shake up" my students' perceptions of schooling and learning. As I talked about negotiating the course,
my students reacted initially to my invitations with bewilderment, confusion, and resistance. Understanding that years of being in classrooms had
taught them to expect teacher-talk, imposed curriculum, and a prescribed
way of learning, I sought ways to change these deeply ingrained beliefs.
Additionally, since I knew this notion of sharing power was new to my students, I realized that in the beginning it would have to be my agenda and
regardless of how I presented the idea, students would see it as teacher-
imposed. At the same time, my critical pedagogy called for explicit anti-bias
content and a different way of reading and writing.

Looking back, I had begun the course with my notion of a critical practice—reading, writing, and discussing challenging texts about racism and
sexism in a dialogic (Shor, 1992, 1996) classroom where all would engage
intellectually with tough issues and consider possibilities for change. Interestingly, I had not foreseen my students' passionate convictions about the
need for change in the basic skills program; and, in this sense, the agenda
for our class *had* become student-imposed.

Imagining such a dialogic classroom had been exciting. Putting this
idea into practice had become exhausting and difficult. In the end, I had
realized the critical importance of power and voice—it was only when ways
were found to share power *and* to enable all to speak that such a critical
practice would work.

Course Curriculum

Concepts/Issue	Texts	Essay Topics	Outsides Meetings
Meaning of Oppression	**Novel: It Makes Me Wanna Holler**, Nathan McCall	Compare Makes Me Wanna Holler and *A New Vision of Masculinity*.	Poetry Reading and Lecture by Linda McCarriston (class)
DuBois/ The Color Line: Still Present	**Short Stories:** *Requiem* *Tough Boyz*		Lunch at "Doc Street"
Poverty and Race	**Articles and essays:** *Million Man March*	Compare the video, *There Are No Children Here*, *Oppression*, and *Makes Me Wanna Holler*.	Art exhibit, *Life Sentences*, at Eastern State Penitentiary (class)
Inner City Inequity	*Flight to the Burbs*		Lecture at UPenn Sonia Nieto/ Equity and Diversity
White Flight "Making It" in the White Man's World: Who Pays the Price?	*A Room of Your Own: Dubois House*	Argue, using specific examples to show how the media does/does not tell the truth. Argue for/against "Bring your daughter to work" day.	Dinner at my home (Focus group) 9 focus group sessions at Tutoring Center
Black Separatism	**Gender Images, anthology Articles and essays:** *Oppression*		
M/F Differences	*Masculine/Feminine*		
Sexual Harassment/Abuse	*New Vision of Masculinity Victims*	Argue pros/cons for high school nursery to help teenage mothers.	Ethnography Forum, UPenn (Focus group)
Men, Aggression and Violence	*For Women, China is all Too Typical* **Poems:**		Dinner at "Olive Garden" (Focus group)
Basic skills students: A Marginal Population	*Eva Mary, Eva McCarriston* College documents and brochures	Discuss the perception of beauty in college.	
Students' Critiques of Basic Skill Courses			
Advocating for Change: Issues of Power	Past students' interview and Questionnaires Results *City on a Hill*, James Traub Chronicle of Higher Education		

References

Books

Cochran-Smith, M. & Lytle, Susan (Eds.). (1993). *Inside-Outside: Teacher Research and Knowledge.* New York: Teachers College Press.

Ellsworth, E. (1992). Why doesn't this feel empowering? Working through the repressive myths of critical pedagogy. In *Feminisms and Critical Pedagogy.* New York: Routledge.

Freire, P. (1998). *Teachers as Cultural Workers.* Boulder, CO: Westview Press.

Lawrence-Lightfoot, S. (1997). *The Art and Science of Portraiture.* San Franscisco, CA: Jossey-Bass.

Rose, M. (1990). *Lives on the Boundary.* New York: Penguin Books.

Shor, Ira. (1992). *Empowering Education.* Chicago: The University of Chicago Press.

Shor, Ira. (1996). When *Students Have Power.* Chicago: The University of Chicago Press.

Journals

Pratt, M.L. (1991). Arts of the contact zone, *Profession 91* (pp. 33–40). New York: Modern Languge Association.

Case #18 Student-Athlete
or Athlete-Student?

ADRIENNE LESLIE-TOOGOOD, MARILYN KAFF
AND TERESA MILLER

This case describes a student-athlete in football at a mid-western university. There is a conscious intent to illustrate both the unique aspects of being a student-athlete, and the distinctive elements of this individual person. Various spheres of Anthony's life are included, which all interact to create his particular college experience. These spheres include: his past life experience (providing the lens through which he views college), the campus community, academics, sports and family/social support. Short vignettes follow depicting interaction in these areas.

Case Narrative

Anthony is a twenty-year-old African American male. He comes from Los Angeles, California. He is the oldest of three children, with two younger twin sisters. His mother is an executive with a major insurance company and his father is deceased. Anthony loves football and has been playing since the age of eight. He was a star running back for his high school team and led them to two consecutive high school championships. He was recruited to play football at a large mid-western university. Unfortunately, his grade point average from high school was too low to qualify for acceptance at the school, so Anthony attended a community college in order to improve his academic skills, and then transferred to the university.

Academic Characteristics

At present, Anthony is a sophomore. He struggles to maintain a GPA of 2.0. He loves being a student athlete, but because academic work is hard for him, he puts off writing papers and then becomes despondent and skips class. His coach has repeatedly told Anthony to take care of business on and off the field. Anthony is close to losing his eligibility due to poor academic grades.

Anthony enjoys school and likes learning although he reports some difficulty with schoolwork. He reports having difficulty with classes that involve long and detailed lectures. He can read and comprehend the material in his classes, but has a great deal of difficulty organizing his work and putting his thoughts on paper.

Anthony has been identified as having a learning disability in written language. He is a visual learner and does best when presented with visual materials paired with auditory input. His academic functioning is well below what would be predicted by his aptitude. He has difficulty reading but is capable of understanding what he reads. He will require extensive accommodations and modifications in his written work in order to succeed academically.

The Admissions Process

Sarah has lived in this town for her entire life. She grew up as a huge fan of the sports team and always wanted to attend the university. She was very involved on campus and considered it the best years of her life. After she graduated from college, a job was open in the office where she worked as a student worker. In her position, she is required to make admissions decisions. As a State University admissions officer, she has straightforward guidelines regarding admissions. Admissions decisions are based almost entirely on high school GPA and SAT scores. There are no special points given for areas of diversity or legacy. The one area in which she is required to make some exceptions is when working with applicants flagged by coaches. Over time and after review of thousands of transcripts, she has noticed that many of these applicants may meet the minimum requirements, but often appear significantly less prepared for the university coursework than the other students.

Media Day

Anthony and his teammates are in high spirits. The new season's Media Day was dawning. The program included running a few plays and then signing autographs for their fans. The church he attends has a program that matches players with members of the church as "adopted families" during the player's stay at the university. His new "little sister" would be one of the fans at this Media Day, and he was anxious to see her again. The coaches had been preparing the team, stressing the importance of team solidarity, as well as respect for each other and the community. Everyone was nervous about public speaking and anxious to get these preliminaries over with so they could get the season started.

Following the scrimmage, he waited on the specified line as the fans raced out to the field. He noticed that there was a long line of fans in front of him. He was a bit embarrassed until he saw his little sis, Ashley. He calmed down, and started signing. The first student asked if he would sign, "To Paul, the future star linebacker for the team," and he did that, but was worried about his handwriting and spelling. What if he could not spell their names? Ashley was signature #4, and she just grinned as he signed her football. Forty-eight autographs later, he finished, proud that he was able to get their names right; tired, but happy with his eager fans.

The Classroom

Dr. Johnston teaches the Introduction to Sociology Class. She has made it clear to all of her students that she places strong emphasis on class participation. Her expectations include regular attendance, and participation in the electronic discussion board. She stresses that students who miss more than four classes will have their grades penalized.

The electronic discussion board enables students to engage in an ongoing conversation in and out of the classroom, and to draw connections between concepts and debates over the course of the semester. Students participate on the discussion board in two ways: (1) as a discussant; and (2) as a respondent. In the role of class discussant, students will write a short memo (roughly two to three pages), analyzing and critiquing (not merely summarizing) the assigned readings from class, posting it to the discussion board, presenting arguments briefly to the class (roughly five minutes), and responding to questions and comments.

A team of three discussants will present on the same readings, so groups will meet with Dr. Johnston as a group prior to the class session to discuss memos. Dr. Johnston strongly encourages students to meet on their own and prepare comments in collaboration (e.g., One will provide the overall analysis of the issues, another can address the strengths, the other focus on the weaknesses; one can agree, the other disagree with certain key debates). Each student will, however, submit, an individually written memo.

Dr. Johnston is sitting at her office trying to consider what she should do about Anthony. She thought she had made it clear to him that he needed to work on his writing, turn things in on time and show up for class. She genuinely likes the soft-spoken young man. He works diligently, but does not always show up for class. In addition, he has asked for extension for his discussant assignment twice during the semester. Anthony's discussant group is upset with him.

She met with Anthony after the first incident and talked to him about the concerns of his classmates. He said that his practice schedule was getting in the way, but once the fall schedule started, things would get better. Anthony asked Dr. Johnston to cut him some slack. They mutually agreed that Anthony would be assigned to another discussion group that includes another African American student and an older student. Dr. Johnston believed that the other students would be a positive influence on Anthony. She could not have been more wrong. Both students complained to her that once again, Anthony failed to show up at the agreed upon meeting to discuss their memos. When he did come, it was obvious he had not understood the readings and the memo itself was so poorly written as to be unreadable. To top it off, the students complained that Anthony expected them to help him fix his memo, since he was leaving that morning for an out-of-town game.

Football

Anthony cannot believe the level of play of the other guys on his team. He was always THE player on the team, but now he just feels like one of many. He is not used to feeling this way and is not sure what to do. He does not know how to tell this to his friends and family who idolize him. For the first time he begins to wonder if he will make it to the next level.

The Coach

Coach Anderson has been coaching football for many years. He is an extremely successful coach and has good support from the alumni. He is very demanding and has little time to deal with the athletes, as he relies heavily on his assistant coaches for the day-to-day interactions. The only thing he requires, is a report at mid-semester on his players' progress.

The Academic Advisor

Jim is an academic advisor. He finds that most of his day is eaten up by ensuring that his athletes are eligible. The football coach is pretty demanding, and he often feels the brunt of things when he has an athlete on the brink of eligibility. As part of his job, he sends mid-semester evaluations out to all professors who have student-athletes in their courses. To his surprise, the feedback he received on Anthony is not good. He is frustrated because now he is going to have to provide this feedback to the Head Coach. He knows the Head Coach is busy, that Anthony is a blue-chipper, and that ultimately he is going to look bad once again.

Discussion Question

1. What are the implications of selective admissions for student-athletes on college campuses? What are the responsibilities of the institution?
2. Engstrom and Sedlacek (1991) found that students judged student-athletes negatively simply because they were an athlete. What can student affairs administrators do in order to educate both the general student body and student-athletes?
3. What can be done to facilitate the dialogue between student-athletes, their families, coaches, athletic administrators, and student affairs professionals?
4. Student-athletes who secure an athletic scholarship have invested a lot of time and energy in sport from a very young age. They may be prepared and motivated athletically and less so toward academics. What is the role of the student affairs professional in working with student-athletes? Related to this, student-athletes may select a school primarily for athletic reasons. What do you feel are the implications for the student-athletes who select a school primarily for athletics?
5. What is the institution's responsibility in educating student-athletes about career possibilities other than professional sport? What programming should be implemented to ensure that student-athletes develop the skills they need to function in life after college?
6. What is the responsibility of the student-athletes in their education? What is the role of the institution?
7. Select one of the student development theories in the chapter 2 paper as a framework to discuss this case.

Recommended Readings

Chickering, A.W., & Reisser, L. (1993). *Education and identity*. San Francisco, CA: Jossey-Bass.

Cross, W.E., Jr. (1978). The Thomas and Cross models of psychological Nigrescence: A review. *Journal of Black Psychology*, 5(1) 13–31.

Engstrom, C.M., & Sedlacek, W.E. (1991). A study of prejudice toward university student-athletes. *Journal of Counseling and Student Development*, 70 (1) 189–193.

Solorzano, D. G., & Yosso, T.J. (Fall, 2001). From racial stereotyping and deficit discourse toward a critical race theory in teacher education. *Multicultural Education*, 9 (1), 2–8. [].

For Further Discussion

Hollis, L.P. (2001–2002). Service ace? Which academic services and resources truly benefit student athletes. *Journal of College Student Retention*, 3(3), 265–284.

Howard-Hamilton, M.F., & Watt, S.K. (2001). *Student services for athletes*. San Francisco, CA: Jossey-Bass.

Kuh, G.D., Schuh, J.H., Whitt, E.J., & Associates (1991). *Involving colleges: Successful approaches to fostering student learning and development outside the classroom*. San Fransisco, CA: Jossey-Bass.

Nishimoto, P.A. (1997). Touchdowns and term papers: Telescoping the college student-athlete culture. *College Student Affairs Journal*, 16 (2), 96–103.

Parham, W.D. (1993). The intercollegiate athlete: A 1990s profile. *The Counseling Psychologist*, 21 (3), 411–429.

Pascerella & Terenzini (1996). How college makes a difference: A summary. In F.K.Stage, G.L. Anaya, J.P. Bean, D. Hossler, & G.D. Kuh, G.D. (Eds.). *College students: The evolving nature of research*. Needham Heights, MA: Simon & Schuster.

Scales, J. (1991). African-American student-athletes: An example of minority exploitation in collegiate athletics. In E.F. Etzel, A.P. Ferrante, & J.W. Pinkney (Eds.). *Counseling college student-athletes: Issues and interventions*. Morgantown, WV: Fitness Information Technology

Schlossberg, N.K. (1989). Marginality and mattering: Key issues in building community. In D.C. Roberts (Ed.). *Designing campus activities to foster a sense of community* (New Directions for Student Services, No. 48, pp. 1–15). San Francisco, CA: Jossey-Bass.

Schulman, J.L., & Bowen, W.G. (2001). *The game of life: College sports and educational values*. New Jersey: Princeton University Press.

Simons, H.D., Rheenen, D.V., Covington, M.V. (1999). Academic motivation and the student athlete. *Journal of College Student Development*, 40 (2), 151–162.

Wolf-Wendel, L.E., Toma, J.D., & Morphew, C.C. (2001). How much difference is too much difference? Perceptions of gay men and lesbians in intercollegiate athletics. *Journal of College Student Development*, 42 (5), 465–479.

Young, B.D., & Sowa, C.J. (1992). Predictors of academic success for black student athletes. *Journal of College Student Development*, 33 (4) 318–324.

Case #19 Faith in the Academy: Developing Religious Diversity in a Judeo-Christian Dominant Culture

TED N. INGRAM

When we think about going away to college in search of knowledge and growth for becoming well-rounded students, we generally tend to think of growth in areas of intellectual and personal development, often omitting spiritual growth. This case study attempts to address the issue of religion or faith and how it impacts college student development. Some college students experience some turmoil as they attempt to adapt, adopt, and mediate the challenges of preparing for adult development. When developing new identities their values and faith can be navigators for certain actions.

With this in mind, a person's faith is an influential component in a young adult's life. Moreover, higher education practitioners should be instrumental in cultivating this phenomenon with the educational experience as it relates to a student's development on campus. Nash (2001) indicates that the ability to incorporate spirituality in the field of higher educational is a challenge most resisted by most faculty and administrators in higher education. The role of the faculty member in the promotion of religious diversity is essential in the promotion of cross-campus, multi-faith dialogue on religion. According to Nash (2001), faculty can be a positive force in enacting this project; they must shed their instinctive suspicions of students and others who are not ashamed to go public with assertions of strong religious belief. Faculty can encourage students with strong faith to create an environment or an organization where they can exercise their spirituality while on campus. Public institutions are the best venue to demonstrate a multi-faith society.

Faculty can introduce teaching and faith in the classroom and this union can also be supported by student affairs staff. Faculty and student affairs professionals' efforts should be collaborative and communal in contributing to the maturation of students. Furthermore, Nash (2001) posits that administrators and other professional staff are needed as well in the development of a living-learning community. The living-learning community of a residential state institution attempts to strengthen the interactions between student affairs administrators and faculty while offering development to its constituents.

Students are eager to explore and share the deep meaning and purposes they associate with their sense of calling and purpose yet find few opportunities to do so (Chickering, Stamm, & Dalton, 2004). Such evasion leads to a tense situation among students and cross-campus dialogue on religion; furthermore, spirituality will be terminated before it gets started. In order to prevent uncomfortable situations from reoccurring, educators must remain committed to the paradoxical educational principle that the very best way to teach students how to deal intelligently with religious dissent and compromise is to expose students to as much intense, divergent beliefs as possible. At times in academia there are limitations or avoidance placed on conversation relating to spirituality or religion.

Christian Privilege

When society thinks about religion it often refers to the mainstream religious organizations and often omits the less-popular faiths (Schlosser, 2003). Ironically, the United States is a multicultural society however, there is a constant presence of Christianity as the dominant religion (Schlosser, 2003). Christianity is so well accepted and embedded in Western culture, that other religions become suppressed.

For example in December walking through the mall, it is not uncommon to hear Christmas carols resonating throughout the halls, stores, and dressing rooms. Cashiers, sales persons, and mall personnel smile and extend a "Merry Christmas" when communicating with customers. in the large department store the cashier closes each transaction with "Merry Christmas".

Hardiman and Jackson (1997) feel that social oppression matrix combined with Christianity illustrates how Christian groups' privilege subconsciously or consciously denigrates another social group for its own gains. Christianity is being promoted as the norm and other smaller social groups are being interpreted as abnormal, thus causing followers of minority faiths to become skeptical in their search for truth and become doubtful in their own character.

After his frustrations are heightened with society, the agnostic student chooses to escape the small town mentality of the residents of Kenville by seeking refugee in his residence hall. Upon his return to the building he is greeted by red and gold bells cheerfully accenting the twenty-year-old building. While the student body, which has members of a dominant religion, agrees and happily admires the celebration of the Western tradition, the agnostic student is experiencing doubts about his practice.

The agnostic student is further confused and does not have an outlet to discuss his beliefs. The student begins to formulate questions as to why are they is no evidence of other beliefs being supported by the university. Why is he feeling alone and singled out for not having a strong religious platform? The stress of trying to find meaning and understanding has become a major contributor to the student's stress level. Without an educational environment that encourages discussion on religion it is possible the student may not hold steadfast to his or her belief and may assimilate to the majority or withdraw from any belief in order to avoid additional stress.

Institutional Setting

Southern Jersey University (SJU) in Kenville, New Jersey has been serving students from its home and surrounding states for approximately eighty years. With six academic colleges and a graduate school, Southern Jersey University is a middle-sized university that serves almost 10,000 students distributed among 31 undergraduate majors, 7 teacher certification programs, 25 master's degree programs, and a doctoral program in educational leadership. Currently, SJU is taking steps to expand the campus from thirty-one buildings, eight residence halls and four apartment complexes to a doctoral-granting institution in the immediate future. In 2002, 80% of the students were Caucasians; 9% were African Americans; 6% were Latinos; and less than 4% were Asians, all groups representing the undergraduate and graduate student population of the university.

What is God?

Chase Howard is a white senior residential student from Kenville who attends SJU. Chase is an accounting major who has made the dean's list every semester, since he entered SJU in the fall of 2002. Due to his serious demeanor and academic integrity, Chase is viewed as a loner by his classmates but, he does have regular interactions with a select few individuals from his classes and in his residence hall. For Chase, religion was not something that was a big part in his upbringing. His mother considered herself a Christian, but did not speak of her spirituality nor did she attend church regularly. His paternal grandparents are Buddhist, but he is unsure of what his father's beliefs are. The only religious experiences were contributed to his childhood education in a Lutheran elementary school. Now away at college, Chase has not been challenged to deal with faith, until he met Robin Culpepper from Central Jersey.

Residents from Southern New Jersey, like Chase, stereotyped residents north of South Jersey as uppity people. Robin's parents had her life planned for her, from the college she will attend to the type of man she will marry. Robin was daddy's little girl, who tried to do all her life practices in the best interest of the family's name. She enjoys a life of wearing all the latest name brand clothing, silver Tiffany accessories, and going to the tanning parlor for touches up to her olive Italian complexion. Her faith and the influence of her family play a major role in Robin's identity.

Both students as sophomores taking speech class were assigned to work together on their first group project. Throughout the semester, their partnership shortly turned into a dating relationship. At the age of nineteen years and without a solid religious foundation, Chase already knew he was going against the grain by becoming involved with her. Nonetheless, he did not let this community's ignorance interfere with his decision to court the girl from Central Jersey.

In addition to conversations on their future together, Chase and Robin regularly had discussions on religion. Regardless of her knowledge of his limited spiritual background, Robin elected to probe towards this subject. Unbeknownst to Robin, she was headed down hostile territory. Some of the things Chase said would startle Robin and cause her to stare into his eyes, trying to understand what leads someone to become such a person.

Although knowledgeable on various subject matters, Chase was not confident in his understanding of religion and questioned himself about whether God does exist. He would often tell her that it mattered little whether or not there really was a God—what matters is that people believe there is and thus act accordingly. With SJU being a smaller institution, information will disseminate throughout the student body in a short time. This leads to their separation and pulled Chase further away from fellow students.

Chase wanted to know more about religion but, attending this state institution limits discussion on such a fragile topic. Chase alleged there are other students, teachers or staff members who have the same concerns on religion like he does. Chase believe society has been conditioned to accept things previous generations believed without ever questioning them, particularly as they relate to faith. With this being true, it was strange that educators continue to think this way. After all, are we not encouraged by our prestigious faculty members to think critically? If religion is as sound as it claimed, then should it not be able to withstand the interrogation of inquiring minds? If it was not for fear of the administration or retaliation from the political students of The Christian Student Alliance, Chase would like to begin an organization for people who doubt their religious beliefs. He is certain there are others like himself, who are interested in exploring this journey and welcome any findings. From his experiences with Robin, Chase vowed never to discuss religion with any love interest; he will have to switch the subject in order to avoid an argument or further embarrassment. He will use his remaining time in school to remain steadfast to his goal of graduating with no desire of interacting with other students.

While enrolled in college, Chase has the freedom to explore the meaning of Truth in religion. In school, he is learning to lean less on the vision of God that his mom had and began to formulate his own understanding of certain phenomena and other intangible realities. He begins to reject the dominant religion and starts accepting things that were self-evident. Chase feels little need to believe in the existence of something which cannot be proven. His philosophy is there is no one God; God is in everything that is around him.

Chase believes it is not important to know if there is a God. He understands life to be a cyclical power based on relationships and interaction with others. The more good things one does for others, the greater the likelihood that good things may happen in return, without any guarantees. There is no higher Being looking out for him or protecting him in the conventional way that most religious people like to believe. He further believes citizens are responsible for each other and for providing assistance to those who are less fortunate.

Chase posits if there was a higher Power, he or she would not care about man's attendance record at church. Chase believes these are the factors that people put too much emphasis into, instead of helping the next man.

As he travels through his spiritual development, Chase believes there are people who avoid sinning or do good deeds because they fear the consequences or strive to reap the rewards of their behavior. He hates to be a person whose actions are motivated by fear or a desire to seek recognition. He wants to do the right thing in life, simply because it is the right thing, not for personal gain. Similar to Robin looking for gifts from her parents for obeying their commands, he believes man is looking for rewards for following the majority religion.

International Perspective

Seda Ak is a second-year international graduate student who came to SJU from Turkey. Seda has been studying and practicing English for five years but nonetheless her Turkish accent is prominent in her speech. Seda is the middle child, born into a traditional household where she and her family practice Islam. Her relationship with her mom is as close as any mother–daughter relationship could be. Respect of the family holds meaning to Turks, including Seda, and she greatly misses them as she pursue her doctoral degree in the United States. She will never do anything to bring guilt or shame to her family's name. In Turkey, over 95% of the population is Muslim; being Muslim is "natural". It was not until her arrival to Kenville, that she felt "different" due to her religion.

When she was in her homeland it was customary to worship regularly, join prayers, or fast during Ramadan, because these were traditional familial practices. However, while in the United States, Seda feels lonely and guilty about her religious practice. Her parents are concerned that during her time in America, Seda will lose commitment to her beliefs and Turkey culture. On the contrary, Seda is a believer in Allah and can not imagine living a life without believing in a God. In fact, believing in Him is the source of Seda's strength. There have been times in her life that her belief gave her the reason to live, because she knew that she was not alone.

As a third year doctoral student in school psychology, Seda has been faced with both academic and social challenges while living in the United States for the past three years. The time taken in preparation of her coming to the United States and her nieces are the motivation for Seda's persistence. Surprisingly the campus culture and community also shaped her spiritual development in America.

In the community surrounding the university there are enormous churches with stained glass windows and beautiful landscapes within every half-a-mile of each other. The elaborate structures are constant reminders of how Christianity prevails as a force in Western civilization. Meanwhile, the nearby mosque, for other Muslim worshippers, is thirty miles away across the bridge in the metropolitan city of Metropolis. With the enormous amount of schoolwork coupled with no transportation, Seda must utilize the time in her off-campus apartment to meditate and worship. The lack of space available off campus dictates to Seda that her differences are not part of the campus community and she must practice her religion in her own space.

One aspect of the Muslim faith requires believers to pray five times a day. Seda's ten-hour days on campus and the lack of resources prohibits her from engaging in peaceful mediations throughout the day. Researchers (Constantine, Wilton, Gainor, and Lewis, 2002; Thomas, 2001) state that female college students of color use religion as a coping device. Seda uses mediation to cope with the demands of being an international student in a doctoral program. Thus, she becomes annoyed with how this institution and America contradict their messages of embracing diversity.

Educating American students on Turkish culture and the Islamic faith is another responsibility she has been assigned as an international student. There are a lot of stereotypes and prejudices Americans possess about her people and religion. A lot of the stereotypes are related to the perception of Muslim women and the subservient lifestyle they have been labeled to have in Turkey. Often her friends consider Seda not covering her hair as an expression of Seda's new found American freedom. Turkey is a secular land where freedom of expression is given to the individual; and her hair remains exposed in both countries.

At times she does not mind sharing her experiences with other students in an effort to educate those who may not have the privilege of visiting Turkey. In some way, Seda enjoys sharing a part of her culture with others but there are other times when she is frustrated by American understandings and she does not correct other students' views on Turkish culture.

Summary

Most undergraduate college students explore, establish, and consolidate new personal and professional identities. With this fact in mind, it is important that conversation on religion is further held in the effort for students to develop confidence in their faith as well as academic and social intelligence on the campus of higher education. Moreover, with the conversation of religion, other students will begin to share their various experiences and religions with the goal of integrating and highlighting the different religions that may exist in an intellectual, comfortable, and safe environment that is a reflection of the heterogeneous society we live in.

Institutions can create resources or opportunities on campus that allow students to exercise their faith. Staff, faculty, and other officials who are responsible for the growth of students should investigate strategies to accommodate the diversity of religions so students and religion can exists together. Religion, faith, or institutional values should be reflected in the campus culture.

Discussion Questions

1. What are the primary student development issues in this case study?
2. What student development theories would you draw upon to help students who are less-confident in their faith development?
3. What organizational changes in leadership can be utilized to help SJU and their constituents?
4. How does campus culture contribute to student's spiritual development?

5. How can faculty and/or administrators create a more positive experience for students?
6. What kind of institutional changes can be made to promote religious diversity?
7. Develop a program/activity/project which will explore ways in which spiritual intelligence can inform your practice as a student, faculty or student affairs administrator.
8. How does the campus culture suppress students' growth development, faculty and staff is faith development?

References

Chickering, A., Stamm, L., & Dalton, J. Encouraging authenticity and spirituality in higher education. (2006). San Francisco: Jossey Bass.
Constantine, M.G., Wilson,G., & Lewis,E. L. (2002). Religious participation, spirituality, and coping among African American College Students. *Journal of College Student Development*, 43 (5), 605–613.
Hardiman, R. & Jackson, B.W. (1997) Conceptual foundation for social justice courses. In M. Adams, L.A. Bell & P. Griffin (Eds.). *Teaching for diversity and social justice: A sourcebook*, (pp. 16–19) New York: Rutledge.
Nash, R.J. (2001). *Religious pluralism in the academy*. New York: Peter Lang Publishing.
Thomas, A.J. (2001) African American women's spiritual beliefs: A guide for treatment. *Women and Therapy*, 23 (4), 1–12.

Suggested Readings

Howard-Hamilton, M.F. (2003). Meeting the needs of African American women. New Directions for Student Affairs, 104.
Jablonski, M.A. (2001). The implications of student spirituality for student affairs practice. New Directions for Student Affairs, 95.
Schlosser, L.Z. (2003). Christian Privilege: Breaking a sacred taboo. Journal of Multicultural Counseling and Development, 31, (1), 44–51.
Washington, V.S. (1999). The relationship of spirituality and religious life to the moral development of college students. [(Doctoral dissertation)].

Case #20 Asian American and Pacific Islander Students: A Displaced Minority?

DAISY RODRIQUEZ

While diversity remains a fundamental value and goal for many universities, the conversation and targeted constituencies do not typically include Asian American and Pacific Islander students. This case study explores the questionable status of whether or not Asian Americans and Asian Pacific American Islander, also referred to as APA, are a designated minority group within higher education. The primary objective is to raise critical questions about the criteria that determine who comprises a minority group and who is eligible for minority funding and services at higher education institutions. The issue requires us to examine why a certain group may be considered a minority or underrepresented population in some cases but not in others. For example, APA student organizations are eligible for cultural programming money yet do not qualify for minority scholarships and programs.

Setting

MidAmerica University (MAU) is located in the Midwest section of the United States. MAU is a public, research I institution that is largely residential, with a student population of 27,000 students. The minority student population of 9.3% includes African Americans, Latino, Asian Americans, and Native Americans; 8.45% are international students; and 12.27% of MAU faculty members are African American, Asian American, Latino/Hispanic, or Native American. There are a variety of courses offered at MAU—a selection of over 5000 courses each year—giving students the opportunity to study other cultures and languages in depth. The Department of African American Studies and the Program for Latino/Hispanic Studies underscore MAU's commitment to research and scholarship in the study of minority cultures. At this time an Asian American Studies Program does not exist though efforts to establish an academic program geared towards the APA experience in the United States are underway.

Key Characters

Cedric Davis: the vice president for Academic Initiatives and Multicultural Affairs for the MidAmerica University system. Davis reports directly to the President and holds a significant role in creating policies and programs that carry out the university's mission to promote and establish diversity initiatives. In his efforts to create a campus community that fosters openness, inclusion, and opportunity, he also remains focused on the retention and recruitment of minority and underrepresented populations. In his role, he encounters situations that challenge his personal loyalties with his professional interests.

Additionally, Davis is the highest ranking African American administrator at the campus and the entire system. Steadfast in his commitment to strengthening the overall conditions of the African American experience at MAU for faculty, staff, and students, he garners a great deal of support from the African American community within MAU. White and black campus officials privately question many of his actions, specifically the way he responds to issues that affect APA students. However, white and black campus senior or mid-level officials rarely question his approach to some issues.

Joanna Gonzalez: a Filipina American, serving in her fourth year as the Director of the Center for Asian and Asian American Culture, also referred to as CAAC. The Center for Asian and Asian American Culture provides students a place to hang out and has come to be known as "a home away from home" for several students of Asian heritage, including international and domestic students. It provides educational and cultural programming, academic and emotional support to Asian and Asian American and Pacific Islander students, serves as a resource for the university and local community, and as an advocate for Asian and Asian American student concerns.

Gonzalez is one of three student affairs administrators of Asian heritage. She has strong relationships with members of the university and the local community and actively serves on a number of campus and community committees that address multicultural issues. Though Gonzalez is an advocate for Asian and Asian Pacific American students, her primary concern is the equitable allocation of resources for minority students at MAU.

Steve Marshall: the Director of the Program for Minority Excellence, also referred to as PME, and holds very strong opinions about why Asian Americans should not be eligible to participate in the program he oversees. Steve's staff have had several conversations with staff from CAAC, listening to their concerns while adhering to his beliefs that Asian Americans are well represented and academically successful.

Marshall has worked at MAU for over twelve years, serving primarily in the academic arena. In the past five years, he has taken on a dual role of administrator of PME and faculty member. He is content with the number of students in PME and feels no need to expand the program to include an already successful minority group.

Grace Bautista: a doctoral student in the Higher Education Administration program. When she relocated to MidAmerica to begin school at MAU, she was thrilled by the endless opportunities for involvement with CAAC. As a proud Asian American, she welcomed her chance to make a mark and become connected to the Asian Pacific American community at MAU. Little did she know that her feisty energy would lead to multiple conversations and efforts to change the status of APAs to a recognized minority group. She volunteers at the Center for Asian and Asian American Culture, initiated the Asian American Graduate Organization, and participates in the School of Education's minority graduate organization. During her experience at MAU, she toils over her beliefs for including APAs into minority-based programs and becoming eligible for minority scholarships and fellowships. Several of her APA peers are reluctant to advocate for changing MAU policy to include all APAs because they strongly believe that some subgroups within the APA community are more disadvantaged economically than others.

Case

During the middle of the Fall semester, the Graduate and Professional Student Organization held a Town Hall meeting focused on diversity that would solicit feedback on how their organization could better serve their minority constituency and to hear what concerns existed. To add to the substance of the meeting, Vice President Davis was invited to help facilitate the conversation. The room was filled with primarily graduate and professional students that represented various academic disciplines and a handful of administrators. Several issues were raised as the dialogue occurred. Students, in attendance, voiced the following concerns:

(1) the lack of representation within the graduate and professional student organization;

(2) the matriculation of minority students in their various graduate programs;

(3) university support to graduate minority students.

In a room of about thirty individuals, it appeared that most of the individuals present seemed to understand the challenges articulated and shared in one another's frustrations. Midway through the meeting, Grace Bautista questioned Vice President Davis about why APAs were not considered a minority at the university. He explained that the university looks at the population in the state of a specific ethnic/racial group and compares that number to the enrollment rate for that particular group. Based on this definition, APAs are overrepresented since the overall percentage of students matriculated at MAU exceeds the state population.

Vice President Davis then added that APAs have not been historically discriminated against in ways that African Americans, Hispanic Americans and Native Americans have; this comment infuriated Grace. In a room filled with graduate students, university administrators, and leaders of the graduate and professional student organization who are intellects, social justice advocates, and proponents of diversity, not one person questioned Mr. Davis' statement. Grace left the town hall meeting disgusted and outraged by Mr. Davis' ignorant comments about APAs.

The day after the town hall meeting, Grace stopped by the CAAC and spoke with Ms. Gonzalez. Grace raised many questions about the ambiguous usage of the term minority, as the conversation ensued, the degree of Grace's frustration intensified. To attempt to make sense of the non-minority status of APAs, student coalitions were established within the Minority Education Association to challenge the requirements of the dean of Education's minority fellowship, chancellor's minority fellowship, and the Equal Opportunity scholarship. Due to the limited financial resources offered by MAU to support minority graduate students, the allocation of fellowships and scholarships is at the heart of this discussion.

Later that semester, Ms. Gonzalez initiated a meeting with the Program for Minority Excellence staff to discuss the possibilities for changing the policy to include Asian American students into PME. Mr. Marshall, the Director of PME, argued that Asian American students are a thriving population that does not struggle academically and that advocates for Asian Americans should be pleased at the academic success of these students. Teranishi (2002) acknowledges that "when Asian Pacific Americans (APAs) are brought into the discussion, they are often considered to be educationally successful, overrepresented in higher education, or in general, a 'successful minority'" (p. 17). Mr. Marshall then added that APAs are not in need of the same services as African American, Latino/Hispanic, and Native American students. Mr. Marshall, like many other administrators and students, fails to see the diversity that exists within the APA community.

Asian Pacific Americans represent a broad scope of Asian cultures and communities; each culture contains variations in language, religion, traditions, and values (Sue & Sue, 1990). Within the APA population, the range of ethnic heritages is extensive, including and not limited to Chinese, Filipino, Guamanian, Hmong, Indian, Japanese, Korean, Laotian, Micronesian, Pakistani, Samoan, Singaporean, Taiwanese, Thai, Tongan, and Vietnamese. This begs several questions of who PME targets. Latino and

Hispanic students, like APAs, are not a monolithic group and are "descendants of various ethnic and socioracial groups" (Helms & Cook, 1999, p.55). Latinos/Hispanics represent ancestries from Central America, Latin America, and the Caribbean as well as ethnic groups of Portuguese and other European and Asian heritages.

To help shed greater light on the experience of APAs, the Center for Asian and Asian American Culture held a Symposium on APAs in higher education. The event was held the following Fall. After bringing in a nationally recognized Asian American studies professor and expert as the keynote speaker for the symposium, Mr. Davis voiced his appreciation of the lecture and day of educational workshops. This initiative proved to be somewhat successful as Vice President Davis' understanding of APAs was expanded. For one, the keynote's address touched on the status of APAs as a minority group. Davis was challenged to consider how, on one hand, APAs are invited to minority events, such as cultural and minority receptions and celebrations but in terms of being eligible for minority funding programs or scholarships, they are excluded. Hence, he came to understand some of the inconsistencies of how the determination of minority is blurred.

In the following Spring semester, Mr. Davis participated in an interview by CAAC to be published in the center's newsletter where he stated that APAs would be allowed to participate in the PME. This article raised a tremendous amount of hope for Asian Americans in being eligible for acceptance into PME and felt like a victory for CAAC and the students involved in the efforts to change the policy. The CAAC begin informing prospective APA students of PME as a recruitment tool. However, this raised tremendous concern for the staff and student participants of PME. Black students voiced their ambivalence for this change because it could eliminate financial aid opportunities for Black and Latino/Hispanic students. Many underrepresented student populations rely heavily on financial aid; the role of loans and monetary assistance promote and sustain college attendance (Fenske, Porter, & DuBrock, 2000; Volkwein, Szelest, Cabrera, & Napierski-Prancl, 1998). Moreover, most studies do not identify APAs as a group that relies heavily on financial assistance and often use APAs and white students as a comparison group to Blacks and Latino/Hispanic students needing aid. This framework can be problematic as the APA student population varies in economic circumstances.

After a few months following the article, CAAC staff noticed that changes on the PME application and website were not made to reflect the addition of APA students. Grace was angered by the disparity in Davis' verbal commitment and the actual implementation of the PME policy change. From that moment on, Grace as well as other Asian American students question Davis' sincerity and loyalty to the APA student community at MAU. Davis' actions are incongruent with his conceptual understanding because of the pressures he encounters from external and internal forces that dissuade him from the expansion of the program. Without a critical mass of Asian APA faculty, staff, or Alumni to apply substantial pressure to implement this change, the reality of such a measure seems impossible.

Environmental Factors

This section highlights environmental factors to consider in understanding the situation at MAU.

1. The way the university has defined a "minority" or "underrepresented" student is based on the percentage of the state population compared to the percentage of students matriculated.
2. The percentage of residents within the state MAU is located that identify as APA is 1.2% and the enrollment of APA students is 3.1%.
3. The vice chancellor for Academic Support and Diversity is a member of the African American community and encounters situations where there is a conflict of interest.
4. Due to a proliferation of racial incidents in the university community, MAU has a heightened awareness of issues that affect black students. Moreover, the historical presence and experiences of the different underrepresented racial groups in the state and MAU are vastly different. The disparity contributes to the tension between the different racial groups in terms of access to scholarships as they all vie for the same limited amount of financial aid.

Diversity is at the forefront of the university's agenda with a steadfast commitment to providing a campus climate and community that promotes a welcoming atmosphere for minority students. While various support services and programs exist to serve the underrepresented, APA students are displaced. The university's fact book states that the university utilizes the definitions of minority ethnic group classifications used by the United States Office of Civil Rights, which include African American, Hispanic, Native American, and Asian. If this in fact is true, then APA students should be included in all minority-based programs and be eligible for all minority scholarships.

The term "Asian Pacific American" is too broad and does not recognize the heterogeneity amongst APAs, in terms of immigration and socioeconomic status. For instance, the model minority designation is actually based on the economic and educational success of Chinese Americans, Japanese American, Korean Americans, and South Asians from India and Pakistan. Higher poverty rates and lower levels of education exist for immigrants and their children from Southeast Asia (Vietnam, Cambodia, Laos,

Thailand), the Philippines, and Indonesia. The existing category of APAs is problematic because it does not differentiate among Asian immigrants who arrived at higher levels of education and socioeconomic status and those who did not.

Currently, the university appears to utilize university-wide enrollments to determine which groups are underrepresented. This does not present a problem for African American, Latino/Hispanic, and American Indian students. However, though Asian Americans constitute 3% of student enrollment, there are many academic departments at MAU where the APA enrollment is negligible at both the undergraduate and graduate levels. For instance, in the Curriculum and Instruction and Counseling departments in the School of Education, only one APA is enrolled in each of those departments. Another example is the history department which enrolls approximately 200 students a year, of which none are APA. The explanation for this is unclear and MAU's lack of attention to this is troubling. Perhaps, APA students are not applying to the history program, the program does not attract APA students, or they are not being admitted. However, these explanations are not used to justify the low enrollment of APA graduate students.

Moreover, a few perceptions of the general student population of Asian ancestry exist that compound this institutional dilemma. First, due to the large matriculation of Asian International undergraduate and graduate students it visibly appears as though there a substantial number of APAs matriculated at MAU. Though these two student groups are markedly different, they are often viewed as the same by both administrators and their peers. The fact that their citizenship differs is overlooked by the similarity of their physical features. Second, university administrators and students believe that all APA students are academically successful and are not in need of the services provided for other minority populations. Many MAU administrators and faculty members buy in to the model minority characterization of APA students. As suggested by Kim and Yeh (2002), the belief in the model minority myth takes for granted the heterogeneity of the economic and educational success levels between and within the APA student group or their varied backgrounds with respect to acculturation or immigration to the United States. Third, the perception of APA experience in the United States is not commonly associated with their history of exclusion or of being disadvantaged. This population is not perceived to be an oppressed group.

Similar to other racial minority groups, APA students encounter a lack of campus belongingness, alienation, marginalization, and loneliness (Lee & Davis, 2000). A sense of belonging is critical for all students of color. Though most research has focused on Black, Latino/Hispanic, and Native American students, this finding also relates to the experiences of APA students who face similar challenges of feeling connected. For example, many

Southeast Asian American and Hispanic/Latino students struggle with college adjustments issues and academic success (Stage, 2000).

Discussion Questions

1. What factors should be taken into consideration when defining an underrepresented minority group in terms of eligibility for minority scholarships and fellowships, as well as prestigious minority programs?
2. How should a university determine the minority or non-minority status of a particular racial group?
3. What conclusions are drawn by whom about APAs that lead to the assumption that they are entitled to "a piece of the pie"?
4. If APAs were included as minority group, who would supply the financial resources to expand the monies for financial aid and academic support so other minority groups do not feel shortchanged?
5. What responsibility, if any, does the university have in providing institutional support to APA students? How would that support be explicitly communicated and demonstrated?
6. Has the African American community with its moral authority derived from resisting oppression, bought into the exclusion of other underrepresented racial groups that have integrated into the majority white population more easily? Have the oppressed assimilated elements of the oppressor?
7. What limitations and possible consequences are influencing the campus' perceptions of Latinos/Hispanics and APAs as monolithic groups? Are there elite subpopulations within these groups? If so, should members of these elite sub-groups be eligible to receive the same services and resources as non-elite members of these groups?
8. What limitations and possible consequences are influencing Davis' decision to not include Asian Americans into PME?

Recommendations

When developing and implementing programs, activities, policies, and programs, universities need to be clear on how the term minority is defined at their respective institution, and the specific implications of this definition. Additionally, question whether or not the university's policies are able to:

● Recognize the complexities within the APA community (including Southeast Asian, South Asian and Pacific Islanders) into one category and the problematic nature of grouping these subgroups together.

- Distinguish between the socioeconomic impact on more recent immigrants and APAs who have resided in the U.S. for generations, as well as the implications for why different groups have immigrated.
- Disaggregate the data for more accuracy; what are the individual percentages for the various APA subgroups?

It is not only necessary but critical to the purposes and goals of higher education that colleges and universities of all types and in all regions of the United States focus more energy and attention on the growing APA student populations especially in light of the higher participation rate of this population in higher education, which is at a greater proportion than any other ethnic group. The challenge that universities will continue to face is recognizing that this student population is not homogenous and differs across immigration history, class levels, and academic abilities.

Conclusion

When discussing minority students in higher education, an inconsistency exists in who is considered a "minority". Research on minority students and minority-based student services tends to focus on Native Americans, African Americans/Blacks or Hispanic Americans. According to the United States Department of Education (2001), minority membership includes American Indian/Alaska Native, Asian/Pacific Islander, Hispanic, and Black, non-Hispanic. Moreover, Cushner, McClellan and Safford (2003) define a minority group as "a social group that occupies a subordinate position in a society" (p.37) whereas APAs are a subordinate group in the United States who lack social and political power. This case raises the question of how a universitiy's determination of a minority is blurred. On the one hand, MAU celebrates the ethnic and racial composition of the student body but denies one of the racial group's eligibility for minority funding. The question of the equitability of the allocation of financial resources to students of color who are underrepresented in their academic programs is incongruent with the university's appreciation of the racial diversity that exists at MAU.

References

Cushner, K., McClelland, A., & Safford, P. (2003). *Human diversity in education: An integrative approach* (4th ed.). Boston: McGraw-Hill.

Fenske, R.H., Porter, J.D., & DuBrock, C.P. (2000). Tracking financial aid and persistence of women, minority, and needy students in science, engineering, and mathematics. *Research in Higher Education*, 41 (1), 67–94.

Helms, J.E. & Cook, D.A. (1999). *Using race and culture in counseling and psychotherapy: Theory and process*. Boston, MA: Allyn and Bacon, p.55.

Kim, A. & Yeh, C.J. (2002). *Stereotypes of Asian American students*. New York: ERIC Clearinghouse on Urban Education.

Lee, R.M. & Davis, C. (2000). Cultural orientation, past multicultural experience, and a sense of belonging on campus for Asian American college students. *The Journal of College Student Development*, 41 (1), 110–115.

Stage, F. (2000). Predictors of college adjustment and success: similarities and differences among Southeast Asian American, Hispanic, and White students. *Education*, 120 (4), 731–740.

Sue, D.W. & Sue, D. (1990). *Counseling the culturally different: Theory and practice* (2nd ed.). New York, NY: John Wiley & Sons.

Teranishi, R. (2002). The myth of the super minority: misconceptions about Asian Americans. *College Board Review*, 195, 16–21.

U.S. Department of Education (2001). *Minority definition*. Retrieved from the world wide web: *http://nces.ed.gov/pubs2001/100 largest/methodology. asp*

Volkwein, J.P., Szelest, B.P., Cabrera, A.F., & Napierski-Prancl, M.R. (1998). Factors associated with student loan default among different racial and ethnic groups. *The Journal of Higher Education*, 69 (2), 206–233.

Case #21 Higher Education in Transition: Gender Identity on College Campuses

Jeffrey S. McKinney

Introduction

Jane Pelley is a third-year student at a large, public, four-year institution in the Midwest region of the United States. Jane, a transgender student, has begun to explore her identity during the last year of school and has encountered some obstacles at the University of the Midwest (UMW). Five years ago, UMW funded the opening of the Gay, Lesbian, and Bisexual (GLBT) Support Office on campus, reporting to the vice president for Student Affairs and the dean of Students Office. A growing trend in recent years prompted UMW to add "Transgender" to the GLBT Support Office two years ago, although little thought was given concerning the issues of transgender college students. David Kent, the director of the GLBT Support Office, has some knowledge on transgender issues and has attempted to incorporate programming on campus, but little information and knowledge is readily available. Donna Anderson, vice president for Student Affairs at UMW, has provided some resources to the GLBT Office director, but is not knowledgeable about transgender issues. Recently, Jane has become more vocal on campus and has been speaking about her experiences as a transgender student at UMW.

Institutional Setting

University of the Midwest is a large public university located approximately ninety minutes from a major metropolitan city. Situated in a small city of 60,000 residents, the university is the major employer in town and most of the community revolves around the activity of the school. The university is not the state's flagship institution, but has been known for its academic programs in the region. it has slightly more than 22,000 students, both undergraduate and graduate and 85% of those students are white. During the course of the last five years, UMW has begun to discuss issues of diversity in a more open fashion, but little, if any, discussions about transgender issues have taken place. To date, there have been no campus-wide programs offered to discuss transgender issues or students. Efforts to increase the number of students and faculty of color have been marginally successful, yet more needs to be done. Student retention initiatives have recently focused on low-income and first-generation students.

UMW Administration

The administration at UMW consists of mostly white males but does include Don James, an African American male who is vice president for Diversity, and Donna Anderson, a white female who is vice president for Student Affairs and dean of Students. The Board of Trustees is comprised of eight white males, one African American female and one Latino male. The President has shown some interest in diversity initiatives, but many on campus believe that these initiatives are mostly superficial in nature. The current administrative team has been intact for the last five years.

Campus Climate

Ten years ago, the University of the Midwest conducted a campus climate study to determine how students, faculty, and staff of color were experiencing campus life. Results from that assessment painted a troubling picture for UMW administrators and the Board of Trustees. Students of color reported consistent incidents of harassment and a lack of faculty that "resembled the student body." Students of color shared some common campus experiences with GLBT students in that both groups of college students have felt marginalized by UMW. These similarities have become very apparent over the last few years in terms of resources available on campus and the lack of programming on such issues.

Soon after this campus climate study was released, gay and lesbian students became more vocal at UMW and persuaded the VP for Student Affairs to provide funds for a similar climate study that would help the campus better understand the lives of GLB students on the campus of UMW. Results from that climate study were also troubling. Many students, faculty, and staff identified (confidentially) as gay, lesbian, or bisexual and many of them reported negative experiences with faculty, students, and colleagues. As a result of this study and the motivation of students, faculty, and staff,

UMW's administration on the Board of Trustees funded a position and the operating costs of the Gay, Lesbian, and Bisexual Support Office on campus. David Kent was hired by Donna Anderson to direct this office. Simultaneously, sexual orientation was added to the campus non-discrimination policy. Both of these efforts were heavily protested by some students and many alumni.

Donna Anderson: vice president for Student Affairs and dean of Students has been at UMW for nearly twenty years. She has generally been supportive of diversity initiatives and efforts at UMW, but does not fully understand the issues of transgender college students. She was supportive when the GLBT office was opened five years ago, yet more reluctant to add "transgender" to the official name of the office when it was proposed two years prior. During meetings, she regularly asks "How many transgender students do we actually have on campus?" This question is generally answered by those in the room with "we are not sure, but maybe a handful of students." With only a few possible students on campus identifying as transgender, Donna Anderson has been reluctant to offer added resources to the GLBT Support Office budget and her office has not sponsored any campus-wide programming or presentation addressing transgender or gender identity issues. She fully supports the efforts of David Kent, the Director of the GLBT Support Office.

The Gay, Lesbian, Bisexual, and Transgender Support Office

Since its opening, David Kent, a gay male, has directed the efforts of the GLBT Support Office. He acknowledges that transgender issues have not been addressed in a meaningful way on campus but is unclear on how to proceed. When the issues were raised two years ago, he was supportive when "transgender" was added to the GLBT office, but admits he was mostly swayed by his colleagues in similar positions around the country. Recently, more students, faculty, and staff have been approaching the office in search of information concerning transgender and gender identity issues. Currently, only a few resources exist in the office library, including some books and videos, but the offerings are less than comprehensive. There are no current plans to offer transgender programming and no student groups exist on campus in support of transgender students.

Recently, David Kent has been approached by Jane Pelley, transgender student who has embarked on a personal journey in the last year to more fully understand her identity. She has visited the office many times for information, but has often left disappointed by the lack of knowledge in the office that is supposed to support her and her peers. She has asked David Kent to start a student group, support her efforts to add transgender to the school's non-discrimination policy, and to offer more programming on campus. David Kent, although sympathetic, has realized that he may lack the experience and skills necessary to help Jane and students with similar issues on campus.

Like many other units on campus, David is concerned about budgets and available resources, and wonders how many students are in need of such support.

Character

Jane Pelley is like many other college students, she studies, works on campus, and participates in a healthy social life. However, the last year of college has been a difficult journey. During early childhood, Jane (then Jack), often felt that she was not quite the same as her friends. Although these feelings persisted, Jane kept telling herself that it was only a phase. Eventually, she thought, things would change and the feelings she had would go away. When entering college, Jane applied for admission under her male name (Jack), and was admitted to UMW and placed in the residence hall system. This was the beginning of a real journey for Jane. As Jack, she was placed in a residence hall with a male roommate, making her feel uncomfortable and somewhat out of place. Jane approached her Resident Assistant (RA), only to be referred to the counseling center. However, Jane was not ready for this step at this point in her life. Although uncomfortable, Jane continued to live in the residence hall for the remainder of her first year. Jane was unable to be honest with her roommate and continually had to hide from him, often taking much of her energy and time. Jane often felt quite alone during her first year of college and was not an engaged student on campus. This isolation often brought pain, anxiety, and depression. Jane felt trapped in her living situation and did not find a place on campus that could support her during this period of inner turmoil and exploration.

During her second year, she moved off campus with some close friends, but still kept her identity issues to herself. These friends were both male and female, and people she had come to trust, at least to some extent. She often felt helpless and alone, but was not ready to make her feelings and thoughts public. After another year of struggling with her identity, Jane ended her second year of college on a somewhat disappointing note, receiving a 2.0 grade point average. During the summer after the second year of college, Jane decided to start the next part of her personal journey. She began to discuss her feelings with her very close friends. Her close friends were confused and unable to fully comprehend her feelings and thoughts, but were supportive of Jane and encouraged her to seek counseling on campus. They had many questions about Jane's identity and her exploration.

Her female friends were more open to this new person than were her male friends. They were more uncomfortable around Jane after her disclosure, but to their credit did not stop being friends with Jane. During the summer, Jane visited the Counseling Center at UMW and began to discuss her feelings with a professional. This new journey was tough for Jane. She had not been able to trust many people on campus, especially those on campus who were meant to support students in times of need. Although she knew she needed to go to the counseling center, she also began to think of all the negative possibilities that visiting the center may bring. Will they contact her parents? Will they out her to others on campus? Would they be able to help? What would they think of her? Were they even qualified to help her in this personal journey? (Few more details need to flesh out the story) Her experiences at the counseling center were anything but positive. While talking with David Kent, Jane conveyed her experiences with the Counseling Center:

> I tried to get counseling through the campus resources and was eventually told that I need to find a counselor familiar with gender issues. I continued to look for a counselor but nobody on campus has experience dealing with trans issues. None of the counselors were even able to refer me to anyone in the local community. Eventually they referred me to a counselor in the city who might be able to help with trans issues, but that is going to be at least 50 miles away and I am not sure I will be able to see her very often. What can I do to get counseling here on campus?

Given David's lack of experience with transgender issues, he was not able to help in a way that Jane needed. The GLBT Support Office, set up to assist students like Jane, was not a resource that Jane could count on in her identity exploration. David Kent was not knowledgeable on transgender issues and the office had only a handful of resources available for transgender students. The most they could really offer were referrals to the counseling center or a few mental health professionals in town. While well-intentioned, David Kent and his staff, and limited budgets, just could not support transgender students in a meaningful way. He also privately insisted that only a handful of students would need such support on campus.

Frustrated by her experiences with the counseling center, Jane was resolved to find support on campus. After much reading and chatting on the internet, Jane was determined to begin hormone therapy and was hoping to get that support on campus. After her experiences at the counseling center, Jane was less than optimistic about approaching the Health Center at UMW. She was determined to start her transition on campus, setting an appointment to see a doctor on campus. During her appointment, Jane explained the reasons for her visit, "I want to begin female hormone therapy. I am a transgender student and have begun the process of transitioning here on campus." Puzzled, the doctor looked at Jane with astonishment and replied, "I am not sure what we can do. I do not have any experience with this issue and I am not sure any of my colleagues have any experience either." She has since tried other doctors at the health center but continues to face obstacles in getting the support and care she needs to make her transition.

Once again, Jane was frustrated with available resources on campus and discussed her frustration with her friends:

> I keep getting a lot of "no, we cannot help you here." I am determined to get help on campus. I cannot afford to go to other doctors in the community or travel to the city to get the help that I need. I was almost ready to stop trying until I finally found a doctor to prescribe me some hormones. I put up with her ignorance about trans issues because I get what I need from her but I would never really trust her medical opinion. If it were not for the hormones, I would probably completely avoid the Health Center here. Every time I go in the health center for an appointment, it seems like I have to educate everyone there about my issues. It is getting very tiresome to "tell my story" during every visit to the Health Center. I am not sure where to turn.

> These hormones are not covered in our student health insurance so I have started working more hours so that I can at least get that part of my transition covered. Some of Jane's friends were outraged at this, while others still did not quite understand the situation. Jane continued to feel frustrated at the situation, but felt that the support she was receiving from her female friends could help her keep going in her journey. Her male friends are still in need of more education, but still remain supportive to some extent.

Jane's frustration with the health care system is all too common, according to others that Jane has met online. She recently met another student on campus who is dealing with the same issues and has found that support to be very helpful. At least for now, she does not feel totally alone on campus. Her network of friends, her new acquaintance, and some GLBT allies have begun to meet and discuss transgender issues, yet the group is not formally recognized as an official student group by the university. In fact, after many pleas, the GLBT office still does not announce or list their monthly meetings.

During the Fall semester of her third year in college, Jane decided to change her name legally. She knew this would be an issue, but walked in to the Student Legal Services Office to find help. She was pleasantly surprised to find support their from a male law student. This student, John Reynolds, agreed to help Jane legally change her name from Jack to Jane. While this was a difficult process, Jane became her legal name just before returning home for the holidays. For the moment, the support she received from John renewed her hope in the UMW system of student support. She eagerly awaited the new semester so that she could change her name with the registrar, the bursar, and her professors.

As Jane arrived back on campus in early January, she entered the office of the registrar the first day classes began. The first person she spoke to about her name change was less than helpful. Armed with copies of her legal name change certificate and her new driver's license, Jane was sure that this process would prove to be less troublesome than finding supportive counseling and health care. While waiting for the representative in the registrar's office, Jane overheard people laughing in a cubicle a few yards behind the counter. Once again, her transition would provide another roadblock. Once again, Jane felt alone and disheartened after this encounter. She wondered if she should begin to think about transferring to another school or leave college life all together. After returning to the counter, the representative told Jane that they were unsure how to help and would have to consult the registrar in an afternoon meeting. Jane's first class was only a few minutes away, and she was anxious to talk with her first professor.

After Jane's first class, she approached the professor about the name she was called at the beginning of class. After explaining her situation to the professor, Jane was once again shocked at the response. Surprised by the event, the professor said, "I cannot do anything about this until I hear from the registrar. Is this something that can even be done here at UMW? Forgive me, but I do not know how to handle this situation. I wish I could be more helpful, but there is nothing that I can do at this point. Let me know when you hear from the registrar's office." Jane was a little stunned at this response, yet not totally shocked. In her mind, she believed that a professor would be more supportive of her and be sensitive to her needs to be known as Jane instead of Jack. Frustrated with the entire UMW system, Jane left campus for her apartment, so that she could attempt to comprehend her struggles with campus. Overwhelmed by the gravity of her current obstacles, Jane struggled through tears as she discussed these struggles with her roommates and friends.

The next day, she approached the GLBT office to discuss the situation with David Kent and the other staff working that day. She was angry with the system, including the lack of support from the office that was supposed to be her advocate. Jane was upset and not sure how to keep working with a system that had been only marginally supportive of her efforts to transition. Beginning with her first encounter with her RA in the dorms, it seems as though few people on campus could understand the issues that Jane deals with on a daily basis. Holding back tears, she said to David, "I am not sure how to continue here at UMW. Every time I turn around, I get blocked, laughed at, or turned away. I am not sure what I can do next! It could be time for me to leave UMW. Is there anything you can do to help?" Somewhat embarrassed and frustrated with the limited support that the GLBT office offers in regards to transgender issues, David Kent agreed to have a conversation with the GLBT Support Office Advisory Board, of which Donna Anderson is a member.

Not totally satisfied with the response from David Kent, Jane decided to gather friends, allies from the GLB student groups, and supportive staff, faculty, and a few graduate students who had spoken about the issue. Jane found many students on campus who were experiencing the same types of frustration with campus life. Finally, Jane had found other transgender students on campus. It was a positive time for Jane to know that she was not alone in her personal struggles or alone on campus. Jane formed an action group named Transgender Action Group (TAG) and called her first meeting in February of the spring semester. She discussed her experiences with the group of concerned campus community members. Much to her surprise, some of the students and staff began to discuss their experiences with gender identity issues on campus. A handful of those in the group had also experienced difficult times on campus, especially in the health and counseling centers. This sense of support is something Jane has been searching for during her time at UMW. This group of supportive allies empowered Jane to fight for some real change on campus. As a group, they began to draft some proposals that they eventually wanted to present to Donna Anderson, David Kent, and other administrators on the UMW campus. They set dates for a series of TAG group meetings and developed a set of objectives, goals, and milestones. Jane and the group were ambitious and outlined a plan for the UMW campus.

David Kent and Donna Anderson had several conversations about transgender issues but were unclear on how to proceed with their work. They decided to explore the issues in more detail but declined to name a formal task force or group to investigate the issues in more detail. They were still unclear how many students on campus were actually affected by the lack of transgender resources available at UMW. After consulting with other members of administration, residence halls staff, and a handful of faculty members, they agreed to listen to the students, allies, and friends who had formed TAG.

Intent on achieving their goals and objectives, TAG formulated a set of resolutions to address the treatment of transgender individuals on campus. The following list of recommendations was presented to the GLBT Support Office Advisory Board, including Donna Anderson:

1. Work to include gender identity in the non-discrimination policy at UMW.
2. Develop training and educational programming for the entire UMW community.
3. Train all staff, including doctors, at the UMW Health and Counseling Centers.

4. Provide resources to the GLBT office to better address transgender issues.
5. Train all Student Affairs staff on the issues faced by transgender students.
6. Train all faculty, including non-tenure track and adjunct faculty members.
7. Train all residence halls staff, including all resident assistants
8. Provide gender-neutral restroom facilities on campus.
9. Provide gender-neutral recreation facilities on campus.
10. Provide support for a student group to support transgender students.
11. Develop a student records process for transgender students.
12. Develop forms, such as admissions applications, that are gender-neutral.

Jane and the rest of TAG do acknowledge that the recommendations are ambitious, but believe that they are necessary to begin some much needed campus reflection and dialogue.

Discussion Questions

1. Common barriers for transgender students on campus have been raised by Jane Pelley and her action group, TAG, including:

   - Lack of support from GLBT Support Office
   - Lack of adequate counseling at the Counseling Center
   - Lack of adequate health care at the Health Center
   - Lack of adequate programming for transgender issues
   - Lack of knowledge among Student Affairs staff
   - Lack of knowledge among faculty on campus
   - Lack of support from dean of Students office
   - Little, if any, safe space for transgender students
   - Lack of gender-neutral housing, restrooms, or recreation

   Describe how each of the above mentioned barriers work against Jane and her peers in their development as human beings and as college students.

2. What suggestions do you offer David Kent and Donna Anderson to better support Jane Pelley and other transgender students on campus?
3. Where do you see potential conflicts on campus in addressing transgender issues? What suggestions do you have to resolve such potential conflicts?
4. How can Donna Anderson and David Kent advocate for transgender students without knowing how many students are in need of campus services and support?

5. Where can UMW find resources to better serve the needs of transgender students?
6. What strategies can David Kent consider in better supporting UW's transgender students?
7. How can the faculty better support Jane and her peers? What are the potential barriers in securing faculty support for these issues?
8. How can Jane and TAG work to build support for the equitable treatment of transgender students?
9. What are some possible programs and initiatives UMW can consider?
10. What are strategies that UW can utilize to communicate with the larger university community, including the local community, alumni, and donors? (Case would better if we had several students who had similar perceptions and experiences on campus?) What are the pluses and minuses of families who live in these areas?

Recommended Readings

Beemyn, B. (2003). Serving the needs of transgendered college students. *Journal of Gay and Lesbian Issues in Education*, 1(1) 1–26.

Brevard, A. (2001). *The woman I was not born to be*. Philadelphia, PA: Temple University Press.

Carter, K.A. (2000). Transgenderism and college students: Issues of gender identity and its role on our campuses. In V.A. Wall & N.J. Evans (Eds.). *Toward acceptance: Sexual orientation issues on campus*, (pp.261–282). Lanham, MD: University Press of America.

Devor, H. (1997). *FTM: Female-to-male transsexuals in society*. Bloomington: Indiana University Press.

Eddy, W. & Forney, D.S. (2000). Assessing campus environments for the lesbian, gay and bisexual population. In V.A. Wall & N.J. Evans (Eds.). *Toward acceptance: Sexual orientation issues on campus*, (pp.131–154). Lanham, MD: University Press of America.

Evans, N.J. & Wall, V.A. (2000). Parting thoughts: An agenda for addressing sexual orientation issues on campus. In V.A. Wall & N.J. Evans (Eds.). *Toward acceptance: Sexual orientation issues on campus*, (pp.389–403). Lanham, MD: University Press of America.

Feinberg, L. (1996). *Transgender warriors*. Boston, MA: Beacon Press.

———— (1998). *Trans liberation: Beyond pink and blue*. Boston, MA: Beacon Press.

Lark, J.S. (1998). Lesbian, gay, and bisexual concerns in student affairs: Themes and transitions in the development of the professional literature. *NASPA Journal*, 35 (2) 157–168.

Lees, L.J. (1998). Transgender students on our campuses. In R.L. Sanlo (Ed.). *Working with lesbian, gay, bisexual, and transgender college students: A handbook for faculty and administrators*, (pp.37–43). Westport, CT: Greenwood Press.

McKinney, J.S. (forthcoming). On the margins: Transgender college students. *Journal of Gay and Lesbian Issues in Education*.

Namaste, V.K. (2000). *Invisible lives: The erasure of transsexual and transgendered people*. Chicago, IL: University of Chicago Press.

Pauly, L.B. (1998). Gender identity and sexual orientation. In D. Denney (Ed.). *Current concepts in transgender identity*, (pp.237–248). New York: Garland Press.

Pusch, R.S. (2003). *The bathroom and beyond: Transgendered college students' perspectives of transition.* Unpublished doctoral dissertation. Syracuse University.

Rankin, S.R. (2003). *Campus climate for gay, lesbian, bisexual, and transgender people: A national perspective.* New York: National Gay and Lesbian Task Force Policy Institute.

Rogers, J. (2000). Getting real at ISU: A campus transition. In K. Howard & A. Stevens (Eds.). *Out and about campus: Personal accounts by lesbian, gay, bisexual, and transgendered college students*, (pp.12–18). Los Angeles: Alyson.

Sanlo, R.L. (Ed.). (1998). *Working with lesbian, gay, bisexual, and transgender college students: A handbook for faculty and administrators.* Westport, CT: Greenwood Press.

Sanlo, R., Rankin, S., & Schoenberg, R. (2002). *Our place on campus: Lesbian, gay, bisexual, and transgender services and programs in higher education.* Westport, CT: Greenwood Press.

Schlossberg, N.K. (1989). Marginality and mattering: Key issues in building community. In D.C. Roberts (Ed.). *Designing campus activities to foster a sense of community* (New Directions for Student Services, no. 48, pp.5–15). San Francisco, CA: Jossey-Bass.

USA Today (June 22, 2004). Gender-neutral comes to campus, p. D2.

Case #22 LGBTQ: Finding Our Place

Nancy M. Gimbel

The OutCoalition, a campus organization for lesbian, gay, bisexual, transgender and questioning (LGBTQ) students, invited the College Conservatives, the College Liberals and the College Libertarians to debate the topic
of gay marriage. The College Conservatives agreed to the debate, but
decided not to participate a few days before the event, noting that their
viewpoints were vilified during last year's debate on gay marriage. To
decline the invitation, the College Conservatives sent the following letter
to OutCoalition via campus email:

Dear OutCoalition:
Thank you again for your invitation, but the College Conservatives is declining
your offer to participate in the debate on gay marriage. We don't think gay marriage is a legitimate issue, which is best represented by our choosing not to participate. There are several reasons why we will not participate.

First, we feel like the event last year in which we participated was intentionally
designed to make us look bad. As a result, we see no reason to participate again.
We felt that we were not given an equal chance to put forth our viewpoints in a
fair and unbiased forum. Basically, your "forum" is a farce that seeks only one
thing: to uplift those groups who support your viewpoint, while simultaneously
bashing groups that stand opposed to you. This is rather ironic, coming from a
group who is supposedly fighting tooth and nail for tolerance, diversity, and
"equal rights".

If gays want to be tolerated, they should knock off the political propaganda.
Those in the gay community aren't doing themselves any favors when they
flaunt their lifestyle and push for public celebration of it. If you expect not to be
judged according to who you like to have sex with, then you shouldn't define
yourselves by it! We refuse to help the gay community impose their lifestyle on
the rest of society.

We believe that this is a politically motivated event by a small group of people at
the university who are trying to persuade the rest of the university community to
change their views on a variety of issues. While we don't agree with homosexuality, we don't think that this should really be an issue at all. Simply put, we feel

that this is wrong and a gross misuse of both our time and others'. Whether or not a person is gay does not and should not affect how we view them, but we feel that being subjected to a constant barrage of homosexuality is quite inappropriate. You don't see straight people encouraging people to announce to the world that they are indeed heterosexual, but if you happen to be gay and participate in the same type of act, you are applauded and protected. This heinous double standard is one with which we would rather not be associated.

We believe that the fact that the Student Government Association actually funds your organization and pays for your events is absolutely ludicrous. We do not accept a dime from SGA, and we feel like a political organization such as yours whose sole purpose is to convince others of your views should not receive money either. An event such as this will only serve to damage the reputation of the university and present a misguided and immature image to the community, alumni, and professional institutions. What kind of an impression do parents receive when they come to visit their child for Parents' Weekend and are inundated with advertisements for a group that publicly advertises its sexual preference? What does this say about our priorities? The school has recently canceled a number of summer classes in the science curriculum due to lack of funding. Is it more important to provide students a top-notch science education or is it more important to provide students with an event at which they can ask witty questions about sex? Some might say that the university's priorities are misguided and perverted.

As an organization, we don't really care if you're gay or not, but nor should we have to hear about it constantly. As conservatives, we feel that sex is something sacred and private, and should therefore be kept that way. A person's homosexuality is a private matter to be discussed privately, not something that should be flaunted to the public. To support an organization whose only purpose is to unite members based on their common sexual preference is not only distasteful but a gross misuse of the university's resources. Not only is it morally questionable for the university to fund a sex club, it is also fiscally irresponsible to refuse funding to groups that support long standing American values in favor of funding a fringe group that can't even manage to be tasteful.

While the OutCoalition promotes itself as a social club, this distinction is misleading at best. Your goal is to push a political agenda supported by radical homosexual and leftist organizations and to convince people that homosexuality should be more acceptable and that gay marriage should be legal. Since we disagree with your views, we have no reason to help you in furthering them.

Sincerely,

The Executive Board of the College Conservatives

Many of the members of OutCoalition were offended and upset by the letter, which they considered hateful and full of stereotypes about the gay community. Several members of OutCoalition talked with Dean Christina Brassey, the director of Multicultural Affairs in the Dean of Students Office, requesting that the Office respond publicly to the College Conservatives. Dean Brassey decided against responding publicly, noting that her goal is to retaliate by providing more education and outreach so similar situations do not occur in the future. She mentioned to another administrator that a response would be a conflict of interest since she was the unofficial advisor for both the College Conservatives and the OutCoalition.

The OutCoalition president formulated a letter of response to the College Conservatives, posting the response and the original letter to the Out-Coalition website. Some OutCoalition members saw the letter as a weak rebuttal, mainly focusing on SGA funding and ignoring the "offensive" gay stereotypes. Several OutCoalition members felt that the administration had ignored their concerns and wondered if the Dean of Students Office would have responded publicly if a similar "hateful" letter had been sent to an African American student organization. Other members saw the Dean of Students Office response as "par for the course", typical of the administration's attitude towards LGBTQ students on campus.

The OutCoalition members decided to bring their concerns to the vice president of Student Affairs, who oversees the Dean of Students Office. In a letter to the vice president, the group members wrote that they felt "unacknowledged by the university" due to the university's lack of response to the letter from the College Conservatives, noting that the lack of response "shows ignorance of their concerns". The group noted that while LGBTQ students are not physically harassed on campus, the letter and the administration's lack of response to it are representative of a social climate on campus that does not accept LGBTQ students. The letter also charged that the administration ignores, through lack of resources and programming, complex identity issues of certain populations on campus, including African American LGBTQ students and transgender students. The letter concluded with a list of requests, including: 1) a public response to the College Conservatives' letter, 2) office space and resources for a LGBTQ center and 3) a designated staff person on campus to address LGBTQ concerns, a position that is currently nonexistent. OutCoalition is awaiting a response.

Institutional Setting

The state university, located in the southeast and founded in the late 1890s, is classified as a Doctoral/Research University—Extensive Institution on the *Carnegie Classification of Institutions of Higher Education*. There are approximately 16,000 undergraduate and graduate students on campus. Approximately 70% of students major in the sciences, although there is a significant liberal arts population on campus. Like many universities, it originally admitted only white, male students, until it opened its doors to women in the 1950s and African American students in the early 1960s. The first female faculty member was hired in the mid 1960s. Currently, male students comprise 69% of the undergraduate student population. Eighty-one percent of the faculty is male and 30% of faculty members are people of color. The approximate racial and ethnic breakdown of the undergraduate student populations is as follows: 68% white, 8% African American, 15% Asian, 3% Hispanic, .2% Native American, .6% multiracial, and 5% international. Ninety-two percent of the undergraduate population is between the ages of seventeen and twenty-three years. The average SAT of the most recent incoming freshman class was 1300.

Dean of Students Office and Director of Multicultural Affairs

The Dean of Students Office is comprised of the dean of students, three associate deans of students, two assistant deans of students, three coordinators, three directors, and seven administrative support people. The Office oversees student organizations, volunteer programs, disability services, student conduct and honor code violations, the judicial process, student programming, Greek affairs, diversity programming and education, the women's center, alcohol and drug awareness programs, student media, the counseling center, and student/faculty mediation. Each staff person is assigned a variety of responsibilities although no one in the Office or on campus is assigned to oversee outreach to or assess the needs of the LGBTQ students on campus. The counseling center, which is overseen by the Dean of Student's Office, has facilitated a well-attended support group for LGBTQ students for several years.

Christina Brassey, the director of Multicultural Affairs within the Dean of Students Office, is charged with the broad mission of reaching out to all student organizations to encourage them to partake in diversity education organized by the Dean of Students (DOS) Office. Brassey, who defines herself as "African American with French and English ancestry", is also the unofficial contact person on campus for students who feel they have been affected by racism, sexism, or homophobia. Although she is not assigned to oversee outreach to LGBTQ students, she serves as the volunteer advisor for the OutCoalition and the Coming Out Week planning committee.

When Dean Brassey joined the DOS Office seven years ago, she was charged with launching the university's first Office of Multicultural Affairs after founding a similar office at another southeastern public university. She earned her undergraduate degree in the liberal arts and a graduate degree in Student Personnel Services in Higher Education and worked in numerous student affairs divisions during the last fifteen years, including residence life, counseling, multicultural affairs, student activities, disability services, and women's affairs. Graduate students at the university recently recognized her as the Administrator of the Year and an opinion writer for the student newspaper wrote, "We should look to

Christina Brassey's efforts in fostering true diversity as an example of the right way to do things."

Although the Dean of Students Office has not assessed the LGBTQ population on campus to understand their numbers or specific needs, Dean Brassey, based on her interactions with LGBTQ students, knows they "need more resources" and attention. Due to her heavy workload, she reported that she would not have time to address LGBTQ programming needs even if the students or the university identified their specific needs; she barely has time to provide the diversity training and programming requested. One example Dean Brassey provided to illustrate the shortage of resources is the university's Safe Haven program, a program that has trained more than 200 faculty and staff members to serve as resources for LGBTQ students on campus. The DOS Office recently "inherited" the maintenance of the Safe Haven program when the student leader who launched the program three years ago recently graduated, leaving the program without a leader or a continuation plan. The program has not held a training event in almost two years.

Dean Brassey said the Safe Haven Program is illustrative of the way student concerns are addressed on campus. Students present a problem, like the lack of LGBTQ advocates on campus, and the students, with DOS support, solve the problems themselves by creating programs like Safe Haven. She described the university as a place where administrators encourage students, including OutCoalition leaders, to take ownership of the concerns and meet with the appropriate administrators to seek advice and resolution. She reported that on several occasions she attempted to assist the Out-Coalition leadership with strategizing their events and presence on campus but that the group has not taken advantage of her offers.

OutCoalition

The OutCoalition has existed in some form on the campus since the late 1980s. It started as an underground network of gay students on campus, but evolved into a group of approximately twenty to thirty students, that, according to one officer, is "decidedly apolitical". Their mission is to serve as a source of information, to promote a positive self-awareness, and to provide a social outlet for Gay, Lesbian, Bisexual, Transgender, Questioning people and their allies within the university community. The group is currently comprised of male students. Each year the group holds approximately six social events, several group meetings, and the October Coming Out Week celebration.

An officer reports that the group does not know how to attract female members and that when women attend group meetings he thinks they are "overwhelmed by the testosterone in the room". His perception is that there are not many lesbians on campus.

The group has Student Government Association funding of several hundred dollars, equal to other similarly sized groups, and always receives a fully enclosed student group office due to the privacy needs of the organization. There is some frustration among OutCoalition members since they share their office space with another organization, limiting the privacy the office was supposed to grant. The group recently lost their volunteer advisor who was very active with the group but left the university to accept a position at another college. He was instrumental in supporting the Safe Haven program and helping LGBTQ students organize. The group has not yet found an advisor, but is concerned that since it is a voluntary position, they might not find someone who is as dedicated as their former advisor.

In response to how the group is perceived on campus, an OutCoalition officer said that "it's not that the campus is anti-gay, it's just that students don't invest time in thinking about it or many important issues; they're too busy with school. If they're against it, they just ignore the OutCoalition programming. Protests are minimal on campus and often ignored."

The OutCoalition officer's comments mirror what some campus student leaders report about the apathy surrounding involvement in student activities. Although the campus boasts more than 300 student organizations, most students on campus are not intensely involved in student activities. The majority of students on campus are enrolled in schools focusing heavily on rigorous mathematic and scientific study, which, according to students, leaves little time for extracurricular activities. A survey of freshmen at the end of their first year revealed that before coming to college, 35% of students participated in an organized demonstration, but only 18% participated in one during the first year of college. In the first week of class only 18% of freshmen said they felt overwhelmed by all they had to do, but by the end of freshmen year that was up to 47%. In high school, 31% discussed politics but by the end of freshmen year only 18% had discussed it in the last year. The director of student activities cited the intense academic workload for the decrease in involvement and noted that students have little time or incentive to learn about cultures outside their own.

Campus Climate and Resources for LGBTQ Students on Campus

Consensus among several campus student affairs administrators who volunteer with LGBTQ students was that the resources for LGBTQ students were "scattered at best", leading to a climate where the letter from the College Conservatives could remain unaddressed because the institution lacks a staff person tasked with advocating for LGBTQ students. Two student affairs administrators noted that they looked to the Dean of Students Office for a response to the letter since the upper administration of the president's and provost's offices take a "hands off" approach to student affairs, allowing the DOS Office to address student diversity issues. This uninvolved stance frustrates some administrators and students; one student affairs administrator described a "missed opportunity" in which the president's office decided against providing a note of support for inclusion in the annual Coming Out Day advertisement. Although seemingly removed from LGBTQ student concerns, the administration has been described as avidly supporting the employee-driven movement to gain healthcare benefits for same-sex partners and include sexual orientation in the non-discrimination policy. The movement led to the university's decision to provide some domestic partnership benefits to LGBT faculty and staff, although the State Board of Higher Education prohibits the institution from providing full medical or retirement benefits for same-sex couples. The administration supported the non-discrimination and domestic partnership policies in an effort to remain competitive with peer institutions with which it competes for new faculty members. These different approaches to addressing LGBTQ student and faculty needs is a topic of discussion among LGBTQ student advocates who believe these students need to hear similar messages of inclusion from upper administration.

In describing the campus climate for LGBTQ students, the director of student activities noted that the general political climate in the state, whose citizens recently approved an amendment outlawing gay marriage, makes LGBTQ students feel isolated, like their concerns have been negated. She added that most staff members on campus, even those with graduate degrees in higher education, do not understand the phases of sexual orientation identity development and how this development manifests into behaviors. She noted that this could be one reason why LGBTQ student concerns or needs are not understood or addressed appropriately on campus.

Another student affairs administrator and LGBTQ student advocate added that the LGBTQ students have a magnified response to the normal feelings of disconnectedness that exist within the campus culture. A recent "Your First Year Survey" reported that only 57% of the university's freshmen men and 56% of freshman women were satisfied or very satisfied with the "overall sense of community among students", almost twenty percentage points lower then their peer institutions. According to an LGBTQ advocate, the disconnected environment is made more difficult for LGBTQ students due to a conservative political climate and rigorous curriculum on campus, both of which encourage students to put addressing sexual identity issues "on the back burner" until they finish college.

Dean Brassy noted that in this conservative campus environment, more students are closeted or in the questioning phase of their sexual orientation identity development, leading to fewer "out" students, students who could serve as resources for questioning students who may not feel comfortable visiting the counseling center or the Office of Multicultural Affairs.

The psychologist in the counseling center who oversees the sexual orientation support group noted that most students on campus "don't care if you're gay; they just don't want to see it". She also said that lesbians on campus experience a sort of "double minority"; they stay in the closet because they already feel different as a woman on campus and coming out makes them more different and isolated. Lisa Eades, the Director of the Women's Resource Center on campus, also noted that she was concerned about lesbian and bisexual women on campus because they are mainly invisible. On an anonymous survey of 700 women on campus, only 6 identified as lesbian or bisexual. She said she tries to make the Center a place for all women, regardless of sexual orientation and tries to show the students through individual conversations and programming that the center welcomes lesbians, bisexual women, and questioning women. She thinks it is possible that the general conservative culture on campus negates the accepting environment they find in the women's center, encouraging them to stay in the closet.

In responding to a question about the climate for LGBTQ students on campus, a member of the OutCoalition said that the residence halls, the places where new students start to understand how LGBTQ students are perceived and should be treated on campus, have become one of the most supportive places for LGBTQ students. According to the student, Residence Life organizes diversity trainings in the halls and responds quickly to reports of harassment. There are several "out" gay and lesbian staff members and more than 40% of the staff belong to the Safe Haven program.

Climate for Women and Students of Color on Campus

The following sections describe the social climate for women and students of color on campus and the programs directed at retention of these populations. Since the climate and degree of advocacy for LGBTQ students on campus may be linked to the university's response to other underrepresented groups on campus, these sections are included for reference and discussion of this case.

Climate for women on campus: In the 1990s, the president and provost supported several campus initiatives aimed at addressing the growing concerns of female faculty, staff, and students on campus. These concerns focused on the harassment and disregard for female students in the classroom, the scarce programs and activities directed towards female students, the reported differences in the tenure process, resources, and committee work for female faculty, and the small number of women in higher administrative positions.

The 1990s saw the first female dean on campus and the first female chair of an academic program. In the late 1990s, female students mobilized to secure funding from the university president for a one-room women's center. The Center recently moved to a large office suite with a library/study area, student assistant workroom, conference room, and director's office. The university first celebrated women's history month in 1994.

In the 1990s several academic programs focusing on the sciences launched retention programs aimed at female students. Additionally, two academic programs launched research centers specifically focusing on women within their disciplines. A mandatory faculty gender equity training program was started and met with incredible resistance by the faculty who felt it was not necessary.

Lisa Eades, the Director of the Women's Center reports seeing less faculty harassment of female students and more male students harassing female students, making comments that they are not qualified for the university's science programs. She added that the climate for women at the university exceeds that of its peer institutions, which are also male dominated, but still have some progress to make.

A recent freshman year survey showed that among females, self-ratings of academic ability declined more than twice as much as their male counterparts over the first year. In the beginning of the year, 96% of male freshmen and 92% of female freshmen rated themselves "above average" or "Highest 10%" compared with the average person in their age group. By the end of freshman year, the percentages were 90% for male students and 77% for female students. The survey also showed that 65% of female students reported feeling intimidated by their professors verses 46.2% of male students. The percentage of female students reporting that they were intimidated by their professors was significantly higher than that of peer schools. Female intellectual self-confidence was somewhat lower than that of students at peer schools.

Climate for Students of Color: The university voluntarily integrated in the 1960s, allowing African American students to enroll before the date mandated by the state. Through directed and aggressive admissions and retention efforts, the school has become one of the top schools of choice in the country for African American students looking to specialize in the natural sciences. The campus has an Office of Academic Support and Retention (OASR), founded in the 1980s, which provides academic success and retention programming directed at underrepresented students of color on campus, including college transition assistance, tutoring, mentoring, writing assistance, and honors recognition. Currently, this mission of OASR does not include programming for LGBTQ students.

Dean Brassey, the director of Multicultural Affairs, works closely with students of color on campus. Although the university dedicates significant resources to attracting and retaining students of color, and African American students in particular, Dean Brassey noted that the African American students do not have the same "love" for the university as white students. She noted that few will buy class rings, which are popular at the university, and they will not be as financially generous after graduation. They feel somewhat disappointed with the university, like it was not "all that it could have been for them." The African American students she works with say that they try to "get out of the university as soon as possible". They "stick it out" because of the tremendous reputation and earning potential of a degree from the university. According to the director of Multicultural Affairs, the average black student has the following attitude: "People here don't understand my culture or understand who I am and I'm tired of telling them, so I'll just play along." She says there is significant self-segregation of students of color, especially African American students, because "after a full day of sitting in class where you're the only student of color, you want to hang out with your own on your breaks."

Dilemma

The vice president of Student Affairs met with the deans and directors within the Dean of Students Office to strategize a response to the three OutCoalition requests, which included (1) public response to the letter from the College Conservatives, (2) office space and resources for a LGBTQ center and (3) a designated staff person on campus to handle LGBTQ concerns.

The staff was most divided on the demand to respond publicly to the College Conservatives' letter. Some staff members feel that the administration should not respond to the letter since a public response could result in a backlash against gay students, resulting in harassment and increased homophobia. These administrators feel the situation will dissipate over time and that the Office should respond with more education on campus. Several administrators argued that the letter is only a minor dispute between two organizations that could be resolved internally, without public response. Others say no response is needed since student problems usually resolve themselves through the public forum of the student newspaper and campus debate. One administrator who supports publicly responding to the College Conservatives' letter noted the LGBTQ students should not be asked to educate other students alone and argued that one of the goals of the DOS's Office was to respond to acts of intolerance on campus and make sure all students feel protected; not responding sends a message of support to the College Conservatives. Several administrators are concerned that admonishing the College Conservatives about their letter could infringe on the group's freedom of speech. Another issue raised is that a response to the letter could be seen as the DOS Office supporting or favoring OutCoalition over the College Conservative. The staff remained undecided on publicly responding to the letter.

In debating the requests for a LGBTQ student center and a designated staff person to oversee LGBTQ student outreach, the group acknowledged that a lack of statistics about LGBTQ students on campus hinders action on these requests. The campus has not surveyed LGBTQ students to understand their numbers or their needs.

As for possible placement of LGBTQ support services, several DOS administrators argue that LGBTQ concerns should be addressed through the Office of Multicultural Affairs. Other administrators cite the overburdened schedule of the director of Multicultural Affairs as an obstacle to adding LGBTQ needs to her responsibilities. One associate dean indicated discomfort with lumping LGBTQ concerns with other underrepresented populations, adding that there are unique challenges LGBTQ students face as a "hidden population". Some support channeling all LGBTQ advocacy issues through the counseling center, since anecdotal evidence illustrates that many LGBTQ students on campus are struggling with the exploratory phases of their sexual orientation identity development, a sensitive phase that could demand much psychological support. One staff member objected, noting that situating LGBTQ support services in the counseling center stigmatizes students, feeding into the myth that LGBTQ people are psychologically deficient. This same staff member advocated for placing LGBTQ support services with the DOS Office, which maintains a neutral, non-stigmatizing status on campus. At the end of the meeting, a response to the OutCoalition was still unformulated.

Discussion Questions

1. In this case, how do organizational structures and roles impact how the campus addressees, does not address, or partially addresses issues that impact LGBTQ students?
2. What suggestions would you offer the vice president of student affairs for addressing the three OutCoalition requests? Include in your suggestions ways to address the concerns voiced by staff members in the Dilemma section.

3. What freedom of speech issues are present in this case and how can the administration respond to student groups' rights to voice their opinions on controversial issues?

4. What are the ramifications of responding or not responding to the College Conservatives' letter?

5. If you advise the administration to publicly respond to the College Conservatives, strategize the method of address, the content of the message, the anticipated student feedback, and administration's response to this feedback.

6. At this university, student movements brought about the creation of the women's center, Coming Out Week, and the Safe Haven program. To what extent should students be responsible for mobilizing to advocate for their own interests? Is the university responsible for anticipating and addressing these concerns first? Are there populations who are unable to advocate for themselves?

7. If the vice president decided to create a LGBTQ student center and hire a designated staff person to address LGBTQ student concerns, what opposition or obstacles could emerge? How would you respond to these obstacles or opponents?

8. What are the long-term consequences of maintaining a campus culture that encourages students to delay sexual orientation identity exploration and development until after college? Does the student's "stage" of sexual orientation identity development affect programming and outreach methods? If yes, how?

Recommended Readings

Evans, N. (2000). Creating a positive learning environment for gay, lesbian and bisexual students. *New Directions for Teaching & Learning*, 82 (Summer) 81–87.

Dunkel, N.W. & Schuh, J.H. (1998). *Advising student groups and organizations. The Jossey-Bass higher and adult education series*. San Francisco, CA: Jossey-Bass.

Henquinet, J., Phibbs, A., & Skoglund, B. (2000). Supporting our lesbian, bisexual, and transgender students. *About Campus*, 5 (5), 24–26.

Love, P.G. (1997). Contradiction and Paradox: Attempting to change the culture of sexual orientation at a small Catholic college. *Review of Higher Education*, 20 (4), 381–398.

Mallory, S.L. (Winter 1997). The rights of gay student organizations at public state-supported institutions. *NASPA Journal*, 34 (2), 82–90.

McRee, T.K., & Cooper, D.L. (Fall 1998). Campus environments for gay, lesbian, and bisexual students at southeastern institutions of higher education. *NASPA Journal*, 36 (1), 48–60.

Mohr, J.L. & Sedlacek, W.E. (2000). Perceived barriers to friendship with lesbian and gay men among university students. *Journal of College Student Development*, 41 (1), 70–80.

O'Neil, R.M. (1997). *Free speech in the college community.* Bloomington, IN: Indiana University.

Ritchie, C.A. & Banning, J.H. (2001). Gay, lesbian, bisexual, and transgender campus support offices: A qualitative study of establishment experiences. *NASPA Journal*, 38 (4), 482–494.

Tierney, W.G. (1992). Building academic communities of difference: Gays, lesbians and bisexuals on campus. *Change*, 224 (2), 40–46.

Van Loon, R. (2001). Organizational change: A case study. *Innovative higher education*, 25 (4), 285–301.

Case #23 Identity Development and Transition Issues in the First-year Experience

FRANK E. ROSS AND JULIA M. LASH

Key Character

Bobby

Getting Out and Getting On

Bobby, actually Robert II, lives in a small southwestern town of 15,000. Bobby was valedictorian of his graduating class and captain of the tennis team. He is very popular with his peers, teachers, and elders in his neighborhood. Bobby is very active in his church and religion is an integral part of his family's life and values. His church is part of a conservative, evangelical, Christian denomination.

Eighteen- year old Bobby is the oldest child in his family. His father works at a nearby power plant and his mother is a secretary at a local legal firm. Bobby's parents are very successful in their work, although neither attended college. The family is relatively financially secure and middle-class. Bobby has received many scholarships due to his academic success, allowing him to attend the college of his choice. Bobby has two younger sisters, aged fifteen and twelve years. They both do well in school. The entire family is very excited about Bobby's plans to attend college. Since Bobby is the first in his family, including his extended family, to attend college, everyone is anticipating his success and looking to him as a role model to his younger siblings and cousins.

Bobby plans to attend Coastal Research University—150 miles from his home town. He plans to major in biology and later attend medical school. Bobby considered attending a nearby Bible college for his undergraduate education, but feared he would appear less competitive to medical schools in the future. He is somewhat nervous about the transition from his small town to the large university.

Bobby is also concerned about his relationship with his girlfriend of two years. Shelly is a year younger and will be a senior in high school. The couple had discussed engagement, but decided to delay that decision at the recommendation of their pastor. Bobby was somewhat relieved at this recommendation, as he is uncertain about the idea of marriage. While he feels very close to Shelly and loves being with her, he does not feel the physical attraction to her that his friends talk about. Bobby and Shelly have not engaged in intercourse, attributing this to their religious values. But, Bobby knows that several of his church friends have been much more physical in their relationships. Bobby wonders if Shelly was the "right woman" for him.

Coastal Research University

Coastal Research University (CRU) is a public research university located in a large city on the west coast, only five miles from the Pacific Ocean. The large campus is home to 174 buildings and sprawls across over 400 acres. The University enrolls nearly 40,000 students, with almost 26,000 undergraduates and over 12,000 graduate students. The university is home to eleven professional schools, in addition to its College of Letters and Science. Currently CRU boasts 200 degree programs for graduate students, with 118 undergraduate programs. In addition, Coastal Research University's library has 7.6 million volumes, and ranks among the top ten university libraries in the country.

Welcome to Campus!

Bobby was nervous, yet excited to move to campus. His entire extended family, including Shelly, loaded up the van and made the nearly three-hour drive to CRU during move-in weekend. Bobby and his family entered the campus to a flurry of student activity—sorority and fraternity members were adorned in matching t-shirts helping new students move-in, returning students were in the courtyard playing volleyball, and hordes of confused new students and their families were wandering around trying to make sense of the new surroundings.

Bobby clutched Shelly's hand and walked into the main lobby of his new home, Paige Hall. His academic advisor during new student orientation advised Bobby to stay in Paige Hall, as it was the themed living community for freshmen students with an interest in science. No one else from Bobby's small high school was attending CRU, and his advisor told Bobby it would help him make friends with other students who had similar interests.

Plus, the advisor mentioned another benefit was the building was co-educational so females were allowed on the men's floors 24 hours a day. Bobby failed to mention that small detail to Shelly or his family.

The group made their way up three flights of stairs to his new home. The stairwell was noisy from sounds of booming music, student laughter and grumblings of his father saying "as much as you pay to go here, you'd think they would have an elevator in this place!" As they reached the third floor, Bobby took a deep breath and wondered how his life would change. 310, 312, 314, 316! They reached room 316, which was located right across the hall from the restroom. The door was decorated with sports paraphernalia, including two crossed chemistry beakers made from construction paper with names reading "Robert" and "Nathan."

Bobby entered his room to find a tall, sun kissed man with curly blonde hair. "Hi! You must be Robert; I'm Nate," he exclaimed, and stuck out his hand. Bobby thought to himself, "Is *this* my roommate?" "Hey, call me Bobby." Bobby introduced his family and Shelly to his new roommate. They discovered Nate was from the Midwest, and was attending CRU on a full-ride scholarship. His charming smile, polite demeanor and incredible manners made the family very comfortable and confident that Bobby was going to have a good roommate. Everyone liked Nate—especially Bobby.

Bobby and Nate became fast friends. They spent all of welcome week together—playing Frisbee, listening to music, working out, and attending student activities on campus. Bobby felt like he had known Nate his entire life. They laughed about how much they had in common, from their favorite movies to sports teams. The more they hung out together, the more Bobby felt this incredible bond to Nate—something he had never felt before.

Bobby had Shelly back home, and at first he talked to her on the phone nightly. Already the transition of being separated from his girlfriend was difficult and he wondered what would happen to them. Nate, on the other hand, was single. His mission during welcome week was to meet as many women as possible. He explained to Bobby that there is nothing wrong with harmless flirting. By the end of welcome week, Nate had invited many CRU women back to their room in the residence hall to party. Bobby was enjoying his time away from home, meeting new people, and hanging out with Nate.

Tau Delta Epsilon

On the last day of welcome week, the student life office organized a student organization fair on campus. This was an opportunity for all new students to get information on all the campus clubs, including social fraternities and sororities. Nate's father and older brother were both members of Tau Delta

Epsilon fraternity and had encouraged him to check out the chapter at CRU. Bobby's family, never having attended college, warned him about the evils of fraternities. Nonetheless, he and Bobby decided to attend the fair together, just to see what it was all about. CRU had a deferred recruitment policy, and did not allow first semester freshmen to join the Greek organizations. But this fair gave new students the opportunity to preview the Greek groups on campus, in preparation for the spring quarter when recruitment would take place.

The pair was very impressed with the Tau Delta Epsilon chapter. The Tau Delt's had the highest over-all grade point average for the fraternities, and consistently ranked above the all-men's average on campus. The chapter's national philanthropic cause was the Pediatric AIDS Foundation, and the men worked many hours annually raising money and awareness for their cause. Tau Delt was known as the preppy jock fraternity on campus. Many of its members participated in high school athletics, which helped them dominate the campus intramural competitions.

Nate and Bobby were both impressed with Tau Delt. Because of his father and brother, Nate was instantly accepted at the house and invited to attend their parties. Although he knew his parents would not approve if they knew, Bobby attended the parties with Nate, which exposed him to all of the evils his mother had warned him about—beer and sorority women. As the weeks progressed, and with more pressure from Nate, Bobby began consuming alcohol. The more that Bobby drank the more fun he and Nate seemed to have. Soon, both Nate and Bobby were leaving the parties with women and bringing them back to their residence hall room. Bobby, who came to CRU a virgin, was beginning to experiment sexually with these women. This pattern continued and often late night parties and next-day hangovers prohibited Bobby from attending his morning classes.

The Incident in Sociology Class

Bobby was enrolled in an introductory sociology class, which met twice a week in the afternoons. This course was much more interesting than the difficult pre-med science course his advisor had placed him in. In fact, Bobby surprised himself in how much he liked the topics he was studying in sociology. He also admired his professor, Dr. Haas, a middle-aged engaging professor who liked to talk about rock and roll and his excessive drug usage during the 1970s. Dr. Haas incorporated stories from his life in class and made the discussion very interesting. Bobby always enjoyed coming to this class.

One day in early October, Dr. Hass invited in a panel of students to the class to talk about diversity at CRU. There were eight students representing various cultural and religious student organizations on campus. Dr. Haas introduced the topic of diversity to the class and then allowed each panel member to introduce himself or herself. One by one, the students talked about their organization and activities they participated in. Coming from a small town, Bobby had not experienced much diversity and was learning a lot from his peers. Then, Curtis spoke.

Curtis was the president of the Spectrum, which he described as the "queer student alliance" at CRU. Bobby suddenly found himself a bit nervous, but very interested in hearing what Curtis had to say. Curtis went on to mention gay, lesbian, bisexual, transgendered and questioning students were all welcome in Spectrum, as were their straight allies. He talked about the advocacy work they do in the community, as well as the campus events they help sponsor with the CRU queer resource center. He finished by handing out a list of the national coming out week events that were scheduled for the next week. Bobby quickly shoved his in his folder.

After the panel concluded, Dr. Haas asked the class if they had any questions. An interesting discussion followed each question. Then, a hand shot up from the back of the room. "Yeah, Dr. Haas, can you tell me why these faggots get a special week and what they are all celebrating? That sounds *gay* to me!" Roars of laughter came from the class. Bobby nervously looked at Dr. Haas, to see what his response to the question would be. Instead of saying anything, the professor simply shook his head and smiled. Curtis promptly spoke up and delivered an eloquent answer, as if he had said it a million times. But Bobby could not focus on that. He became very uncomfortable, and felt as if his heart had stopped. He admired Dr. Haas so much—why did he not say or do anything? Did Dr. Haas think being gay was wrong, too? Bobby was so confused.

Mid-term Week

The week before Fall Break was pretty intensive at CRU. Most professors scheduled mid-term examinations and many class projects were due that week. Bobby was a little nervous because he knew his grades were not as good as they could be, and he did not want to disappoint his parents. He figured he could make up for lost time with good exams this week. While he had good intentions, Bobby found himself very distracted and not able to concentrate.

There was a long-standing tradition at CRU of *the* Thursday night. To celebrate the end of mid-term week, and to give a proper send-off to Fall Break, every mid-term week ended on Thursday night with major campus-wide parties in all of the fraternity houses. This year was no exception. Nate and Bobby started drinking in their room, and decided to finish a six-pack before they made their way to the Tau Delt house. Bobby was not happy with his performance on exams this week, but Nate reminded him that this was the night to forget about it all. The roommates finished their last can and made way across campus.

The Tau Delt house was more crowded that night than the guys had ever seen. Being regulars, they were recognized at the front door and welcomed inside by brothers offering them can after can of cheap beer. Midterms were over; Bobby was hanging out with his best friend; girls from their favorite sorority were there. This was a night to celebrate!

A Tau Delt party tradition occurs at midnight when all the brothers lock arm-in-arm and form a circle on the dance floor. Nate and Bobby, who both had shown interest in pledging next spring, had been pulled into the circle tonight. They scream a favorite fraternity cheer, which is typically loaded with derogatory words toward a rival fraternity on campus, chug a beer and finish with a group hug. Nate looked over at Bobby, smiled, and yelled "I love you, man!" In that moment of intoxicated excitement, Bobby finally felt like he belonged.

The drunken pair walked back to Paige Hall, loudly singing Tau Delta Epsilon songs at the top of their lungs. They fumbled their way in the side entrance of the residence hall and up the stairs to their room. The pair decided to keep partying, and both cracked open another can of beer. Loud music and more fraternity chanting drew the attention of Shane, the resident assistant. Shane entered the room prepared to offer a warning regarding the noise, and finds a trash can full of empty beer cans, with opened cans in the hand of both intoxicated residents. The "night they would never forget" ended with an alcohol violation and noise violation for both residents. That night as he was falling asleep, all Bobby could think about was the party and Nate hugging him and telling him that he loved him. "I love you, too, Nate," he whispered. At that moment, everything seemed to feel right.

Fall Break

With everything that had been happening, Bobby was a bit relieved to be going home for fall break. He was confused and distressed. He hoped time with his family, Shelly, his church, and his old friends would "straighten" him out. Everyone was excited to see him and hear about his experiences. Bobby put on a happy face and told his family and friends about his academics and the parts of his social life he thought he could share.

Bobby wished he could talk with his parents about his confusion, as he had when deciding about college and discussing his potential engagement to Shelly. But, he knew how they felt about homosexuality. His uncle Charlie was gay, at least that is what Bobby thought; the family had not seen Charlie for twenty years and on the rare occasions his name was mentioned, they shook their head and uttered a prayer for his salvation. Uncle Charlie had attempted to contact Bobby to congratulate him on graduation, but Bobby heard his father tell Charlie over the phone that he did not want him to have any contact with his son. When Bobby asked why, his father replied that uncle Charlie had "chosen a sinful way of life."

Bobby and Shelly went out with friends on Saturday night. On the way home, Bobby felt very uncomfortable. He knew he had been intimate with other women, and Shelly was beginning to talk about having sex. But, Bobby did not feel the same type of attraction and excitement that he felt about Nate. He cared about Shelly, and did not want to hurt her. So, he used his old excuse, and told Shelly they would need to wait until marriage. He knew that would never happen.

On Sunday morning, Bobby and Shelly attended church with the rest of Bobby's family. When Bobby walked into the church, many people came to hug him. He was glad to see so many familiar and loving faces. Then it hit him, "Would they love me and hug me if they knew?" Bobby used to love singing the hymns in church, but today, he only mouthed the words. A sense of sadness and shame fell over him. Then Pastor Tom began the sermon. As was often the case, he spoke about the difficulties of walking on "God's path" in the midst of the "sinful world." Today, however, his choice of "sinfulness" was homosexuality. Pastor Tom was talking about recent Gay Pride celebrations on the west coast, and warned the congregation about the attempts of homosexuals to "seduce young boys." Bobby suddenly felt ill. Pastor Tom exclaimed, "We must protect our children, until God damns these sinful people to an eternal hell!" Bobby's heart raced, he became pale, he began to sweat, and he felt like he could not breathe. Bobby ran from the church and vomited in the parking lot. As his mother came to comfort him, he simply said, "I have the flu."

Bobby spent much of the rest of the day in bed. That evening, he joined his family at the dinner table. As the family talked, laughed, and enjoyed the togetherness, Bobby began to relax. Then, his father asked, "Bobby, do you see any of 'those people' at that university?" Bobby knew what his father meant, and began to feel ill again. His father said, "I hope you don't have to deal with any of them, and, even though I have taught you not to fight, you do whatever you have to if one of *them* even looks at you!" Bobby just said, "Yea Dad" and excused himself to return to his room. He left for school early the next morning.

Back to School

When Bobby returned to CRU, he found a note from the Residence Hall Director to meet with him as soon as possible. Bobby went to his room, and went to bed. When he finally went to see the Director two days later, he saw Bobby immediately. Mr. Winston told Bobby he was very concerned about him. Of course, he mentioned the intoxication incident before break. He also had been contacted by Bobby's first year seminar class instructor, who told Mr. Winston that Bobby had missed nearly half of the class meetings. Mr. Winston informed Bobby that there would be disciplinary actions due to his residence hall behavior. However, he also told Bobby he was very concerned about him and asked Bobby if there was anything troubling him. Bobby informed Mr. Winston that he was considering leaving CRU and going to the local Bible College back home because he no longer thought he was capable of becoming a physician. Mr. Winston was confused, as Bobby's grades had remained well above average, despite his lack of consistent attendance. Bobby began to cry. As Mr. Winston put his hand on Bobby's shoulder to comfort him, Bobby jumped up and ran from the office. Later that day, Bobby's resident assistant, Shane, knocked on his door and handed Bobby a brochure about the Campus Counseling Center.

Counseling?

The next day, Bobby felt like he had nowhere else to turn and felt totally alone for the first time in his life. He picked up the phone and called the Campus Counseling Center. He was told he could come in that afternoon to talk to a counselor. Bobby was nervous and not sure what he would actually tell a counselor. Would they tell him he was sick? Would they tell him he was going through a phase? Would they tell him to go experiment? Would they tell him to give up his religion? Would they tell him he was crazy? Would they tell him to go home?

Bobby was surprised. The counselor listened, did not judge, and did not tell Bobby what to do. He discovered that his "flu" symptoms at church were likely caused by a panic attack. Bobby attended counseling weekly and felt like the counselor actually understood his confusion and conflicts. After about four weeks, the counselor brought out a list of GLBTQ groups and activities on campus and in the city. As she handed this list to Bobby, he suddenly felt afraid. The counselor told Bobby that she wanted him to attend at least two activities on that list before the next session. Bobby began to feel ill, sweat, shook, and felt like he could not breathe. The counselor barely noticed, and Bobby left the session.

Bobby knew he could not go to any of these events. But, he was afraid his counselor would be disappointed in him. So, he did not return to counseling the next week, or the next. One day, Bobby received a phone call from his counselor and she invited him to schedule an appointment. When

he told her he was not sure if he wanted to continue, his counselor suggested he come in to talk about his uncertainty. When Bobby entered his
counselor's office, he began to cry and told her that he did not attend any
events. He apologized for not complying and disappointing her. The counselor said she was not disappointed, and actually apologized for not talking
the assignment through with Bobby before he left the last appointment.
They began to discuss how Bobby felt about attending GLBTQ activities,
and how he was feeling about himself.

Discussion Questions

1. What are the relevant issues of identity development and conflict
    for Bobby? Discuss the following issues:
    a. transition to college
    b. transition to an urban environment
    c. alcohol issues
    d. religion issues
    e. desire to belong ("mattering")
    f. first generation to college
    g. others?
2. Describe Bobby at the beginning, middle, and end of this scenario
    based on our knowledge of:
    a. Student development theory
    b. Gay identity development theory
    c. Other models of identity development
3. What were significant aspects of the incident in sociology class?
    What would you recommend Mr. Haas have done differently?
4. List and discuss any ethical concerns related to:
    a. The first year seminar instructor's contact with Mr. Winston
    b. Mr. Winston's actions when talking with Bobby
5. If you were the Resident Assistant, how would you have approached
    Bobby with information about the Counseling Center?
6. How can you explain Bobby's reluctance to follow his counselor's
    recommendation that he attend GLBTQ activities? How would you
    suggest the counselor have handled that situation differently?

Recommended Readings

Alexander, C.J. (Ed.). (1996). *Gay and lesbian mental health: A sourcebook for practitioners.*
    Binghamton, NY: Harrington Park Press.
Alexander, C.J. (1997). *Growth and intimacy for gay men: A workbook.* Binghamton, NY:
    Harrington Park Press.

Dworkin, S.H. & Gutiérrez, F.J. (1992). *Counseling gay men & lesbians: Journey to the end of the rainbow.* Alexandria, VA: American Association for Counseling and Development.

Evans, N.J. & Wall, V.A. (Eds.). (1991). *Beyond tolerance: Gays, lesbians, and bisexuals on campus.* Alexandria, VA: American College Personnel Association.

McEwan, M.K. (2003). New perspectives on identity development. In S. Komives & D.B. Woodard and Associates (Eds.). *Student services: A handbook for the profession* (4th ed., pp. 203–233). San Francisco, CA: Jossey-Bass.

Sanlo, R., Rankin, S., Schoenberg, R. (2002). *Our place on campus: Lesbian, gay, bisexual, transgender services and programs in higher education.* Westport, CT: Greenwood Press.

Part V *Student Affairs and External Relations*

Case #24 Student Affairs Unit's Stepchildren: Black Greek Letter Organizations Receive Unsatisfactory Advising

O. GILBERT BROWN AND CHRISTOPHER RIDDICK

Institutional Setting

Russet University is located in the scenic town of Haysville. The university is the largest employer of the town. The population is an estimated 70,000. Apart from the University, the next largest employers in the town are Frieght-com Industrial (an escalator parts manufacturer) and Whar-Al (a farming and produce co-op). Whites constitute 87% of the town's population. One local establishment, the Water Cooler Lounge and Bar is known, by word of mouth, for its unfriendly demeanor towards Latinos and African Americans.

Russet University is a large mid-western Research I university. Russet is especially known for its premier business programs, particularly its evening MBA program. Other notable graduate programs include journalism and education. While considered a tier-two institution, Russet is still strong in various undergraduate programs including English, secondary education, and sports management.

The student population consists of approximately 34,000 undergraduate, graduate, and professional students. White students constitute the majority population of Russet. Respectively, the student percentage is white 83%, Asian 7%, black/African American 4%, Latino 2%, Native American 1%, and other 3%. The majority of Russet's student population (73%) consists of in-state students while the remaining 37% are out-of-state. Underrepresented (Native Americans, Latinos, and African Americans) students share a common view that Russet has an unfriendly campus climate for students who look like them.

Campus Climate

Students' perceptions of the campus climate are often different depending on their racial and ethnic backgrounds. White students walk around campus with the unspoken impression that Russet is their campus and Haysville's bar strip belongs to them. White students are more than likely to select terms of "warm", "sunny", and "clear skies" to describe their satisfactory experiences about pursuing their undergraduate degrees at Russet.

Definitely, there is a small subculture of African American students who are satisfied with their collegiate experiences at Russet, however, on aggregate black students have been the most vocal in their unsatisfactory views about the campus climate. African American students are more than likely to select terms of "chilly", "cold", and "partly cloudy" to describe their partially satisfactory to unsatisfactory perceptions of Russet. Some contributing factors to Black undergraduates' partially unsatisfactory views are:

- Institutional tradition of unsatisfactory responses to hate crimes, racial bigotry, and discrimination in the campus and surrounding community
- "Black Out" appears to be the order of the day with the institution's first black president and men's basketball coach being forced to resign due respectively to pressure from white faculty, donors, and alumni.
- Campus and the surrounding community failure to develop a cultural (beauty and barber shops)infrastructure that reinforces the black presence
- White and black students primarily interact in the classroom, laboratories, and studios. Social isolation primarily exists between white and black students outside of the classroom.
- Lower graduation rates of African American students compared to white, Asian, and Latino students

Student Engagement

The Higher Education and Student Affairs literature has long supported that undergraduates who perceive satisfactory academic and social (collegiate) experiences compared to undergraduates who perceive unsatisfactory collegiate experiences tend to have higher rates of persistence, academic achievement, and graduation at residential campuses (Kuh, Branch Douglas, Lund, & Gyurnek-Ramin, 1994; Kuh, Kinzie, Schuh, & Whitt, 2005; & Tinto, 1993). Purposeful student engagement is critical to undergraduates' having satisfactory collegiate experiences. Briefly, engagement is a concept that describes undergraduates' devotion of time and energy toward educational purposeful activities (in-class curriculum and out-of-class curriculum) which impacts their collegiate experiences and degree attainment (Kuh, Schuh, & Whitt, 1991; Kuh et.al. 1994).

Greek Letter Organizations

Greek letter organizations are one of the main institutional recognized and supported peer groups that foster students' engagement with the institution (Kuh et al. 1991; Kuh et al. 1994; Pike, 2000). In general, traditionally white Greek letter organizations (TWGLOs) and historically black Greek letter organizations (HBGLOs) provide members opportunities to acquire leadership experiences, cultivate sisterhood or brotherhood, network with academic and potential career networks, impact the campus and the larger community through their community and service projects (Dungy Jordan, 2003; Hammrick, Evans, & Schuh, 2002; Harper 2005; 2006). However, TWGLOs' and HBGLOs' contributions to members, students, institution, and the larger community should be placed in the context of the uneven (financial assets and quality of institutional advising/support) playing field that exists for majority organizations (more assets) and underrepresented organizations (less assets) at most traditionally white institutions (TWIs) (Kimbrough, 2003; Ross, 2000). For the purposes of this case, we will interchangeably use the socially constructed terms of African American or black Americans to describe the descendants of former West African slaves in the United States.

Student Affairs

Student Affairs has four general roles at institutions of higher education (IHEs). A major responsibility of the division is cultivating and sustaining a partnership between Academic and Student Affairs. Also, the division is responsible for the creation and management of programs and services which sustain and enrich students at the campus. Next, the division serves as the institutional administrative unit responsible for fostering and supervising student engagement with institutional recognized student organizations. Finally, divisional leaders collaborate with students and faculty to create and maintain a campus climate that welcomes and supports diverse learners. Briefly, Student Affairs' combined roles cumulatively impact undergraduates' attainment of their BA/BS degree at IHEs (Dungy Jordan, 2003; Hammrick, Evans, & Schuh).

At many campuses, Student Affairs' portfolio includes Student Activities and Greek Affairs units which are the division's entities with direct responsibility for collaborating with students to gain leadership experiences in recognized campus organizations. Russet's Student Affairs division has historically treated TWGLOs as its natural children and HBGLOs as the step children in the campus's Greek letter organization family.

Office of Student Organization and Involvement (OSIO)/ Greek Affairs

OSIO is the Student Affairs unit with responsibilities for undergraduates' out-of-classroom experiences including Greek letter organizations. OSIO governs the more than 250 recognized student organizations including Greek organizations and the student government. Russet is a Greek oriented campus where 5000 of 34,000 students are members of Greek letter organizations. Dan Elfman is the Assistant Dean of Students and OSIO Director. He has been the Director for seven years. Elfman came to Russet having served as an Associate Director of Student Activities for three years at another institution. He obtained his undergraduate degree from Russet which was seen as a plus when he was hired. It has been no secret that Elfman has been searching for a new job at another institution for the past year.

Perhaps feeling burned out from serving at the same institution for several years, Elfman has developed a reputation as a nonchalant administrator especially by his interactions with Latino and Black Greek letter organizations. For unknown reasons, Elfman still has his position in the face of the widespread perception across the campus about his general malfeasance. Elfman reports to the legendary Vice President for Student Affairs Butler Crenshaw who held his position earlier in his career.

Butler Crenshaw has served the university for over thirty years in different capacities ranging from Elfman's Assistant Dean position, Associate Dean, and now Vice President for Student Affairs. Crenshaw virtually created OSIO during his tenure as Assistant Dean. He is very "careful" in making decisions. Dean Elfman directly answers to him. Crenshaw has conflicted feelings about Elfman's performance as Assistant Dean. On the one hand, Crenshaw really appreciated Elfman's energy and performance as Assistant Dean during his first three years on campus. On the other hand, the Vice President believes Elfman is not performing at the level required to provide leadership to all spheres of his unit. Since Crenshaw continues to give him satisfactory evaluations and raises, Elfman believes that he is still performing beyond expectations. Crenshaw partially addressed his concerns about Elfman by working around him by interacting directly with Rowland Fisher who is the Assistant Director of OSIO and Director of Greek Affairs.

Fisher was Dean Elfman's first hire. He has been the Director of Greek Affairs for the past five years. He focuses mainly on the programmatic, philanthropic, and academic endeavors of the councils. Fisher's Iranian ethnic heritage and precollege socialization as an adopted child in a white family allows him to understand aspects of both the "White perspective" and "racial minority's perspective." The Director of Greek Affairs reports to the Assistant Dean for OSIO and he is responsible for supervising the four councils that govern different subcommunities within the Greek system:

- Intercultural Greek Council (ICGC)
  ICGC is the self-governing body that represents the four students of color Greek letter organizations not affiliated with Black Greek Association Council. The council oversees two historical Latina sororities, an Asian American interest sorority, an Asian interest fraternity, and an Intercultural sorority. Greek Affair's graduate advisor (ten dollar hour/ten hours) serves as advisor to ICGC. ICGC organizations have between 20–30 members most years. The different chapters do not have fraternity or sorority houses and they must hold business and social meetings in university facilities.
- Greek Fraternity Council (GFC)
  GFC is a self-governing body representing the 26 fraternities on campus. The Council works to accomplish its goals through a committee structure focusing on different areas including chapter development, scholarship, community development, member education, alumni relations, and public relations. Greek Affair's graduate assistant advises the six member executive committee. The different chapters have fraternity houses on Greek row.
- Sorority Alliance (SA)
  SA oversees all 19 women's chapters and constantly encourages the women to go above and beyond personal and communal expectations. Greek Affair's graduate assistant advises SA. The different chapters have sorority houses on Greek row.
- Black Greek Association (BGA)

BGA is a self-governing unit of the Divine Nine which are the historically black Greek letter organizations. BGA establishes guidelines for how each organization brings in new members and it provides a structure to each organization's founding week. Eight/nine organizations currently have chapters on campus. Depending on the year, the entire BGA population varies between 60–80 members. On the whole, HBGLOs perceive that OSIO has failed to provide them with comparable satisfactory leadership training, advising, and infrastructure support as received by their white counterparts. Thus, these student organizations believe that they have had bifurcated (academic satisfaction and mixed social fulfillment) collegiate experiences at Russet.

Black Greek Stepchildren in Student Affairs

OSIO's professional staff has provided unsatisfactory advising, mentoring, and leadership development functions to BGA in the following areas: (1) Uneven governance advising support, (2) Inadequate leadership training and development (3) Shifting OSIO advising/mentor roles to Dr.Elaine Washington, (4) providing uneven logistical support to BGLOs scheduling weekend parties in campus facilities, and (5) Symbolically OSIO is absent at BGLOs' academic and social programming.

Uneven Governance Support

Elfman and Fisher have devoted more staffing and training resources toward advising the mainstream Greek Fraternity Council and Sorority Alliance while devoting inadequate resources toward BGA. The offices hired and appointed two graduate Assistants (.50 FTE) assigned to advise the Greek Fraternity Council and Sorority Alliance while they hired and appointed a (.25 FTE) graduate assistant to advise BGA. Historically, the Greek Affairs positions are highly sought after graduate assistantship by Masters students in College Student Personnel Administration. Thus, the Assistant Dean and Greek Affairs Director usually get to select the cream of the crop of prospect graduate positions to work with these two councils. Career minded graduate students realize the market value of their experiences and they tend to keep the assistantship during their two year program. Previous graduate students appointed to these positions interact frequently with the Assistant Dean and Director of Greek Affairs. A perk of the positions is graduate students are encourage to participate in the nationally recognized Greek Leadership Seminar held every summer at Russet. Career minded graduate students are able to network with Dean level staff who will be searching for Greek Affairs staff during the next hiring cycle.

OSIO's and Student Affairs' constant reorganization of the BGA advisor position has contributed to the position loosing some of its luster within the graduate application pool. Twenty years ago, OSIO and Student Affairs hired a twelve month (100 FTE) staff person to provide advising/mentoring support to BGA. Several years later, senior leaders reorganized the position into a ten month (100 FTE) position. The change from twelve month to ten month contract prompted the incumbent advisor to seek employment at another institution. For a couple of years, OSIO and Student Affairs supported BGA with a full-time person in the academic year only. After his departure, OSIO and Student Affairs re-organized the advisor position from a full-time to graduate fee remission assistantship (50% FTE). OSIO hired different graduate assistants to serve as BGA advisor. Several years later, OSIO and Student Affairs perceiving budgetary problems reorganized the advisor position from a graduate fee remission assistantship to its current graduate hourly position (ten hours a week at ten dollars per hour).

OSIO's staffing approach for BGA showed several patterns. BGA advisors were all African Americans who were alumni members of different Divine Nine organizations. Also, OSIO often paid inadequate attention to staff selection, training, and supervision, and mentoring of the BGA advisor. Thus, OSIO would have a black face in the office, but the staff person work was not meeting BGA's multiple needs (leadership training, membership in-take process, and knowledge of best practices in chapter development). Over the past 15 years, OSIO has had personnel turn-over in its Assistant Dean and Director of Greek Affairs positions, however, the personnel changes did not result in a new and positive approach toward fostering the growth and development of black Greek letter organizations.

For different reasons, OSIO's BGA advisor position is not considered a plum position among graduate students from the College Student Personnel Program. OSIO's position is not a fee remission position which would attract a strong applicant pool among graduate students. Thus, personnel turnover is closely associated with the BGA advisor position. NOW, the position typically attracts a graduate student who has an assistantship in another office, but he or she seeks to supplement his or her earnings with another part time position on campus. BGA advisor, unlike the other graduate staff, typically does not receive the all-around graduate assistantship experiences that enhance the resume which results in the person being highly marketable in entry level positions following graduation. Previous advisors perceived that OSIO's leadership expected much out of them in terms of advising/mentoring BGA while the office inadequately compensated, unsatisfactorily supported, and irregularly supervised them.

Nuts and Bolts Leadership Training

Many BGA members believe white organizations are Student Affairs/ OSIO's s natural children and thus the primary beneficiaries of the campus support, while they think African American organizations are the stepchildren who receive modest support from the Student Affairs/OSIO.

Student Affairs and OSIO devote more divisional resources (staffing, supervision and training) towards helping advisors work more effectively with majority Greek leaders. OSIO's Nuts and Bolts Leadership training seeks to help student leaders understand how to be effective internal leaders (consensus style of making decisions, resolving conflicts, and developing a mission) with members while also helping the organization accomplish its goals with different stakeholders (other student organizations, admininistrative offices, and private vendors) inside and outside the university. OSIO routinely schedules Fall and Spring Nuts and Bolts Leadership Training and Event Planning Workshops for the traditional White Greek Fraternity Council and Sorority Alliance. Traditionally, BGA and the Intercultural Greek councils are usually not encouraged to participate in this leadership training.

Logistical Support

HBGLOs' historical roots orient them to service to the campus and larger community. The chapters regularly organize academic and service programs to the campus and larger community. However, HBGLO's most visible programming focus is their weekend dances which attract students from the campus and surrounding institutions. They believe that OSIO has given them inconsistent assistance in acquiring resources and facilities for their weekend parties. HBGLO unlike TWGLO do not have fraternity and sorority houses on campus. Majority Greeks make use of their houses in multiple ways including, serving as a residence for the members, site for chapter business meetings, hosting parent and alumni events, and place for holding weekend (Thursday–Saturday) parties. While, HBGLO must hold their chapter meetings, parent functions, and alumni events in the student union. Chapters' weekend parties are held as one member described it as "in catch as catch can" locations at the union, in residence hall dining rooms, skating rings, and other off-campus venues. The chapters financially struggle to host the weekend events due to the weight of the overhead costs (venues deposits, D.J.'s fees, and security) on their meager chapter budgets.

BGA chapters really resent Student Affairs security requirement as a condition for holding "open to the public" dances in university facilities. Chapters really resent having to pay for several security officers to be present at the dances held on campus. More important, the chapters believe the policy is racist, since the only student organizations that regularly use campus facilities to hold dances are African American and most of the guests at the dance are black.

Most academic and administrative units that have leased facility space to HBGLOs for weekend dances, have privately complained to each other that the organizations usually do a poor job with most aspects of the reservation process. Some facility mangers have gone beyond whispering to each other about the above problems and they have, in writing and verbally, shared the negative feedback with OSIO's Director and Assistant

Director. Specifically, facility leaders whisper among themselves that "these organizations"

1. Attempt to reserve prime facility space two or three days before the events
2. Neglect to complete their reservation process with the OSIO and the local facility manager
3. Ignore or wait until the day of the event to arrange through OSIO for campus or private security
4. Regularly overlook to schedule facility orientation and walk through meetings with facility mangers
5. At the end of their terms, current student leaders' knowledge of the reservation process doesn't get passed on to their successors
6. BGA's individual chapter accounts often lack the funds to pay for the events

During/after the event, facility managers observed that BGA

1. Chapters, Russet students, or guests cause significant damage to the facilities and they are often tardy in making restitution arrangements with facility managers
2. Habitually sponsoring chapters fail to clean up the facilities after events
3. BGA leaders overlook communication protocols between co-sponsoring chapters and between the chapters, police or security units.
4. During the reservation process, sponsoring chapters commit sins of omission by failing to share that the group is sponsoring a step-show (coordinated dance routine) and a dance. Thus, the organizations change the facility set up from a dance venue to a viewer venue in order to allow everyone to see the step-show. Thus, facilities are damaged by untrained student groups adjusting the venue's set up or current students and or guests seeking to get a better view of the step-show adjust the venue's set up.
5. BGA groups routinely extend the parties past the facilities regular weekend closing time.

Behind closed doors, OSIO's leaders recognized the complaints have some validity. Elfman and Fisher have been hesitant to share development and corrective feedback to BGA advisor and executive leadership. Yet, OSIO's leadership has not shown a lot of interest in collaborating with the groups to offer Nuts and Bolts Leadership training for the council and members which might help them identify and correct the causes of the chapters' uneven event planning/execution process. Dr. Elaine Washington began to take an interest in BGA due to the convergence of BGA leaders seeking an advisor and Vice President Crenshaw's concerns about negative publicity coming from fights at some BGA chapter's weekend dances.

Shifting OSIO Advising/Mentor Role to Dr. Elaine Washington

Elaine Washington is an Associate Dean of Students within the Division of Student Affairs. Elaine's is an African American who has added diversity not only in color to the upper administration of the Student Affairs division, but in sexual orientation and gender as well. She brings a wealth of experience as an administrator and faculty member that students and the Division can draw upon. Elaine is an alumni member and former chapter advisor for one of the Divine Nine organizations. For unknown reasons, Crenshaw has been hesitant about developing a portfolio for Washington that is commensurate with her experience and education. However, Washington believes Crenshaw wants her to be visible on campus as a known asset (tokenism) of Student Affairs especially during crises that involve African American students.

Elaine's formal Student Affairs generalist functions do not include working with African American or other Intercultural student organizations. Elaine routinely observed that OSIO's staff preferred to advise, mentor, and train White Greek letter organizations while they were failing to offer Latinos and especially HBGLOs basic advising, administrative, and leadership development support. In Student Affairs cabinet meeting, OSIO's Assistant Dean routinely gave colleagues an update on his office functions which routinely included TWGLOs' activities and excluded HBGLO's activities. Serendipitously, Elaine begins an informal relationship with BGA's executive leadership that resulted in her interacting with them in the areas listed below:

- Mentoring student leaders, especially the BGA chairperson
- Serving as an advocate for BGA with senior African American and White institutional leaders
- Advocating for regular Nuts and Bolts Leadership training for BGA's executive leadership
- Working with leaders to develop a proposal to secure educational and social programming funds from the Student Activity fee
- Serving as a judicial officer involving chapter violations of campus rules and regulations
- Attending chapters' different educational and social events
- Partnering with chapters to secure campus facilities for weekend dances

All in All, BGA leaders routinely praised Elaine for her efforts to help the council and individual chapters. Elaine sent emails to OSIO's leadership suggesting that they meet to discuss how to more effectively support BGA. Also, she sought meetings with the Vice President to gain his assistance in helping OSIO assume more responsibility for providing comprehensive support to BGA. In one meeting, Elaine brought the subject up with the Vice President who promptly told her that "I appreciate your actions in filling a void and doing things that have helped BGA and the Intercultural Greek Councils." Next, he promptly changed the discussion away from BGA to talking about problems in the Residence Halls. Later, Elaine thought to herself, "The facts on the ground show that I have been doing many of the things that OSIO's leadership should be doing on a regular basis with BGA. I developed the rough draft of the student activity fee proposal, basic curriculum for the Nuts and Bolts Leadership Workshop, and I attend the council's educational and social programs. Why isn't the Dean demanding that Elfman and his staff give the black students what I am giving them?"

Symbolically OSIO is Absent at BGLOs' Academic and Social programming

Student Affairs sends BGA a mixed message about how the division values their presences and role on campus. On the hand, Vice President Crenshaw makes cameo appearance at many student organizations including BGA's academic and social programs. Thus, his personal stock is high with black unaffiliated (non-members) leaders and Greek organization leaders.

On the other hand, Assistant Dean Elfman is constantly at Greek Fraternity Council events and he is adored by the women of the Sorority Alliance. BGA is concerned with the lack of visibility and attention that Elfman seems to give them. From a visibility standpoint, Eflman rarely has attended any BGA events. His no show reputation is in stark contrast to Butler Crenshaw's (his supervisor) reputation of attending all student organizations' events. Whenever there is a concern involving BGA, Crenshaw tosses the hot potato to Elman, Eflman acts like it is a hot potato and tosses the issue to Fisher, who in turn tosses the hot potato to the latest BGA advisor. OSIO's senior leadership does not respond to phone calls or emails from colleagues regarding HBGLO.

Discussion Questions

1. What campus traditions have allowed the OSIO to make a priority of assisting white Greek Letter organizations while not making assisting black Greek organizations a priority? What are the observable symbols of the campus priority system? What impact would additional advising staff resources play in Greek Affairs providing better advising to BGA chapters?
2. Crenshaw has been cautious in directing performance feedback to Elfman.What impact has the campus culture and Crenshaw's

supervisory style assumed in the Vice President's approach with his Assistant Dean?

3. What steps could Student Affairs take to learn about BGA members' views and feelings about OSIO's contributions to their organizations?

4. What factors impacted Student Affairs' decisions to allocate most of their advising resources to help GFC and SA while they assign fewer resources to help BGA?

5. What are the similarities and differences in Student Affairs' supervision of professional and graduate student staff depending on the race of the supervisor and the race of the supervisee?

6. If race still matters, how is the racial divide manifested in the Student Affairs Division's supervision and management of the OSIO relationship with BGA?

7. What are the short and long terms implications of allowing Elaine Washington to fill the leadership void with BGA?

8. How can you relate the support of BGA's social and programming endeavors with the retention of black students and its positive effects on white students?

9. Why has Student Affairs allowed Elaine to fill the leadership vacuum with BSA?

10. What lessons should Elaine draw to avoid allowing Student Affairs to situationally make use of some of her assets while showing disinterest in her other professional strengths?

11. What organizational, typology, environmental, and student development theories would you draw upon to help guide the practice decisions you would make for the entire student body?

References

Dungy Jordan, G. (2003). Organization and functions in student affairs. In S. Komives, D. Woodward, Jr., and Associates, (Ed.), *Student Services: a handbook for the profession*, (4th ed., pgs 339–357). San Francisco: Jossey Bass Publishers.

Hammrick, F., Evans, N., & Schuh, J. (2002). Foundations of Student Affairs Practice: How philosophy, theory, and research strengthen educational outcomes. San Francisco: Jossey Bass.

Harper, S., Byars, L., & Jelke, T. (2005). How black Greek-letter organization membership affects college adjustment and undergraduate outcomes. In T. Brown, G. Parks, & C. Phillips, (Ed.). *African American Fraternities and Sororities: the legacy and the vision*, (pp. 393–416). Lexington, Kentucky: The University Press of Kentucky.

Harper, S. & Harris III, F. (2006). The role of black fraternities in the African Male Experience. In M. Cuyjet and Associates (Ed.), *African American men in college*, (pp. 128–153). San Francisco: Jossey Bass Publishers.

Kimbrough, W. (2003). Black Greek 101: The culture, customs, and challenges of black fraternities and sororities. Danvers, Mass.: Rosemont Publishing & Printing Corp.

Kuh, G., Schuh, J., & Whitt, E. (1991). Involving Colleges: Successful approaches to fostering student learning and development outside the classroom. San Francisco: Jossey Bass Publishers.

Kuh, G., Douglas Branch, Lund, J., & Gyurnek, Ramin, J. (1994). Student learning outside the classroom: Transcending artificial boundaries. ASHE-ERIC Higher Education Report, no.8. Washington, D.C.

Kuh, G., Kinzie, Schuh, J., Whitt, E., and Associates. (2005). Student success in college: Creating conditions that matter. San Francisco: Jossey Bass.

Pike, G. (2000). The influence of fraternity or sorority membership on students' college experiences and cognitive development. Research in Higher Education, 41 (1), 117–139.

Ross, L. (2000). The Divine nine: The history of African American fraternities and sororities. New York, NY: Kensington Publishing Corp.

Tinto, V. (1993). Leaving college: Rethinking the causes of student and cures of student attrition. Chicago and London: The University of Chicago Press.

Recommended Background Reading

Hurtado, S., Milem, J., Pedersen-Clayton, A., & Allen, W. (1996). Enhancing campus climates for racial/ethnic diversity: educational policy and practice. In C. Turner (Ed.). *Racial and ethnic diversity in higher education*, (pp. 671–685). Boston, MA: Pearson Custom Publishing.

Kimbrough, W. (2003). Black Greek 101: the culture, customs, and challenges of black fraternities and sororities. Danvers, Mass.: Rosemont Publishing & Printing Corp.

Kuh, G. & Whitt, E. (1988). The invisible tapestry: Culture in American colleges and universities. Washington, D.C.: ERIC Clearing on Higher Education.

Love, P. (2003). Advising and consultation. In S. Komives, D. Woodard Jr., and Associates (Ed.). *Student services: A handbook for the profession*, (4th ed., pp.507–524). San Francisco, CA: Jossey Bass.

Miller, T. (2003). CAS: The book of professional standards for higher education. Washington, D.C.: Council for the Advancement of Standards in Higher Education.

Rogers, J. (2003). Leadership. In S. Komives, D. Woodard Jr., and Associates (Ed.). *Student Services: A handbook for the profession*, (4th ed., pp.447–465). San Francisco, CA: Jossey-Bass.

Roper, L. (2003). Teaching. In S. Komives, D. Woodard Jr., and Associates (Ed.). *Student services: A handbook for the profession*, (4th ed., pp. 466–483). San Francisco, CA: Jossey-Bass.

Case #25 Blue Diamond University Campus Climate and Student Life: Becoming Greek

Darnell G. Cole

Many college student administrators have focused much of their attention, professional development, and program planning on efforts designed to increase diversity and create culturally and racially sensitive environments. As such, diversity has become synonymous with recruiting students from diverse racial/ethnic backgrounds. Little attention is paid to retention and even less to developing tolerance and acceptance across racial/ethnic groups. Further, differences between and within groups, based on gender, religion, socioeconomic status, and gay/lesbian/bisexual/and transgender issues are on the margins, barely considered as integral components of diversity efforts on campus. Therefore, creating a context where all students are challenged to consider how they may expand their perceptions of race/ethnicity as complicated by within group differences often goes overlooked.

Institutional Setting

Blue Diamond Valley University (BDV) is a public, doctoral-granting university with slightly over 20,000 undergraduate and graduate students. The University offers a growing assortment of degree programs ranging from theatre, which has surprisingly becoming quite reputable, to mediocre science and engineering programs, to flailing education programs. Given external pressure to meet new state standards, programs in education have been vigorously prepared for their next NCATE accreditation. The University is also on the cutting edge of technology and offers easy access to computer clusters in almost every building on campus. Consequently, most students surf the World Wide Web for educational, occupational, and personal information; though, much of the computer use is still electronic mail and Napster.

The University is located within a fifteen-minute bus ride of down-town in the state's largest metropolitan city, Blue Diamond Valley, where opportunities for social outings, adventurous travel outdoors, and multi-national cultural events are numerous. Blue Diamond Valley, in co-sponsorship with the city's chamber of commerce offers a smorgasbord of plays, operas, orchestral recitations, and comedy shows. Student organizations are quite active on-campus, inviting national renowned speakers, poets, and politicians. Other social activities on-campus and in adjacent neighborhoods are usually sponsored by fraternities and sororities.

The University has been in existence since 1895, first as a normal school, then as a teacher's college, and now as a university. The university's growth has been a reflection of Blue Diamond's history and progress as a metropolitan city. It has recently earned fame and recognition across America for its racial/ethnic diversity, a few highly ranked and prestigious academic programs, opportunities to view nationally recognized athletic events, and service to the local community. As the fastest-growing university in the state, students are beginning to travel from different parts of the country to attend BDV and become a part of its burgeoning tradition. Though actively recruiting students from across the country, BDV mainly enrolls students from local communities and nearby states.

When compared to the population in Blue Diamond, BDV is more than representative in terms of race/ethnicity. In fact, a slightly larger percentage of minority students, approximately 40%, attend BDV. The slight over-representation, in part, is due to other prestigious institutions in the area that draw an increasing number of white students from surrounding suburbs and local townships. Less stringent entrance requirements and aggressive recruitment strategies complement the competition from nearby universities, also allowing BDV to enjoy a great deal of success in achieving a racially/ethnically diverse campus environment.

The Greek System

Students who join the Greek system represent a significant portion of the student body and hold many of the student-elected positions on campus. Almost all of the fraternity and sorority houses on campus in an area called the "Blue Diamond Chain" are predominantly white organizations. A black fraternity and a Latina sorority also have houses on campus. They are not located on the "Chain", but around the corner. There are two councils operating to unite, organize, and self-govern fraternities and sororities. Although these councils now work together, they were distinguished historically by race. Inter-fraternity council currently has representatives from each fraternity and sorority. The Pan-Hellenic Council has representatives from each Black fraternity and sorority and symbolizes a collective voice that was desperately needed before BDV became a racially diverse campus. These two councils still struggle with preventing overlapping social events, the type of fund-raising activities, and supporting their members in student elections. These disagreements sometimes split the groups along racial lines.

The two fraternities usually at the core of such conflict are Tri-Nu (NNN) and Beta Nu Pi (BNΠ). As old rivalries, these two organizations typically engage in fierce competition in intramural sports and the yearly 3-on-3 basketball tournament. There has yet to be any physical altercations, but during the finals in last year's tournament both organizations were suspended from participating this year due to unsportsmanlike conduct.

Becoming Greek

The rush/pledge process has become more regulated given recent hazing incidents that have resulted in local chapter fines and suspension. Each chapter is still responsible for recruiting, selecting, and initiating its new members, but usually in accordance with rules and regulations imposed by the chapter's national headquarters and the University as a charter requirement.

Reports of hazing and other violations, however, still occur. Last week during Tri-Nu's rush process; the new initiates called the "13 Bricks" were given the traditional Tri-Nu Scavenger Hunt. The "Hunt" had two parts: 1) a written list, which contained twenty items (see Appendix A)and 2) an unwritten list of items, called the "Orals". The oral list was an opportunity to gain extra bonus points; the greater the risk, the greater the points. However, this list has never been revealed beyond the members and pledges of Tri-Nu. The "Hunt" was to be completed in ten hours, starting at 2:00pm on Friday and ending at mid-night. If the "hunt" was incomplete by 12:01am Saturday, the Tri-Nu wrath (i.e., a ritual hazing events where pledges are paddled and forced to eat food similar to items eaten by participants on the reality TV show—Fear Factor) would be invoked for each initiate.

During the course of the "hunt", the 13 Bricks split up into two teams, against direct orders from Tri-Nu brothers. If they were caught separated into groups by any Tri-Nu brother, the initiates would have to face the Tri-Nu wrath. Each group took a portion of the written list and designated the "Lucky Oak Tree" as a central meeting place after completing their part of the "hunt". Lucky Oak was an enormously old tree located on the Northwest end of campus, typically decorated with lights and ornaments during the Christmas holiday. In the course of the evening and in pursuit of Beta Nu Pi's letter N (see Appendix B), team 1 broke into the Beta Nu Pi (BNΠ) house. Getting into the Beta house was relatively easy because it was under renovation and was closed off to the public. As team 1 was exiting the Beta house, BDV campus police screamed "Freeze . . . put your hands up". As their hands rose to the sky in panic, the initiates yelled "don't shoot, we are students here!" Once campus police determined that they were not members of Beta and that they were Tri-Nu initiates on a scavenger hunt, they were arrested for breaking and entering.

Administrative Response

When the Director of Student Activities, Lin Sue, heard of this news on Saturday afternoon, she immediately reported the series of events to the Dean of Student Affairs, Lloyd Peterson. On Monday morning, BDV campus paper and *Blue Diamond Observer* had scandalous headlines reading, "Sexist Scavenger Hunt Leads to Jail Time" and "Racism is Still Alive and Well at BDV". After reading the morning paper, in consultation with the director, Dean Peterson temporarily suspended the fraternity pending further investigation. On Tuesday, a part of the list was leaked to the press and circulated to almost every student on campus via electronic mail. Women, Muslim, GLBT, and various racial/ethnic minority student groups were in uproar and demanded permanent action from the campus administration. In the days to follow, students, community members, and some faculty were protesting the actions of Tri-Nu on their front lawn. The campus was chaotic! This event created several pockets of discussion about the intersections of race, gender, religion, and GLBT issues all over campus. The growing controversy found its way to the attention of national media, which painted a picture reminiscent of the 1960s student-led protests. As such, a press conference was held by Dean Peterson on the Friday following the incident. Dean Peterson stated that "Blue Diamond Valley University takes diversity seriously and this situation will be dealt with swiftly."

Institutional Challenges

Currently, there are several problems facing BDV. First, the university has less than 15% percent of its faculty from the aforementioned ethnic groups. Second, the university has just hired a new president and has started to downsize several overlapping offices and personnel. Third, enrollment of African American, Latino (a), and Native American students is unusually low but still over 25% of the incoming undergraduate and graduate class. This is mostly likely due to the state instituting a high school exit exam and BDV's increase in entrance requirements (e.g., High School GPA and SAT/ACT scores). Fourth, the city in which BDV is located has a recognizable

Muslim population that the university has catered to prior to 9–11. After 9–11 the relationships have been slightly different.

Decision Options

Beyond Tri-Nu's reprimand from their national organization, there appear to be two main decision options: (1) to suspend the fraternity for hazing and several of its members responsible for participating and/or organizing the Scavenger Hunt; or (2) to put the fraternity and the members participating and/or organizing the "Hunt" on probation. This option would also consist of multicultural awareness and sensitivity training for all of its members.

The Problem

Action: Option 1

You are Dean Peterson and Director Lin Sue, and have decided to suspend the fraternity and a few of members. You justified your positions by citing campus hazing violations and Tri-Nu's national organization suspension ruling. The following are important questions you should consider in the case:

Action: Option 2

You are Tyrone Stone and Claude Blacksmith, and have been invited to assist Professor Allen by creating and presenting a series of sessions, workshops to promote multicultural awareness to members of Tri-Nu. The media will be present at the first few workshops.

Questions (Environmental Issues; Student Development Theories; Leadership; etc.)

Discussion Questions

The following are important questions you have to answer.

1. What issues do you think Tyrone Stone and Claude Blacksmith will face by taking on this challenge? From the general student population? Other minority students and faculty?
2. If you were recruited to assist Professor Allen what would you present as a first workshop? Or plan for a series of workshops and other events? Also state why?

3. How might theories of multicultural education help inform you about presenting these issues to students using such a list?
4. How would you handle the media and students watching what happens when students behave in this way?
5. How would you turn this into a campus discussion and action for change?
6. What are long-term effects of this situation and how it will be dealt with?
7. What are other issues that will arise as this situation continues to unfold?

Key Characters

NNN (Tri-Nu): the largest and most racially diverse fraternity on campus with over 100 members. This fraternity was the first fraternity on BDV's campus in 1888. Several members hold leadership positions in student government and the university's programming board.

13 Bricks: the name of the pledge line consisting of thirteen first year (second semester) students. These racially mixed group (e.g., 2 Asian, 3 black, 2 Latino, and 6 white) of young men are attempting to become full members of NNN (Tri-Nu) Fraternity, Incorporated.

Peter Greenburg: an upperclassman majoring in Biology and President of NNN Fraternity, Incorporated.

Tyrone Stone: a senior majoring in Education and Coordinator of the NNN Rush Process.

Beta Nu Pi (BNΠ): the largest predominantly black fraternity on campus and has one of two Greek houses occupied by a racial/ethnic minority group. There are a total of 40 members on campus, all of whom are not African American.

Director Lin Sue: the director of student activities has only been at the institution for two years. She is not completely familiar with all of the institutional challenges and past political battles on this campus. Lin Sue does hold a MA from a highly accredited program in student affairs.

Dean Lloyd Peterson: has been the Dean of Student Affairs for the last twelve years and is familiar with campus issues. Peterson has a Ph.D. and several years of experience primarily on this campus.

Blue Diamond News: student operated newspaper.

Blue Diamond Observer: the Blue Diamond city paper.

Professor Quentin Allen: a Ph.D. in Clinical Psychology. He has been at this institution for the past fifteen years and is regarded with high esteem by his colleagues, respected by administrators, and well liked by students. Professor Allen has held several administrative positions during his tenure here at BDV which allowed him to develop strong relationships with students and administrators. Professor Allen is also an African American and graduate member of Beta Nu Pi (BNΠ).

Tyrone Stone: a graduate student preparing for comprehensive qualifying exams in counseling psychology. Tyrone has taught high school social studies with special emphasis on African American economic and political development. Tyrone is also an African American and graduate member of Beta Nu Pi (BNΠ).

Claude Blacksmith: a graduate student in Higher Education Administration with a minor in sociology. Claude supervised a residence hall at a large public school in the East. He has organized and presented several workshops on communication skill development, conflict resolution, and multicultural awareness.

Recommended Background Reading

Allport, G. (1954). *The nature of prejudice.* Cambridge, MA: Addison-Wesley.

Anaya, G. & Cole, D. (2001). Latina/o student achievement: Exploring the influence of student-faculty interaction on college grades. *Journal of College Student Development,* 42 (1), 3–14.

Burkard, A., Cole, D., Ott, M., & Stoflet, T. (2005). Entry-level competencies of new student affairs professionals: A delphi study. *NASPA Journal,* 42 (3), article 2. http://publications.naspa.org/naspajournal/vol42/iss3/art2.

Chang, M.J. (1999). Does diversity matter? The educational impact of a racially diverse undergraduate population. *Journal of College Student Development,* 40, 377–395.

Chang, M. J., Witt-Sandis, D., & Hakuta, K. (1999). The dynamics of race in higher education: An examination of the evidence. *Equity and Excellence in Education,* 32(2), 12–16.

Cole, D. (In Press). Do Interracial Interactions Matter?: An examination of Student Faculty Contact and Intellectual Development. *Research in Higher Education.*

Cole, D., & Ahmadi, S. (2003). Perceptions and experiences of Muslim women who veil on college campuses. *Journal of College Student Development,* 44(1), 47–66.

Cole, D. & Jackson, J. (2005). Racial Integration in Higher Education and Students' Educational Satisfaction 50 Years Beyond Brown. In Byrne, & N. Dara (Eds.). *Brown v. Board of Education: Its' Impact on Public Education 1954–2004.* New York, NY: The Thurgood Marshall Scholarship Fund.

Gurin, P., Dey, E. L., Hurtado, S., Gurin, G. (2002). Diversity and Higher Education: Theory and Impact on Educational Outcomes. *Harvard Educational Review,* 71, 3, 332–366.

Gurin, P., Peng, T., Lopez, G., & Nagda, B.A. (1999). Context, identity, and intergroup relations. In D. Prentice & D. Miller (Eds.), *Cultural divides: Understanding and overcoming group conflict* (pp. 133–172). NY: Russell Sage.

Hurtado, S. (1992). Campus racial climates: Contexts for conflict. *Journal of Higher Education,* 63, 539–569.

——— (2001) Linking diversity and educational purpose: How diversity affects the classroom environment and student development. In G. Orfield (Ed.), *Diversity chal-*

lenged: Evidence on the impact of affirmative action (pp. 187–203). Cambridge, MA: Harvard Education Publishing Group and The Civil Rights Project at Harvard University.

Hurtado, S. & Carter, D.F. (1997). Effects of college transition and perceptions of the campus racial climate on Latino college students' sense of belonging. *Sociology of Education,* 70(4), 324–346.

Hurtado, S., Milem, J., Clayton-Pederson, A., & Allen, W. (1999). *Enacting diverse learning environments: Improving the climate for racial/ethnic diversity in higher education.* San Francisco: Jossey-Bass.

Jones, L., Castellanos, J., & Cole, D. (2002). Examining the Ethnic/Minority Student Experience at Predominantly White Institutions: A Case Study. *Journal of Hispanic Higher Education,* 1(1), 19–39.

Milem, J. & Hakuta, K. (2000). The benefits of racial and ethnic diversity in higher education. In D.J. Wilds (Ed.), *Minorities in higher education, 1999–2000, seventeenth annual status report* (pp. 39–67). Washington, D.C.: American Council on Education.

Nora, A. & Cabrera, A.F. (1996). The role of perceptions of prejudice and discrimination on the adjustment of minority students to college. *The Journal of Higher Education,* 67, 119–148.

Rankin, S. (1998). Campus climate for lesbian, gay, bisexual, transgendered students, faculty, and staff: Assessment and strategies for change. In R. Sanlo (Ed.). *Working with lesbian, gay, and bisexual college students: A guide for administrators and faculty* (pp. 277–284). Westport, CT: Greenwood Publishing Company.

Sedlacek, W.E. (1994). "Issues in Advancing Diversity Through Assessment," *Journal of Counseling and Development,* 72, 549–553.

Tatum, B.D. (1999). *Why are all the Black kids sitting together in the cafeteria?: And other conversations about race* (Rev. ed). New York, NY: Basic books.

Tierney, W.G. (Ed.). (1990). *Assessing academic climates and cultures.* San Francisco, California: Jossey-Bass, Inc.

Tinto, V. (1993). *Leaving college: Rethinking the causes and cures of student attrition* (2nd ed.). Chicago: University of Chicago Press.

Appendix A

Deeznuts Scavenger Hit List

You are all young ambitious men. Your job tonight is an important one; it requires secrecy, focus, persistence, and skill. You must continue a great tradition, every member of NNN had done it and you will too. The task failure of this task will have serious consequences—The Tri-Nu Wrath. These written items must be collected by midnight. You must complete them together! If you stray, you'll pay!

Time limit: _____

Start Time: _____

End Time: _____

Special items

1. A Milli Vanilli cassette tape.
2. The Biggest panties you can find (must be a size 24 or larger).
3. Get a copy of any porn video from a Tri-Nu brother.
4. Used condom (in a plastic baggy, please).
5. Impression of a chick's nipple in a bowl of Jell-O pudding.
6. A blow-up doll.
7. An Arab women's head wrap.

Portraits

8. Picture of a Muslim women without her scarf.
9. Picture of a guy reading a gay porn magazine (extra credit if person reading porno is Black).
10. Picture of all pledges and a towel head.
11. Hottest Latin, black, Asian, and white chick in dorm and phone numbers.
12. Ugliest Latin, black, Asian, and white chick in dorm and phone numbers.
13. Pledge member with an entire burrito in mouth, no help.
14. Picture of two or more chicks kissing (No clothes, you win!).
15. Picture of pledge urinating on Beta Nu Pi's front lawn.
16. Any terrorist looking Arab (get them to hold or point to a picture of the twin towers, extra-points).
17. A MIDGET (Latin midget super-extra credit).
18. The prestigious Nu Greek letter that hang on the outside wall of Beta Nu Pi fraternity house.

Case #26 Divine University

M. Queen

Questions have surfaced regarding the possibility that the Office of Admissions at Divine University will pay for thirty-two African American high school seniors to fly in and visit the campus. These students have applied and been accepted to the university, it is simply a matter of their making the commitment to attend Divine. One year later, the Affirmative Action plan is challenged and the University Admissions Office is up in arms about how to best diversify the incoming class and simultaneously work against Affirmative Action. The Executive Administration and the Dean of Admissions are questioned about wanting to have this event.

Institutional Setting

Divine University is a small, private, liberal arts and sciences school with 2500 undergraduate students and 200 graduate students. Undergraduate students may receive a Bachelor of Arts or a Bachelor of Science in an array of fields. For graduate students, Divine offers programs of study in selected professional areas. The university prides itself on offering a quality education and experience for students. It has national recognition and regional prestige as each year *U.S. News & World Report* has proclaimed Divine to be the "best in the west" for the past twenty-five years. Although Divine operates independently, it has a long-standing relationship with the Protestant church.

For thirty years, President Marcus Sonner, the former President worked arduously to build the caliber of the institution so that it would have the reputation, academic rigor and financial means to provide a quality education, attract highly talented students, and be staffed by esteemed faculty and competent professionals. Today, Divine has achieved its goal and the current president, President Reginald Harbrough, is maintaining the institution's status and working to increase its national recognition.

Divine is located in the historical district of the highly populated southern city, Azucar. Of Azucar's one million plus population, 67% are

Hispanic, 23% Caucasian, 7% African American, 1.4% Asian and 1.6% other. The city is also home to a large public institution, two religiously affiliated universities and a well-established community college system.

Divine is a residential campus with a collegial atmosphere. Respectively, amongst students, Caucasians make up 81% of the population, Hispanics are represented at 11%, 3.8% are Asian, Blacks constitute 1.2% of the population, and Native Americans represent at 5%. Lastly, 2% of the student body is international. The university has made a commitment to facilitate an environment of academic talent and scholarship amongst its students. By requiring students to live on campus for three years, Divine is also promoting community. The average classroom ratio of 14:1 allows for relationships amongst faculty and students to be created. Students will receive more personalized attention, which in turn contributes to their undergraduate success.

Key Characters

Harbrough: the president has served for five years and is approaching an evaluation period. In his address to the university community, he has stated important matters to be addressed, maintained, or changed in the coming years. Those items include a continued emphasis on SAT scores, more improvements in technology, new faculty lines and renovation of select facilities. These were at the top of his priority list. He praised the talent of the former incoming class of students, the quality of students being produced and sent off to graduate programs and careers of the highest caliber and acknowledged the new diverse class of scholars that joined the faculty. He went on to express the importance of diversity and Divine's commitment to facilitate an atmosphere of diversity and inclusiveness. President Harbrough encourages the campus community to be open minded about diversity and think of it in terms of more than race, ethnicity, and gender, but also talents, experiences, backgrounds and more.

Office of Admissions

The Office of Admissions reports to the Vice President of Academic Affairs. The Admissions Counselors recruit in a few local high schools, primarily magnet, and private schools. Its recruitment arm extends throughout its home state, and beyond to the east and west and finally reaches overseas to attract international students. Many of the Admissions Counselors are alumni or have experience at similar institutions so they do a fantastic job representing Divine to prospective families and students. In application review, the staff follows the university's standards and selects students with strong grade point averages, high standardized test scores, extracurricular activities, and quality of high school, among other factors. During the process, they work to make sure that the pool of admitted students will bring unique and different experiences to Divine University.

Realizing the underrepresentation of black students, the Office of Admissions conducted an evaluation of black students who applied to Divine University but declined admission. Upon compilation of the data, Admissions found that black students were denied admissions for several reasons, primarily because of financial aid packaging, low numbers of black students and faculty, and their lack of knowledge about the university and all it has to offer amongst other reasons.

Due to the feedback received from former prospective black students, the university's commitment to diversity and the need to add to the black community, the Office of Admissions decided to fully fund a visit from thirty two admitted black students. They represent the north, south, east and west regions, with high standardized test scores, solid grade point averages and involvement in extracurricular activities at their respective high schools.

Current Black Students

Of the 2500 undergraduate students, there are thirty black students working to receive their Baccalaureate degree. Their majors vary from English and Religion to Business and Biology. Some participate in intercollegiate athletics, although none receive athletic scholarships for their participation because Divine is categorized under Division III. Many of them participate in the Association for Black Students (ABS), a student organization that has periodic meetings and special events for the Martin Luther King Jr. holiday and February's Black Heritage Month. Other than that, they exist within the campus community, have friends across racial groups, ethnic and culture lines and at least wave hello when passing another black student on campus.

They are not well represented on university committees nor are they very involved in many campus life activities or organizations other than ABS events. They can only walk around campus and see two black faculty members and one black student affairs administrator. Academically, black students mirror the grade point average of the overall student population. In fact, there is a higher retention rate amongst black students, when compared to white students.

Office of Campus Life, Diversity Coordinator

The Diversity Coordinator, Ms. Yvonne Jenkins, operates under the Division of Student Affairs. Ms. Jenkins is working on several initiatives to improve campus climate with regards to diversity. Currently, she convenes the diversity committee in the Office of Academic Affairs to increase diversity amongst faculty, particularly black faculty members. Once a plan is prepared or in place for increasing black faculty representation, the committee will begin working on student recruitment and retention with a special focus on recruitment of black and Native American students.

If the Office of Admissions receives approval to fly in prospective students, Ms. Jenkins will partner with Admissions to ensure a successful visit for the students. Along with asking for support from President Harbrough, Ms. Jenkins is promoting the event and gathering support from faculty, students, and, staff to guarantee a successful weekend.

Key Facts

- Black students exist in small numbers at Divine University. In order for Divine to be successful in evolving into a more inclusive and diverse campus, it needs to pay particular attention to certain groups.
- The Office of Admissions does not use Affirmative Action in its admissions process.
- Over the past three years, the number of black students enrolling in Divine University has decreased by 10%.
- Faculty, staff, students, alumni and community members are calling upon the University to increase its number of enrolled minority students.
- The Office of Admissions has an increase in applications from black students this year and wants to capitalize on the opportunity. Admissions is waiting to receive approval and funding from the Executive Administration to fly in the 32 black students.
- During the weekend visit, special activities, classroom visits, meetings with faculty, financial aid counselors and the diversity coordinator will take place. Additionally, these prospective students will participate in a day-long workshop with 150 other students who have been accepted to Divine. This workshop is an in depth introduction to Divine University, its degree programs, faculty, various opportunities available in campus life, and the caliber of current students and graduates of Divine.
- This is the second fiscal year that departments did not receive an increase in their "supplies and expenses" lines, salary increased minimally and renovation requests from two departments were put on hold.
- The university is in the process of undergoing a major renovation of its primary academic and administrative building. This will be a

multi-million dollar project, in which much of the funding will be obtained from the endowment.

Faculty

Select members of the faculty are openly supportive of increased enrollment of black students. These same members are vocal about the need for black faculty members as well. The question posed was "how can we recruit and retain black students if we are fatigued in the number of black faculty on our campus?" Nonetheless, they recognize the opportunity available to the university and fully support the initiative. If the weekend visit is approved, they will be supportive and available as resources to the prospective students. On the other hand, they have asked how the event would be funded, given the president's caution about budgets and spending. Currently, they are working to receive salary increases and additional funding for departmental and research resources.

Admissions

Being able to bring in students and provide them with a firsthand experience of Divine University at no expense to their family is a powerful, yet expensive recruitment tool for Admissions Counselors. By hosting this weekend, the Admissions staff is giving life to the university's commitment to diversity. Divine University is an institution that offers an excellent education, a quality campus life experience, innumerable educational resources, an accomplished faculty and a highly capable staff. Unfortunately, when recruiting and presenting the Divine University experience, Admissions Counselors face the challenge of revealing the small community of black students that exists. It has been difficult for counselors to sell the university because one of the first questions asked by prospective black families is about diversity and the presence of black students and faculty.

Current Black Students

The campus climate for black students needs to be improved. They often refer to their experience at Divine as simply getting an education and graduating. Voicing their frustrations, black students discuss being the only person of color in most, if not all, of their classes, sometimes feeling like they have to represent for the entire black community and not completely feeling a part of the Divine family. They do, however, realize that Divine has a lot to offer and that they can greatly benefit from it, but they are still searching for their niche.

In response to the possibility of flying in prospective black students, the current students expressed excitement and a willingness to assist the Office of Admissions in hosting for the weekend. President Baya Anise, of ABS, volunteered her time to support the Admissions initiative to ensure that the prospective students would feel welcome, gain a clear picture of Divine University and understand their attendance is greatly desired. The current students understand the potential that can be attained from an increase in the number of black students. They are anxious to gain a greater presence on campus and believe it will strengthen the black community and add volume to their collective voice.

Current White Students

As they have received word of the possible visit, they have expressed some apprehension that special attention and privileges are being given to prospective black students. A major worry is that all students are not receiving the same benefits, which leads to their belief that black students are receiving unfair advantages in admission to Divine University and potentially preventing other qualified students from attending. If the Office of Admissions was not fully funding the trip, they would be less concerned but they believe that their $26,000 tuition money could be put to better use. If the black students qualify for admission to Divine University then it should be their decision to attend just like every other prospective student and family. Almost 20% of the campus population is made up of minorities and compared to similar schools, Divine is a leading institution in terms of diversity.

Executive Administration

The President and Vice Presidents are in theory supportive of the opportunity to fly in the prospective students, but are concerned about the cost to successfully implement the program. In a year where budgets remained flat and a major renovation project will soon be underway, they are trying to determine if the financial investment is worth it. They have resolved that the university will benefit from a greater presence of black students and not simply because of their race or ethnicity but because of the unique talents and experiences they have to offer. In order to achieve the desired level of national recognition and to be equipped to prepare the evolving student of today, the Administration realizes the importance of diversity. Their major concern is how to communicate the importance of such an event to university constituents without backlash, especially regarding funding.

Making the Decision

1. Executive Administration can approve the visit and allow for it to be fully funded. If this is the case, they can choose to openly inform the campus of this initiative and communicate its importance to the accomplishment of Divine University.
2. The visit can be approved but not funded. The Office of Admissions will then communicate to prospective students and families the importance of a special extended visit to campus and how the experience can better inform their decision in choosing a university.
3. Executive Administration can deny the special visit and suggest that students try and make a campus visit on their own. The Office of Admissions will be encouraged to find creative ways to present the opportunities and advantages the students will receive if they attend Divine University.

In making the decision, it is important for the Administration to remember the purpose and benefit of reaching out to these prospective students. They must understand the importance of diversity and use it as a lens through which they manage the University. Being able to clearly define their actions, if choosing to conduct this event, in lieu of recent federal rulings on the use of Affirmative Action is critical to the success of the event. For opponents, Executive Administration must either create buy in or be prepared to counter the questioning of whatever decision is made.

Discussion Questions

1. What are all of the factors that should be considered in making a decision?
2. How can Executive Administration prepare to respond to the University constituents regarding their decision?
3. How will they respond to questions regarding the practices of Admissions in enrolling minority students, especially in lieu of getting rid of Affirmative Action policies in selection and enrollment?
4. How can they find the funding to fly in the students and still make the faculty feel comfortable with and confident in the decision made to fund the weekend event?
5. Is a fully funded visit to campus a strategic tool for recruiting underrepresented students? Why or why not?
6. Is a special recruitment weekend for these students valuable to the University? In the short term? In the long term? What is that value?
7. Does such an effort contribute to the future of higher education? If so, in what way? If not, why?

8. What kind of campus climate will be facilitated in the event of an increased number of African American students? For black students? For majority students?

9. Would the campus climate be impacted if students had knowledge of the recruiting tool used to attract black students? How so?

Recommended Background Reading

Astin, A.W. & Helen S.A. (2000). *Leadership reconsidered: Engaging higher education in social change.* Battle Creek: W.K. Kellogg Foundation.

Eckel, P., Green, M., & Hill, B. (2001). *On change V: Riding the waves of change: Insights from transforming institutions.* Washington, D.C.: American Council on Education.

Hurtado, S., Milem, J., Pedersen-Clayton, A., & Allen, W. (1996). Enhancing campus climates for racial/ethnic diversity: Educational policy and practice. In C. Turner (Ed.). *Racial and ethnic diversity in higher education,* (pp.671–685).

Kuh, G. & Whitt, E. (1988). *The invisible tapestry: Culture in American colleges and universities.* Washington, D.C.: ERIC Clearing House on Higher Education.

Read: Executive summary, threads of executive institutional culture, and institutional cultures.

Miller, T. (2003). CAS: *The book of professional standards for higher education.* Washington, D.C.: Council for the Advancement of Standards in Higher Education.

Peterson, M.W., Dill, D.D., Mets, L.A. & Associates. (1997). *Planning and management for a changing environment.* San Francisco, CA: Jossey-Bass.

Tinto, V. (1993). *Leaving college: Rethinking the causes of student and cures of student attrition.* Chicago and London: The University of Chicago Press.

West. C. (1993). *Race matters.* Boston, MA: Boston Press.

Case #27 Set Up for Failure?

Joshua B. Powers

Cameron Walker, Associate Director of the Wells Memorial Student Union, shuffled into his office, shut the door, and slumped into his chair. Returning from an emergency meeting with the Dean of Students, he sat silently, numb from the import of what was shared. With no inkling about the topic of the meeting, he dutifully attended the 8:30am summons where he was shocked to discover that his boss, Dr. Samia Sherron, Director of the Wells Union, had just resigned effective immediately and that a university official would be soon coming to pack up her personal belongings. Cameron would be expected to serve in an Acting Director role, although most of Dr. Sherron's responsibilities would be shifted to the Associate Dean of Students, Dr. William Sloane, the person to whom Dr. Sherron reported. No explanation was given as to the reason for the resignation.

A million thoughts went through Cameron's mind, chief among them being that people just don't "resign effective immediately" unless something very serious had occurred. All he could conclude was that it might have something to do with the recent financial audit of the Union's books and the secretive way the auditors seemed to pursue their work. Dr. Sherron had been completely open throughout the audit after assurances from her boss that there was no special reason to be concerned that the audit came a year earlier than was typical. "Don't worry," Dr. Sloane had repeatedly said to her, "this happens from time to time." She took him at his word and complied. Cameron's other main feeling was one of disappointment, bordering on betrayal. Why had Samia, someone he had come to call a friend as well as a colleague/supervisor/mentor, done such a thing without telling him first? They had been partners in the leadership of the Union, he the white male from rural Vermont and she, the African American female from the tidewater area of Virginia. She had taught him so much about racism, ignorance, whiteness, and how to be an ally for underrepresented students of color on the historically white North Carolina campus. He reciprocated by helping her to build a Union Program where all students felt welcomed and supported and together led many workshops on diversity-related topics. Now it looked like that relationship was over, or at least destined to be drastically altered.

As these varied emotions engulfed him, he was shocked to external alertness when the phone on his desk rang. "Hello, this is Cameron," he responded.

"Cam, this is Samia." I assume by now you know what's up."

"The Dean called an emergency meeting this morning to share that you had resigned, effective immediately. But that's all that he said other than now I am the Acting Director with most of the responsibilities being shifted to Bill Sloane."

With a cracking voice, Dr. Sherron responded, "Cam, I was set up. They claim I embezzled money and misused university funds. What's worse, they threatened to press charges if I didn't resign immediately. I can't go through all that. The University is a powerful force and I just couldn't bear to go through the humiliation of a public courtroom lynching."

"Oh my God," is all that Cameron could muster in response.

"Cam, they told me you would be bringing a box of my personal items to the house this afternoon. They also told me I had to give you any university-owned items I may have at home including the cell phone. I'll have them ready for you." With voice quivering, "I don't know what to do . . . the community will be devastated. Many will call it racism and frankly, that's what it feels like to me. Once again, a successful black professional gets dragged down. All I can say is watch your back. The administration will expect you to line up behind them on this one but will be suspicious of you because of your closeness to me. No doubt that's why they are having Bill take over many of the Director's responsibilities rather than you, even though you are eminently qualified to handle things . . .. I'll see you later today."

With that, Dr. Sherron hung up, leaving Cameron even more confused than before. Was it really racism? Certainly he'd seen countless examples of that. Dr. Sherron had educated him well on those issues as well as white privilege. Yet, detail management had never been Dr. Sherron's strong suit and perhaps she did treat the finances too loosely or even inappropriately. She was a visionary and a powerfully symbolic leader, especially for the issues of students of color, but was not an especially good manager and not very good at asking those above her for help at those times she really needed it. Frankly, because she didn't fit into the "traditional" culture of the institution's largely white male leadership and had such close ties to the black community and they did not, he sensed that she was a threat to them. It appeared to him that the administration feared a wrong move on their parts would label them racist. As a result, they tended to treat her with kid gloves and rarely gave her the supervision she needed to be successful with the managerial responsibilities of her position. But, if she did in fact embezzle as was alleged, does that excuse her behavior? How was he to think about these issues? Could he and or should he raise these concerns with Dr. Sloane or others in the administration and help educate them on how their behavior may have contributed in part or in full to her downfall?

Fairmont University

Fairmont University, a four-year private university with Presbyterian roots was founded in 1847 in south central North Carolina. Named after its founder, a wealthy landowner with a prosperous cotton and tobacco growing business, it began as a school where wealthy Presbyterians from the South and North could send their sons to college in a bucolic setting and refine them into gentlemen. Following the Civil War, it fell upon hard times for a period of years but was resuscitated by a dedicated group of local businessmen who bought it from the Presbyterian Church and proceeded to integrate new programs in the mechanical arts and applied sciences that proved beneficial to the growing textile industry in the area. It retained its image as a gentlemen refining school but also as a place where young men who wished to become involved in the field of textile manufacturing could jumpstart a career in that industry.

By the turn of the century, Fairmont had established a strong regional reputation while continuing to attract students from as far away as Chicago and Boston. Following the Second World War, it, like many campuses in the United States, grew substantially in size as servicemen (GIs) returned from Europe and the Pacific desiring to obtain a college education. By the mid-1950s, it had over 1100 male students enrolled in a wide variety of fields within the arts and sciences, engineering technology, and business. In 1960, life began to change for Fairmont like it did for many institutions of higher education as the Civil Rights Movement spread in earnest across the country. On February 1st of that year, four freshmen at historically black North Carolina Agriculture Technical (A&T) sat down at the then whites-only lunch counter at the local Woolworths in Greensboro and proceeded to launch a movement of sit-ins across the state and elsewhere in the segregated South. Students and others from colleges and universities around North Carolina joined in support of the sit-in protesters, including some students from down the road at Fairmont. This action prompted a heated debate on Fairmont's campus, though, as students debated the appropriateness of the "Greensboro Four's" actions. As the Civil Rights movement gained momentum, colleges and universities throughout the country found themselves having to liberalize policies to accommodate students' desires for greater freedom and choices on the college campus. Fairmont was no different in this regard and began to admit black male students to the college by 1967. Inevitably, students began demanding that the institution also begin admitting women, something that the board resisted for a number of years but finally relented to doing so in 1973.

By the mid-1980s, Fairmont's female population reached parity with the male population and the combined enrollment had reached 3000 students. However, while there had been growth in enrollments among African American students, it increased much more slowly such that by 1989, the year that Dr. Sherron was hired, it was only at 6%, much smaller than the percentage of college-aged (eighteen to twenty-five-year-old) African-Americans in the state or the South in general. Although there had been some efforts at recruiting underrepresented students such as African Americans to the campus, it had not borne much fruit, in part frustrated by the fact that the institution's faculty and administration had failed to diversify—no members of the president's cabinet were non-white and only two females were at that level, one who was dean of the College of Education and the other who was vice president for Research. Furthermore, of a faculty of 200 persons, just 3% were non-white and 20% were women.

Apartheid and Campus Protests

In late March 1986, Fairmont's campus was rocked by protests over the institution's policies toward investment in companies that did business with South Africa. A vocal contingent of students, consisting of an amalgam of interest groups including the Black Student Alliance, erected a shanty town on the central campus and refused to take it down or vacate it until the university agreed to divest all of its endowment holdings in companies that did business with South Africa. At first the campus administration seemed to be tolerant, perhaps even proud of their students who seemed to rally to a cause such as apartheid. However, when days stretched into weeks, and weeks into a second month and then the summer, the high hopes that the students would loose steam and simply disassemble their "village" and go away when the school year ended disappeared. Although the protest numbers had dwindled considerably, a vocal few held out. Exasperated by the students' persistence, the eyesore that had been created, and an alumni weekend that was looming, the university simply tore it down one afternoon on the auspices that it was a fire hazard and in violation of the city health ordinance. This action immediately erupted into a firestorm of anger, especially from the black community, since it was a single black student who happened to be present when the shanties were torn down and was almost run over by a large dump truck who did not see the sleeping individual inside of a cardboard box (or as some had alleged, sought to terrorize the youth on purpose). Despite it being summer, a number of students, the largest group of whom were from the Black Student Alliance, briefly held a sit-in at the president's office followed by a much larger protest that Fall.

The protests and passionate attacks against university policies and a racist administration finally died down in late Fall when the trustees agreed to review their investment policies and decided to only invest in companies that had endorsed the Sullivan Principles that explicitly sought to improve the living conditions of South Africa's black population. Nevertheless, the experiences of the previous months had left a bad taste in the mouths of Fairmont's African American students and an administration weary of bad publicity and a lighting rod for student anger over perceived institutional racism.

The Hiring of Dr. Samia Sherron

Because the responsibility for "managing" the student protests had fallen largely on the shoulders of the Dean of Students, the campuses chief student affairs officer, and because some of the student—administration interactions that had occurred did not go well, it became painfully clear that something had to be done to bolster the Division's skill sets in working with students of color. The problem was exacerbated by the fact that the Dean of Students did not have an especially good relationship with the Director of the Black Culture Center, a person who reported through the academic side of the university's administration but did not hold a cabinet level position. During the protests, the Director of the Black Culture Center often came down on the side of the students and seemed to have the ear of the president and many of the Dean's colleagues on the president's cabinet on what to do at various times. He seemed to know the students involved much better than the Dean of Students, something that privately irritated the dean and made him feel uncomfortable when issues of diversity were discussed in cabinet meetings. In the end, though, as the dean's colleagues on the cabinet came to feel that the Black Culture Center Director's advice was more self-serving than institutionally helpful, no one bothered to confront or to discuss the issue with him. Instead, they simply politely heard what he had to say, left him alone to run his Center located on the periphery of the campus, and made such decisions related to the protest as they felt were best.

Troubled by the less-than satisfactory resolution to the protest, its simmering aftermath, and his own lingering anxieties over the "diversity problem", the dean decided in the Spring of 1987 that the solution would be to hire the Division's first high level African American who could advise on issues related to diversity and play a leadership role in working with students of color. At that time, the director of the Wells Union position was open following the retirement the previous year of a long-time and well-liked white male Director. Rather than conduct the typical search—posting the position in the *Chronicle of Higher Education* and possibly talking to a few colleagues in his network—the dean impressed upon his staff that they all would need to assist with this effort and go beyond the usual recruitment approaches. One idea that was floated was to call student union directors on historically black college campuses and encourage them to apply for the position. The Associate Dean, Bill Sloane, indirectly knew through a colleague that the Union Director at an historically Black college in a nearby state was well respected and accomplished at building student leadership programs, something that was central to the mission of the Wells Union. Furthermore, she was believed to be well connected among African American celebrities, people like Maya Angelou, Oprah Winfrey, and Arthur Ashe among others. If enticed to Fairmont, she might be instrumental in bringing major African American speakers and musical events that would do much to build positive feelings for the community. Bill agreed to attend the annual meeting of the College Union's Association, and make contact with Dr. Sherron who was very active in the group.

Bill Sloane returned very upbeat about his chat with Dr. Sherron. He had "bumped" into her at the conference social and chatted amicably about their mutual colleagues and other things that they seemed to have in common including teenage children, a love of reading, and a desire to see students become leaders of their campuses and later their communities. Bill worked the conversation around to the fact that they had an opening in the Wells Union which Dr. Sherron seemed to know about from the Association posting. From there, he went into his full court press on how the institution was in need of the kind of leadership that Dr. Sherron could offer in the college union area and that the institution was committed to the issues of diversity. Dr. Sherron casually raised that she had heard some negative reports as it regarded the institution's recent handling of the shanty town crisis, but seemed to be mollified by the explanation for the difficult decisions that had to be made and the institution's desire to move forward in positive ways. She even ventured some commentary that it had been a difficult year for many historically white institutions across the country on this very issue. They left the conversation on a positive note with Dr. Sherron indicating some guarded interest in the position as she was ready for a change and had some family in the area.

With this news, the Dean of Students called Dr. Sherron and mentioned it to the director of the Black Culture Center who also called to encourage her to apply. In the end, Dr. Sherron was persuaded to apply and ultimately received an invitation for a finalist interview. Amidst a beautiful early April day complete with flowering dogwoods and blooming daffodils, Dr. Sherron met with a variety of campus stakeholders and came away impressed. Despite some misgivings about making a move to an historically white institution from her familiar historically black campus roots, the staff, faculty, and students with whom she met seemed genuine and the opportunities to do substantive and positive work for the African American student community was very attractive as was the sizable bump in salary. One week later she was offered the position, and after thinking about it for a few days, she accepted.

Early Honeymoon

Dr. Sherron began her position on July 1, 1987 to much fanfare. The Dean of Students graciously introduced her to members of the Division and held an open house for professional staff and faculty who came by to meet her, including the president and other members of his cabinet. Although she felt that she stuck out like a sore thumb in the sea of white faces and white hands thrust out to meet her, she nevertheless felt buoyed by this seemingly genuine affection and appreciation for who she was and the kinds of values and talents that she would bring to the administrative table. All wished her well and suggested that if she ever needed anything that she should feel free to call. "Fairmont is really a great place to work, people are so friendly and caring of one another, a real family atmosphere," seemed to be the most common refrain that she heard from those she met.

A few weeks later, she sought out the two members of the Black Student Alliance who happened to be on campus taking classes that summer so she could begin building that relationship. They seemed surprised to hear that someone who looked like them was hired for the Union Director job and no one in the Dean of Students Office seemed to have notified them who was hired, despite their having participated in the on-campus interviews. Nevertheless, they too seemed genuinely pleased to see her. "We are really glad you are here," they both said, "and look forward to working with you to bring about positive change for the Black community."

Over the rest of the month and into the Fall semester, Dr. Sherron got to know the students, her Union staff from top to bottom, and her senior level colleagues in the Dean of Students Division. Her presence, values, and vision became apparent to all very quickly. She was committed to the concept of multiculturalism, for her a term that meant that organizations needed to reflect the diversity of society and that the visible and invisible power differentials that existed based on color and gender needed to be recognized and eliminated. One immediate action she took in this regard was to insist on the recruitment and hiring of a diverse group of student employees, in some cases, intervening herself to be sure it occurred. In her mind, the visibility of students of color and women in positions of leadership as managers and area supervisors in the Union would be an important and symbolic first step in showing that things had changed in the college union. Second, she worked with the student program board to diversify their programming and helped them to land high profile student events featuring black musical artists and educational speakers, including Maya Angelou. Lastly, and most notably, she played an instrumental role in responding to an alleged gun fire incident that happened at an off-campus black Greek party. The police responded to the incident, arrived in force in riot gear, and proceeded to tear gas the crowd that happened to be loitering around outside of the rented facility. In order to get out in front of the incident, she quickly arranged a town hall meeting in which the students could voice their concerns about the racist response of the police and convinced the university police and the Dean of Students Division that these kind of events should be sponsored on campus in university facilities since the white Greek community had their own university-owned houses to have parties and the black Greeks did not. Furthermore, she assured everyone that she could work with the community to ensure that these events were safe, appropriately staffed, and without the need for metal detectors since this would also seem racist given that they were not required for white student events. For all this work, the Dean of Students and Associate Dean Sloane provided private and public praise for Dr. Sherron and basked in the light of positive energy that was building on the campus for the work of the Division.

Diversifying the Professional Staff and Leadership Style

As luck would have it for Dr. Sherron, both assistant director positions were open and she wasted no time in pursuing a national search to fill them. For the assistant director of Operations, she selected a rising African American female professional who had worked in the Union Operations area for five years. She would be responsible for much of the Union operation program including the student employees, Housekeeping, the Room Reservations Office, and the Maintenance Department. For the other position, the assistant director for Programs, she selected Cameron Walker, a white male with four years of experience working with student program boards at a major private institution in the Midwest. She was initially reluctant to hire Cameron, but a confluence of factors—his program staff was already diverse (a gay man and a Jewish woman served as Program Advisors), he came with excellent experience dealing with contracts and college major event production, her boss really liked him, and he seemed to have the kind of personality that students would warm up to quickly. "Perhaps we need our token white male around here if we are to embody multiculturalism," she joked.

With her full professional staff in place by the summer of 1988, it became clear that it was a good fit for all. Dr. Sherron was fiercely and publicly loyal to those who worked most closely with her, the two assistant directors. She had a very open style of management, inviting her assistant director colleagues into her decision-making sanctum, encouraging opinion sharing, and making herself vulnerable by sharing when she was not sure what to do on certain matters. This stimulated great reciprocal loyalty, especially because of how highly she was respected outside of the Wells Union as a visionary and a champion for issues of diversity and multiculturalism. Furthermore, it was evident that Dr. Sherron wished to mentor both of her assistant directors. In the case of her assistant director for Operations, she helped her with her writing skills and encouraged her to be more assertive, especially when working with challenging employees. For her other Assistant Director, Cameron Walker, she worked to deconstruct and to rebuild him into the ally of diversity that he would need to be successful in a multicultural world. To this end, she forced him to make the hard choices necessary for greater diversity among the leadership of the Student Program Board as well as their program offerings. Furthermore, she put him in charge of developing and managing the new late night party policy by which African American student groups could hold on-campus parties. This caused Cameron to go through a series of soul-searching exercises in which he need to be both firm and nurturing of the relationship between the Union and the African American student community while coming to understand their need for a social outlet that was inclusive of the black community outside of the student body, typically the source of problems when they occurred.

By the end of his first year, Cameron was immensely satisfied in his new job, in large part due to the kind of relationship that was developing between Dr. Sherron and himself. She had opened his eyes to a new way of thinking, seeing, and responding to the world around him by helping him to see how he accrued certain benefits that she and others who shared her skin color did not. Yet, she did it in a way that forced him to move past feelings of guilt to a higher level of thinking and feeling that emphasized empathy and action. For example, she would relay personal stories of discrimination, racism, or simply ignorance—being followed around an upscale department store, getting stopped by police for no apparent reason, being accused of being the hired help when standing too close to the punch bowl at a university function—and then relaying how she did not let those regular occurrences beat her down but rather motivate her to a higher level of commitment for change. The outcome of these efforts led to a deepening level of trust between the two as Cameron began to put words into action—a new policy for late night parties that led to safe and inclusive events, a diverse line-up of programs and events coming out of the Student Program Board, and most of all, diversity workshop co-facilitation efforts between the two of them. This latter experience was especially meaningful because partnering on such projects by persons who were themselves diverse seemed to increase the potential impact on session participants.

Harbingers of Trouble

While Dr. Sherron was completely or nearly completely transparent in her interactions with her direct reports and willing to share her own vulnerabilities and doubts, including that she was not especially good with details, this was not true in public settings or with those to whom she reported. In public, she was viewed as a strong-willed, assertive (some would say aggressive), and visionary leader and she did much to nurture this image. When probed by Cameron how her public and private side often seemed so starkly different, she responded with, "for the sake of the community, it is important that we not show our weaknesses nor take actions that might reflect badly on the community as a whole. That is why it was so difficult to watch the Anita Hill/Clarence Thomas debate—she was forced to air dirty laundry that pitted the community against each other."

This divergence of persona was also evident in her relationship with her boss, William Sloane. A genuinely nice white man with a good sense of humor, Dr. Sloane had been at the University almost as long as the dean and had built a strong reputation as a powerful persuader. He had an uncanny ability to break seemingly complex problems down into their rational parts and then address them with a generally structural response—if we put more resources here, outcome X will occur, if we reorganize unit Y in this way, we can achieve our goal, etc. Dr. Sherron, on the other hand, tended to see complex problems in political or symbolic terms and often took action based upon an emotional or gut feeling approach. Thus, their one-on-one meetings on Union related issues tended to involve Dr. Sherron venting about a particular issue or concern and Dr. Sloane offering structural response suggestions. Dr. Sherron was not especially receptive, in part because she was not necessarily looking for answers and in part because accepting those suggestions at times felt like she was not being strong enough to fix problems on her own. This "clash" of styles was apparent in a growing line of issues that got discussed with her boss.

First, about a year and a half into Dr. Sherron's tenure at Fairmont, it became clear to her that the secretary she had inherited, Helen Wilks, had to go. Over a period of months, Helen was becoming increasingly recalcitrant about doing her work. She would complain under her breath about how much typing she was having to do and often took longer to type letters and other material than their agreed upon 24 hour turn around time for such tasks. Furthermore, Helen seemed to lose documents with growing frequency and then claim she never received them in the first place. Of greatest irritation to Dr. Sherron, however, was the fact that she suspected Helen was losing the documents on purpose to make Dr. Sherron look bad and sensed that Helen was chatting excessively with her friends on the phone when Dr. Sherron was not around and passing on confidential information to them of a nature that was designed to undermine Dr. Sherron's credibility. Helen also seemed to treat the students of color who came to the office with a certain condescension that she did not seem to exhibit with the white students or staff who visited. Unfortunately, these latter behaviors were ones she could not clearly document but rather fell under the vague category of "employee attitude". To Dr. Sherron, Helen had come to represent "poor, racist white trash" who was now threatened that the tide had turned with the hiring of an African American to direct the organization. Dr. Sherron complained about Helen to her boss, Bill Sloane, and sought his support in firing Helen. His response was typically centered on some adaptation of exercising caution and to be sure not to violate Helen's due process rights. This generally made Dr. Sherron angry because he failed to empathize or affirm that racism could be at the root of the problem. The issue simmered until finally it resolved itself when Helen was badly hurt in an automobile accident and had to take permanent disability.

The second issue emerged more slowly and centered on Dr. Sherron's judgment around issues of financial management. For instance, she seemed to delegate all of the tasks related to organizational budgeting to her senior finance director, Cindy Devron. On one level, this demonstrated her strong confidence in Cindy who Dr. Sherron had hired fresh out of a high quality MBA program from the public flagship institution in the state. Yet, on seemingly routine matters of budgeting, Dr. Sherron seemed to be out of touch with the basics of accounting procedure beyond her insistence in having adequate "rainy day" reserves. Her response to Cindy on questionable organizational expenditures and requests from other staff in the building of a financial nature was often to "use your best judgment" or "run it by Bill Sloane to see what he thinks". In budget meetings with her boss and the other deans, she also seemed to be somewhat vague on details, choosing instead to justify her requests on larger issues of principle, often tied to her vision for making the Wells Union an inclusive facility where diversity was respected.

The third issue was more complex and involved how to best supervise the assistant director for Operations. After two years in the position, it became clear that she was not cut out for the job. Not only was it very difficult for her to write well-written memorandum and policy documents, she also had great difficulty standing up to her white male housekeeping supervisor who seemed to resent that he worked for a much younger woman. On this issue, Dr. Sherron would confide in private with Cameron about being very conflicted as to what to do since she wanted to see this African-American woman be successful yet at the same time could see how it was undermining the work of the Union. After a while, though, others outside the Union, including Dr. Sloane, got wind of the problem and raised the concern. When it came up in their meetings, Dr. Sherron would respond in defense of her assistant director and usually with some adaptation of "I'm dealing with it." Finally, Dr. Sherron told her Assistant Director in a letter that her contract would not be renewed at the end the academic year and then met with her only infrequently on work related issues after that. Because Cameron's assistant director colleague would often confide in him how much this cut-off of the relationship hurt, he at times probed Dr. Sherron about it in one of their frequent one-on-one meetings. At first she would respond with, "I know, I'll make plans to take her to lunch." However, it never occurred. Sometime after the assistant director for Operations had left and Cameron had been promoted in title to assistant director, taking on many of the Operations area duties, he raised the issue again. In an introspective mood, Dr. Sherron relayed that she felt that she had failed in her mentoring obligations in this case and felt powerless to do anything about it once she made the decision to let the assistant director for Operations go. Thus, she avoided her to keep her own hurt and guilt to a minimum.

Nearing the End

Despite the warning signs, in many other ways, Dr. Sherron seemed destined for greatness at the institution. On a number of occasions over the four years that Cameron had worked for her, she had been out in front of crisis issues involving race in the community. Furthermore, she had become centrally important to new student orientation for which she had developed a core of student diversity educators who then led discussion sessions on the topic during Freshmen Week. Most especially for Cameron, he himself was a first responder to a hate incident in which someone had defaced the flyer of an African American candidate for Student Council President with the word "nigger". The flyer was found on the office door of the Black

Student Alliance, just down the hall from Cameron's office. When the students brought it to his attention, he immediately called the campus police, quelled a near riot when the police officer responded belligerently to the gathering phalanx of students who were hearing about the incident, and engaged in crisis counseling before other allies in the black community including Dr. Sherron arrived an hour later. Being able to remain calm and professional, yet empathetic to the group and the student whose flyer was defaced, were skills that Dr. Sherron had clearly provided him.

At the same time, however, Dr. Sherron seemed to continue to have a sputtering relationship with her boss as they seemingly talked past each other. She would complain about his style or about the way he would respond to the issues she raised that needed attention, and then be resistant to what she heard in response. Cameron would also talk with Dr. Sherron about issues that needed to be raised at the dean's level. In casual conversation with Dr. Sloane, though, Cameron often discovered that the associate dean had heard nothing from Dr. Sherron about the issue. Finally, it seemed as if the two of them simply had fewer and fewer regular meetings.

Toward the end of her tenure at Fairmont, Dr. Sherron was also doing a lot of consulting work around the country. She was a gifted speaker in national demand and often would be away for two or three days at a stretch making both university and corporate presentations. It was during this time that she purchased a cellular phone with university funds for her car since she was on the road a lot and this allowed her to continue to do the work of the university even though she was not physically present. Her rationale for the purchase was based upon the positive PR that her work was bringing the University, the fact that it allowed her to do her work from a distance when she was away for short periods, and that other high profile administrators, particularly the Health Center Director, were actively consulting on high profile issues of their own. Cameron generally agreed that what she was doing did bring positive benefits to the University but worried aloud to her on occasion that for some, including her colleagues in the Dean of Students Office who did no consulting, that they might be resentful over her success but probably wouldn't dare say this to her face out of fear of being labeled racist. She assured Cameron that the "Deans" were fully aware of her work and supported it.

During one of the times that Dr. Sherron was away, the auditors "swooped" down on the Union, copied files from her office computer as well as the director of Finance, and began private interviews with all members of the finance staff. At first, Dr. Sherron was livid and let her boss know it. However, after his reassurances, she calmed down and cooperated, only to be forced out of her job shortly thereafter.

Decision Time

Amidst this backdrop, Cameron Walker took stock of his circumstances and pondered what to do. Knowing that Dr. Sherron's warnings were likely true, his first concern was self-preservation. Had he ever done anything illegal, even just unethical, that could put his job in jeopardy? He had a pregnant wife at home and could not afford to get fired, let alone get accused of any crimes. All he could think of was the few times he made personal copies on the office photocopier. "I'll never do that again ever," he thought, "and every pen, sticky note, and scotch tape dispenser stays right here." Thus, laying low and doing his job, no more, no less, struck him as a very appealing course of action.

However, there appeared to be a higher duty needed. He really had not done anything wrong and his record would stand on its own. His closeness to Dr. Sherron and first hand knowledge of what can happen to undermine and then cutoff the very thing that the institution had sought to nurture put him in the unique position to be able to educate his white senior colleagues. They surely did not have the luxury of seeing and experiencing the complex issues of style and culture difference, the overlay of supervision, and how to tune into key warning signs that may lead a person of color to fail in an historically white context as he had. Most especially, it was doubtful that they had as rich a perspective on institutional racism as he did.

Yet, to do the latter would require his ability to separate the facts of the case as the administration seemed to see it (a person who appeared to commit a crime or who they could accuse of committing a crime as a means of forcing her out), from the issues he wanted to get across (how the "system" may have been culpable in full or in part for what happened). This solution was a tall and potentially risky order indeed.

Reaching for his desk drawer Cameron thought, "My head is spinning right now—where's the damn aspirin?"

Discussion Questions

The central decision question of this case was presented at the end of the introductory section. In summary, how should Cameron think about and respond to Dr. Sherron's "resignation"? As you think about and discuss this question with others, you will find it helpful to explore these questions as well:

1. How would you describe the institutional culture? What role does history and tradition likely play?
2. How would you describe Dr. Sherron's management and leadership style? How does that contrast with the style of her boss, Bill Sloane?

3. How has race and racism likely shaped Dr. Sherron's attitudes toward management and leadership and influenced the way that she interprets meaning from others' behaviors or institutional values and events?

4. What preventative steps might the institution and/or the Dean's Office have taken to avoid the ultimate outcome? What might they have done differently during the search process? What might they have done differently during Dr. Sherron's transition? What might they have done in response to perceived "warning signs"? As you think about these questions, consider them in light of the racial issues at play in the case from the perspective of the majority white culture and the perspective of historically underrepresented persons in general and African Americans in particular. Furthermore, be sure to discuss the realities of personnel supervision and the mechanisms for giving and receiving constructive feedback.

5. What might Dr. Sherron have done differently to avoid the ultimate outcome? Where might she have turned to for help? What are the learning insights for persons of color working at majority white institutions?

Recommended Readings

Cohen, G., Steele, C.M., & Ross, L.D. (1999). The mentor's dilemma: Providing critical feedback across the racial divide. *Personality and Social Psychology Bulletin*, 25 (10), 1302–1318.

Estrada, D., Frame, M.W., Williams, C.B. (2004). Cross-cultural supervision: Guiding the conversation toward race and ethnicity. *Journal of Multicultural Counseling & Development*, 32 (4), 307–319.

Helms, J.E. (1993). *Black and white racial identity: Theory, research, and practice*. Westport, CT: Greenwood.

Johnson-Bailey, J., Cervero, R.M., Baugh, S. (2004). Mentoring in black and white: The intricacies of cross-cultural mentoring. *Mentoring & Tutoring*, 12 (1), 7–21.

Jones, L. (2001). *Retaining African Americans in higher education: Challenging paradigms for retaining black students, faculty and administrators*. Sterling, VA: Stylus.

Kirwan, W.E., Hale, F.W., & Hale, F.W. Jr. (2003). *What makes racial diversity work in higher education: Academic leaders present successful policies and strategies*. Sterling, VA: Stylus.

Kuh, G.D. & Whitt, E.J. (1988). *The invisible tapestry: Culture in American colleges and universities*. San Francisco, CA: Jossey-Bass.

Mabokela, R. & Green, A.L. (2001). *Sisters of the academy*. Sterling, VA: Stylus.

Author's postscript

In memory of a loved colleague. Although the story is fictionalized, the basic premise remains true to life.

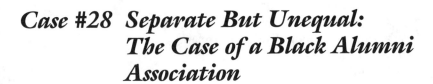

Case #28 Separate But Unequal: The Case of a Black Alumni Association

ANGELA DAVIS

Institutional Setting

Western Technical University is a mid-size, four-year public university in the Southwestern region of the United States. It was founded by the state legislature in 1873, and blacks were not permitted to attend the university until 1905. At that time many blacks had began to migrate from the Deep South to the Southwestern region of the country in search of a better quality of life. The university has gained global notoriety because of its technical educational programs and the success of its graduates.

Currently, WTU has the highest number of blacks enrolled in its history. The total number of students attending is 14,217 with 9.2% being black. However, the Southwestern region's black population has increased to 14.2% in the past twenty years. Moreover, retention rates of black students have been decreasing for the past five years.

Western Technical University Alumni Association

Founded in 1893, the WTU Alumni Association mission is to support the advancement of the university and offer benefits to its alumni. The Association is to be the catalyst to bridge the university and alumni as a support to the institution—professionally, financially, and in other ways that would promote WTU's growth.

The WTU Alumni Association is comprised of a thirty member board of directors that represents the approximately 80,000 alums who live in all fifty states and in 125 countries around the world. Of the 30 current board members, two are African Americans, one of whom is also a member of the

WTU Black Alumni Alliance. Currently there were 5065 annual members and 3304 life members of the WTU Association. The organization with the assistance of the Alumni Relations staff hosts many annual events all over the country to reach out to its alums.

Examples of the events sponsored by the WTU Association include:

1. Scholarship Golf Outings
2. Ice Cream Socials
3. Vacations to England, Germany, Ireland
4. Churchill Downs
5. Sock Hops
6. Basket Bingo
7. Badminton Tournament
8. Outstanding Alumni Awards Banquet

The WTU Association offers two types of membership: annual, which cost $50 yearly or life membership for $700. The group also receives $50,000 from the University to fund its programming, postage, and alumni scholarship program.

Ms. Renee Brown has been a computer software programmer at a prestigious Fortune 500 company. She has been employed with the company for almost ten years, and has received national recognition for several of the software packages she has developed. Renee has said many times that she has been successful in her professional career because her parents, who did not attend college, instilled in her the importance of higher education.

Renee graduated from Western Technical University (WTU) in 1995 with a degree in Computer Programming. Since her graduation from WTU, Renee has been active with WTU Black Alumni Alliance. The organization is comprised of Black Alumni who graduated from WTU. The Alliance has been in existence for forty years, and is acknowledged by the Office of Alumni Relations and the university. However, it is not affiliated with the "official" WTU Alumni Association, which was founded over one hundred years ago.

In recent years, there has been some conflict as to why WTU has two alumni associations. As financial resources at institutions of higher education face sustainable budget restraints, the Office of Alumni Relations has asked if it is feasible to support two alumni groups in its budget. A committee has been formed to discuss possible solutions to the situation. Renee has been asked to sit on the committee since she is a member of both organizations.

WTU Black Alumni Alliance

Founded in 1964, the WTU Black Alumni Alliance was formed by ten alums that graduated in the 1930s. Two of the alums were physicians, one a lawyer and the others were successful business men and women. These alumnae had lobbied for many years to gain membership into the WTU Alumni Association. Historically, for African American graduates to become a member of the WTU Alumni Association, a current member needed to sponsor the application of the interested person. However, because it was an association that consisted of only white alumni, African American participation was absent due to the lack of sponsorship from their white counterparts. On the other hand, the only requirement for white members was that they graduated from WTU.

The African American attorney alum decided to bring a discrimination suit against the WTU Alumni Association and Western Technical University. Just before the case went to court African American alums were admitted to the Association. Once they became members, however, they were never appointed or elected into positions of power within the organization. This became very frustrating for the alums; hence they formed their own group, WTU Black Alumni Alliance. The university was so relieved that the black members had left the WTU Alumni Association that they supported the group's application to be recognized as a university organization.

The Alliance was comprised of a steering committee that would oversee the business of the organization. The cost of membership was $20 annually and $200 for a life membership. Currently there are 2989 annual members and 1342 life members of WTU Black Alliance. The mission of the Black Alliance is to support the needs of Black Alumni and currently enrolled African American students at WTU, which includes financial, professional, and emotional support. Another thrust of the Alliance is to support African American faculty who may serve as mentors on campus for students.

The Alliance received $10,000 from the university's budget, and very little support from the Alumni Relations staff. Those funds are earmarked for printing, and supplies. The other needs such as recruiting, scholarships, care packages and programming of the group are met by the fund-raising events sponsored by the Alliance which include:

1. Annual Step show and Dance
2. Card/Spades Party
3. Homecoming Family Weekend
4. Scholarship Banquet
5. Internships for Black Students

We Are All Alums, Right?

The current WTU Administration was adamant that the Office of Alumni Relations should give its support to one united alumni association. The committee formed by the president of the university consisted of Bob

Johnson, Vice President of the WTU Alumni Association; Misty Burns, Alumni Development Officer; Jan Perkins, member WTU Black Alliance; Brent Rosenberg, member of the WTU Alumni Association; Renee Brown, member WTU Alumni Association and WTU Black Alliance; and ex-officio member Roger Nixon, Executive Director of the Office of Alumni Relations.

The first meeting of the committee was held on campus in the Office of Alumni Relations in mid-July. The goal was to resolve the consolidation question by October's Homecoming Weekend. The WTU President was on hand to give the committee the charge to resolve the issue. After the President exited the meeting, John Nixon gave a brief overview of the mission of the WTU Alumni Association. When he concluded his opening statements, Bob Johnson stated that "He never understood why the university funded both organizations." Brent Rosenberg agreed and added "Black alumni are not contributing to the Annual Fund in great numbers, making it cost effective to eliminate it."

Breaking the silence in the room, Jan Perkins said "The WTU Black Alliance is not just a line item in the university's budget; it has value to its members, and future African American students." Renee Brown took this opportunity to remind everyone of the purpose of meeting. Renee asked the committee "If anyone besides Jan knew why the WTU Black Alliance was founded?" No one raised a hand or said a word. Renee saw this as her moment to plead her case for the Black Alliance.

Passionately, Renee told the story of the Black Alliance like a professional storyteller would on Broadway. She began with the founders of the organization and its early struggles. These early trailblazers did not let the fact that they could not join the WTU Alumni Association keep them from fellowshipping with their WTU brothers and sisters. The Black Alliance began giving scholarships to up and coming blacks to attend WTU one year after it was founded. Other activities the organization undertook in the early years were: bringing high school students to campus, mentoring current students, supporting the African American Center.

Renee also did not want the committee to forget that the university recognized the Black Alliance in its infancy, and did so to keep the WTU Alumni Association segregated. Moreover, the Black Alliance has its own traditions, events, and programs to promote its love for WTU. Even today, Renee added that the WTU Alumni Association has not been viewed as very welcoming to black alumni.

Jan revealed that she had spoken to many Black Alliance members, and if the WTU administration withdrew its financial support it would still survive. Jan proudly stated that the Black Alliance would have more fundraisers and remain active without "technical" affiliation with the Office of Alumni Relations. The room was once again silent. Renee excused herself from the meeting to get some fresh air. She saw several current WTU students eating lunch and talking at the courtyard on campus. Renee thought to herself how refreshing it is to see a racially mixed group of students enjoying themselves. Mr. Nixon, came outside and touched Renee's shoulder and told her, the meeting was about to recommence.

A Foot in Both Worlds

Renee Brown: born on a hot summer day on July, 15, 1960 in Enterprise, Mississippi was the first of five children born to Tyrone and Essie Brown. Renee's father was a skilled blacksmith, a trade that was passed down to him from his father and his father's father, who was a slave. Miss Essie stayed at home to raise her children; however, to earn extra money for their large family she would take in laundry from the rich white families in town. Early in her childhood, Renee was very curious and asked her mother why they had to use a different bathroom and drinking foundations from white folks. Miss Essie told her first born "That's the way it's been for hundreds of years," and looked at the child and said "Someday it might change, but not here in Mississippi."

Tyrone had dealt with segregation all his life, and did not want his children to live with it in Mississippi. Renee's parents have seen small changes with the beginning of the Civil Rights Movement, but felt the best way to give civil rights to their family was by moving. Both Tyrone and Essie attended school only to the sixth grade, and wanted better for their kids and decided to relocate west. The Brown's were able to find a modest home for their family in a racially mixed neighborhood when Renee was twelve years old. Raising their children in an integrated area was something Renee's parents felt was imperative for their children to succeed. They wanted Renee and her young siblings to have friends that were not just black like in Mississippi, but white, yellow, and brown.

Renee's parents worked very hard to provide a good living for their family; they didn't have structured education, but instilled its importance in their children. Renee, being the oldest saw how hard her mother worked as a maid, and her father at the local car factory. This motivated Renee to earn excellent grades in school to become the first member of her family to attend college.

Mr. and Mrs. Brown were so happy to have their children's friends of different cultures come to their home, and "hang-out." All the parents in the neighborhood loved having their kids at the Brown's home; the parents would come over too. There would be neighborhood cook-outs, birthday parties, and many dinners where traditional foods from many countries would be served.

When it was time to choose a college to attend, Renee's parents were so excited that their firstborn would have the opportunity to pursue higher education, something they only dreamed about in Mississippi. Western Technical University was known for its state of the art computer science program. It was about six hours away from home by car and two hours by plane. Renee, with her excellent academic record received a full scholarship from the WTU Black Alumni Alliance. The Black Alliance even gave her funds to use for books and supplies she needed. Renee was fortunate enough to receive a book scholarship for all four of her years at WTU.

Renee was one of only three blacks in her major; this did not bother her because she had friends from all nationalities. From her first day, Renee became involved in a number of organizations, and was well known on campus. As she completed her second year, Renee was required to complete an internship for the summer. Many of Renee's cohorts were sought out by some of the top computer companies from around the country. Renee was finding it very difficult to secure one.

The WTU Black Alumni Alliance had a mentoring program Renee remembered, she connected with several members of the Black Alliance. Unfortunately, there were no members of the Black Alliance that were in the computer science field. However, one of the alumni suggested she contact the WTU Alumni Association. Renee was successful in her pursuit of an internship; the Alumni Association was able to pair Renee with the top computer company in the West. The president happened to be an alum of WTU, and an office holder for the WTU Alumni Association.

After completing her internship, Renee continued to work at the company during every break she had from school. She was eventually offered a full-time position because of her hard work and dedication. Renee became the first black woman junior executive in the company. The entire Brown family attended Renee's graduation, and Renee proudly presented her degree to her parents. As a graduation gift, Renee's boss gave her lifetime membership to the WTU Alumni Association and she became very active with the group. Moreover, Renee never forgot the WTU Black Alumni Alliance who provided her with her scholarships, and helped in obtaining her internship. She bought a full life membership to the Black Alumni Alliance and worked diligently for the group. Renee proudly held memberships in both organizations.

Where Does WTU go from Here?

The Office of Alumni Relations did not want this situation to turn into a disaster for Western Technical University. The university has been know for its strong support from all its alumni, and did not want to see that diminished. Furthermore, extreme care had to be used by the staff to resolve the situation. The Office of Alumni Relations should:

1. Use the services of WTU's Department of Counseling to arrange focus groups consisting of WTU Alumni Association members, WTU Black Alumni Association members, and a final group that would have members of both organizations.
2. Create a survey with the assistance of the WTU Department of Information Technology that would be postal mailed, and e-mailed to all alumni, not just those paid members of the organization. The results would also be tallied by the Department of Information Technology.
3. Gather research on other universities to attain the trend on alumni specialty clubs.
4. Attend the meetings and events of both the WTU Alumni Association and the WTU Black Alumni Alliance.
5. Brainstorm financial alternatives to meet the budgetary needs of the Office of Alumni Relations.

Possible Solutions

Seed of Change

The norm at the Office of Alumni Relation over the past five decades included two alumni organizations. However, the time has come to re-examine this practice at Western Technical University. The current Administration has given the Office of Alumni Relations the task to reduce funding. Rather than offend alumni, perhaps the Office of Alumni Relations should pursue other funding sources. This could include: private foundations, grants, alumni fundraising.

Inclusive Alumni Organization

Many colleges and universities have organizations for different constituency groups. Perhaps, the WTU Alumni Association could make its organization more inclusive to all alumni. Black alumnus should be sought out, not just for quota purposes. Bridges should be built to include and welcome all WTU alumni. If the WTU Black Alumni Alliance wanted to remain a club without funding from the university, then it should be allowed to do so without alienating the Office of Alumni Relations.

New Opportunity

The Office of Alumni Relations could use this opportunity to engage more alumni by redeveloping itself into overseeing one new alumni organization.

The leadership and the design of the organization would begin with former members of each group. This would give the buy-in necessary for the new alumni organization to be successful. Members like Renee Brown should play pivotal roles in promoting the new association to their counterparts.

Discussion Questions

1. Would you recommend the combination of two organizations, knowing the history of its founding? Why or why not?
2. What suggestions would you give the Office of Alumni Relations in handling this situation?
3. Could conflict among the two Western Technical University alumni groups have been avoided?
4. What advantage is it to the Office of Alumni Relations to have Renee Brown serving on the committee?
5. How could Renee's background guide her on the committee?
6. Is it possible for the WTU Black Alumni Association to disband and join the WTU Alumni Association without losing its founding principles?
7. How could this situation be used as a positive change for the Office of Alumni Relations?

Recommended Reading List

Cross, W.E., Jr. (1978). The Thomas and Cross models of psychological Nigrescence: A review. *Journal of Black Psychology*, 5, 13–31.

———— (1991). *Shades of black: Diversity in African American identity*. Philadelphia: Temple University Press.

———— (1995). The psychology of Nigrescence: Revising the Cross model. In J.G. Poterotto, J.M. Casas, L.A. Suzuki, & C.M. Alexander (Eds.), *Handbook of multicultural counseling* (pp. 93–112). Thousand Oaks, CA: Sage.

Gasman, M., Anderson-Thomkins, S. (2003). *Fund Raising from Black-College Alumni: Successful Strategies for Supporting Alma Mater*. Washington D.C.: CASE Books.

Herndon, M.K., Hirt, Joan, B. (2004) Black Students and their Families: What Leads to Success in College. *Journal of Black Studies*, 34 (4), 489–513. Thousand Oaks, CA: Sage.

Lewis, A. (2003) *Race in the Schoolyard: Negotiating the Color Line in Classrooms and Communities*. New Brunswick: Rutgers University Press.

Willie, S.S. (2003). *Acting Black: College Identity, and the Performance of Race*. New York: Routledge Press.

Case #29 Student Governance and the Politics of Race

MICHELE SCOTT TAYLOR AND SARA SADHWANI

Student involvement in campus life has a positive impact on student learning and development. (Astin, 1985) The extent to which students are engaged in the university community speaks greatly of an institution's ability to offer opportunities for student involvement and interaction. Student organizations serve as a primary venue for students to explore various interests, gain valuable leadership development skills, and apply critical and analytical thinking processes that directly impact the situations in which they are engaged.

Pennsburg University has an atypical classification system of student organizations. Student governments represent the highest level of leadership opportunities available to students. These students are elected to represent the student body at large. The Associated Student Government (ASG) is the governing body for the entire undergraduate population, and the Professional and Graduate Student Government Association represents all the graduate and professional students. Pennsburg also has student organizations classified as "governance groups." Governance groups are student organizations that represent key student subpopulations on campus and have unlimited resources for their programming efforts. In the early 1960s organizations such as the Resident Student Association, the Inter-Fraternity Council and the Pan-Hellenic Association were the only groups to have "governance" status. But by the late 60s, the Black Action Society, an organization addressing the needs and concerns of African American students, fought and gained recognition as a governance group.

All other student organizations, ranging from sports clubs to honorary groups to cultural organizations, make up the bottom of the hierarchy. With more than three hundred student organizations, these groups have a limit to their budget expenditures and must join a lottery system for office space within the student union. Creating a new organization simply requires ten students and a written constitution defining the goal and mission of the organization. In recent years, the number of new organizations has greatly increased, putting pressure on the already limited resources for student groups.

As the University approached the new millennium, other subgroups of students, particularly cultural groups, began growing disenchanted with the lack of support for diversity programming. The waning student activity fee—the money for programming and other student activities—meant a reduction in the volume and quality of cultural programs sponsored by student organizations. Talk of governance status began circulating amongst concerned students and ignited the Asian Cultural group's campaign for governance group status.

Institutional Context

Situated in the Midwestern state of Ohio, Pennsburg University is a large, urban research institution with approximately 40,000 undergraduate and graduate students. Offering a diverse selection of academic and professional programs, the University attracts highly qualified students from a variety of backgrounds. While Pennsburg is located on an urban campus, only 13% of the student population is made up of students of color. African American students represent 8% of the population, while Asian American students only represent 4%.

Given the increased selectivity of students who are accepted into Pennsburg, questions regarding students' access have arisen. Pennsburg has always made diversity an institutional priority, most recently evidenced in a statement released supporting the Supreme Court decision made in the University of Michigan's Affirmative Action case. In February 2003, prior to the ruling, Pennsburg officials filed an amicus curia supporting an institution's right to choose its admissions policy. In its statement, Pennsburg wrote, "Not every college or university faces identical enrollment management issues. Therefore, it clearly is not desirable for the nation to be governed by a 'one size fits all' approach to access higher education. Instead, it is important that individual institutions have the freedom to design admissions programs that meet their particular challenges and effectively advance their own goals." (*Pennsburg Times*)

In 1994, the institution wrote a diversity statement that articulated, "Pennsburg University, as an educational institution, an employer and a good citizen of the community, values equality of opportunity, human dignity, and racial/ethnic diversity and will continue to take steps to support and advance these values consistent with the University's mission." Not only has the institution publicly acknowledged diversity as being critical to the educational enterprise, but noticeable advances have been made in terms of increasing staff, students, faculty, and programming efforts related to diversity.

Background of Governance Groups

Currently there are two types of governance groups; those affiliated with an academic unit, including the Business Student Council, the Engineering Student Council, and the Nursing Student Association. The second type includes co-curricular organizations that serve as a primary programming function for the Student Life Office, such as the Resident Student Association, the Inter-Fraternity Council and the Pan-Hellenic Association. The Black Action Society, a co-curricular organization, gained its status as a result of the turbulent 1960s civil rights movement when students demanded recognition and enhanced services for black students.

Since the Black Action Society, Student Affairs has not received any requests for governance status review, and consequently policymaking for governance groups has fallen through the cracks. While governance groups have an unlimited funding potential from the ASG, in an ad hoc manner the Office of Student Affairs has awarded additional resources such as offices, technology, and professional staff including secretaries and professional advisors.

No real policy exists for approving governance status or for evaluating an organization's continued status. What policy does exist is unclear and ambiguous, but does indicate that student organizations requesting governance status need to petition the Vice Chancellor of Student Affairs following the protocol established by the Vice Chancellor's Office and through the ASG.

The Vice Chancellor of Student Affairs recently received a formal inquiry from the Asian Cultural group requesting consideration for governance status. The Associate Vice Chancellor prepared a document after receiving the inquiry describing student governance groups as compliments to ASG in that they "allow for greater self-governance among the various student constituencies, and increase student participation in the University Community".

Mounting Tensions

The ASG has authority to allocate money to governance groups and student organizations for programs and activities that are geared toward the members of their organizations. Since the last student activities fee increase five years ago, the number of student organizations has increased 20%, reducing the pool of money per student organization.

Talk of the cultural climate on campus has created a buzz among students. The recently elected board creates the most diverse ASG board in the history of Pennsburg University. Certain underrepresented groups, feeling disenfranchised and powerless, began forming loose coalitions in an effort to increase the cultural programming produced by and for the students. Winning the majority of seats, the diverse ASG board is comprised of members from the Black Action Society, the Rainbow Alliance (the Lesbian, Gay, Bisexual, and Transgendered students), the Asian Cultural group and the Women's Association. Being most concerned with increasing diversity and diversity programming, the board began denying requests from organizations such as the ski club, the polo club, and outdoors club. At public hearings, the non-cultural based organizations began making public statements denouncing the board's decisions and accusing ASG of reverse discrimination in its allocation decisions. The ASG and the cultural groups backing them retorted, arguing they had a duty to fund programs that ought to have institutional support.

The Black Action Society Experiment—Building the Rationale

In 1968, students concerned for the needs and interests of black students assembled in Bally Hall to discuss the lack of courses dealing with the black experience and the history of blacks across the diaspora. Led by Dr. Shaw, who taught underground classes to provide students with such education, the students decided to form the Black Action Society based on the fundamental question asked by Dr. Shaw, "What are we about?" and the students answered, "Action!".

From that meeting, demands were presented to the Chancellor for an increase in black students, faculty, and staff; governance status, including an office with a secretary; and a campus-wide community service office to serve the majority-black community surrounding the university.

Today, the Black Action Society receives a substantive allocation from ASG, has an office in the student union, a secretary who serves the administrative needs of the organization, as well as a professional advisor who assists with the programming initiatives of the Black Action Society and the overall development of its members. While the Black Action Society is a co-curricular organization, it is also a cultural and advocacy group. Strong similarities have developed between the vision and mission of the Black Action Society and the Asian Cultural Group. For that reason the Black Action Society serves as an example and a justification for the Asian Cultural Group's campaign for governance status.

The Coveted Governance Status

Denise Williams, a politically active member of ASG, believed in affecting change from within. Being of both Asian and African American descent, she was collaterally involved in the Black Action Society and the Asian Cultural Group.

Her involvement with the Black Action Society familiarized her with the opportunities that a governance group was able to afford its constituency and the greater campus community. Denise wanted similar opportunities for the Asian Cultural Group. As a member of ASG, she understood the funding structure of student government and the board would be receptive to the idea of a cultural organization requesting governance status.

Serving also as vice-president of the Asian Cultural Group, whose primary purpose is to provide cultural programming and awareness of Asian and Asian American issues, Denise decided that the organization must become more politically active. She encouraged the members of the group that Asian and Asian American issues and concerns were similar to issues broached by groups like the Black Action Society, and even the Rainbow Alliance. With growing global tensions, Denise convinced the Asian Cultural Group that their role was to educate students and the wider community on the rich histories and diverse cultures of the Asian populations whose presence in the United States continues to grow.

Implications of a New Governance Group

The Advisor for ASG updated the Associate Vice Chancellor and the Vice Chancellor for Student Affairs of the recent planning session held by ASG in which Denise posed the question of the Asian Cultural Group petitioning for governance status. Apparently some members of ASG believe that governance status does not complement the role of ASG but encourages separation among subgroups of students. Additionally, since other student organizations can only apply for $2000 per program, awarding another student organization with governance status, in which there is no ceiling in funding requests, could have an impact on the budget and the amount of money other organizations can request.

One board member stated, "We already give the Black Action Society 15% of the overall student activity fee, they have an office that is bigger than ours, they have a secretary and an advisor, as if they were equal to us. Now what are the Asians going to want?"

Denise and the Asian Cultural Group have planned a public hearing where they will present the vice chancellor, governance group advisors, and other Student Affairs administrators with their case for governance status.

The members of all the other cultural organizations plan to be in attendance to support the Asian Cultural Group and Denise has requested that a formal decision be made by the administration within five days of the public hearing.

The Problem

You are a Student Affairs administrator who reports directly to the Vice Chancellor. The Vice-Chancellor is looking for your consultation in regards to the Asian Cultural Group's request for governance status. What decision or recommendations will you make? Use the questions below as a guide in your decision-making process.

Discussion Questions

1. What Student Development theories will inform your decision?
2. What are the structural issues (categorization of organizations, representation of student subpopulations, role of university programming) in this case vs. the environmental considerations (quality of campus life, organizational programming)?
3. How will your decision develop and impact the role of governance groups on campus in the future?
4. How will you justify your response?
5. What implications will your decision have on the greater campus community?
6. Knowing you will be responsible for the impacts of the decision, what kinds of responses will you expect and must you be prepared for?
7. What will your communication strategy be to inform the campus community of your decision?
8. How will you respond to the student constituency?
9. How will you respond to the Student Affairs staff?
10. How will you respond to the university community?

Facilitator's Guide

1. Utilize student development theories such as racial identity development, character development, cultural assimilation theories, organization development theories, and fiscal management policies.
2. In this case, the structure of governance groups and the idea of governance status need to be reconsidered. Perhaps finding a more representative form of student government would better serve the different student subpopulations while creating a more equitable

finance structure of the student activity fee. What kinds of representative student governments are there? From an administrative position, how might you include and foster students in making that decision and creating a more representative governing system? Participants may also consider raising the activity fee (which had not been raised in five years).

3. Administrators need to be acutely aware of the consequences of their actions. By denying the Asian Cultural Group governance status, the Vice Chancellor and Student Affairs administrators run the risk of criticism for racism or discrimination—a serious media darling topic that could ruin the institution's reputation, as well as damage the campus climate with student outcry resulting in picketing, rallies, marches, and other anti-administration protests.

4. Yet administrators must also be held accountable for student spending and budgetary restrictions. Granting the Asian Cultural Group governance status will result in a serious draining of funds. Campus climate is also an issue in granting governance status because other cultural groups may follow suit and demand the same opportunities, in addition to current governance groups, like some members of the ASG who have already commented on the unfairness of the system.

5. Whatever the decision, a careful communication strategy must be in place.

Recommended Readings

Astin, A.W. (1985). *Achieving educational excellence.* San Francisco, CA: Jossey-Bass.

Ponterotto, J.G., Casas, M.J., Suzuki, L.A., & Alexander, C.M. (Eds.). (2001) *Handbook of multicultural counseling.* Thousand Oaks, California: Sage.

Helms, J.E. (1990). *Black and white racial identity: Theory, research and practice.* Westport, CT: Greenwood.

Kohatsu, E.L. & Richardson, T.Q. (1996). Racial and ethnic identity assessment. In L.A. Suzuki, P.J. Meller, & J.G. Ponterrotto (Eds.). *Handbook of multicultural assessment,* (pp.611–650). San Francisco, CA: Jossey-Bass.

Cross, W.E., Jr. (1995). The psychology of nigrescence: Revising the Cross model. In J.G.Ponterotto, J.M. Casas, L.A. Suzuki, & C.M. Alexander (Eds.). *Handbook of multicultural counseling,* (pp.93–122). Thousand Oaks, CA: Sage.

Rogers, Reuel R. (2004). Race based coalitions among minority groups: Afro-Caribbean immigrants and African-Americans in New York City. *Urban Affairs Review,* 39 (3), 283–317.

Soneshein, R. (2003). The prospects for multiracial coalitions: Lessons from America's three largest cities. In R.P. Browning, D.R. Marshall, & D.H. Tabb. (Eds.). *Racial politics in American cities,* (3rd ed., 333–354). New York: Longman.

Waggaman, John. (2001). Strategies and consequences: Managing the costs in higher education. ASHE-ERIC Higher Education Report (8). Washington, D.C.: George Washington University.

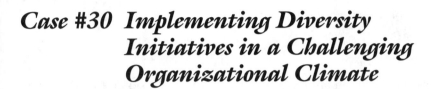

Case #30 Implementing Diversity Initiatives in a Challenging Organizational Climate

MONICA GALLOWAY BURKE

Diversity initiatives are becoming commonplace at several universities in light of the shifting demographics of college campuses and society, the legal challenges of Affirmative Action policies and discrimination, and the increase of racially motivated incidents and crimes. At Ballowett University the implementation of initiatives to improve the campus climate for diversity into the university's student affairs structure has been met with some resistance and opposition. Moreover, old alliances from some members of the Student Affairs Division's top leadership have created frustration, confusion, and barriers.

Institutional Setting

Ballowett University is a medium-size public institution located in the unassuming southern town of Lovell, a predominantly white community of approximately 70,000 people. It offers a broad range of baccalaureate programs with over sixty undergraduate majors and approximately forty master's degree programs to over 24,000 students across seven disciplines. The demographic makeup of the institution is 87% white, 7% black; 2% hispanic; 1.5% Asian American/Pacific Islander; .94% Native American; and the remaining 1.11% represents the international students at the university. A high percentage of the students reside on campus and there is a high level of student activism on campus. However, the minority students tend to not be very involved in these types of activities. There are approximately 1200 faculty and staff members at the institution, of which 9% are ethnic minorities.

In the past year, the university hired a new Vice President of Student Affairs, Dr. Evan Lewis. Dr. Lewis is a fairly young vice president and an advocate for making his division extremely innovative as well as promoting a campus climate that embraces diversity at all levels for students. He has introduced a new theme, a new thrust, a new sense of change, and a new direction. However, his administrative cabinet consists of eight individuals who have been at the university an average of 14.2 years.

The Obstacles

The realism of the situation in the Student Affairs Division is that Dr. Lewis, the Vice President of Student Affairs is encountering obstacles involving several of his initiatives. Within his administrative cabinet, power linkages have been formed by some of the directors with more resistance coming from Dr. Calvin Kelson, the Director of Housing and Residence Life and Dr. Peter Johnson, the Director of Student Activities and Programs who have each been at the university for over nineteen years respectively. They have seen three Vice Presidents of Student Affairs come and go and have concurred to wait out the time of this new energetic and active Vice-President. In addition, some of the other directors have clearly and openly verbalized their disagreement with most of the proposed initiatives, particularly those involving diversity.

The Framework for Change

At his first Administrative Directors Meeting, Dr. Lewis issued an overview of his vision and outlined his five-point plan for diversity and initiatives for the Division of Student Affairs. His plan supports the evolution of his division through innovation and recognition with emphasis on students' experiences, intellectual foundation, programming, and diversity throughout the campus community. In terms of diversity, Dr. Lewis stated that he wanted to pursue diversity in a sustained and comprehensive manner. Ultimately, he envisions a supportive, inclusive environment for all students in which diversity is embraced in all aspects of the campus culture and where the importance of democratic citizenship is imparted to each student. Dr. Lewis wanted to promote the Student Affairs Division to reflect the ideals of an equitable and democratic society through instruction, programming, and opportunities for interaction and learning.

Prior to establishing his goals and initiatives to accomplish his objective for diversity, Dr. Lewis performed a "culture audit" to gain a sense of organizational culture, team spirit, perceptions, and overall satisfaction. He also obtained status reports from each unit in the Student Affairs Division.

Through the assessment of the diversity paradigm and focus groups with staff members and minority students, several initiatives were developed that encompassed the creation of a special committee for diversity issues; diversity being included as a criterion on annual evaluations; the incorporation of training seminars for faculty, staff, and students; encouraging programming to provide opportunities for dialogue, interaction, and learning across the campus; and the incorporation of all-inclusive efforts to retain students and staff of color at the university.

Diversity: The Implementation Phase

Dr. Lewis has expressed that he wants his five-point plan for diversity to be integrated into the university's structure. He developed a blueprint for action and change that encompassed a multi-year approach with activities, strategies, and programming that involved every unit of the Student Affairs Division; an emphasis on providing information, addressing intolerance, altering assumptions, encouraging dialogue and teaching collaboration; and a comprehensive and uniform focus on students and staff and their experiences. The five areas of focus included (1) vision, planning, and implementation; (2) staff education, training, professional development, and community development; (3) performance evaluation and review of policies and procedures; (4) student education, programming, and outreach; and (5) communications and marketing. To accomplish the incorporation of diversity throughout the Student Affairs structure, Dr. Lewis delegated projects and objectives to each member of his administrative cabinet. This was in addition to the incorporation of a professional development series and a mandatory sensitivity training seminar for all professional staff in the division, requiring assessment and reports for each unit's initiatives; and required presentations of each unit's services to all student orientation courses.

Dr. Lewis charged the Director of Student Activities and Programs with including diverse students in activities to increase students' involvement in campus life, implementing activities that increase dialogue and build bridges across populations of difference, and maintaining an evaluative process for diversity initiatives. Many members of the Student Activities and Programs staff, in concurrence with the director, are particularly upset because they see these initiatives as creating more work for them as well as being unnecessary. Most complaints involve the platform that the Office of Multicultural Affairs should be responsible for these types of initiatives and these efforts impose some form of separatism amongst the students. The Director of Residence Life is also not pleased with having to create a committee that will focus on incorporating cultural programming in the residence halls. He has openly verbalized his discontent with creating another standing committee in his unit, stating that his staff is already overworked, and that this initiative is redundant since the minority students already have their own programming through the Greek system and minority-oriented student organizations.

Out with the Old?

At the core of Dr. Lewis' difficulties is the old paradigm that was established by the previous vice president. A couple of unpleasant incidents involving minority students had gone awry because of poor responsive actions from some members of the Student Affairs Division. In addition, a strong, close relationship between the prior Vice President of Student Affairs and Dr. Beverly Stallworth, the Vice President of Academic Affairs, had created a situation of mistrust and vulnerability for many members of the Student Affairs division. Several efforts proposed by directors in Student Affairs had been thwarted if Dr. Stallworth felt it interfered with her division's image or goals and/or she personally disliked the point person of any project or program. Furthermore, Dr. Kelson and Dr. Johnson were golfing buddies, fellow church members, and close friends with the former Vice President of Student Affairs, and often openly refer to "how things used to be" in administrative cabinet meetings. This created an uncomfortable environment filled with tension.

To create an environment that would change the perception of the division throughout campus and amongst members of the division of Student Affairs, Dr. Lewis wanted to cultivate a culture that valued the identification and addressing of problems in students' experiences and interactions as well as in the quality of work experience for members of his division. He also wanted to incorporate proactive measures to avoid similar circumstances of conflict and feelings of estrangement for minority students that had occurred in the past.

The Conflict with Academic Affairs

The Vice President for the Division of Academic Affairs has expressed her concern that the new Vice President of Student Affairs is stepping on her toes when attempting to implement his initiatives to promote the development of democratic citizenship of students throughout campus. She feels that the academic arena is the primary locale to promote this and that Student Affairs should just focus on the social aspects of Ballowett's students. Dr. Stallworth met with Dr. Lewis and Dr. Calvin Cook, the President of Ballowett University, where she informed them that the Assistant Director of Academic Programs, Harold Samuels, had devised a plan to promote diversity and democratic citizenship in students. "The Democracy and Diversity Project" was developed to increase the matriculation of students and to engage them in critical-thinking activities and community service. She praised this program as being a premier approach to embracing and promoting diversity in all aspects throughout the campus.

The "Democracy and Diversity Project" developed by Harold Samuels identifies three primary goals for enhancing diversity on the campus. The outlined goals are to increase cultural, ethnic, and racial diversity within the student body, faculty, and staff through continuous attention to recruitment, hiring, and retention; to promote avenues to foster discussion, understanding and appreciation for diversity in the campus community; and to provide programs which enhance interactions with and pragmatic learning about other cultures and people.

Mr. Samuels is a former graduate assistant of Dr. Stallworth who was personally recruited by her for his current position. Prior to coming to Ballowett, he was a customer service associate for a major airline and a receptionist for a small Business Development Center. He is seen as being a very loyal friend to Dr. Stallworth and they often spend time together outside of work.

In his current position, Mr. Samuels is responsible for coordinating faculty workshops; maintaining a faculty database; preparing reports; providing faculty handbooks and other needed materials to faculty offices; maintaining course syllabi and resource listings; and assisting with curriculum planning meetings. He has become known by a number of faculty and staff members as someone who "talks out of both sides of his mouth" and as often being pretentious and abrupt when communicating with others. Several faculty members have, to not avail, complained to Dr. Stallworth about his attitude and performance.

Same Song-Second Verse

Dr. Michael Thomas, the Associate Vice President of Multicultural Affairs, requested a meeting with Dr. Lewis and expressed his concerns about the "Democracy and Diversity" Project. He admitted that there had been tension in the past between him, Dr. Stallworth, and Harold Samuels that developed when he refused to hire Samuels for a vacant position in his office. Dr. Thomas stated that he had since had to deal with attacks about his unit's performance and about him personally. He informed Dr. Lewis that he usually likes to avoid these "political plays" with them but that this was the "last straw". He outlined his concerns, which included that the goals conflicted with the Office of Multicultural Affairs' goals and initiatives; mixed messages will occur with these two programs in existence; Harold Samuels lacks skills and experience and he and his staff are less qualified to deal with diversity issues; accountability was not present in the outline; and that he suspects that there will not be increased funding and support for his unit because resources will now be diverted to the "Democracy and Diversity" Project. Furthermore, he questioned whether this project was really in the best interest of faculty, staff, and students or whether it had more to do with job security and control for Samuels and Stallworth.

At the Crossroads

Dr. Lewis is now sitting in his office frustrated but undeterred from attempting to implement his five-point plan in his division. He would like to have a collaborative relationship exist between Student Affairs and Academic Affairs and for his division to take an active role in implementing the vision he has for it. However, he is now questioning if this collaboration would be more of a detriment than an asset. As he sits at his desk and prepares for his upcoming meeting with the President and his administrative council, he is pondering several issues about his initiatives, responsibilities, and his next action.

Discussion Question

The following are key areas and issues that should be considered regarding this case:

The Present Environment and the Implementation of Diversity Initiatives

1. What are some of the environmental issues that are present in this case study?
2. What would provide a better framework for improved operations in the Student Affairs Division? How would you implement this in the tense environment that is present in this case study?
3. What student development theories would support Dr. Lewis' concept of the importance of enhancing a diverse environment and encouraging democratic citizenship in students?

Leadership and the Organizational Climate

1. Why is Dr. Lewis encountering such opposition? Is the real problem with the implementation of diversity initiatives or with change in general?

2. What leadership theory do you think would best work for Dr. Lewis? What organizational theory do you think would work best?
3. What should Dr. Lewis do to ensure "buy in" to change the culture to accept his initiatives?

Conflict Management among Leadership in the Student Affairs Division

1. What are the conflicts and constraints that impede the implementation of the initiatives proposed by Dr. Lewis?
2. What are the aims and interests of all the involved parties that underline the conflicts in this case? How do these interests collide?
3. What steps can Dr. Lewis take to pull his staff together to adopt "his vision"?
4. What leadership style/approach should Dr. Lewis use to manage the conflict in his division?

A Collaborative Relationship Between Student Affairs and Academic Affairs

1. What are Dr. Lewis' options to deal with issues presented by Dr. Stallworth and Dr. Samuels in Academic Affairs?
2. What foreseeable barriers and consequences would you see with forming collaboration with Academic Affairs?
3. How should Dr. Lewis handle the situation with the attacks on Dr. Thomas (the Director of Multicultural Affairs) by Dr. Stallworth and Mr. Samuels?

Influencing Change

1. What leadership style/approach should Dr. Lewis use to influence change in his division?
2. What coalition-building strategies should Dr. Lewis develop?
3. What are effective means for incorporating accountability in relation to implementing the five-point plan?

Recommended Readings

The Campus Environment and Diversity

Astin, A. (1982). *Minorities in higher education.* San Francisco, CA: Jossey-Bass.

Brayboy, B. (September 2003). The implementation of diversity in predominantly white colleges and universities. *Journal of Black Studies,* 34 (1), 72–86.

Feagin, J., Vera, H., & Imani, N. (1996). *The agony of education: Black students at white colleges and universities.* New York: Routledge.

Filling the pipeline: A look at enrollment and employment trends in public higher education. (2002). (Special Report). Washington, D.C.: American Association of State Colleges and Universities. (ERIC Document Reproduction Service No. ED 472 500).

Sacks, D. & Thiel, P. (1998). *The diversity myth: Multiculturalism and political intolerance on campus.* Oakland, CA: The Independent Institute.

Smith, D., Wolf, L., & Levitan, T. (Eds.). (1994). Studying diversity in higher education. New Direction for Institutional Research, 81.

Steele, C. (2000). Stereotype threat and black college students. *About Campus,* 5 (2), 2–4.

Leadership and the Organizational Climate

Clement, L. & Richard, S. (1992). *Effective leadership in student services.* San Francisco, CA: Jossey-Bass.

Komives, S. & Woodard, D. Jr. (Eds.). (1996). *Student services: A handbook for the profession* (3rd ed.), San Francisco, CA: Jossey-Bass.

Kuh, G. (Ed.). (1993). *Cultural perspectives in student affairs work.* Lanham, MD Maryland: University Press.

Morgan, G. (1989). *Creative organization theory: A resource book.* Newbury Park, California: SAGE Publications.

Winston, T. Creamer, D. & Miller, T. (2001). *The professional student affairs administrator: Educator, leader, and manager.* New York: Brunner-Routledge.

Sandeen, A. (1991). *The chief student affairs officer: Leader, manager, mediator, educator.* San Francisco, CA: Jossey-Bass.

Conflict Management Among Leadership in the Student Affairs Division

Carnall, C.A. (1995). *Managing change in organizations* (2nd ed.). London: Prentice-Hall.

Cowher, S. Summer 1996). A power development model for managing and preventing conflict. *Guidance and Counseling,* 11 (4), 18–22.

Guttman, H. (January 2004). The art of managing conflict. *USA Today Magazine,* 132 (2704), 62–63.

Spencer, J. (1998). *Who moved my cheese?* New York: Putnam.

A Collaborative Relationship Between Student Affairs and Academic Affairs

Berquist, W.H. (1992). *The four cultures of the academy: Insights and strategies for improving leadership in collegiate organizations.* San Francisco, CA: Jossey-Bass.

Gurin, P., Nagda, B., & Lopez, G. (2004). The benefits of diversity in education for democratic citizenship. *Journal of Social Issues,* 60 (1), 17–34.

Kezar, A., Hirsch, D., & Burack, C. (Eds.). (Winter 2001). *Understanding the role of academic and student affairs collaboration in creating a successful learning environment.* New Directions for Higher Education, No. 116. San Francisco, CA: Jossey-Bass.

Schuh, J. & Whitt, E. (Eds.). (Fall 1999). *Creating successful partnerships between academic and student affairs.* New Directions for Student Services, No. 87. San Francisco, CA: Jossey-Bass.

Influencing Change

Fried, J. (1995). *Shifting paradigms in student affairs: Culture, context, teaching, and learning.* Lanham, MD: University Press of America.

Kezar, A. (Ed.). (2001). *Understanding and facilitating organizational change in the 21ˢᵗ century:* Recent research and conceptualization. ASHE-ERIC Higher Education Report, 28 (4). San Francisco, CA: Jossey-Bass.

Woodard, D., Jr., Love, P., & Komives, S. (Winter 2000) Organizational change. New Directions for Student Services, San Francisco, CA: Jossey-Bass, No. 92, Volume 2000, 61–70.

Index

Questions about the Purpose(s) of Colleges and Universities

Norm Denzin,

Joe L. Kincheloe,

Shirley R. Steinberg

General Editors

What are the purposes of higher education? When undergraduates "declare their majors," they agree to enter into a world defined by the parameters of a particular academic discourse—a discipline. But who decides those parameters? How do they come about? What are the discussions and proposed outcomes of disciplined inquiry? What should an undergraduate know to be considered educated in a discipline? How does the disciplinary knowledge base inform its pedagogy? Why are there different disciplines? When has a discipline "run its course"? Where do new disciplines come from? Where do old ones go? How does a discipline produce its knowledge? What are the meanings and purposes of disciplinary research and teaching? What are the key questions of disciplined inquiry? What questions are taboo within a discipline? What can the disciplines learn from one another? What might they not want to learn and why?

Once we begin asking these kinds of questions, positionality becomes a key issue. One reason why there aren't many books on the meaning and purpose of higher education is that once such questions are opened for discussion, one's subjectivity becomes an issue with respect to the presumed objective stances of Western higher education. Academics don't have positions because positions are "biased," "subjective," "slanted," and therefore somehow invalid. So the first thing to do is to provide a sense—however broad and general—of what kinds of positionalities will inform the books and chapters on the above questions. Certainly the questions themselves, and any others we might ask, are already suggesting a particular "bent," but as the series takes shape, the authors we engage will no doubt have positions on these questions.

From the stance of interdisciplinary, multidisciplinary, or transdisciplinary practitioners, will the chapters and books we solicit solidify disciplinary discourses, or liquefy them? Depending on who is asked, interdisciplinary inquiry is either a polite collaboration among scholars firmly situated in their own particular discourses, or it is a blurring of the restrictive parameters that define the very notion of disciplinary discourse. So will the series have a stance on the meaning and purpose of interdisciplinary inquiry and teaching? This can possibly be finessed by attracting thinkers from disciplines that are already multidisciplinary, for example, the various kinds of "studies" programs (women's, Islamic, American, cultural, etc.), or the hybrid disciplines like ethnomusicology (musicology, folklore, anthropology). But by including people from these fields (areas? disciplines?) in our series, we are already taking a stand on disciplined inquiry. A question on the comprehensive exam for the Columbia University Ethnomusicology Program was to defend ethnomusicology as a "field" or a "discipline." One's answer determined one's future, at least to the extent that the gatekeepers had a say in such matters. So, in the end, what we are proposing will no doubt involve political struggles.

For additional information about this series or for the submission of manuscripts, please contact Joe L. Kincheloe, joe.kincheloe@mcgill.ca. To order other books in this series, please contact our Customer Service Department at: (800) 770-LANG (within the U.S.), (212) 647-7706 (outside the U.S.), (212) 647-7707 FAX, or browse online by series at: www.peterlang.com.